THE LITERARY ANIMAL

THE LITERARY ANIMAL

Evolution and the Nature of Narrative

Edited by

Jonathan Gottschall
and David Sloan Wilson

Forewords by

E. O. Wilson and Frederick Crews

Northwestern University Press
Evanston, Illinois

Northwestern University Press
www.nupress.northwestern.edu

Printed in the United States of America

10   9   8   7   6   5   4   3   2   1

ISBN 0-8101-2286-3 (cloth)
ISBN 0-8101-2287-1 (paper)

Library of Congress Cataloging-in-Publication Data

The literary animal : evolution and the nature of narrative / Edited by Jonathan Gottschall and David
    Sloan Wilson ; forewords by E. O. Wilson and Frederick Crews.
        p. cm.
    Includes bibliographical references.
    ISBN 0-8101-2286-3 (cloth : alk. paper)—ISBN 0-8101-2287-1 (pbk. : alk. paper)
    1. Literature and science.   2. Evolution (Biology) in literature.   3. Human beings in literature.
    4. Narration (Rhetoric)   I. Gottschall, Jonathan.   II. Wilson, David Sloan.
PN55.L39 2005
809'.9336—dc22

                                                                                    2005004290

Contents

Foreword from the Scientific Side

E. O. Wilson

The cleavage between naturalism and social constructivism in literary theory highlighted by the essays to follow extends to the foundation of knowledge itself. The essence of the matter, I believe, is as follows: Either the great branches of learning—natural sciences, social sciences, and humanities—can be connected by a web of verifiable causal explanation or they cannot. Either existence can be mapped as a continuum with the aid of science, as the naturalistic theorists suggest, or science is "only one way of knowing," as the constructivist theorists believe, with many other disjunct truths arising from cultural and personal happenstance.

The naturalistic theorists have at the very least clarified and framed the issue. If they are right and not only human nature but its outermost literary productions can be solidly connected to biological roots, it will be one of the great events of intellectual history. *Science and the humanities united!* The opposing opinion is equally interesting. If the naturalistic quest consistently fails to the extent that the constructivist default position earns general acceptance, that would be an even greater advance in intellectual history. *Existence is not consilient!* In this case, the constructivists guessed right, but the would-be unifiers will have forced the issue and provided the crucial evidence. There is only one way to settle the issue: Go there and find out; utilize Francis Bacon's dictum that truth comes more easily out of error than out of confusion.

Confusion is what we have now in the realm of literary criticism. The naturalistic ("Darwinian") literary critics have an unbeatable strategy to replace it. They do not see the division between the great branches of learning—the natural sciences on one side and humanities and humanistic social sciences on the other—as a fault line between two kinds of truth. They do not consider it a line at all but rather a broad expanse of mostly undiscovered phenomena awaiting cooperative exploration by scholars from both sides. This conception has the enormous advantage that it can be empirically proved to be either right or wrong or, at worst, unsolvable.

An analogy exists between the current contest of ideas and the history of geographic exploration. The first geographic explorers were Columbian: they searched for continents and archipelagoes. The second wave of explorers were

Magellanic; synthesizers by nature, they encompassed the whole. The third wave were cartographic: they pressed on into the details of coastlines and rivers, of cordilleras and inland tribes. The naturalistic literary theorists are would-be Columbians. Embattled, even scorned, by tenured constructivists, they have launched their frail caravels on an uncertain sea. Who will gamble against them? If there is any chance of success, who with any courage and ambition would not want to join them—or at least lend support?

Their ultimate key to success is the understanding of mind. Twenty-five centuries of philosophy have not succeeded in what Darwin once aptly termed the assault on the citadel. Indeed, much of the history of philosophy up to present day has consisted of failed models of the brain. Freud, Jung, and the psychoanalytic schools they inspired were naturalistic in approach. But they also failed. There was not enough neuroscience and evolutionary biology in their time to build sound models of the brain. The psychoanalytic theorists also sought independence from biology, causing them to go further astray (see Dylan Evans's "From Lacan to Darwin," this volume).

Nowadays neuroscientists, cognitive psychologists, and evolutionary biologists appear to have gained an entrée in the assault. Their painstaking, bottom-up approach—process by process, circuit by circuit—is at last disclosing the multiple workings of the brain. They seem likely to attain, perhaps within a decade or two, at least a rough answer to the question universally regarded as premier in the natural sciences: What is the mind?

As the properties of mind are clarified empirically, it will also be possible to define human nature with greater precision. That there is a human nature is no longer in doubt. Until recently great controversy raged over the question of whether the brain is wired to predispose certain patterns of learning and behavior, or the brain is a blank slate, free of all but the most elemental drivers and ready to be molded almost entirely by culture and personal history. The blank-slate model could be tested empirically. It lost. The evidence from the biological and behavioral sciences converged to establish that the brain is in fact intricately wired from birth. Human behavior is determined by neither genes nor culture but instead by a complex interaction of these two prescribing forces, with biology guiding and environment specifying.

In the light of modern biology, what is then human nature? It is not the genes, which prescribe human nature. Nor is it just the universal traits of culture, such as the creation myths, incest taboos, and rites of passage, possessed by all societies. Rather, it is the inherited regularities of sensory and mental development that animate and channel the acquisition of culture. The number of genes in the human genome, about thirty-six thousand, is too small to encode more than a minute fraction of the variants of human behavior. Obviously the spectacular efflorescence of cultures is based on learning. Yet for all its achievements, and for all its prodigious variety, human behavior is severely constrained relative to the combined behavioral repertories of other animal species. At base we have remained true not only to our origins as primates but as savanna-dwelling African catarrhines. We possess no ability to see the ultraviolet light that guides butter-flies, no electrical sense by which electric fish organize their lives, none of the echolocation by which bats and whales hunt and orient, and not a trace of the magnetic sense by which songbirds migrate at night. We are also microcosmic idiots, having almost lost the sense of smell so exquisitely refined in the vast majority of animals. Our cultures and values seem highly variable to us but in fact are very specialized and very epigaeic and diurnal mammalian. Here, for example, are several of the values that we could expect to characterize termite cultures if they had attained the intelligence threshold of civilization: loving dank darkness, photophobic, with a refined taste for lignin and cellulose and for music consisting of sophisticated pheromonal song, faithful to the taboo against reproduction by any caste but royalty, and devoted to the duty of consuming injured and dead nestmates. Civilized termites, I feel certain, would consider the very conception of human existence a nightmare.

The mind is a narrative machine, guided unconsciously by the epigenetic rules in creating scenarios and creating options. The narratives and artifacts that prove most innately satisfying spread and become culture. The societies with the most potent Darwinian innovations export them to other societies. In the process of gene-culture evolution, genes affect which scenarios and memes are created, and the cultures thereby generated affect which genes survive. The long-term interaction of genes and culture appear to form a cycle, or more precisely a for-ward traveling evolutionary spiral, of the following sequence:

Genes prescribe epigenetic rules, which are the regularities of sensory perception and mental development that animate and channel the growth of culture.

Culture helps to determine which of the prescribing genes survive and multiply from one generation to the next.

The brain develops its activity and thence mind and culture by epigenetic rules of thumb that channel learning. Incest is avoided, for example, by the West-ermarck effect, an automatic inhibition that occurs between two people who live in domestic proximity during the first thirty months in the life of either one or both. That imprinting is the foundation of an important part of our moral code—and the production of literary themes. In another realm, that of aesthetics, the brain is activated most sharply by abstract patterns with about 20 percent redun-dancy, which perhaps not coincidentally is the amount put into much of abstract art. Also, as color vocabularies grow more complex across cultures, those with two terms usually designate black and white; those with three colors black, white, and red; green or yellow makes a fourth; next comes green plus yellow; and so forth.

Successful new genes or gene combinations alter the epigenetic rules of the populations.

The altered epigenetic rules change the direction and effectiveness of the channels of cultural acquisition.

Scientists and other scholars have begun to map a few of the connections between genes and culture. But the details of the coevolutionary spiral cannot be predicted from knowledge of the genes or even the circuitry of the brain alone. It can only be adduced by joining the relevant data of cognitive psychology, the social sciences, and the humanities with those of biology.

The time has come to bring science into closer contact with epistemology. Science is the organized, systematic enterprise that gathers knowledge about the world and condenses it into testable laws and principles. In addressing phenomena that range all the way from the origin of the universe to the workings of the brain, science is distinguished from pseudoscience by five qualities. The first is repeatability of the observation, preferably by different observers using different techniques. The second is economy: the accounts provided by the best of science are those that are simplest (and, usually, most aesthetically pleasing) and also yield the largest amount of testable information. The third diagnostic quality is mensuration: the best science comes from phenomena that can be measured repeatedly by generally employed scales and tested for likelihood by statistical inference. The fourth quality is heuristics: the best discoveries are those that raise new questions and stimulate further inquiry. The fifth diagnostic quality of true science is consilience: the explanations of different phenomena most likely to survive are those that can be connected and proceed consistent with one another.

Science is neither a philosophy nor an ideology. It is a way of exploring the tangible world that conferred understanding and power beyond the imaginings of prescientific people. Although born in Europe at a particular time, during the seventeenth century, modern science is not in any sense an idiosyncratic contrivance of Western civilization. The knowledge it generates is the most inclusive and transparent, as well as democratic, available to all of humanity. (Tibetan Buddhism and postmodern constructivism are also among the many ways of thinking available to all of humanity but have none of the diagnostic characteristics of science.)

Naturalism is a conviction, based upon the spectacular successes of science continuing to the present time, that scientific inquiry can be taken to any level of detail, including the productions of mind and culture. In accepting this world view myself, and as a biologist, I like to reflect on the parallel between the productions of organic evolution expressed in ecosystems and the productions of the brain expressed in cultures. Each species of the millions (when bacteria are included) that compose ecosystems, like each defining element of every culture, is worthy of a lifetime of study. Each has unique biological traits that can be understood in depth. Such is the level of competence of individualistic biology at the present time. But how species are assembled into ecosystems and how the ecosystems sustain themselves as higher level entities are only partly understood. And so it is, a fortiori, with mind and culture.

The substance of the creative arts is of course the work itself. In creating literature, visual art, or music successful innovators have no need of theory. We may even hope that authors who generate literature of genuine originality, who use language to transmit images and feeling directly from one mind to the other with aesthetic and emotional power, will remain, as they have ever been, largely unencumbered by theory. To explain what they have accomplished, or have not accomplished, and why and, further, how literature evolves and, finally, the role it plays in culture—all that is the responsibility of the literary theorist. Those who take the naturalistic approach stand apart from science in important ways but have much to accomplish if they draw upon all it has to offer.

Foreword from the Literary Side

Frederick Crews

Among the routines common to literary critics and their nearest evolutionary cousins, the chimpanzees, perhaps the most conspicuous is the grooming behavior of back scratching. In one species a partner plucks out fleas with the Triversian expectation of a symmetrical favor; in the other, buddies write prefaces and blurbs for buddies who will be likely to reciprocate. But wait a minute. The people who have requested this foreword are familiar with me only by reputation, and the most pertinent thing they know about me is that I recently poked some fun at their school of practice.[1] Ergo, these cannot be typical critics; they must have something better in mind than the usual partisan posturing. Could it be open dialogue about new analytic horizons and neglected principles of inquiry?

Although I am not a champion of evolutionary criticism, I do happen to be a committed Darwinian—more of one, I believe, than some well-known evolutionists who patrol a Maginot line between scientific and religious truth.[2] As Darwin well understood, and as Daniel Dennett has articulated in our time, natural selection is an acid that burns through every myth about ordained purposes and meanings. Those of us who embrace Darwinian knowledge without cavil are convinced that all existence is unplanned and therefore quite pointless, leaving humanity with the task of *rendering* its life dignified in moral, intellectual, and aesthetic ways scrounged and adjusted from our evolved heritage of repertoires. When the gods have been shipped back to fairyland to rejoin the Easter Bunny, we can direct our awe toward beings who actually deserve it—Shakespeare, Rembrandt, Beethoven, Einstein—without cheapening their achievements by ascribing them to mysterious infusions of spirit.

Enough pontificating. The topic at hand is literary study and its possible refreshment by a Darwinian outlook that can generate fruitful new questions and throw a useful light on some old ones. I hope that this movement will succeed. When I waxed satirical over it in *Postmodern Pooh*, I was merely expressing reserve about the claim that critical Darwinism is *the* answer to the antiempiricism that has reigned over literary theory for the past three decades. To my mind, evolutionary criticism is just one among many avenues of legitimate inquiry in our field, and one that needs to branch out from its early, potentially monotonous, preoccupation with the survival of Pleistocene psychology in modern works of art. Exactly such a widening of focus is assayed in this book.

It will be important, of course, for "human nature" critics to bear in mind that consilience across disciplines does not require the surrender of one field to the goals and methodological habits of a more basic one. Literary study is not about laws of mental functioning but about a body of heterogeneous texts. And the social value placed on the most prized of those texts is associated more with their distinctiveness than with their membership in a lawfully governed class. Thus a science of literary criticism, strictly construed, may be neither desirable nor feasible at all.

On the other hand, it should be mentioned that closeness to literary texture is not a summum bonum by which every enterprise must be judged. The essays below include some learned, boldly stimulating inquiries into the possible functions of literature as a category of endeavor and experience. Although such discourse looks nearer to anthropology and psychology than to criticism per se, its breadth of perspective and its marshaling of solidly grounded research put to shame what usually passes for interdisciplinarity in literary study.

The Literary Animal is valuable not only in its own right but also as a corrective to questionable assumptions and practices that have long been ascendant in literary study. Let us be clear, however, that old-boy humanism, with its aversion to everything that smacks of theory, plays no part in this extended critique. Your contributors actually share some assumptions with the "social constructionists" or "constructivists" who have often been denounced as enemies of art. Insofar as those theorists unearth motives of self-interest and domination where more tender-minded observers saw only values and beauties, they could well be regarded as honorary Darwinians. The adversary justly targeted in this book isn't constructivism *tout court* but its most brittle branch, a sociopolitical determinism so thoroughgoing as to rule out any allowance for biological commonalities.

As many of us have learned to our chagrin, however, the rejection of biological universals often partakes of a more general scorn for the empirical attitude. For three decades now, our field has been warped and demoralized by cynicism about the very possibility that intellectual controversies can be resolved on evidential grounds. The reason I feel comfortable with the contributors to this book, whether or not they are pursuing an evolutionary theme at any moment, is that they always write as open-minded empiricists.

Although these innovative scholars aren't conducting science as it is usually understood, they believe, as I do, that humanists ought to play the knowledge game according to the ethical rules that apply throughout the sciences. In brief: test and compare hypotheses, attend to negative as well as positive evidence, put partisan loyalties in abeyance when weighing that evidence, fairly confront objections, and prefer Ockham's razor to, say, Derrida's mallet to the skull.

It is not the case, of course, that only avowed evolutionists accept these imperatives. Even when quantitative methods are not employed, much contemporary discourse on any number of literary topics shows a scrupulous regard for the empirical ethos. The writers of such books and articles ought to be counted as allies and encouraged to join the Darwinians in defending their shared scruples against irrationalism. Our common aim, I would hope, is not to render literary criticism drier and more technical but to reclaim governance of the field—its appointments and promotions, its curricula, its standards for publication, its manner of debate—from the fast-talking superstars who have prostituted it to crank theory, political conformism, and cliquishness.

Here, I feel sure, my fellow foreword writer E. O. Wilson will experience a sense of déjà vu. As the founder of what has now become evolutionary psychology, he was once subjected to a low campaign of misrepresentation and vilification, led, appallingly, by colleagues in his own great university who were quick to resolve a scientific issue on ideological grounds. His forbearance and perseverance during and after that episode have been exemplary.

If Professor Wilson has now largely prevailed in gaining a fair hearing for his views, however, the credit does not belong exclusively to him. The scientific world can be relied upon to disavow kangaroo courts once it has been made aware of them. Not so the literary-critical world, in which ad hominem tactics and nakedly political justifications of theory go largely unrebuked and are even sanctioned by the profession's flagship journal.[3] Hence the need for explicit, even militant, affirmation of the standards that Darwinian critics share with many others who have been reluctant to speak out.

Meanwhile, Darwin's own example can be serviceable to those of us who lack either the aptitude or the opportunity to practice science. He was tireless in gathering data and patient in deciding what to make of it; he squarely faced anomalies that threatened to overturn his theory; and instead of exaggerating his originality and demeaning the character of his rivals, he built upon and acknowledged the work of predecessors and contemporaries whose expertise compensated for gaps in his own knowledge. In a word, Darwin conducted himself like a member of a disciplinary community held together by a common regard for truth. We can do the same, and it is in that spirit that I salute the authors of the essays that follow.

Notes

1. Crews 2001a.
2. Crews 2001b, 2001c, 2002.
3. Crews 2003.

Introduction:
Literature—a Last Frontier
in Human Evolutionary Studies

Jonathan Gottschall
and David Sloan Wilson

This book attempts to understand the nature of literature from an evolutionary perspective. We call literature one of the last frontiers because it is an easily documented fact: choose any subject relevant to humanity—philosophy, anthropology, psychology, economics, political science, law, even religion—and you will find a rapidly expanding interest in approaching the subject from an evolutionary perspective. The specific hypotheses are often controversial and frequently prove to be false. Science, like evolution itself, involves many failures for each success. Nevertheless, the evolutionary perspective has become part of the normal discourse for each of these subjects and is increasingly proving its worth, not only by delivering specific insights that turn out to be correct but also by providing a single conceptual framework for unifying disparate bodies of knowledge. Darwin himself studied an amazing array of subjects, from sex in barnacles to morality in humans. His ability to function as an extreme integrationist was due partially to his personal genius but also to his theory, which provides a common framework for studying all things animate and their productions, therefore all things human. We might not share Darwin's personal genius, but we can make use of his theory to reverse the trend of extreme specialization of knowledge that has taken place in the absence of a unifying conceptual framework.

Against the background of this tumult, as exciting for the general reader as for the specialist, the study of literature stands apart. Numerous evolutionists and literary scholars have become interested in exploring this territory, but it has not become part of the normal discourse for the field of literary studies as a whole. Indeed, the exclusion of evolution from the otherwise diverse array of perspectives within literary studies serves as a microcosm for why the human sciences as a whole initially lagged behind biology in embracing Darwin's theory. The best way that we can explain this is by relating our own stories of how we became interested in literature from an evolutionary perspective—Jon as a graduate student in literature who contracted "the evolution bug" on his own, and David as an established evolutionary biologist eager to add literature to other human-related subjects that he was already studying.

Jon's Story

I came down with the "evolution bug" in 1996 during my second year of graduate work in Binghamton University's English department. I happened across a dusty copy of the English zoologist Desmond Morris's 1967 best seller *The Naked Ape* in a used bookstore and purchased it for its provocative title and its graduate-student-friendly price of fifty cents. While the specifics of *The Naked Ape* were outdated by this time, its general attitude toward exploring human behavior was not: humans have complicated culture and stunning capacity to learn, yes, but this does not change the fact that we are also animals, vertebrates, mammals, primates, hominids, and great apes. Aspects of our culture, intelligence, and symbolic behavior make us different from the other apes, but they do not emancipate us from our evolved biology or lift us above other animals onto an exalted link of the chain of being. Therefore, zoologists can apply basically the same theoretical and methodological concepts to the study of human behavior that they apply to the behavior of other animals. Morris argued that the behavioral characteristics of the human animal, just like the morphological and physiological ones, should be understood as end results of an unfathomably long evolutionary process. Morris did not claim that all other perspectives on human behavior were thus engulfed and rendered obsolete. Rather, he claimed that an important fact had been neglected in studies of human behavior to the detriment of our understanding: people are apes; that we are bizarrely furless, and that we are smart and possess culture, does not change the fact.

At exactly the same time I was picking up Morris, I was again picking up Homer's great war poem, the *Iliad*, as required reading in a graduate seminar on the classic epics. As always Homer made my bones flex and ache under the weight of all the terror and beauty of the human condition. But this time around I also experienced the *Iliad* as a drama of naked apes—strutting, preening, fighting, tattooing their chests, and bellowing their power in fierce competition for social dominance, desirable mates, and material resources. Far from diminishing my sympathy for the characters, the revelation of timeless evolutionary logic behind all the petty jealousies, infidelities, spats, lies, cheats, rapes, and homicides that comprise the plot of the poem imparted, for me, a new kind of dignity to it. As Darwin wrote, and as all evolutionists intimately know, there is grandeur in this view of life.

As I continued to read Homer, and to work my way through the broad and interdisciplinary literature associated with sociobiology and evolutionary psychology, I became convinced not only that an evolutionary perspective could bring something new and useful even to a poem that had been picked over by scholars for twenty-five hundred years but that it could do the same for literary analysis generally by providing it with its first truly scientific theory of human psychology and behavior. I believed at the time that what ultimately drew most people to study literature was a desire to explore the behavior and psychology of human beings—a desire to play one's humble role in the ancient project of seeking the nature of the human. And here was a theory of why, ultimately, humans think and act as they do, a theory based not in intuitive speculations but in the bedrock of evolutionary theory and scientific method. Since most literary scholars spend their lives engaged in the study of why people (i.e., characters, authors, and readers) act and think as they do, the potential benefits for expanding understanding of literary phenomena seemed almost boundless. True, evolutionary psychology was a young science in the midst of a sometimes ungainly adolescence, but it had also demonstrated substantial power in predicting and explaining aspects of human behavior and psychology, and, together with cognitive science, behavioral genetics, and other fields, it had decisively undermined the scientific respectability of tabula rasa views of human nature.[1]

But tabula rasa theories had not lost their respectability in the humanities, and when I approached my epics professor with a plan for a seminar paper on male conflict in Homer from the perspective of evolutionary theory and research, he flatly forbade me to write it on the grounds of absurdity and irrelevance. Instead, he authorized me to write a paper based on what I had been learning in another seminar called "Psychoanalytic Criticism Applied"; I could study male conflict in Homer, as I had hoped, but I would do it from the perspective of Freud and Lacan, not Darwin.

What just happened? For my professor, as for virtually all of the other graduate students and professors in the English department, psychoanalysis was considered respectable (cutting edge in the case of Lacan; see Evans, this volume), despite the fact that psychology and other fields had long since rejected it. In fact, as in most English departments around the country, Binghamton University's was tolerant of a profusion of different disciplinary, ideological, and theoretical approaches. Students and professors moved fluidly from feminism to Marxism, to queer theory, to psychoanalysis, to continental textual theory, to structuralism, to poststructuralism, and to historicism; they moved across all the warring tribes of philosophy and across all the battling factions of literary theory and criticism; they drew upon theory and data from sociology, psychology, anthropology, and history; and they drew upon new thinking in chaos theory and quantum physics. Of course, there could be intense disagreement and debate over these topics, but the ideas were generally considered intellectually and politically respectable, and people were largely tolerant of the diverse ideas and perspectives represented in the program.

This tolerance reached its limits, however, when it came to evolutionary theories of human behavior and psychology, toward which students and professors evinced nothing but skepticism, hostility, and, most of all, fear. Older professors, like my epics professor, seemed to see "the naked ape perspective" as a churl's insult to humanity and to great art. The younger professors, as well as my fellow graduate students, saw it as something far worse. I quickly learned that when I spoke of human behavior, psychology, and culture in evolutionary terms, their minds churned through an instant and unconscious process of translation, and they heard "Hitler," "Galton," "Spencer," "IQ differences," "holocaust," "racial phrenology," "forced sterilization," "genetic determinism," "Darwinian fundamentalism," and "disciplinary imperialism." Once, discussing Baudelaire's *Les Fleurs du Mal* in seminar, the "fact" that gender was an arbitrary social construct was announced by a classmate with typical casual confidence. Contrary to a policy formed under hard experience, I noted that, actually, a confluence of different sources of evidence, deriving from an impressive array of disciplines, consistent with the expectations of evolutionary theory, and borne out in cross-cultural research, suggested that this constructivist orthodoxy was wrong—the dimorphic behavioral and psychological tendencies observed in populations of men and women were as much a product of biology as culture. A close female acquaintance seemed to speak for the whole seminar when she turned to me, shaking her head with a mixture of sadness, pity, and stubborn hope: "You can't really believe that, Jon, can you?"

I did believe it. I believed that the hard social constructivism that dominated the humanities had been definitively exposed by numerous and redundant studies as a failed theory. And I felt that fears about the baleful political and ideological ramifications of an evolutionary perspective were misplaced and misguided. So I went on to write a dissertation on Homer, male conflict, and evolution, but I was obliged to accomplish this in de facto exile from the English department. After failing to identify an English professor who both understood my perspective and who was neither intellectually nor morally put off by it, I formed a dissertation committee consisting entirely of professors outside my department. One was a classicist, one was an economist, and one was a well-known evolutionary biologist named David Sloan Wilson.

David's Story

When Jon first entered my office and related his story to me, I was somewhat surprised. I had been teaching a popular course on evolution and human behavior for many years that was open to all majors and cross-listed with the philosophy, psychology, and anthropology departments in addition to the women's studies program. I was conversing and collaborating with colleagues across a broad array of disciplines, at Binghamton University and elsewhere, and I knew that the evolutionary perspective had become firmly established in most branches of the human sciences. Controversies abounded, and I myself was considered a town heretic among my own evolutionary colleagues, but the days of declaring evolution off limits for the study of human behavior were over. Given such a healthy—and heady—dialogue, why were evolutionary perspectives discouraged, if not effectively off limits, in the English department at my own university?

I became even more perplexed when I considered how much evolution had already established a presence among contemporary writers. Books such as E. O. Wilson's *On Human Nature*, Jonathan Weiner's *The Beak of the Finch*, and Jared Diamond's *Guns, Germs, and Steel* had won Pulitzer Prizes, while many others with evolutionary themes appeared on best-seller lists and were avidly discussed in intellectual circles, including literary forums such as the *New York Review of Books*. The flamboyant literary agent John Brockman was routinely securing six-figure advances for his stable of evolutionary authors. A major novel influenced by evolutionary thinking had even appeared. Not only did Ian McEwan's *Enduring Love* feature a science journalist reporting on the new science of evolutionary psychology but the novel itself was an exploration of an important evolutionary theme, and McEwan acknowledged his gratitude to the very evolutionary biologists who had inspired Jon's study of the *Iliad*. Given all this interest, I could understand why the evolutionary perspective might be *controversial* in the field of literary studies—but effectively *off limits*?

When Jon asked me to become a member of his Ph.D. committee, I jumped at the opportunity because of my own lifelong interest in literature. My father was the well-known novelist Sloan Wilson, author of *The Man in the Grey Flannel Suit* and *A Summer Place*, and I often regarded myself as a novelist trapped inside the body of a scientist. I knew that there was essentially no difference between my father's passion to understand the human condition and my own. The difference was in the methods. My father didn't have to prove anything that he said. The only proof that mattered was the degree to which his books rang true in the minds of his readers. I, on the other hand, had to bear the tedious burden of proof for every important statement that I wanted to make about humans or any other species. Nevertheless, my hard-won results, combined with those of others, accumulating over time like the grain-by-grain construction of a termite mound, became something magnificent that cannot be found in literature—a body of knowledge upon which all reasonable people must agree.

To make this laudatory statement about science is not to disparage literature. Indeed, when a work of literature rings true in the mind of a reader, there is likely something that *is* true; it simply has not been proven. Anyone who wants to seriously consider what it means for something to "ring true" will quickly be plunged into some of the very philosophical and psychological issues that I and my colleagues are trying to address scientifically, from an evolutionary perspective, and which will be encountered in the pages of this book. The important point is that there is more than one pathway to knowledge. The human mind, individually and collectively in the form of culture, is impressively adapted to derive conviction without proof. Proof is a luxury that is usually too expensive to afford in the real world. The advantages of certainty aren't worth the time and effort required to obtain them. That is why science is such a recent institution that exists only in the most affluent societies. When science does flourish, it validates and extends as much as it overturns the uncertain knowledge derived by other means. For this reason, literature does not diminish in value when approached from a scientific perspective. The relationship between the two bodies of wisdom can and should be mutually reinforcing.

Just as Jon had experienced the themes of *The Naked Ape* leaping from the pages of the *Iliad*, I could not escape my work when I turned to the pages of literature. The evolutionary themes were everywhere. Perhaps my most memorable experience came during an extended trip to Japan, a culture that is supposed to be very different from our own. I asked my hosts to suggest their favorite Japanese plays, novels, and short stories, which I purchased in English translation and read during the course of my stay. The evolutionary themes were everywhere, cultural differences notwithstanding. One short story by Shiga Naoya entitled "Han's Crime" involved a Chinese circus performer who erred by a fraction of an inch during his knife throwing act, killing his wife. During the trial to determine if he was guilty of murder, the following dialogue takes place between the man and the judge. The judge speaks first:

"Have you never loved your wife at all?"
"From the day I married her until the day she had the baby, I loved my wife with all my heart."
"Why did the child become a source of discord?"
"Because I knew it wasn't my child."
"Do you know who the father was?"
"I have an idea it was my wife's cousin."
"Did you know the man?"
"He was a close friend of mine. It was he who suggested that we get married. He introduced me to her."
"Was there a relationship before she married you?"
"Of course there was. The baby was born the eighth month after the marriage."
"The stagehand said it was a premature birth."
"That's because I told him it was."
"The baby died shortly afterwards?"

"Yes."

"What was the cause of death?"

"It choked at the breast."

"Was that a deliberate act of your wife's?"

"She said it was an accident."

"Did your wife tell you about the relationship?"

"No, she didn't. Nor did I ask her about it. I felt that the baby's death was a judgment on her for what she'd done. I thought that I myself should be as forgiving as possible."

"But in the end, you couldn't forgive her?"

"That's right. My feeling remained that the baby's death wasn't enough of a judgment. At times, when I thought about it by myself, I could be rather forgiving. But then, my wife would come in. She would go about her business. As I looked at her, at her body, I could not keep down my displeasure."[2]

In another short story by the same author entitled "Kuniko," a playwright tries to explain to his wife why he is tempted to have affairs with other women despite his sincere love for her:

"Stop it," I told her, unable to take any more. "You overestimated me. Weren't you well aware that when I was single I did a lot of that kind of thing? During that time, I was a companion of your 'animals.' And I can't say even now that I'm not. I'm not trying to absolve myself, but most men have that 'animal' in them. The only difference is whether to let it roam free or bind it with chains. . . . To put it strongly, that 'animal' *is* man. . . .

"It's strange to say this to you, but from the beginning I've only thought of women like Yukiko as lead. Why a man who has gold or silver in his possession should also lust after lead is beyond my ability to explain. But unless you believe at least this much, I won't feel right about myself. You must believe that if you were silver, I never thought of Yukiko as anything more than the lead. I recognize that what I did was bad. At the same time, please believe that from the start my feelings were only of that degree."[3]

These tales of sexual conflict could have come from any culture and are highly compatible with cross-cultural research on sexual conflict from an evolutionary perspective. As for sexual conflict, so also for other major themes that we associate with the human condition.

I had one final interest in studying literature from an evolutionary perspective: I was increasingly using narrative as a research method by having participants read and respond to fictional scenarios whose elements I systematically varied. It was amazing how easily they became engaged in the briefest of stories and how sensitive they were to even single-word alterations. It was as if the human mind is constructed to think in terms of stories, a possibility that I develop from an evolutionary perspective in my own contribution to this book.

The Literary Animal

When we decided to collaborate on editing this book, our experience became a story in its own right. We quickly assembled what we regarded as a first-rate cast of authors but then encountered extraordinary difficulty finding a publisher. Time after time, the science editor of a given press would express great interest, only to encounter the resistance of the literary studies editor, whose reaction was much like what Jon experienced with some of his English professors. We therefore want to express our gratitude to Northwestern University Press for their courage—no other word will do—in publishing our volume.

The other authors in this volume—some (like Jon) from the world of literary studies and some (like David) from the world of evolutionary studies—could tell similar stories. Collectively, they illustrate two key points. First, the study of literature from an evolutionary perspective has enormous potential, which can be perceived by people from either world who become even passably familiar with the other world. Second, resistance to the study of literature from an evolutionary perspective is dominated by fear of the consequences, as if Pandora's box will be opened and its malevolent contents forever unleashed upon the world.

That is why literature as one of the last frontiers is a microcosm for the more general reluctance to approach human nature from an evolutionary perspective. Every branch of knowledge that we mentioned earlier—philosophy, anthropology, psychology, economics, political science, law, and religion—had to overcome similar resistance to evolutionary theory based on fear about Pandora's box. However, these fears proved groundless. The world hasn't become less moral, although we better understand the nature of morality. The importance of culture and learning has not diminished, although we better understand these subjects as well. Nonevolutionary perspectives have not become obsolete; the task of integration is much more interesting and symbiotic than simple replacement. Pandora's box has been opened—and surprise! Instead of malevolent forces, out flew an important set of conceptual tools, which, like all tools, can be used for good or ill. There is no question that evolutionary theory, like God and Country, has been linked to objectionable social and political agendas, but it is the job of intellectuals of all stripes to see through and challenge such linkages rather than declaring the entire subject off limits.

This book has multiple goals, in keeping with the broad audience for which it has been written. For the academic audience, we aim to forever establish evolution as part of the normal discourse in literary studies, while directing the attention of evolutionists to literature (and other art) as a fundamental product of human nature, as a source of insight, and even as a source of data that can be analyzed quantitatively. The alert reader will quickly discover that we do not all speak with the same voice. It is a myth to think that there is some monolithic evolutionary perspective, malevolent or otherwise. One reason for our diversity of opinion is because science is all about disagreement. If we all spoke with the same voice, we wouldn't be breaking new ground. Another reason is because evolution is a complicated process that leads to diverse outcomes. A given trait such as a spot on a guppy might be an important product of natural selection that increases fitness or a nonadaptive byproduct with no function at all. If adaptive, it might have evolved by natural selection or sexual selection. It might reflect the direct influence of genes or an open-ended process in which the influence of genes is more remote. These and other outcomes of evolution are possibilities for literature, no less than for spots on guppies.

The essays in this book reflect at least three major themes, which we will briefly summarize before letting the authors speak for themselves.

First, what is literature about? This question might seem extraordinarily naive, perhaps appropriate during the early days of literary theory but irrelevant to the current scene. On the contrary, rethinking literary studies requires returning to the basics. The problems of survival and reproduction are "on the minds" of all species that have minds and should dominate the stories of the one species that speaks and writes. This basic prediction has far-reaching implications for the contents of literature that are novel against the background of both early and modern literary studies.

Second, what is literature for? As we have seen in the case of spots on guppies, the properties of an organism need not be "for" anything. Literature could be a mere reflection of our natures without having any important influence. On the other hand, literature could have a profound effect on how we think and act through psychological and cultural processes in which the role of genes is remote. A third possibility, which could never be entertained without an evolutionary perspective, is that literature is a product of sexual selection, somewhat like a peacock's tail.

Third, what does it mean for a seemingly nonscientific subject such as literature to be approached from the perspective of a scientific discipline such as evolution? Fear and mistrust of evolution in literary studies is frequently accompanied by an even greater fear and mistrust of science in general. Both are unwarranted. As the evolutionary historian Frank Sulloway remarked, "science is not a subject but a *method*,"[4] and it can be applied to subjects such as history and litera-ture as well as those traditionally associated with science. All intellectuals, includ-ing literary theorists, make assertions—otherwise known as hypotheses—that they support on the basis of evidence. A typical example for literary studies is "The association of witchcraft with females, including the representation of witches in literature, is an effort to limit the social role of females to that of the good wife."[5] Sometimes an assertion can be so strongly supported on the basis of descriptive information that scientific methods aren't worth the effort. Other-wise, scientific methods extend our ability to accept or reject hypotheses on the basis of evidence that is collected systematically and analyzed with statistics. These methods refine intellectual discourse but do not change its fundamental character. They are a welcome addition to all subjects, and two of our authors show how they can be employed to good advantage in literary studies.

Evolution will eventually become part of the normal discourse in literary studies, as in any other subject relevant to humanity. This book has all the prom-ise associated with the word "pioneering"—and all the uncertainty. The articles we have collected represent early words on their subjects, not last words. It is cer-tain that we have made errors. Many of these will be the stumbles that occur in interdisciplinary projects as authors attempt to move outside of their specialties. Other errors will be much larger, given that we often come to different conclu-sions on which not everyone can be right. Where we make errors we trust that they will be productive errors—errors that lead to honest criticism, debate, rethinking, and, ultimately, more satisfactory responses to the broad variety of thorny questions we confront. We hope that our readers share our excitement of discovery, some so much that they decide to join our effort.

Notes

1. See Pinker 2002; Ridley 2003.
2. Naoya 1987, 50.
3. Naoya 1987, 147, 163.
4. Sulloway 1996.
5. Brauner 2001.

THE LITERARY ANIMAL

PART I

Evolution and Literary Theory

The subject of literary studies is ultimately the human mind—the mind that is the creator, subject, and auditor of literary works. The prime activity of literary critics of all theoretical and political slants has been to pry open the craniums of characters, authors, and narrators, climb inside their heads, and spelunk through all the bewildering complexity to figure out what, ultimately, makes them tick. What are they trying to say? What does all this mean? When engaged in these activities literary scholars lean hard on theories of human nature. Sometimes these theories are explicitly codified, as they are, for instance, in some Marxist, feminist, and psychoanalytic schools. Sometimes they are not, as when traditional literary critics base their judgments on personal intuitions about the regularities and rhythms of human psychology. But at the core of all the classes and orders of literary scholarship are assumptions about the nature of human beings: our capacities, our limits, our ultimate motives, our wants and needs, our strengths and weaknesses.

The theories of human nature that have dominated humanities scholarship over the last several decades are based on the nearly limitless capacity of what Durkheim called "the social factor" to mold and manipulate the biological factor. In these models, human behavior, psychology, and culture are seen as products of arbitrary social conditioning with none but the most gossamer and inconsequential ties to our evolved biology. These "hard" versions of social constructivism cannot stand up to the evidence—theory and data from biology, behavioral genetics, psychology, cognitive science, cross-cultural anthropology, and other fields have definitively cut the legs from beneath the tabula rasa perspective.[1] The psychoanalytic theories that remain current in the humanities, although generally allowing somewhat greater scope for inborn biological tendencies, also fail in the face of the evidence. In short, the theories of human nature that have dominated literary theory and criticism since the 1960s now only exist in the humanities. While literary scholars are often suspicious of concepts like "right" and "wrong" or "true" and "false," the dominant theories of human potential in literary studies have been falsified. This is now a matter of scientific "fact," as the term is defined by Stephen Jay Gould: "Confirmed to such a degree that it would be perverse to withhold provisional consent."[2]

The articles in this section represent attempts to grapple with some of the problems and opportunities presented by the collapse of the constructivist foundations of contemporary literary theory. These articles represent attempts to explore specific problems in literary theory from the perspective of the evolution-based theories of human nature that are now replacing extreme social constructivist versions. However, none of these authors suggest that social constructivism in a more reasonable form is dead. In fact, the nature-nurture dichotomy is a false one—a more restrained version of social constructivism is fully compatible with the emerging evolutionary models of human nature.

Notes

1. Pinker 2002.
2. Gould 1994, 254.

Literature, Science, and Human Nature

Ian McEwan

Greatness in literature is more intelligible and amenable to most of us than greatness in science. All of us have an idea, our own, or one that has been imposed upon us, of what is meant by a great novelist. Whether it is in a spirit of awe and delight, duty or scepticism, we grasp at firsthand when we read *Anna Karenina* or *Madame Bovary* what people mean when they speak of greatness. We have the privilege of unmediated contact. From the first sentence, we come into a presence, and we can see for ourselves the quality of a particular mind; in a matter of minutes we may read the fruits of a long-forgotten afternoon, an afternoon's work done in isolation, a hundred and fifty years ago. And what was once an unfolding personal secret is now ours. Imaginary people appear before us; their historical and domestic circumstances are very particular, their characters equally so. We witness and judge the skill with which they are conjured. By an unspoken agreement, a kind of contract between writer and reader, it is assumed that however strange these people are, we will understand them readily enough to be able to appreciate their strangeness. To do this, we must bring our own general understanding of what it means to be a person. We have, in the terms of cognitive psychology, a theory of mind, a more-or-less automatic understanding of what it means to be someone else. Without this understanding, as psychopathology shows, we would find it virtually impossible to form and sustain relationships, read expressions or intentions, or perceive how we ourselves are understood. To the particular instances that are presented to us in a novel we bring this deep and broad understanding. When Saul Bellow's Herzog stands in front of a mirror, as characters in fiction so often and conveniently do, he is wearing only a newly purchased straw hat and underpants.

> [His mother] wanted him to become a rabbi and he seemed to himself gruesomely unlike a rabbi now in the trunks and straw hat, his face charged with heavy sadness, foolish utter longing of which a religious life might have purged him. That mouth!—heavy with desire and irreconcilable anger, the straight nose sometimes grim, the dark eyes! And his figure!—the

long veins winding in the arms and filling in the hanging hands, an ancient
system, of greater antiquity than the Jews themselves. . . . Bare legged, he
looked like a Hindu.

A reader may not understand from the inside every specific of Herzog's condition—a mid-twentieth-century American, a Jew, a city dweller, a divorcé, an
alienated intellectual—nor might a young reader sympathize with the remorse of
early middle age, but self-scrutiny that is edging toward a reckoning has a general
currency, as does the droll, faux naive perception that one's biology—the circula-
tory system—predates and, by implication, is even more of the essence of being
human than one's religion. Literature flourishes along the channels of this unspoken agreement between writers and readers, offering a mental map whose north
and south are the specific and the general. At its best, literature is universal, illu-
minating human nature at precisely the point at which it is most parochial and
specific.

Greatness in science is harder for most of us to grasp. We can make a list of
scientists we've been told are great, but few of us have had the kind of intimate
contact that would illuminate the particular qualities of the achievement. Partly,
it is the work itself: it does not invite us in; it is objectifying, therefore distancing,
corrupted by difficult or seemingly irrelevant detail. Mathematics is also a barrier.
Furthermore, scientific ideas happily float free of their creators. Scientists might
know the classical laws of motion having never read Newton on the matter or
grasp relativity from textbooks without reading Einstein's special or general theories or know the structure of DNA without having—or needing—a firsthand
knowledge of Crick and Watson's 1953 paper.

Here's a good case in point. Their paper, a mere twelve hundred words, published in the journal *Nature*, ended with the famously modest conclusion: "It has
not escaped our notice that the specific pairing we have postulated immediately
suggests a possible copying mechanism for the genetic material." "It has not
escaped our notice"—the drawing-room politesse of the double negative is
touchingly transparent. It roughly translates as "Look at us everybody! We've
found the mechanism by which life on earth replicates; we're excited as hell and
can't sleep a wink." "It has not escaped our notice" is the kind of close contact I
mean. It is not easily come by at firsthand.

However, there is one preeminent scientist who is almost as approachable in
this respect as a novelist. It is perfectly possible for the nonscientist to understand
what it is in Darwin's work that makes him unique and great. In part, it is the
sequence of benign accidents that set him on his course, each step to be measured
against the final achievement. And partly it is the subject itself. Natural history, or
nineteenth-century biology generally, was a descriptive science. The theory of
natural selection is not, in its essentials, difficult to understand, though its impli-

cations have been vast, its applications formidable, and the consequences in scientific terms quite complex—as the computational biology of the late Bill Hamilton shows. Partly too because Darwin, though hardly the greatest prose writer of the nineteenth century, was intensely communicative, affectionate, intimate, and honest. He wrote many letters and filled many notebooks.

Let us read his life as a novel, like *Herzog*, driving forward toward a great reckoning. The sixteen-year-old Charles is at the university in Edinburgh and beginning to show disillusionment with the study of medicine. He writes to his sisters that he is "going to learn to stuff birds, from a blackamoor." Charles took his lessons in taxidermy from one John Edmonstone, a freed slave, and found his teacher "very pleasant and intelligent." Edmonstone recounted to the young Darwin his experiences as a slave and described the wonders of a tropical rain forest to him. All his life, Darwin abhorred slavery, and this early acquaintanceship may have had some bearing on the relatively neglected book of Darwin's I want to discuss. The following year Darwin comes in contact with the evolutionary ideas of Lamarck and, in the Edinburgh debating societies, hears passionate, godless arguments for scientific materialism. He spends days foraging along the shores of the Firth of Forth looking for sea creatures, and in an 1827 notebook he records detailed observations of two marine invertebrates.

Since Charles did not warm to the prospect of becoming a physician, his father "proposed that I should become a clergyman. He was very properly vehement against my turning an idle sporting man, which then seemed my probable destination." So he studied at Cambridge, where, at the age of eighteen, his love of natural history is becoming a passion. "What fun we will have together," he writes to his cousin. "What beetles we will catch, it will do my heart good to go once more together to some of our old haunts . . . we will make regular campaigns into the Fens; Heaven protect the beetles." And in another letter, "I am dying by inches from not having anybody to talk to about insects." In his last two terms his mentor, Henslow, professor of botany, persuades him to take up geology.

After Cambridge, the offer comes through Henslow to be the naturalist and companion to the captain on board the *Beagle*, making a government survey of South America. We may follow the wrangling as he persuades his father, with the help of Uncle Josiah Wedgewood. "I must state again," implores the earnest Charles, "I cannot think it would unfit me hereafter for a steady life." Many weeks of delay, then after two false starts, he sets sail on December 27, 1831. Days of seasickness, then the *Beagle* is prevented by quarantine measures from landing in La Palma in the Canaries. But Charles has a net in the stern of the ship; the weather is fine, and he catches "a great number of curious animals, and fully occupied my time in my cabin." Finally, landfall at St. Jago in the Cape Verde Islands, and the young man is in ecstasy. "The island has given me so much instruction and delight," he writes to his father, "it is utterly useless to say anything about the scenery—it would be as profitable to explain to a blind man colors, as to a person who has not been out of Europe, the total dissimilarity of a tropical view. . . . Whenever I enjoy anything I always look forward to writing it down. . . . So you must excuse raptures and those raptures badly expressed."

He enjoys working in his cramped cabin, drawing and describing his specimens of rocks, plants, and animals and preserving them to send them back to England to Henslow. The enthusiasm does not die as the expedition proceeds, but to it is added a growing scientific confidence. He writes to Henslow:

Nothing has so much interested me as finding two species of elegantly coloured Planariae, inhabiting the dry forest! The false relation they bear to snails is the most extraordinary thing of the kind I have ever seen . . . some of the marine species possess an organization so marvellous that I can scarcely credit my eyesight. . . . Today I have been out and returned like Noah's ark, with animals of all sorts. . . . I have found a most curious snail, and spiders, beetles, snakes, scorpions ad libitum. And to conclude, shot a Cavia weighing one hundredweight.

With vast quantities of his preserved specimens preceding him, and already being described, and with his own theories about the formation of the earth and of coral reefs taking shape in his mind, Darwin arrives back in England five years later, at the age of twenty-seven, already a scientist of some standing. There is something of the thrill and illumination of great literature when Darwin, at the age of twenty-nine, only two years after he had returned from his voyage on the *Beagle* and still twenty-one years before he would publish *The Origin of Species*, confides to a pocket notebook the first hints of a simple, beautiful idea: "Origin of man now proved. . . . He who understands baboon would do more towards metaphysics than Locke."

And yet *The Origin of Species* itself does not allow an easy route into an understanding of Darwin's greatness. Read as a book rather than as a theory, it can overwhelm the nonspecialist reader with a proliferation of instances—the fruits of Darwin's delay—and it is significant that the most frequently quoted passages occur in the final paragraph.

Darwin was the sort of scientist whose work completely permeated his life. His study of the earthworms in the garden at Downe is well known. He attended country markets to quiz horse, dog, and pig breeders, and at country shows he sought out growers of prize vegetables. Always a warmly devoted father, he recorded in a notebook, "My first child was born on December 27th 1839, and I at once commenced to make notes on the first dawn of the various expressions which he exhibited." Long before an innate theory of mind had been postulated, Darwin was experimenting with his eldest child, William, and reaching his own conclusions:

When a few days over six months old, his nurse pretended to cry, and I saw that his face instantly assumed a melancholy expression, with the corners of the mouth strongly depressed. Therefore it seems to me that an innate feeling must have told him that the pretended crying of his nurse expressed grief; and this, through the instinct of sympathy, excited grief in him.

While out riding, he stops to talk to a woman and notes the contraction in her brows as she looks up at him with the sun at his back. At home he takes three of his children out into the garden and gets them to look up at a bright portion of the sky. The reason? "With all three, the orbicular, corrugator, and pyramidal muscles were energetically contracted, through reflex action." Over many years, while engaged in other work, Darwin was researching *The Expression of the Emotions in Man and Animals*, his most extraordinary and approachable book, rich in observed detail and brilliant speculation, beautifully illustrated—one of the first scientific books to use photographs, including some of his own baby pouting and laughing—and now available in a third edition, prepared and annotated by the great American psychologist of the emotions, Paul Ekman. Darwin not only sets out to describe expressions in dogs and cats as well as man—how we contract the muscles around our eyes and reveal our canine teeth when we are angry and how, in Ekman's words, "we want to touch with our faces those we love"—he also poses the difficult question, Why? Why do we redden with embarrassment rather than go pale? Why do the inner corners of the brow lift in sorrow, and not the whole brow? Why do cats arch their backs in affection? An emotion, he argued, was a physiological state, a direct expression of physiological change. In pursuit of these questions, there are numerous pleasing digressions and observations: the way a billiard player, especially a novice, tries to guide the ball toward its target with a movement of the head or even the whole body; how a cross child sitting on his parent's knee raises one shoulder and gives a backward push with it in an expression of rejection; the firm closure of the mouth during a delicate or difficult operation.

Behind this wealth of detail lay more basic questions. Do we *learn* to smile when we are happy, or is the smile innate? In other words, are expressions universal to all cultures and races, or are they culture specific? He wrote to people in remote corners of the British Empire asking them to observe the expressions of the indigenous populations. In England he showed photographs of various expressions and asked people to comment on them. He drew on his own experience. The book is anecdotal, unscientific, and very clear-sighted. The expressions of emotion are the products of evolution, Darwin argued, and therefore universal. He opposed the influential views of the anatomist Sir Charles Bell that certain unique muscles, with no equivalent in the animal kingdom, had been created by God in the faces of men to allow them to communicate their feelings to each other. In a footnote, Ekman quotes from Bell's book: "The most remarkable muscle in the human face is the corrugator supercilii which knits the eyebrows with an enigmatic effect which unaccountably but irresistibly conveys the idea of mind." In Darwin's copy of Bell's book, he has underlined the passage and written, "I suspect he never dissected monkey." Of course, these muscles, as Darwin showed, existed in other primates.

By showing that the same principles governing expression applied in primates and man, Darwin argued for continuity and gradation of species—important generally to his theory of evolution and to disproving the Christian view that man was a special creation set apart from all other animals. He was intent too on demonstrating through universality a common descent for all races of mankind. In this he opposed himself forcefully to the racist views of scientists like Louis Agassiz, who argued that Africans were inferior to Europeans because they were descended from a different and inferior stock. In a letter to Hooker, Darwin mentions how Agassiz had been maintaining the doctrine of "several species"—that is, of man—"much, I daresay, to the comfort of slave holding Southerns."

Modern paleontology and molecular biology show Darwin to have been right and Agassiz wrong: we are descended from a common stock of anatomically modern humans who migrated out of East Africa perhaps as recently as two hundred thousand years ago and spread around the world. Local differences in climate have produced variations in the species that are in many cases literally skin deep. We have fetishized these differences to rationalize conquest and subjugation. As Darwin puts it:

All the chief expressions exhibited by man are the same through out the world. This fact is interesting as it affords a new argument in favor of the several races being descended from a single parent stock, which must have been almost completely human in structure, and to a large extent, in mind, before the period at which the races diverged from each other.

We should be clear about what is implied by the universal expressions of emotion. The eating of a snail or a piece of cheddar cheese may give rise to delight in one culture and disgust in another. But disgust, regardless of the cause, has a universal expression. In Darwin's words: "The mouth is opened widely, with the upper lip strongly retracted, which wrinkles the side of the nose." The expression and the physiology are products of evolution. But emotions are also, of course, shaped by culture. Our ways of managing our emotions, our attitudes to them, and the way we describe them are learned and differ from culture to culture. Still, behind the notion of a commonly held stock of emotion lies that of a universal human nature. And until fairly recently, and for a good part of the twentieth century, this has been a reviled notion. Darwin's book was out of favor for a long time after his death. The climate of opinion has changed now, and Ekman's superb edition was a major publishing event and has been enthusiastically welcomed.

As must be clear by now, I think that the exercise of imagination and ingenuity as expressed in literature supports Darwin's view. It would not be possible to read and enjoy literature from a time remote from our own, or from a culture that was profoundly different from our own, unless we shared some common emotional ground, some deep reservoir of assumptions, with the writer. An annotated edition that clarifies matters of historical circumstance or local custom or language is always useful, but it is never fundamentally necessary to a reading. What we have in common with each other is just as extraordinary in its way as all our exotic differences. I mentioned at the beginning the parochial and the universal as polarities in literature. One might think of literature as encoding both our cultural and genetic inheritance. Each of these two elements, genes and culture, have had a reciprocal shaping effect, for as primates we are intensely social creatures, and our social environment has exerted over time a powerful adaptive pressure. This gene-culture coevolution, elaborated by E. O. Wilson among others, dissolves the oppositions of nature versus nurture. If one reads accounts of the systematic nonintrusive observations of troops of bonobo—bonobos and common chimps rather than baboons are our closest relatives—one sees rehearsed all the major themes of the English nineteenth-century novel: alliances made and broken, individuals rising while others fall, plots hatched, revenge, gratitude, injured pride, successful and unsuccessful courtship, bereavement and mourning. Approximately five million years separate us and the bonobos from our common ancestor—and given that a lot of this coming and going is ultimately about sex (I'm talking here about bonobos *and* the nineteenth-century novel), that's a very long time during which, cumulatively, successful social strategies effect the distribution of certain genes and not others.

That we have a nature, that its values are self-evident to us to the point of invisibility, and that it would be a different nature if we were, say, termites was a point E. O. Wilson was trying to make when he invented a highly educated Dean of Termitities, who delivers a stirring commencement day address to his fellow termites:

> Since our ancestors, the macrotermitine termites, achieved 10 kilogram weight and larger brains during their rapid evolution through the later Tertiary period and learned to write with pheromone script, termitistic scholarship has refined ethical philosophy. It is now possible to express the deontological imperatives of moral behavior with precision. These imperatives are mostly self-evident and universal. They are the very essence of termity. They include the love of darkness and of the deep saprophytic, basidiomycetic penetralia of the soil; the centrality of colony life amidst a richness of war and trade among the colonies; the sanctity of the physiological caste system; the evil of personal reproduction by worker

castes; the mystery of deep love for reproductive siblings, which turns to hatred the instant they mate; rejection of the evil of personal rights; the infinite aesthetic pleasure of pheromenal song; the aesthetic pleasure of eating from nestmates' anuses after the shedding of the skin; the joy of cannibalism and surrender of the body for consumption when sick or injured. . . . Some termitistically inclined scientists, particularly the ethologists and sociobiologists, argue that our social organization is shaped by our genes and that our ethical precepts simply reflect the peculiarities of termite evolution. They assert that ethical philosophy must take into account the structure of the termite brain and the evolutionary history of the species. Socialization is genetically channeled and some forms of it all but inevitable. This proposal has created major academic controversy.

That is to say, whether it is a saga, a concrete poem, a bildungsroman, or a haiku, and regardless of when it was written and in what colony, you would just *know* a piece of termite literature as soon as you had read a line or two. Extrapolating from the termite literary tradition, we can say that our own human literature does not define human nature so much as exemplify it.

If there are human universals that transcend culture, then it follows that they do not change, or they do not change easily. And if something does change in us historically, then by definition it is not human nature that has changed but some characteristic special to a certain time and circumstance. And yet there are writers who like to make their point by assuming that human nature is a frail entity subject to sudden lurches—exciting revolutionary improvements or deeply regrettable deterioration—and defining the moment of the change has always been an irresistible intellectual pursuit. No one, I think, has yet exceeded Virginia Woolf for precision in this matter, though she does allow a certain ironic haziness about the actual date: "On or about December 1910," she wrote in her essay "Character in Fiction," "human character changed." Woolf of course was preoccupied with the great gulf, as she saw it, that separated her generation from her parents'. The famous anecdote may or may not be true, but one hopes it was. It has Lytton Strachey entering a drawing room in 1908, encountering Virginia and her sister, pointing to a stain on Vanessa's dress, and inquiring, "Semen?" Virginia wrote, "With that one word, all barriers of reticence and reserve went down." The nineteenth century had officially ended. The world would never be the same again.

I remember similar apocalyptic generational claims made in the 1960s and early 1970s. Human nature changed forever, it was claimed at the time, in a field near Woodstock in 1967, or in the same year with the release of *Sgt. Pepper*, or the year before on a certain undistinguished street in San Francisco. The Age of Aquarius had dawned, and things would never be the same again.

Less light-headed than Virginia Woolf but equally definitive was T. S. Eliot in his essay "The Metaphysical Poets." He discovered that in the seventeenth century "a dissociation of sensibility set in, from which we have never recovered." He was, of course, speaking of English poets, who "possessed a mechanism of sensibility which could devour any kind of experience," but I think we can assume that he thought they generally shared a biology with other people. His theory, which, as he conceded, was perhaps too brief to carry conviction, expresses both Eliot's regret (this dissociation was not a good thing) and his hopes (this dissociation could be reversed by those modern poets who would redefine modern sensibilities to his prescription).

Jacob Burkhardt defining his own choice moment, in *The Civilization of the Renaissance in Italy*, discerned a blossoming not simply in human nature but in consciousness itself: "In the Middle Ages," he wrote, "both sides of human consciousness—that which was turned within as that which was turned without—lay dreaming or half awake beneath a common veil. Man was conscious of himself only as a member of a race, people, party, family, or corporation. . . . But at the close of the thirteenth century, Italy began to swarm with individuality; the ban laid upon human personality was dissolved."

The French historian Philippe Aries defined a radical shift in human emotions in the eighteenth century when parents began to feel a self-conscious love for their children. Before then, a child was little more than a tiny, incapable adult, likely to be carried off by disease and therefore not worth investing with too much feeling. A thousand medieval tombstones and their heartfelt inscriptions to a departed child may have provided the graveyard for this particular theory, but Aries's work demonstrates a secondary or parallel ambition in the pursuit of the defining moment of change in human nature—that is, the aim of locating the roots of our modernity. This is more or less central to the project of intellectual history—to ask at which moment, in which set of circumstances, we became recognizable to ourselves. At least some of these candidates will be familiar to you: the invention of agriculture ten thousand years ago, or, perhaps closely related, the expulsion from the Garden of Eden, or the writing of *Hamlet*, which features a man so anguished, bored, indecisive, and generally put upon by the fact of his own existence that we welcome him into our hearts and find no precursor for him in literature. We can fix the beginnings of the modern mind in the scientific revolution of the seventeenth century; the agricultural or industrial revolutions which gathered populations into cities and eventually made possible mass consumption, mass political parties, mass communication; with the writings of Kafka, a most artfully or willfully dissociated sensibility; or with the invention of writing itself a mere several thousand years ago which made possible a geometrical increase in the transmission of culture; or with the publication of Einstein's special and general theories, the first performance of the *Rite of Spring*, the publication of Joyce's

Ulysses, or the dropping of a nuclear weapon on Hiroshima after which we accepted, whether we wanted it or not, stewardship for the whole planet. Some used to plump for the storming of the Winter Palace, though I'd prefer to that the radically unadorned, conversationally reflective early poetry of Wordsworth; or by association, the French Enlightenment and the invention of universal human rights.

The biological view, on the other hand, is long and, by these terms, unspectacular, though I would say no less interesting: one speaks not of a moment but of an immeasurable tract of irretrievable time whose traces are a handful of bones and stone artifacts which demand all our interpretative genius; with the neocortex evolving at the astonishing rate of an extra teaspoon of gray matter every hundred thousand years, hominids made tools, acquired language, became aware of their own existence and that of others and of their mortality, and took a view on the afterlife and accordingly buried their dead. Possibly the Neanderthals, who fell into extinction thirty thousand years ago, were the first into the modern age. But they just were not modern enough to survive the pace.

You could say that what is pursued in all these accounts is the secular equivalent of a creation myth. Literary writers seem to prefer an explosive, decisive moment, the miracle of a birth, to a dull continuum of infinitesimal change. More or less the whole time span of culture can be embraced when we ask, Who is the oldest, who is the ur—modern human being, mitochondrial Eve, or Alan Turing?

Our interest in the roots of modernity is not just a consequence of accelerating social change; implicit in the idea of the definitive moment, of rupture with the past, is the notion that human nature is a specific historical product, shaped by shared values, circumstances of upbringing within a certain civilization—in other words, that there is no human nature at all beyond that which develops at a particular time and in a particular culture. By this view the mind is an all-purpose, infinitely adaptable computing machine operating a handful of wired-in rules. We are born tabula rasa, and it is our times that shape us.

This view, known to some as the Standard Social Science Model and to others as environmental determinism, was the dominant one in the twentieth century, particularly in its first half. It had its roots in anthropology, especially in the work of Margaret Mead and her followers, and in behavioral psychology. Writing in *Sex and Temperament in Three Primitive Societies*, published in 1935, Mead said: "We are forced to conclude that human nature is almost unbelievably malleable, responding accurately and contrastingly to contrasting cultural conditions." This view found endorsement across the social sciences and solidified in the postwar years into a dogma that had clear political dimensions. There was a time when to challenge it with reference to a biological dimension to existence would be to court academic, and even social, pariah status. Like Christian theologians, the cultural relativists freed us from all biological constraints and set mankind apart from all other life on earth. And within this view, the educated man or woman pronouncing on a favored date for the transformation of human nature would be on firm ground epistemologically—we are what the world makes us, and when the world changes dramatically, then so do we in our essentials. It can all happen, as Virginia Woolf observed for herself, in the space of a generation.

The famous behaviorist John Watson, professor of psychology at Johns Hopkins, published an influential book on child rearing in 1928. As Christina Hardyment showed in her marvelous book *Dream Babies*, there is hardly a better window into the collective mind of a society, its view of human nature, than the child-care handbooks it produces. Watson wrote:

> Give me a dozen healthy infants, well-formed, and my own specified world to bring them up in and I'll guarantee to take any one at random and train him to become any kind of specialist I might select—doctor, lawyer, merchant chief, and yes, even beggarman and thief, regardless of his talents, penchants, tendencies, abilities, vocations, and race of his ancestors.

Human nature was clay in his hands. I cannot help feeling that the following passage from Watson's child-care book *The Psychological Care of Young Infants*, beyond its unintentional comedy, reflects or foretells a century of doomed, tragic social experiments in shaping human nature and shows us a skewed science devoid of evidence and no less grotesque than the pseudoscience that perverted Darwin's work to promote theories of racial supremacy:

> The sensible way to bring up children is to treat them as young adults. Dress them, bathe them with care and circumspection. Let your behavior always be objective and kindly firm. Never hug and kiss them. Never let them sit in your lap. If you must, kiss them once on the forehead when they say goodnight. Shake hands with them in the morning. Give them a pat on the head when they make a good job of a difficult task. . . . Put the child out in the back yard a large part of the time. . . . Do this from the time that it is born. . . . Let it learn to overcome difficulties almost from the moment of birth. . . . away from your watchful eye. If your heart is too tender, and you must watch the child, make yourself a peephole, so that you can see without being seen, or use a periscope.

Watson's book, hugely successful at the time, was pronounced by *Atlantic Monthly* to be "a godsend to parents."

The ideas of Mead and Watson, who were simply prominent figures among many promoting the near infinite malleability of human nature, found general acceptance in the public and in the universities, where their descendants flourish today in various forms, including the political correctness movement, which holds that since the human condition is a social construct which in turn is defined by language, it is possible and desirable to reform the condition by changing the language. No one should doubt that some good impulses lay behind the Standard Model. Margaret Mead in particular, working at a time when the European empires had consolidated but had not yet begun to crumble, had a strong antiracist element to her work, and she was determined to oppose the condescending view of primitive inferiority and to insist that each culture must be judged in its own terms. When Mead and Watson were at their most active, the Soviet revolution still held great hopes for mankind. If learning makes us what we are, then inequalities could be eliminated if we shared the same environment. Educate parents in the proper methods of child care, and new generations of improved people would emerge. Human nature could be fundamentally remolded by the makers of social policy. We were perfectible, and the wrongs and inequalities of the past could be rectified by radical alterations to the social environment. The cruelties and absurdities of social Darwinism and eugenics and, later, the new threat posed by the social policies of Hitler's Germany engendered a disgust with the biological perspective that helped entrench a belief in a socially determined nature that could be engineered for the better of all.

In fact, the Third Reich cast a long shadow over free scientific inquiry in the decades after the Second World War. Various branches of psychology were trapped by intellectual fear, deterred by recent history from considering the mind as a biological product of adaptive forces, even while, in nearby biology departments, from the 1940s onward, Darwinism was uniting with Mendelian genetics and molecular biology to form the powerful alliance known as the modern synthesis.

In the late 1950s, the young Paul Ekman, who had no firm convictions of his own, set off for New Guinea with head and shoulder photographs of modern Americans expressing various emotions—surprise, fear, disgust, joy, and so on. He discovered that his sample group of Stone Age Highlanders, who had had no, or virtually no, contact with the modern world, were able to make up easily recognizable stories about each expression. They also mimed for him the facial expressions in response to stories he gave them—for example, you come across a pig that has been dead for some days. His work, and later his cleverly designed experiments with Japanese and Americans which took into account the display rules of the different cultures, clearly vindicated Darwin's conclusions. As Ekman writes:

Social experience influences attitudes about emotion, creates display and feeling rules, develops and tunes the particular occasions which will most rapidly call forth an emotion. The *expression* of our emotions, the particular configurations of muscular movements, however, appear to be fixed, enabling understanding across generations, across cultures, and within cultures between strangers as well as intimates.

Before leaving for New Guinea, Ekman had paid a visit to Margaret Mead. Her firm view was that facial expressions differ from culture to culture as much as customs and values. She was distinctly cool about Ekman's research. And yet toward the end of her life she explained in her autobiography in 1972 that she and her colleagues had held back from the consideration of the biological bases of behavior because of anxieties about the political consequences. How strange, this reversal of historical circumstances, that for Mead universality in expression or in human nature should appear to lend support to racism, while for Darwin such considerations undermined its flimsy theoretical basis.

Mead and her generation of anthropologists, arriving at a Stone Age settlement with their notebooks, gifts, and decent intentions, did not fully understand (though Darwin, along with most novelists, could have told them) as they exchanged smiles and greetings with their subjects what a vast pool of shared humanity, of shared assumptions, was necessary and already being drawn on for them to do their work. As the last of these precious cultures have vanished, the data have been revisited. Donald Brown in his book *Human Universals* compiled a list of what human individuals and societies hold in common. It is both long and, given the near infinite range of all possible patterns of behavior, quite specific. When reading it, it is worth bearing in mind Wilson's termite dean. Brown includes—I'm choosing at random—tool making, preponderant right-handedness, specific childhood fears, knowledge that other people have an inner life, trade, giving of gifts, notions of justice, importance of gossip, hospitality, hierarchies, and so on. What's interesting about Brown's characterization of what he calls the "Universal People," who incorporate all the common, shared features of mankind, is the number of pages he devotes to language—again quite specific—for example, Universal People language has contrasts between vowels and contrasts between stops and nonstops. Their language is symbolic and invariably contains nouns, verbs, and possessives. Extra proficiency in language invariably confers prestige. This surely, at the higher level of mental functioning, is what binds the human family. We know now that no blank-disk, all-purpose machine could learn language at the speed and facility that a child does. A three-year-old daily solves scores of ill-posed problems. An instinct for language is a central part of our nature.

On our crowded planet, we are no longer able to visit Stone Age peoples untouched by modern times. Mead and her contemporaries would never have wanted to put the question, What is it that we hold in common with such people?

And anthropologists no longer have the opportunity of first contact. We can, however, reach to our bookshelves. Literature must be our anthropology. Here is a description—twenty-seven hundred years old—of a woman who has been waiting for more than two decades for her beloved husband to come home. Someone has told her that he has at last arrived and is downstairs and that she must go and greet him. But, she asks herself, is it really him?

> She started down from her lofty room, her heart
> in turmoil, torn . . . should she keep her distance,
> probe her husband? Or rush up to the man at once
> and kiss his head and cling to both his hands?
> As soon as she stepped over the stone threshold,
> slipping in, she took a seat at the closest wall
> and, radiant in the firelight, faced Odysseus now.
> There he sat, leaning against the great central column,
> eyes fixed on the ground, waiting, poised for whatever words
> his hardy wife might say when she caught sight of him.
> A long while she sat in silence . . . numbing wonder
> filled her heart as her eyes explored his face.
> One moment he seemed . . . Odysseus to the man, to the life—
> the next, no, he was not the man she knew,
> a huddled mass of rags was all she saw.

So, still uncertain, Penelope tells Odysseus they'll sleep in separate rooms, and she gives orders for the marriage bed to be moved out of the bedroom. But of course he knows this bed cannot be moved—he knocked it together himself and reminds her just how he did it. Thus he proves beyond doubt he really is her husband, but now he's upset that she thought he was an imposter, and they're already heading for a marital spat.

> Penelope felt her knees go slack, her heart surrender,
> recognizing the strong clear signs that Odysseus offered.
> She dissolved in tears, rushed to Odysseus, flung her arms
> around his neck and kissed his head and cried out,
> "Odysseus—don't flare up at me now, not you,
> always the most understanding man alive!
> The gods, it was the gods who sent us sorrow—
> they grudged us both a life in each other's arms
> from the heady zest of youth to the stoop of old age.
> But don't fault me, angry with me now because I failed,
> at the first glimpse, to greet you, hold you, so . . .

In my heart of hearts I always cringed with fear
some fraud might come, beguile me with his talk.

Customs may change—dead suitors may be lying in the hallway with no homicide charges pending—but we recognize the human essence of these lines.
Within the emotional and the expressive we remain what we are. As Darwin put
it in his conclusion to *Expression,* "the language of the emotions . . . is certainly of
importance for the welfare of mankind." In Homer's case we extend Ekman's
"understanding across the generations"—a hundred and thirty of them at least.

The Human Genome Sequencing Consortium concluded its recent report in
Nature with these words: "Finally, it has not escaped our notice that the more we
learn about the human genome, the more there is to explore." This form of
respectful echoing within the tradition must surely appeal to those who admire
literary modernism. And as the sequencing of the human genome is completed, it
is reasonable to ask just whose genome was this anyway? What lucky individual
was chosen to represent us all? Who is the universal person? The answer is that
the genes of fifteen people were merged into just the sort of composite, plausible,
imaginary person a novelist might dream up, and here we contemplate the
metaphorical convergence of these two noble and distinct forms of investigation
into our condition, literature, and science. That which binds us, our common
nature, is what literature has always, knowingly and helplessly, given voice to.
And it is this universality which the biological sciences, now entering another
exhilarating phase, are set to explore further.

Evolutionary Social Constructivism

David Sloan Wilson

Evolutionary theory has been controversial throughout its history for reasons that go beyond religious matters. Even among nonbelievers, something momentous and contentious appears to be at stake. The controversy also transcends knowledge of the subject. It has not quieted over the decades, despite tremendous advances in knowledge, and it currently divides the foremost authorities on evolution, as the pages of professional journals and popular intellectual forums such as the *New York Review of Books* attest.

Among the sophisticates, the controversy does not center on the basic fact of evolution but on certain consequences, such as the importance of natural selection and especially the relevance of evolution to human affairs. The intellectual positions most fiercely opposed to "sociobiology" and "evolutionary psychology" include social constructivism, postmodernism, and deconstructionism. These positions are different from each other but united in their commitment to the idea that individuals and societies have enormous flexibility in what they can become, in contrast to the inflexibility and determinism attributed to evolutionary approaches to human behavior. I will refer to this core idea as social constructivism, with apologies for obscuring the differences between the positions referred to above that are important in other contexts.

These debates usually become so polarized that they reveal the worst aspects of tribalism in our species. Each side regards the other as the enemy whose position has no substance or rational basis, other than being ideologically driven. The middle ground becomes a no-man's-land into which no one dares to venture. Given this kind of intellectual trench warfare, it is no wonder that ideas can stagnate for years, decades, and even centuries.

This essay attempts a more productive exploration of the middle ground. I will try to show that the heart of social constructivism can be given an evolutionary formulation. Social constructivists have more to gain from adopting an evolutionary perspective than by avoiding it, and sociobiologists need to incorporate large elements of social constructivism into their own framework. This is not an exercise in empty diplomacy in which everyone continues to think as they did before. Instead, it is an attempt to genuinely occupy the middle ground that requires fundamental movement on both sides.

Why should a chapter on evolutionary social constructivism appear in a book on evolution and literature? One reason is that literary studies have historically been dominated by social constructivist perspectives. Skepticism toward a genre of evolutionary literary studies is fueled by the larger issues, with literature the battleground rather than the battle. Another reason is that evolutionary social constructivism relies fundamentally upon narrative. The reason that individuals and societies have a capacity for change is largely because of the importance of stories in psychological and cultural evolutionary processes.

Three Evolutionary and Two Social Constructivist Positions

I will begin by outlining three evolutionary (E) and two social constructivist (S) positions. The evolutionary positions are as follows:

E1. The minds of all organisms are genetically adapted to their ancestral environments. Because there are many adaptive problems to solve, all minds consist of a collection of specialized adaptations rather than a single all-purpose adaptation. Understanding the human mind is complicated by the fact that genetic evolution has not kept pace with the social and environmental changes brought about by the advent of agriculture. We therefore often behave maladaptively in our current environments, much as a rain forest lizard would behave maladaptively when transported into the desert. To understand the human mind and its products, we need to examine their adaptedness in ancestral environments, not in modern environments. This is the position most often associated with the term "evolutionary psychology."[1] When related to literature, a typical hypothesis emanating from this position might be "sex differences and sexual relationships in literature should reflect adaptive male and female reproductive strategies that evolved in ancestral environments and are part of our human nature."

E2. There is more to evolution than genetic evolution. Physiological, psychological, and cultural processes can also be evolutionary in the sense that alternatives are created and selected on the basis of given criteria. The immune system is a well-known example of a physiological evolutionary process. Antibodies are created at random, and those that successfully bind to antigens replicate faster than those that don't. The late social psychologist Donald Campbell never tired of using the phrase "blind variation and selective retention" to describe the essence of evolution and its relevance to psychological and cultural processes, including the process of scientific inquiry, in addition to genetic evolution.[2] When related to literature, a hypothesis emanating from this position might be "narratives have a powerful effect on human behavior and adaptation to current environments proceeds in part through the creation and selection of alternative narratives."

E3. There is more to evolution than adaptation. Evolving systems are often poorly adapted to their environments for a host of reasons, including genetic drift; phylogenetic, developmental, and genetic constraints; and more, all of which have counterparts in nongenetic evolutionary processes.[3] When related to literature, a hypothesis emanating from this position might be "literature is a form of play in humans, and adult play exists not as an adaptation in its own right but as part of selection for juvenile characters in general (neoteny). Neotonous behaviors such as play got dragged along with neotonous morphological characters that enabled us to have big heads and stand upright."

Here are the social constructivist positions.

S1. Individuals and societies have enormous flexibility in what they can become, which is largely unconstrained by human biology. This flexibility is reflected in the diversity of behaviors that we observe within and among societies around the world and throughout history. People have almost no instincts and obtain their behaviors through learning and cultural transmission. Current inequities that are often justified as part of human nature, therefore inevitable, are nothing of the sort and usually reflect the efforts of powerful elements of society to dominate less powerful elements. When related to literature, a typical hypothesis emanating from this position is "The association of witchcraft with females, including the representation of witches in literature, is an effort to limit the social role of females to that of the good wife."[4]

S2. Individuals and societies have such enormous flexibility that anything—absolutely anything—goes. For example, all possible combinations of sex roles can exist and have been observed in societies around the world. Words for categories that seem weird to us, such as "red hats worn on the same day that broccoli is eaten" or "second cousins who commit unspeakable acts with barnyard animals," can be found in other cultures, just as our words and categories appear weird to them. When related to literature, it is difficult to provide a hypothesis emanating from this position, precisely because anything goes.

Positions S1 and S2 agree about flexibility but disagree about whether it leads to sensible versus nonsensical outcomes. Critics of social constructivism often portray the S2 version but I think that a more sympathetic reading is closer to S1. Social constructivists are first and foremost trying to imagine and implement a better world. What they imagine may strike some as naively optimistic or wrongheaded, but it is perfectly sensible, even in biological terms—equality, respect, basic necessities for all, the end of repression, and so on. When social constructivists say that anything goes, it is usually in the context of saying that their desired outcome is possible. This is the form of social constructivism that I will defend, and indeed the only form that I think is worth defending. Who would want to defend a view in which absolutely nothing winnows the functional from the dysfunctional?

Our question therefore becomes, what is the potential for incorporating the social constructivist position S1 into the three evolutionary positions E1, E2, and E3? Ever since the publication of *Sociobiology* in 1975, critics have taken refuge primarily in E3.[5] The reason that first sociobiology and then evolutionary psychology are fatally flawed, say the critics, is because they rely excessively on adaptationism. I regard this as an unfortunate wrong turn on the part of the critics. As an evolutionary biologist, I am perfectly comfortable with the fact that there is more to evolution than adaptation. It is definitely the middle ground that needs exploring as far as the general subject of evolution is concerned. However, the nonadaptive side of evolution provides little comfort for S1, the social constructivist position that we are trying to place on an evolutionary foundation. Since S1 involves the achievement of goals that are desirable, therefore adaptive at least in the everyday sense of the word, biologically nonadaptive processes can only accomplish these goals as a happy coincidence, by accident so to speak. Before we rely excessively on a happy accident argument, let us see if a stronger foundation can be found in E1 and E2.

It might surprise some readers to learn that E1, the position most closely associated with sociobiology and evolutionary psychology, provides substantial support for S1, even before we proceed to E2. The key concept that provides a link between E1 and S1 is *behavioral flexibility*, also called *phenotypic plasticity*. No organism is so simple that it is instructed by its genes to "do x." Even bacteria and protozoa are genetically endowed with a set of if-then rules of the form "do x in situation 1," "do y in situation 2" and so on. These rules enable organisms to do the right thing at the right time, not only behaviorally but physiologically and morphologically. The literature on nonhumans is full of wonderful examples of caterpillars that look like twigs in spring and leaves in summer, fish that grow streamlined bodies in the absence of predators but flattened bodies in their presence to exceed the gape of their jaws, frog eggs designed to hatch prematurely at the approach of a snake, salamanders that morph into big-jawed cannibals when food becomes short, and on and on.[6] In all of these cases, information from the environment is combined with a set of predetermined if-then rules to determine the structure and behavior of the organism, much as your tax-preparation software branches off in different directions depending upon the information that it prompts you for.

This kind of adaptive behavioral flexibility provides an intriguing twist to the concept of genetic determinism. Let's assume for the moment that we are driven by our genes to obey the following set of if-then rules.

In this situation . . .   *. . . behave this way*

A   A'

B   B'
C   C'
Etc.   Etc.

Each behavior is adaptive for its respective situation and maladaptive for the other situations. For these if-then rules to evolve, all of the situations must exist in the overall ancestral environment. For example, birds that evolve in environments where predators may or may not be present have evolved to modify their behavior accordingly. In contrast, birds that evolve in environments where predators are always absent do not behave appropriately when the first ones appear. The first sailors to set foot on the Galapagos Islands were surprised when the birds acted as if they were trees rather than predators.[7] To pick an example more relevant to humans, we might be psychologically adapted to live in groups that vary in size from ten to a thousand but genetically unprepared for the megagroups of modern life.[8]

As surprising as it might seem, the genetic determinism of if-then rules provides at least a partial foundation for the social constructivist position S1. Suppose that we regard behavior C' in the above list as socially desirable. We will never achieve behavior C' in situations A and B, but behavior C' will be inevitable if we can implement situation C. The key to achieving the desired social outcome is therefore to change the *situation*, an environmental intervention more reminiscent of social constructivism than genetic determinism as it is usually imagined.

My favorite example of this important concept is a study by evolutionary psychologists Margo Wilson and Martin Daly on risk-taking in men and age of first reproduction in women in the city of Chicago.[9] Unlike most cities, whose neighborhoods are subject to a rapid turnover of residents, Chicago neighborhoods tend to be demographically stable. They also vary greatly in their quality of life, which is reflected in life expectancies that range from the mid-fifties for the worst neighborhoods to the mid-seventies for the best neighborhoods. Wilson and Daly showed that violent risk-taking in men and age of first reproduction in women correlate very strongly with life-expectancy. Of course, both of these are perceived as social problems. Politicians talk endlessly about reducing violence and teenage pregnancies, especially in our inner cities. However, when women from the worst neighborhoods were asked why they had children so young, they gave an answer that can only invoke sympathy: they said that they wanted their mothers to see their grandchildren and in turn wanted to see their own grandchildren. They used the term "weathering" to refer to the aging process that they observed in themselves and their loved ones all around them. If everyone around you was weathering and dying at an average age of fifty-five, wouldn't *you* want to start having children early (as a female) or take great risks to obtain the status and resources required to reproduce (as a male)?

We can portray this example in terms of hypothetical genetically determined if-then rules as follows:

In this situation . . .	*. . . behave this way*
Low life expectancy	Reproduce early (women)
	Take high risks (men)
	Heavily discount the future (both)
High life expectancy	Reproduce later (women)
	Take fewer risks (men)
	Long-range planning (both)

The female and male strategies both fall under the more general categories of discounting the future when life expectancies are low (because there might not be a future) as opposed to foregoing short-term benefits in favor of future benefits when life expectancies are high. If we provisionally accept these if-then rules as the dictates of our genes, then we can derive a straightforward prediction and plan of action: to solve the problems of early pregnancy and violence in our worst neighborhoods, increase life expectancy and otherwise provide a stable social environment with a future to plan for. Of course, this is the kind of solution that a self-described social constructivist and critic of biological determinism might advise.

Genetic determinism contributes positively to social constructivism in this hypothetical scenario, at least in some respects. It leads to a clear plan of action, in contrast to the "anything goes" version of social constructivism. To achieve any given behavior in the right column, simply create the corresponding situation in the left column. In addition, the "anything goes" version of social constructivism can lead to scary outcomes, such as brainwashing people in our worst neighborhoods to be docile and childless. As many critics of social constructivism have observed, it is naive and illogical to think that "anything goes" leads consistently to "socially desirable." The idea of an evolved human nature that fights tenaciously for adaptive outcomes provides a firmer foundation for the optimistic brand of social constructivism (S1) than the "anything goes" portrayal of human nature.

I am not the first person to point out that adaptive behavioral flexibility turns the implications of genetic determinism topsy-turvy. Numerous self-described sociobiologists and evolutionary psychologists have made the same points and justly feel misunderstood by their social constructivist critics who continue to associate evolution with inflexibility.[10] Here, then, is an important meeting ground in which social constructivism can be placed on an evolutionary foundation.

However, I will argue that it does not go far enough. The evolutionary position that I have designated E2 provides even more scope for social constructivism.

Innate Psychology and Nongenetic Evolutionary Processes

"Learning" and "culture" have always been the alternatives to "evolution" for those who reject evolutionary approaches to human behavior. However, learning and cultural change are themselves evolutionary in the sense that alternative behaviors are created and selected according to certain criteria. They are "blind variation and selective retention" processes, as Campbell put it.[11] What separates learning and culture from genetic evolution is not their evolutionary character but their speed. Learning and cultural evolution adapt organisms to their environment quickly, while genetic evolution is so slow that its products are essentially fixed over the time scales that matter most in contemporary human affairs. Another potential difference involves the criteria for selection. Perhaps nongenetic evolutionary processes favor the same behaviors that would evolve by genetic evolution, given enough time, but perhaps they favor a different set of behaviors.[12]

For much of the twentieth century, learning and cultural evolution were invoked so heavily to explain human behavior that genetic evolution seemed irrelevant. If people can be made to do anything with the appropriate reinforcement and enculturation, who cares what happened during the Stone Age? Long before sociobiology and evolutionary psychology made the scene, cognitive psychologists were dismantling the notion of the blank slate by revealing the enormously complicated circuitry that was required to perform such "simple" acts as seeing, hearing, and remembering. It went without saying that this circuitry was largely innate and a product of genetic evolution. However, no cognitive psychologist to my knowledge has interpreted this kind of innateness as denying the existence of nongenetic evolutionary processes.

The cognitive revolution in psychology tended to focus on basic faculties such as vision, hearing, memory, language, and so on. These traits (with the exception of language) are obviously required for survival and reproduction, but what about other traits such as mating, foraging, cooperation, aggression, and migration? According to evolutionary psychologists such as Leda Cosmides and John Tooby, these traits are like vision in their requirement for an elaborate innate circuitry. Just as different circuits are required for vision and hearing (although they must also be integrated with each other), different circuits are required for the evaluation of long-term mates, the evaluation of short-term mates, response to infidelity, the detection of cheaters in social exchange, and so on. The list of specialized cognitive adaptations is not endless but runs into the hundreds and thousands, covering all of the important behaviors that helped us to survive and reproduce in ancestral environments.[13]

This is a startlingly different conception of the mind that will be important even if only partially correct. In its extreme form, however, it has led to the denial of learning and culture as open-ended evolutionary processes in their own right. If this were true, then modern evolutionary theory would provide justification for E1 but not E2, and the only evolutionary foundation for social constructivism would be the innate if-then rules described in the previous section.

The argument upon which the denial is based goes like this: All cognitive adaptations must be specialized to be smart. The first artificial intelligence researchers naively thought that they could build smart general-purpose learning machines, but they soon discovered that the only way to make a machine smart is to make it specialized for a particular task. Chess-playing computers are smart at playing chess but can't do anything else. Similarly, your tax-preparation software can calculate your taxes only if you give it exactly the right information, which it is designed to process in exactly the right way. The world is so full of potential information, which can be processed in so many ways, that all cognitive adaptations must be like your tax-preparation software in its specialized perception and processing of information.

To see why this argument fails, consider the mammalian immune system. Just like the mind, it can be regarded as a collection of genetically evolved mechanisms for helping us to survive and reproduce in our ancestral environment. The number and sophistication of mechanisms that comprise the immune system are mind-boggling when understood in detail.[14] Nevertheless, the centerpiece of the immune system is an open-ended process of blind variation and selective retention. Antibodies are produced at random, and those that successfully fight invading disease organisms are selected. Diseases are so numerous and evolve so fast with their short generation times that the only way to fight them is with another evolutionary process.

The immune system shows that genetic evolution and elaborate innateness do not invariably lead to the kind of modularity that excludes open-ended processes. Indeed, when the pace of environmental change becomes too fast and the number of challenges too great, genetically fixed if-then rules break down and must be supplemented by rapid nongenetic evolutionary processes that generate and select new solutions to current problems. As for the immune system, so also for psychological and cultural processes.

These observations are elementary but profound in their implications for placing social constructivism on an evolutionary foundation. They mean that *whatever the virtues of the evolutionary position outlined in E1, they do not exclude the evolutionary position outlined in E2*. Put another way, all metaphors make a connection between two things that are valid in some respects but not others. My love is a rose even though she is not red and thorny. The blank slate metaphor might be a total failure as a mechanistic conception of the mind but still be perfectly valid with respect to the open-ended nature of individual and societal change.

It would be a mistake to take this reasoning too far. Our eating behaviors provide fine examples of evolved predispositions that were adaptive in ancestral environments, have become maladaptive in modern environments, and are difficult to change. Religions encourage and often achieve altruism at a scale that never existed in ancestral environments, but they don't say that it's easy. There is a difference between *potential* for individual and societal change and *equi-potential*. If by "blank slate" we mean "anything can be written with equal ease," then that part of the metaphor is false.

My argument for placing social constructivism on an evolutionary foundation can be summarized as follows: Those who feel strongly about the potential for individual and societal change need not feel threatened by evolutionary theory. Even the elaborate innateness of the immune system does not exclude and indeed makes possible the potential for open-ended change, leading to new solutions to current problems. However, fulfilling the valid aspects of the blank slate metaphor requires abandoning the invalid aspects. "Potential" does not mean "equi-potential." Realizing potential can be facilitated by a detailed understanding of the mechanisms of genetic evolution and nongenetic evolutionary processes both built by and partially constrained by genetic evolution. In short, the way forward for social constructivism is to become sophisticated about evolution, not to deny its relevance to human affairs.

Evolutionary biologists interested in human behavior, in turn, must realize that there is more to human evolution than genetic adaptation to ancestral environments. The position that I have outlined as E1 does not exclude the position I have outlined as E2, however valid in other respects. Part of our genetic endowment is the capacity for rapid individual and societal adaptation to current environments, which is the heart of social constructivism.

Evolutionary Social Constructivism and Literature

Years ago I asked Napoleon Chagnon, one of the first anthropologists to call himself a sociobiologist, what he found so insightful about evolution.[15] "Because it tells anthropologists to study reproduction instead of pottery!" he snapped back. The simplicity of Chagnon's answer took me aback. He was saying that the study of humans should be centered upon survival and reproduction—and indeed survival only to the extent that it leads to reproduction—just like any other species. We might be playing the reproduction game differently than other species in some respects, but we are playing the same game.

As for anthropology, so also for psychology. David Buss's textbook *Evolutionary Psychology: The New Science of the Mind* has section headings unlike any other psychology textbook: "Problems of Survival," "Challenges of Sex and Mating," "Challenges of Parenting and Kinship," and "Problems of Group Living."[16] This organization reflects the fact that we evolved to do certain things well and that the study of psychology should be organized around those things. As the evolutionary biologist, George Williams, is often quoted as saying: "Is it not reasonable that our understanding of the human mind would be aided greatly by knowing the purpose for which it was designed?"[17]

In many respects, the study of literature from an evolutionary perspective needs to begin with the same refocusing of attention that is already taking place in anthropology and psychology. As Daniel Nettle puts it in his contribution to this volume, if we ask what themes would most interest a nonhuman primate, those are the themes that are most prominently featured in Shakespeare and indeed all literature. I once tested this proposition for myself during a trip to Japan by asking my hosts to provide me with a list of classic Japanese novels, short stories, and plays, which I purchased in their English translations and read during the course of my trip. Even though Japanese culture is often said to be different than Western culture, especially during the times when some of the older works on my list were written, the evolutionary themes leapt off the pages and would have interested our nonhuman primate as much as Shakespeare.

If this volume succeeds in refocusing attention for the study of literature on a par with anthropology and psychology, then it will have accomplished an important task. However, it will not have gone far enough. Stories do more than reflect the ancient concerns of our species, which we hold largely in common with other species. Narratives play an integral role in the nongenetic evolutionary processes outlined in E2 and perhaps even the innate flexibility outlined in E1. Unless we appreciate the importance of narratives in adapting us to our current environments, we will not have a fully developed genre of evolutionary literary studies.

The Genelike Nature of Stories

Genes contain the information about adaptations that have been hard-won by the process of natural selection. Genes are also designed to transmit the information with high fidelity across generations. If nongenetic evolutionary processes exist, the information from those processes must also exist in some form that can be transmitted with high fidelity. Stories have these genelike properties.

Before I elaborate on the meaning of this statement, it will help to establish how scientists and scholars from diverse fields are converging on the importance of narrative in human psychological and cultural processes.

1. Jerome Bruner is one of the fathers of the cognitive psychology revolution that preceded evolutionary psychology. His latest book, entitled *Making Stories: Law, Literature, Life,* is an exploration of the importance of narrative in both the personal and cultural construction of meaning. Some sample quotes: "So why do we want, seek, even find renewal in these unhinging subjunctivized worlds of fiction? Our brain has as many connections among its neurons as there are stars in the Milky Way; it lives and grows by being in dilemmas: we fall asleep when there is not enough to keep those neurons at work, fail to develop our powers." "I want to begin by proposing boldly that, in effect, there is no such thing as an intuitively obvious and essential self to know, one that just sits there ready to be portrayed in words. Rather, we constantly construct and reconstruct our selves to meet the needs of the situations we encounter, and we do so with the guidance of our memories of the past and our hopes and fears for the future. Telling oneself about oneself is like making up a story about who and what we are, what's happened, and why we're doing what we're doing." "So automatic and swift is this process of constructing reality that we are often blind to it—and rediscover it with a cry of 'postmodern rubbish!'"[18]

2. In his book entitled *Love Is a Story,* psychologist Robert Sternberg summarizes his research on the importance of narratives in human relationships. How we behave toward our loved ones depends upon whether we regard love as a fantasy story, a business story, a collector story, a horror story, a pornography story, and so on (twenty-six types of stories are discussed). Our stories and their compatibility with the stories of our partners have a large influence on the quality and length of our relationships. A sample quote: "But a clean separation of fact from fiction simply isn't possible in the context of personal relationships, because we shape the facts of a relationship to conform to our personal fictions. In many ways, we are a composite of our stories. As Immanuel Kant pointed out in *The Critique of Pure Reason,* if there is an objective reality, it is unknowable. All we can know is the reality we construct. That reality takes the form of a story."[19]

3. In his book *Opening Up,* psychologist James Pennebaker summarizes his research on the amazing health effects of keeping a diary. In experiments that have been replicated across age, gender, culture, and social class, writing about important personal experiences in an emotional way for as little as fifteen minutes over the course of three days improves mental and physical health in ways that can be measured objectively, such as college grades and immune function.[20] A sample quote from one of his papers: "The guiding assumption of the present work is that the act of constructing stories is a natural human process that helps individuals to understand their experiences and themselves. This process allows one to organize and remember events in a coherent fashion while integrating thoughts and feelings. In essence, this gives individuals a sense of predictability and control over their lives. Once an experience has structure and meaning, it

would follow that the emotional effects of that experience are more manageable. Constructing stories facilitates a sense of resolution, which results in less rumination and eventually allows disturbing experiences to subside gradually from conscious thought. Painful events that are not structured into a narrative format may contribute to the continued experience of negative thoughts and feelings. Indeed, one of the most prevalent reasons why people begin therapy is because they report suffering from emotional distress. . . . Disclosure is unequivocally at the core of therapy. Psychotherapy usually involves putting together a story that will explain and organize major life events causing distress."[21]

4. In his book *Strangers to Ourselves: Discovering the Adaptive Subconscious*, social psychologist Timothy Wilson summarizes a large body of research showing that people have very little conscious awareness of the psychological mechanisms that cause them to behave as they do. Attempts at introspection not only fail but can actually interfere with mechanisms that are designed to operate subconsciously. Conscious understanding of ourselves must be obtained in the same way that we attempt to understand others: by forming hypotheses (a kind of story) and testing them against experience. The best way to change our behavior is to imagine the kind of person we would like to be and then try to become that person.[22]

5. In his book *The Symbolic Species*, neurobiologist and evolutionary biologist Terrence Deacon argues that we are unique among all species in our capacity for symbolic thought. According to Deacon, the rudiments of symbolic thought do not require a large brain or even a different brain than possessed by our primate ancestors. In fact, it is possible to teach a chimpanzee or bonobo to think symbolically, more like us than their own kind. The problem is that it requires an arduous training process that has no counterpart in nature. Moreover, symbolic thought interferes with more basic forms of associative learning that are adaptive in natural environments. Symbolic thought is like a lofty peak in an adaptive landscape that can be climbed only by first crossing a valley of low fitness. What made humans unique was a natural environmental context that made symbolic thought adaptive in its initial stages, allowing us, and us alone, to cross over to the new adaptive peak. Symbolic thought is above all a system for the generation and selection of mental representations, allowing a form of virtual evolution to take place inside the head.[23]

6. In their article entitled "Evolutionary Psychology and the Emotions," evolutionary psychologists Leda Cosmides and John Tooby themselves stress the importance of narrative in their conception of the modular mind:

Recreating cues through imagery in a decoupled mode triggers the same emotion programs (minus their behavioral manifestations), and allows the planning function to evaluate imagined situations by using the same circuits that evaluate real situations. This allows alternative courses of action to be evaluated in a way similar to the way in which experienced situations are evaluated. In other words, image-based representations may serve to unlock, for the purposes of planning, the same evolved mechanisms that are triggered by an actual encounter with a situation displaying the imagined perceptual and situational cues.[24]

7. People make up their own stories, but they also rely upon stories that come from elsewhere. In modern times stories can be downloaded onto external storage devices such as books and computers, but in ancient times all stories had to be stored in heads and passed from head to head. In his book *Orality and Literacy*, literary scholar Walter Ong shows that the demands of storage and transmission in preliterate societies were so great that they constrained the very nature of human thought. People from oral societies think largely in terms of proverbs that provide guides to action. Discourse consists largely of reciting the proverbs deemed appropriate for given situations. Proverbs are intriguingly modular and provide a system of if-then rules, just as the genetically evolved mind is portrayed in E1. However, proverbs are not innate (however much they require innate mechanisms, as with antibody evolution) but are generated and selected by nongenetic evolutionary processes. We might think that the proverbs of Kahlil Gibran reflect his own poetic genius, but according to Ong, everyone thought and talked that way in his largely oral culture of Lebanon. If the proverbs seem like polished gems, the polishing was accomplished by multiple minds over multiple generations. Moreover, with the advent of writing, our ability to download stories enabled us to use our minds in ways that were impossible throughout our entire evolutionary history, and we were not slow to capitalize on the new opportunities. When the great Russian psychologist Alexander Luria interviewed illiterate peasants, their inability to solve the simplest abstract reasoning problems would have classified them as retarded, but this was simply because they didn't have the luxury to indulge in such idle mental operations in their everyday lives. A cultural innovation (writing) made possible a revolution in human thought, forever changing the way we use our minds.[25]

8. Social psychologist Richard Nisbett is familiar and accepting of the position outlined in E1, but he also appreciates the importance of nongenetic evolutionary processes resulting in profound cultural differences, for example between regions of the United States with respect to violence and between Asian and Western patterns of thought.[26] Nisbett ends one of his coauthored articles with the following reflection on how his own mind has changed over the course of his career:

Almost two decades ago, the senior author wrote a book with Lee Ross entitled, modestly, *Human Inference*. Roy D'Andrade, a distinguished cognitive anthropologist, read the book and pronounced it a "good ethnography." The author was shocked and dismayed. But we now wholeheartedly agree with D'Andrade's contention about the limits of research conducted in a single culture. Psychologists who choose not to do cross-cultural psychology may have chosen to be ethnographers instead.[27]

9. The intensely social nature of human thought, especially in preliterate times when the equivalent of a library was a group of people willing to talk to you, has bound human groups into corporate units throughout our evolutionary history. Conflicts of interest exist within all groups, but the degree to which groups succeed and fail as units also needs to be appreciated. Here again, narrative plays a critical role. As Jerome Bruner puts it:

> I doubt that such collective life would be possible were it not for our human capacity to organize and communicate experience in narrative form. For it is the conventionalization of narrative that converts individual experience into collective coin which can be circulated, as it were, on a base wider than a merely interpersonal one. Being able to read another's mind need depend no longer on sharing some narrow ecological or interpersonal niche but, rather, on a common fund of myth, folktale, "common sense." And given that folk narrative, like narrative generally, like culture itself, is organized around the dialectic of expectation-supporting norms and possibility-evoking transgressions, it is no surprise that story is the coin and currency of culture.[28]

10. Religious stories are taken more seriously than any others. In my own book *Darwin's Cathedral: Evolution, Religion, and the Nature of Society*, I show that religions around the world and throughout history have bound human groups into corporate units.[29] The very word "religion" in our language is derived from the Latin *religio*, which means "to unite or bind together." The genetically evolved mind is unprepared for social life in groups larger than a few hundred or at most a few thousand individuals. Larger groups such as the Hebrew nation were clearly adaptive in their time but existed only by virtue of cultural mechanisms that evolved by nongenetic evolutionary processes and which often took the form of narratives that provide guides for action. A particularly striking example is offered by religious scholar Elaine Pagel's analysis of early Christianity. In her book *The Origin of Satan* she shows that the four Gospels chosen to comprise the New Testament by the orthodox church in the late second century, compared to other Gospels that were branded as "an abyss of madness, and blasphemy against Christ," served as particularly good blueprints for "a practical design of Christian communities."[30] Moreover, the differences between the four Gospels can be

interpreted as alterations in the sacred story adapting particular early Christian communities to their local social environments. Even though the sacred stories in the New Testament became fixed in the second century, their selective use and interpretation make them endlessly adaptable to modern conditions, as in recent efforts to create an environmentally responsible "green" Christianity, perhaps for the first time in its history.[31] In this respect, sacred religious stories are like the proverbs of oral cultures.

11. Modern-day works of literature have the same potent effects on human action as religious stories, at both the personal and cultural levels. In his memoir *Judgement Day*, Nathaniel Branden recalls encountering the novels of Ayn Rand, which were so compelling that he read them again and again.[32] Their glorification of individuals breaking the bonds of conventional society became what he described as a "shield" and a "fortress" that enabled him to resist his own stultifying social environment. He ultimately sought out Rand and became her disciple and lover. During their first meeting he described her books as a "stylized universe," a phrase that delighted her. Although Rand was an avowed atheist, her books have the same powerful organizing effect on behavior as religion and continue to be purchased and discussed in Ayn Rand clubs and e-mail groups around the world. According to Bruner, *Uncle Tom's Cabin* played as great a role in precipitating the Civil War and the Harlem Renaissance played as great a role in promoting desegregation as any legislative or court action by humanizing the plight of those who previously had been dehumanized. As Bruner puts it, "great fiction is subversive in spirit, not pedagogical."[33]

12. In their article entitled "Evolutionary Psychology: A Primer," Leda Cosmides and John Tooby quote with approval Einstein's statement "It is the theory that decides what we can observe" to emphasize the novelty of their perspective against the background of the so-called "Standard Social Science Model."[34] The idea behind this statement is that a scientific theory, like any other narrative, organizes perception, making certain things obvious, others worthy of attention, and still others invisible. A radical new theory, such as Einstein's theory of relativity or evolutionary psychology (in the opinion of Cosmides and Tooby), has such a transformative effect on perception that it literally decides what we can observe. I agree with this statement but I think it leads to a different conclusion than what Cosmides and Tooby had in mind. The position that I have described as E1 does indeed change our perception and reveals many new possibilities that were invisible before, as I have tried to stress throughout this essay. But alas, it also makes other possibilities seem to vanish that were deservedly obvious before. If E1 is interpreted as a denial of E2, that is merely an artifact of its own limited vision.

These examples are not the rantings of naive blank slatists but include some of the most distinguished psychologists and social scientists writing on the basis of extensive research. Their findings show that people are more than tax-preparation software writ large, responding to specific environmental stimuli with preevolved behavioral responses. In addition, people embark upon evolutionary voyages of their own, individually and collectively, arriving at new solutions to modern problems. Furthermore, these evolutionary voyages rely fundamentally upon stories in the creation of new and untested guides to action, the retention of proven guides to action, and the all-important transmission of guides to action from one person to another. In short, stories often play the role of genes in nongenetic evolutionary processes.

What this means for the study of literature is that refocusing attention on the problems of survival and reproduction in our ancestral environment is not enough. A genre of evolutionary literary studies must also appreciate the importance of stories in adaptation to current environments. Giving stories genelike status endows them with the potency and centrality that they have always enjoyed within social constructivist perspectives.

Welcome to the Middle Ground

I began this essay by saying that it is not an exercise in idle diplomacy but a serious attempt to find the common ground between evolutionary theory and social constructivism. The heart of social constructivism is an optimistic belief that people and societies can become better in the future than in the present or past. This belief is not threatened by evolutionary theory. Indeed, evolution is all about change, and only by the strangest of secondary assumptions can it be interpreted as implying an incapacity for change. In particular, if we restrict evolution to genetic evolution and ignore the concept of adaptive behavioral flexibility, then evolution indeed implies an incapacity for change over the time scales most relevant to contemporary human affairs. However, no sophisticated evolutionary biologist would accept both of these restrictive assumptions. The adaptive behavioral flexibility that already occupies center stage in sociobiology and evolutionary psychology provides some scope for the optimistic spirit of social constructivism. Nongenetic evolutionary processes provide even more scope.

Not only should social constructivists feel unthreatened by evolutionary theory, but they should actively learn to use it to achieve their objectives. The blank slate metaphor and the concept of "learning" and "culture" as generic alternatives to "evolution" may crudely capture the spirit of social constructivism, but they fail in every other respect. Evolution is a complicated process, and the factors that constrain adaptation (E3) lurk around every corner. Understanding E2 in conjunction with E1 is even more complicated. After we decide that evolutionary theory is a vehicle that can take us where we want to go, we need to learn how to drive it. The only way forward for social constructivism in a practical sense is to master and advance our knowledge of evolution, the only known process that can create islands of function out of the sea of entropy.

As for evolutionists, it takes an insider to appreciate the diversity of opinion and lack of integration gathered under that term, ranging from nearly exclusive focus on one of the three positions that I have outlined to those who attempt to occupy the middle ground. Perhaps we can understand and sympathize with an excessive focus on E1 as a reaction to its denial in psychology and the social sciences during most of the twentieth century. However, those of us who broadly use the term "evolutionary psychology" think of it not as a counterweight but as a framework for explaining all aspects of psychology from an evolutionary perspective. Evolutionary psychology in its current form, therefore, must take back some of what has been rejected as part of the "standard social science model," in particular open-ended, nongenetic evolutionary processes that adapt individuals and groups to their current environments.

Einstein's quote "It is the theory that decides what we can observe" might seem to imply that every theoretical perspective is like a mask with narrow slits for eyes, providing only a partial view of the world. Perhaps this is true in some sense, but I don't think it explains the kind of narrowness that has existed in the past and need not exist in the future for this subject. Clearly, the middle ground that we have been discussing has remained unoccupied because of perceived implications, not just because of intellectual difficulty. Intellectually it is fully possible to achieve a theory of evolution that acknowledges the importance of all three positions and their relationships with each other and that serves as a resource for individual and societal change. Perhaps before long we will be able to say that the evolution wars are over and the task of reconstruction has begun.

Notes

1. Barkow, Cosmides, and Tooby 1992.
2. D. T. Campbell 1974; 1960.
3. Gould and Lewontin 1979.
4. Brauner 2001.
5. Levins and Lewontin 1987.
6. West-Eberhard 2003.
7. Weiner 1994.
8. Dunbar 1996.
9. Wilson and Daly 1997.
10. Gaulin and McBurney 2001.
11. D. T. Campbell 1960.

12. Plotkin 1994.

13. Tooby and Cosmides 1992.

14. Sompayrac 1999.

15. The publication and controversy surrounding P. Tierney's account of Chagnon in his book *Darkness in El Dorado* represents the kind of battle zone mentality that I described at the beginning of this essay.

16. Buss 1999.

17. Williams 1966, 16.

18. Bruner 2002, 51, 64, 9.

19. Sternberg 1998, 5.

20. Pennebaker 1997.

21. Pennebaker and Seagal 1999, 1243.

22. T. D. Wilson 2002.

23. Deacon 1998.

24. Cosmides and Tooby 2000b, 111.

25. Ong 1988.

26. Nisbet and Cohen 1996; Nisbett 2003.

27. Nisbett, Choi, Peng, and Norenzayan 2001.

28. Bruner 2002, 16.

29. D. S. Wilson 2002.

30. Pagels 1995, 75.

31. A sampling of the Christian environmental movement can be found at the home page of the National Religious Partnership for the Environment: http://www.nrpe.org/.

32. Branden 1989.

33. Bruner 2002, 11.

34. Cosmides and Tooby 1997.

From Lacan to Darwin

Dylan Evans

This is the story of an intellectual journey. It starts with my enthusiastic embrace of the ideas of the French psychoanalyst Jacques Lacan and ends with my eventual rejection of those ideas some five years later. Between those two events, I wrote a book about Lacan, which has since become a standard reference text for those working with Lacanian theory.[1] Nowadays, eight years after the dictionary was published, I occasionally receive e-mails from puzzled Lacanians who have noticed that the author of one of the key reference books in their field has gone on to write other books with such obviously non-Lacanian titles as *Introducing Evolutionary Psychology*.[2] The most interesting thing about these e-mails is not so much their content as their tone, which tends to be one of shock, dismay, or anger that a former disciple should have betrayed the faith so completely. They may not use such religious references explicitly, but it is clear from their vexation that it is more than just an intellectual matter for these correspondents. They do not see my change of mind as the result of an honest and sincere search for truth but as a betrayal, an apostasy, a fall from grace. This essay is an attempt to go beyond such simplistic descriptions to explain exactly how and why I came to change my mind.

Before I begin my story, however, I should perhaps first explain why it belongs in a book about literary theory. Lacan was a psychoanalyst, not a literary critic—a fact that would hardly need stating in those parts of the world, such as France and Latin America, where his ideas are known to more than a tiny minority. Go to a psychoanalytic clinic in Paris or psychiatric hospital in Buenos Aires and chances are you will find a therapist putting Lacan's ideas into clinical practice. In the English-speaking world, however, hardly any therapists have even heard of Lacan. In Britain, the United States, and Australia, the few people who have heard of him tend to be literary critics and cultural theorists. In these countries, Lacanian ideas are used primarily as tools for critiquing works of literature and other cultural artifacts. But to whatever use you put a set of ideas, nothing useful is going to come out if the ideas themselves are fundamentally flawed. Whether used in the clinic or the seminar room, Lacan's ideas are hopelessly inadequate because they are predicated on a false theory of human nature. I came to realize this when I started to treat patients—the clinical reality did not fit with Lacan's theory. Literary scholars are less likely to notice the discrepancy, since textual interpretation is much more malleable than phobias, panic attacks, and other symptoms experienced by real, live human beings. It is my hope that, by sharing my intellectual journey with those literary scholars who still use Lacanian theory, they may also come to realize the inadequacy of Lacan's conceptual edifice.

Lacan in Argentina

I first came across Lacan when I was working in Argentina in 1992. Much to my surprise, I discovered that psychoanalysis was a major cultural force there. In fact, there are more psychoanalysts per capita in Buenos Aires than anywhere else in the world, even New York. The prestige and authority attached to psychoanalysis in Buenos Aires came as quite a shock to me, coming as I did from a cultural milieu in which Freud was almost completely absent and held in low regard. For I had recently graduated from a British university, where I had studied linguistics within a thoroughly Chomskyan framework. In Britain, you can graduate in a cognitive science like linguistics or psychology without ever reading anything by Freud. In Argentina, over 70 percent of a typical psychology degree was given over to psychoanalysis. And much of that was specifically Lacanian.

The different value attached to psychoanalysis in Argentina made me call into question the received view in Britain. Why had I simply gone along with the dismissive attitude to Freud present in my own country rather than judging it for myself? Who was to say that the received view in Britain was superior to the received view in Argentina? I began to suspect myself of being rather ethnocentric in my views about knowledge.

Curious to know more, I teamed up with some Argentinian psychoanalysts who used to meet on a weekly basis to study the works of Lacan. As Lacan drew heavily on both Freud and linguistics, it seemed like a mutually beneficial exchange; they could help me come to grips with Freud, and I could help them come to grips with linguistics. I soon discovered, however, that the sort of linguistics that interested Lacan was very different from the sort that I had studied at the university. Lacan hardly ever mentioned Chomsky's work, and when he did, he didn't seem to think much of it. The linguist to whom Lacan referred most often was Ferdinand de Saussure, whom I had studied in literary theory rather than linguistics proper. So I couldn't contribute much to the weekly meetings after all. But that didn't matter, for by the time I realized this I was already hooked.

Lacan's seminars were an intellectual feast. The range of cultural references was breathtaking and beguiling. One moment Lacan might be dissecting the Sophoclean tragedies with minute attention to detail; the next, he could be offering a satirical reductio of Kant's moral philosophy before diving into a clinical vignette and finishing off with a discussion of a statue by Bernini. And all this without the slightest concession to the beginner! Here was a Renaissance man in command of a vast intellectual landscape, an intellectual of the kind one finds only in France! And he didn't condescend to his audience; he expected his listeners to be as familiar with all these diverse cultural references as he seemed to be. One felt privileged to sit at the feet of such a teacher and listen.

The problem was, of course, that I wasn't familiar with more than a few of these references. Nor were the other members of my study group. So we spent a lot of our time coming to grips with the original sources on which Lacan drew. There were so many that we always felt we were missing something. Lacan's real message was always just out of our reach. It was near enough to make us think we could probably understand it if we just did a bit more studying, but somehow, no matter how much studying we did, his message always seemed to recede, like the end of a rainbow. It was this, of course, that made his seminars so intoxicating, so addictive.

That's when I started to keep notes for myself about the terms of art that Lacan used most frequently in his seminars and writings. It began as a database of citations that I kept on my laptop and gradually expanded as I added glosses and cross-references. In this way, I built up an increasingly detailed map of Lacanian terms and concepts, a document that was simultaneously a record of my own path of discovery. For those who are unfamiliar with Lacan's work, it might be helpful at this point to highlight some of the principal landmarks I observed in this exotic terrain. (Readers who are already well versed in Lacanian theory may wish to skip the next few paragraphs.)

The mirror stage: Lacan was much taken with an observation by the French psychologist Henri Wallon of the different ways that human infants and young chimpanzees react to seeing their reflection in a mirror. According to Wallon, young children are fascinated by their reflections, whereas chimpanzees quickly lose interest. For Lacan, this difference revealed a fundamental human tendency to be mesmerized by visual images, to live in the world of "the imaginary." There are interesting parallels between this idea and Marx's concepts of alienation and ideology, Durkheim's anomie, and even Sartre's "bad faith."

The symbolic order: The only way for people to escape the illusions of the imaginary is to uncover the linguistic symbols that shape those illusions. Just as Marx thought that ideology was a product of and a cover for economic forces, so Lacan saw the imaginary world as a product of and a cover for linguistic forces. *It was not the stream of pictures passing across the mind's eye that determined human behavior, but the unconscious web of words and phrases that lay beneath the images.*

Psychoanalytic treatment was, therefore, principally about speech. Lacan denounced the way that his contemporaries in the psychoanalytic movement had come to neglect the role of speech in psychoanalytic treatment and argued that the treatment should revolve around the linguistic analysis of the patient's utterances. Hence the emphasis Lacan placed on linguistics.

The "subject-supposed-to-know": Lacan did not believe that psychoanalysts should think of *themselves* as experts able to reveal the hidden meaning of the patient's speech, but he did believe that the *patient* should think of the analyst that way. The analyst, in other words, did not really possess a secret knowledge but was merely "supposed" by the patient to posses this knowledge. In the course of the treatment, the patient would come to "de-suppose" the analyst of this knowledge—that is, to lose his faith in the analyst. That, in fact, was the whole point of psychoanalytic treatment. Why, then, did the analyst collude in the original gullibility of the patient rather than simply telling the patient up front that there was no secret knowledge to be had? Because it was only by learning the hard way, so to speak, that the patient could experience the painful process of disillusionment and thereby realize that *nobody* held the key to his life except him.

There were many other curious and intriguing terms in Lacan's baroque conceptual edifice, and as I read more of his work my database of citations and glosses mushroomed into a substantial document. After a year of this rather ad-hoc process, it dawned on me that I had the makings of a publishable reference work, and that is what it eventually turned into.[3]

Lacan in England

My employment in Argentina came to an end in December 1993, and the following month I returned to Britain, where I set about contacting the few Lacanian groups that existed in my native country. The situation was very different from that in Argentina. In contrast to the plethora of paths to becoming a Lacanian analyst in Buenos Aires, there was only one recognized Lacanian training organization in Britain, the Centre for Freudian Analysis and Research (CFAR). In Argentina, training to be a Lacanian analyst was considered to be a rather different and much less formal process than training to be a traditional Freudian or Jungian analyst, but CFAR had implemented a more conventional sort of training regime to make themselves more acceptable to the various bodies that regulated psychotherapy in Britain. I had already been seeing a Lacanian analyst in Argentina for more than a year by the time I returned to Britain, taken a diploma in psychoanalysis at the University of Buenos Aires, and participated in numerous seminars, but CFAR insisted that I start their training course from the beginning, and so I did.

Over the following two years, I busied myself with my training in CFAR and continued my own analysis, this time with a French psychoanalyst based in Paris. Every month I would travel to Paris and pack six or seven sessions into two or three days. At the same time, I also studied for a master's degree in psychoanalytic studies at the University of Kent at Canterbury and continued work on my dictionary of Lacanian terminology. Everything, it seemed, was progressing smoothly, and it was surely only a matter of time before I took the next logical step and became a practicing Lacanian psychoanalyst myself. And that is what I would do for the rest of my life.

Beneath the surface though, doubts were already beginning to brew. I can't remember exactly when I first began to seriously call into question the fundamental principles of the Lacanian worldview. There certainly was no blinding flash of insight, no awful moment when it suddenly dawned on me that I might be dedicating my life to a practice and a theory that were both deeply flawed. It was, rather, a gradual process, in which the inconsistencies in Lacanian theory and the dangers of Lacanian therapy became progressively more obvious to me as my grasp of both became more comprehensive.

As far as the theory was concerned, it was the process of writing the dictionary that was most responsible for my growing skepticism. As I became more familiar with Lacan's teachings, the internal contradictions and lack of external confirmation became ever more apparent. And as I tried to make sense of Lacan's bizarre rhetoric, it became clearer to me that the obfuscatory language did not hide a deeper meaning but was in fact a direct manifestation of the confusion inherent in Lacan's own thought. But whereas most of Lacan's commentators preferred to ape the master's style and perpetuate the obscurity, I wanted to dissipate the haze and expose whatever was underneath—even if it meant seeing that the emperor was naked. In the preface to my dictionary, I wrote:

> This obscurity [of most Lacanian writing] has even been seen as a deliberate attempt to ensure that Lacanian discourse remains the exclusive property of a small intellectual elite, and to protect it from external criticism. If this is the case, then this dictionary is a move in the other direction, an attempt to open Lacanian discourse up to wider scrutiny and critical engagement.[4]

Ironically, it was this attempt to open Lacanian theory up to criticism that played a major role in leading me to reject Lacanian theory myself.

At the same time as I was becoming increasingly skeptical about Lacanian theory, I was also growing more doubtful about the claims made on behalf of the practice of Lacanian analysis. My own analysis in Paris had proved very different from my analysis in Buenos Aires, and much less satisfactory. It seemed that the personality of the analyst played a far greater role in determining the way my analysis proceeded than the theory to which the analyst subscribed. The same lesson was also emerging from my own practice as a trainee analyst. For by 1996 I was seeing my own patients, both privately and in the psychiatric department of a state hospital in South London.

Eight years later, my work as a counselor providing outpatient psychotherapy in the public health-care sector in Britain remains a wonderful source of memories. There are things I learned about human nature then, locked away in a small consulting room, face-to-face with strangers who poured out their innermost secrets to me, that I don't think I could have learned in any other way. It was a humbling, profound, and sometimes harrowing experience. There were times, I think, when I did actually help people. There were other times, I know, when my impact was at best neutral and possibly even harmful. But as I struggled with the dilemmas that so many other therapists have struggled with, one thing did become abundantly clear to me: whenever I did succeed in helping someone, it was always because I had put my Lacanian theory to one side for the moment and simply responded out of intuition, empathy, or common sense. Conversely, whenever I did what I was supposed to do according to my Lacanian training, it rarely helped. In fact, it often left people confused and upset.

When I chatted with my colleagues at lunch and at the weekly group supervision sessions, I was confronted by a welter of different approaches to psychotherapy, each with their own terminology and clinical techniques. Everyone was convinced that their particular approach was best, and yet there seemed no difference in the recovery rates of our patients. We spoke in different languages, without even a common yardstick by which our different perspectives could be judged. Psychotherapy and psychoanalysis were clearly in dire straits. Eventually, I realized I could not continue to practice psychoanalysis or psychotherapy of any kind. I believed then, and still believe today, that it is not ethical for a therapist of any stripe to treat patients with a method that he or she harbors grave doubts about. For this and various other reasons I gradually withdrew from all clinical work and decided to resolve my doubts one way or the other from within the more impartial domain of academic research. I would get a Ph.D.

Lacan in the United States

I applied to various universities, some in Britain and others in the United States. Psychology departments were out of the question, of course. There was no interest in Lacan in any of the decent psychology departments in Britain or the United States. While researching the various other options, I noticed that a prominent Lacanian scholar had a position in a department of comparative literature at the State University of New York at Buffalo. This struck me as a rather odd place for a Lacanian scholar to situate herself, but I put this down to necessity. Surely, I imagined, she had been forced into such a position by the prejudice against psychoanalysis which reigned in Anglo-American psychology departments. While the enlightened psychologists in Argentina were only too happy to let Lacanians into their departments, their blinkered counterparts in Britain and the United States would have none of this. As a result, the misunderstood Lacanians in these countries were forced to take refuge in the only departments that were broad-minded enough to have them—departments of literature and cultural studies. So I resolved to go to Buffalo.

I wasn't really interested in literature or literary theory, but I didn't think that really mattered. The important thing was to work with a supervisor who was familiar with and sympathetic to Lacan's work. Besides, a lot of the research conducted by graduate students and faculty members in the department of comparative literature at Buffalo looked more to philosophy than literary criticism. True, it was continental philosophy rather than analytic philosophy, but it was still philosophy. And that is essentially what I wanted to do. I wanted to conduct an in-depth and rigorous philosophical analysis of Lacan's work to see if I could resolve my nagging doubts about the apparent inconsistencies and fallacies I was increasingly discovering in it.

I soon discovered that such an approach did not fit in well with the academic atmosphere in Buffalo. Neither the graduate students there nor my supervisor seemed particularly concerned to inquire whether Lacan's views were consistent or correct. To them, that was a vulgar question, demonstrating a naive misunderstanding of the Lacanian oeuvre. To them, it was as ridiculous to worry about the factual accuracy of Lacan's work as it was to worry about the factual accuracy of a poem or a symphony. The value of Lacan's work lay not in any ability to describe the facts, but in its power to produce novel ways of interpreting literary texts. For scholars steeped in literary theory, this was, I suppose, a natural response, but to me it seemed clearly at odds with the whole thrust of Lacan's life and work. For Lacan was not a literary critic but a practicing psychoanalyst. Despite the huge amount of time that Lacan spent discussing literary texts in his seminars and writings, he never made a single attempt at literary criticism. Lacan was not the slightest bit interested in literature for its own sake. Every time that Lacan discusses a work of literature, or a piece of art, he does it for one reason, and one reason only: to illustrate a psychoanalytic concept so that other psychoanalysts can understand that concept better and use it in their clinical practice.

To the Lacanians in Buenos Aires and Paris, that was abundantly clear. They were as horrified as Lacan himself was by the way that psychoanalysis had been perverted, as they saw it, by literary critics and cultural theorists in Britain and the United States. Lacan railed against what he saw as the "hermeneuticization" of psychoanalysis, arguing that psychoanalysis was not a general hermeneutics that could be "applied" to any area of inquiry but the theory of a specific domain, namely, the process of psychoanalytic treatment. Lacan did not care about deepening his students' understanding of art and literature; all he cared about was deepening their understanding of psychoanalysis. And psychoanalysis was first and foremost a method for treating patients and second a theory of how that method worked.

Yet most of the Lacanians in Buffalo had no understanding of or any personal experience with that method. They read Lacan entirely within the context of literary criticism and rarely, if ever, thought about its clinical foundation. No wonder they were so unconcerned about the consistency or accuracy of Lacan's ideas. They had completely misunderstood the whole of Lacan's project.

Truth and Evidence

I left Buffalo in disgust and decided to continue my doctoral research elsewhere. I returned to the United Kingdom in 1997 to take up a place in the philosophy department at the London School of Economics, a college of the University of London. The atmosphere there could not have been more different from that in Buffalo. The department of philosophy had been founded by Karl Popper, one of the giants of analytic philosophy, and his influence was clearly visible. The qualities admired in writing here were clarity and concision, not empty rhetorical flourishes and baroque digressions. And above all, people demanded evidence. No matter how obvious (or how weird) your opinions seemed to be, they were worth nothing unless you could back them up.

That's when I began to realize, with growing alarm and shame, that I had never really asked myself what the evidence for psychoanalysis was! I had simply been carried along by the panache and stylistic flourishes of two great word-smiths—Freud and Lacan—without pausing to ask the most important question of all: On what evidence did they base their far-reaching claims? And was that evidence sufficiently solid to support those claims?

With Freud, there was at least some debate to be had here, as was shown by the range of scholarly works dedicated to examining precisely this question. Philosophers of science had been debating the evidential status of case histories versus statistical analysis in general, and the value of Freud's vignettes in particular, for decades. Psychoanalysts themselves had been less willing to subject the founding father of their discipline to such rigorous scrutiny, but some had at least made an effort. Their conclusions might be wrong, but they did acknowledge the question.

With Lacan, matters were altogether different. The question of evidence was not even raised by his followers. Everything the great master wrote was taken on trust, as if it were holy writ. Everything Lacan said was right, just because he said it. Debate in Lacanian seminars was purely a matter of exegesis—what did the master mean by such-and-such a phrase? Nobody ever took the next logical step and asked—was he right? That was simply assumed.

Why was Lacan supposed to be immune from criticism? Was he supposed to have some kind of infallibility like the pope? From where did this infallibility derive? Was it, in fact, merely a projection of his disciples, who put Lacan in the position of the subject-supposed-to-know, Lacan's term for the position of the analyst vis-à-vis the patient? In which case, did a successful "cure" mean discovering that Lacan was a fraud, an impostor, who really had no more access to the truth than anyone else, and probably less?

It took some courage on my part to raise these questions with my Lacanian friends. The response was usually one of faint amusement; "What is truth?" they might reply with a condescending smile. "Surely you don't believe in facts?" It began to dawn on me that, despite all his talk about truth, Lacan didn't really care about it, and neither did his followers. They based their beliefs on their wishes rather than on proper evidence. I was appalled, disgusted by this abnegation of curiosity, by this waste of human intelligence, by this shameless embrace of illusion for illusion's sake. So I began to look around for some better way to go about understanding the mind.

Although I had no idea of this when I first enrolled as a doctoral student at the London School of Economics (LSE), my new place of study had become a breeding ground for a school of thought that many Lacanians would probably see as diametrically opposed to their own. Evolutionary psychology, as it called itself, was by no means universally accepted at the LSE, but its influence was clearly visible, above all in a series of influential public lectures known as the Darwin Seminars. These monthly events, at which academics, writers, and journalists crowded excitedly into packed lecture theaters to hear internationally renowned speakers such as Daniel Dennett and Steven Pinker speak about Darwinian theory, were marked by an intellectual frisson the likes of which I had never witnessed. They were organized by a remarkable woman named Helena Cronin, who was likened by more than one newspaper to the Parisian ladies whose salons were attended by the great philosophers of the Enlightenment.

The Darwin Seminars gave me just what I was looking for—a new way of looking at the human mind, something completely different than the Lacanian quagmire in which I had been bogged down for the previous five years. This changed my intellectual predicament from one in which I had a theory that I knew to be deeply flawed but had nothing to replace it with to one in which I had a choice between two competing theories. So I set about comparing the theories with each other and seeing how each squared up to the evidence.

This is where I want to turn from autobiographical narrative to intellectual discussion. It's not that my intellectual journey became easier at this point or less interesting—far from it. I had a terrible time shedding my Lacanian skin and many agonizing moments when I wondered if my doubts about psychoanalysis were motivated by some repressed wish or other or whether this was not just some kind of "negative therapeutic reaction" or resistance against the process of analysis. But since it was, in the end, the intellectual arguments and empirical evidence, and not any repressed wishes, that finally convinced me to jettison Lacan completely and become an evolutionary psychologist, it is to the arguments and evidence that I must now turn.

Although it is true, as I have already noted, that many Lacanians would see evolutionary psychology as diametrically opposed to their own worldview, there are, in fact, some surprising links between the two. For Lacan was one of the first psychoanalysts to discuss concepts from ethology and cognitive science, the two sciences that would later form the basis of evolutionary psychology. Yes, he was also profoundly critical of these new disciplines and eventually rejected them both in favor of a return to a more traditional Freudian vision, but there were times when he was more sympathetic to them. The reasons for Lacan's change of direction go to the heart of a debate that is still pertinent today—do the new biological and computational theories of mind possess the conceptual resources to deal adequately with emotion and subjectivity, or do these topics require a psychoanalytic understanding? This was the debate into which my encounter with evolutionary psychology plunged me.

Lacan and Ethology

Let's take ethology first. With hindsight, some of Lacan's remarks about ethology can seem uncannily prophetic. When Lacan began to develop his concept of the mirror stage, in the mid-1930s, the scientific study of animal behavior was only just beginning. The work of Konrad Lorenz, the founding father of ethology, was already beginning to attract the attention of many zoologists, but it was completely ignored by psychologists, who still clung to the idea of an "unbridgeable gap" between humans and animals. Later on, after World War II, psychologists would turn increasingly to ethology as they developed a more biologically oriented science of behavior, and John Bowlby would bring these developments to the world of psychoanalysis. But in 1936, Lacan was alone in anticipating this trend. It was in that year that he presented his paper on the "mirror stage" to an astonished audience at the Fourteenth International Psychoanalytical Congress at Marienbad.

Lacan began by describing an experiment called the "mirror test" which his friend, the French psychologist Henri Wallon, had performed in 1931. Wallon had compared the reactions of human infants and chimpanzees to seeing their reflection in a mirror. He found that at around the age of six months both humans and chimpanzees begin to recognize that the image in the mirror is their own. However, Wallon claimed there was an important difference between the subsequent reactions of the human infant and the chimpanzee. The human infant becomes fascinated with his reflection and leans forward to examine it more closely, moving his limbs to explore the relation between image and reality. The chimp, on the other hand, quickly loses interest, and turns to look at other things.

Lacan used this observation as a springboard to develop an account of the development of human subjectivity that was inherently, though often implicitly, comparative in nature. Human subjectivity was only understandable by contrasting it to that of our nearest relative, the chimpanzee. Today, when evolutionary theory is increasingly being recognized as a powerful tool for understanding the human mind, such an approach would not attract much comment. Wallon's observation about the different ways that humans and chimpanzees react to recognizing their own reflections has even become commonplace in the literature. In the 1970s, much was made of an ingenious version of the mirror test that the American psychologist Gordon Gallup devised to test the self-awareness of chimpanzees.[5] But we should not let anachronism prevent us from recognizing the far-sighted nature of Lacan's remarks in 1936. At a time when comparative psychology was still in its infancy, and when most psychologists regarded human-animal comparisons as irrelevant at best, Lacan's decision to invoke Wallon's experiment as the basis for a new psychoanalytic concept was extremely bold.

Interestingly, however, Lacan did not go on to become an enthusiastic proponent of "ethologising" psychoanalysis in the manner of John Bowlby. Rather than taking the concept of the mirror stage into the uncharted territory of evolutionary psychology, as others were to do decades later, he tried to bring it into the fold of Freudianism. During the course of the next decades, Lacan's early remarks about the mirror stage as a phase of biological maturation became increasingly overlain by less-developmental interpretations. By the early 1950s, the mirror stage was no longer simply a moment in the life of the infant but "a permanent structure of subjectivity,"[6] an "essential libidinal relationship with the body image."[7]

These developments in Lacan's concept of the mirror stage are a microcosm of changes in his work as a whole. Other strands in his work show the same shift away from the empirical world of biology to the metaphysical world of "structures." While the early Lacan abounds in references to ethology, these get increasingly sparser as his work develops. In the 1949 version of the mirror stage paper Lacan cites experiments with pigeons and locusts to support his observations about the importance of the image.[8] Five years later, he is still making the occasional reference to ethological concepts such as the "innate releasing mechanism" and citing the names of Lorenz and Tinbergen.[9] Soon after, however, Lacan begins to veer away from ethology. His much-vaunted "return to Freud," announced in 1953, led Lacan to explore those aspects of Freud's work that did not fit so easily with modern biology. When he came to examine Freud's concept of the "death instinct," for example, Lacan quickly realized the impossibility of giving it a biological meaning. But instead of concluding that the Freudian concept was therefore redundant, Lacan tried to rescue it by insisting that Freud had not meant it as a biological concept; the death instinct was "not a question of biology," Lacan now claimed.[10] But Freud's writings were not so pliable; his theory of instincts was couched in an explicitly biological framework. Lacan was therefore forced to invoke tortuous paradoxes to rescue his nonbiological interpretation of Freud; "Freudian biology has nothing to do with biology," he claimed.[11]

But what was this "Freudian biology" if it had nothing to do with real biology? Lacan never said. He went on to rework Freud's theory of instincts in a way increasingly removed from any contact with ethology or comparative psychology. He began to complain that Strachey had betrayed Freud by translating *Trieb* as "instinct," claiming that this blurred Freud's distinction between the human *Trieb* and the animal *Instinkt*. The Freudian term was better rendered as "drive," Lacan argued, to emphasize the contrast between the flexible, culturally determined behavior of humans and the rigid, biologically determined behavior of animals.

The idea of a radical separation between humans and animals, the orthodoxy which Lacan had so boldly questioned in his comments on the mirror stage in 1936, was now beginning to creep into Lacan's own work. By the mid-1950s Lacan was becoming increasingly influenced by the French anthropologist, Claude Lévi-Strauss, who argued that "nature" and "culture" were separated by a massive ontological chasm. This spurred Lacan to pursue his culturalist reading of Freud even further. Every biological term in Freud's work was reinterpreted as a metaphor for some cultural phenomenon. Freud's remarks on the phallus, Lacan claimed, had nothing to do with something so banal as a mere biological organ; they referred to a cultural symbol. Freud's false theory about the "vaginal orgasm" could be rescued by arguing that it was not about biology but about psychological satisfaction.[12]

This strategy was doomed, however. It appeared to save Freud's work from refutation by modern biology, but it did so at the price of removing all empirical import. The biological Freud was wrong, but at least he advanced clear, testable claims. The cultural-linguistic Freud that Lacan invented, on the other hand, was completely untestable. He was not merely impervious to contradictory evidence in biology; he was impervious to any evidence at all. Lacan rescued Freud from a fatal encounter with modern biology by removing him from the world of science altogether.

That is not how Lacan saw it, of course. At the time Lacan began to reinterpret Freud as a cultural theorist; this was not the obviously antiscientific move that it clearly is today. In the mid-1950s, the work of Lévi-Strauss and other anthropologists held out the promise of a truly autonomous science of culture. These anthropologists saw the developing theory of structural linguistics as providing a nonbiological yet equally scientific basis for the study of culture. In line with their emphasis on the distinction between culture and nature, between humans and animals, they divided scientific inquiry into two separate worlds. The natural sciences, including biology, could take their inspiration from physics, but the social sciences would look instead to linguistics for their foundations and methods. The two kinds of science were supposed to be equally scientific but autonomous and independent.

This view of the social sciences has been called the Standard Social Science Model because it dominated anthropology, sociology, and psychology for much of the twentieth century.[13] In the last decade, however, the Standard Social Science Model has begun to fall apart as it is increasingly replaced by a more integrated view of science. The idea of science as a dual-track activity has been increasingly questioned as researchers begin to recognize the idea for what it is—the last refuge for the shaky creationist notion of a radical gap between humans and other animals. Spurred on by the vision of science as a fundamentally unified activity with a single coherent methodology, contemporary researchers are suspicious of any attempt to isolate psychology from biology. Building on the work of the ethologists, evolutionary psychologists are now constructing a unified science of behavior based firmly in biological theory. Their work is increasingly influencing research in anthropology, linguistics, cognitive science, and economics. The Standard Social Science Model is being replaced by a new Integrated Causal Model.

Seen from the vantage point of this contemporary paradigm shift, Lacan's intellectual development acquires a tragic pathos. His early ventures into ethology seem tantalizingly prophetic. If Lacan had pursued them further, he might perhaps have been one of the first to question Freud's hegemony and initiate the move to a more biologically based psychology. Instead, he poured his energy into what would eventually prove to be a historical cul-de-sac—the doomed research program of the Standard Social Science Model.

Lacan's backsliding shows a curious parallel with Freud's own intellectual journey. Freud started out as a biologist. His first publications were papers on anatomy and physiology. He then became interested in neurology, and for a while he sought a way to state psychology in neurological terms. The Project for a Scientific Psychology (1895) was, however, never completed. The fanciful speculations about neuronal connections were impossible to substantiate because there was, at the end of the nineteenth century, no way of looking at the brain at work. Postmortem analyses were the only way to find out more about the structure of the brain, and these had to rely on very weak microscopes. In the absence of such tools as functional Magnetic Resonance Imaging, which can show patterns of activity as they change second-by-second in the thinking brain, or electron microscopes, which can expose the delicate structure of the synaptic cleft, Freud had no option but to pursue a less neurological approach. After the project, he moved further and further away from biology toward in an increasingly cognitive and, finally, a predominantly cultural perspective. If he had been born a century later, things might have been very different. Freud would have been enthralled by the recent developments in neuroscience. With an MRI scanner at his disposal, he may well have never invented psychoanalysis.

Lacan and Cognitive Science

So much for ethology, then. The other pillar of evolutionary psychology is cognitive science, and Lacan was one of the first psychoanalysts to discuss this discipline too. In the 1950s, Lacan became briefly fascinated by the computational model of the mind which lies at the heart of cognitive science. Today, the idea that the mind is a computer is central to much work in artificial intelligence, linguistics, philosophy, neuroscience, and even anthropology, but psychology has been the biggest beneficiary. By providing psychology with a precise language in which testable hypotheses can be clearly formulated, the computational theory of mind has given birth to a new field—cognitive psychology—which is arguably the first truly scientific account of how the mind works.

People have often attempted to understand the mind by comparing it with the latest technology. In the past few hundred years, the mind has been described as a clock, a watch, a telegraph system, and much else. Freud was not immune to this trend. Borrowing heavily from the science of his own time, the nineteenth-century developments in hydraulics, he conceived of the mind as a system of channels and waterways. The waterways could sometimes be blocked, in which case the fluid would soon overflow into another channel. The problem with all these comparisons is that they were little more than interesting metaphors. They did not help very much to advance understanding of the mind because there was no clear way of generating testable predictions from them. In particular, there was no quantitative dimension to these models. The pressure (*Drang*) of the "mental water" in Freud's hydraulic model of the mind was, theoretically, a quantitative (or "economic") phenomenon, but Freud failed to specify a way of measuring it.

All this changed with the "cognitive revolution." Comparing the mind to a computer was different from previous technological analogies because the precise language of information processing allowed testable hypotheses about the mind to be clearly formulated, often in ways amenable to investigation by quantitative methods. Also, there was intuitively much more to motivate the comparison of the mind to a computer than to a clock or an irrigation system. After all, the function of the mind, like that of the computer, is to process information—it is not to tell the time or to distribute water. Unlike earlier comparisons, then, the computational theory of mind could be taken literally; the mind is not just like a computer, it is a computer.

The cognitive revolution swept through psychology in the 1960s, displacing the behaviorist paradigm that had held sway since the 1920s. Its origins, however, lie in the 1950s. If one day had to be singled out as the birthday of cognitive science, it is surely September 11, 1956. It was on that day that three seminal papers were presented at a historic meeting at the Massachusetts Institute of Technology (MIT). Allen Newell and Herbert Simon spoke about a "logic theory machine," inaugurating the modern discipline of artificial intelligence.[14] Noam Chomsky described "three models for the description of language" in a paper that has been described as marking the birth of modern linguistics.[15] And George Miller presented a paper about short-term memory that is now recognized as one of the foundational papers of cognitive psychology.[16]

Lacan's own interest in the computational model of the mind dates from even earlier. In 1955, a year before the birth of cognitive science, and a decade before the cognitive revolution was in full swing, Lacan gave a lecture to the French Psychoanalytic Society on the subject of psychoanalysis and cybernetics.[17] In this lecture, he explored some basic concepts of computational theory, including binary code and the use of AND and OR gates to compute logical functions. Borrowing from Norbert Wiener, the mathematician who, along with Arturo Rosenbleuth, coined the term "cybernetics" in 1947, Lacan urged his audience to think of the mind in information-processing terms and stressed the importance of linguistics in this enterprise.

With hindsight, these remarks seem prophetic indeed. Today, the dominant paradigm in psychology is cognitive. Not only is the mind compared to a computer but also the programs that govern hundreds of specific mental processes have been described in algorithmic detail. And, as Lacan anticipated in 1955, linguistics has played a pivotal role in the cognitive revolution. Chomsky's work, above all, provided the first clear idea of what a whole research program guided by the computational theory of mind would look like.

Yet, as with his early hunches about the importance of ethology, Lacan soon abandoned his interest in cybernetics and computational theory. Perhaps he sensed that the language of information processing did not sit easily with Freud's hydraulic model of the mind. Perhaps he even realized that the digital nature of the former was incompatible with the analog nature of the latter. Whatever the reason, however, Lacan chose to remain with the old Freudian model rather than pursuing the newer computational one. Once again, with the benefit of hindsight, we see Lacan wandering into a historical dead end when he could so easily have helped blaze the trail of a future science.

The turnaround is evident in Lacan's later work, where he increasingly turns away from his 1950s emphasis on Saussurian and Jakobsonian linguistics, back toward a hydraulic model of the mind. By the 1970s, Freud's mythical "mental fluid," the libido, has regained center stage in Lacan's thought in the guise of the term "jouissance." But nowhere is Lacan's change of heart more evident than in his remarks after meeting Chomsky at MIT in 1975. According to one account, Lacan was horrified by Chomsky's approach to the study of language. "If that is science," he commented after his conversation with the great American linguist, "then I prefer to be a poet!"[18]

What was it that Lacan didn't like about Chomsky's scientific approach? His remark about preferring to be a poet might suggest the clichéd "Romantic view of the scientist as murderer of beauty."[19] This certainly seemed to lie behind some of the intense opposition to Chomsky that arose in the foreign language departments of most major American universities in the 1960s. Chomsky's colleagues in the humanities (linguistics was classified as one of the humanities by MIT, where Chomsky worked) condemned his theory of syntax as "dreadful, philistine scientism, a clanking assault by technocratic vandals on the beautiful, unanalyzable, unformalizable subtleties of language."[20] But Lacan's opposition to Chomsky must surely have been motivated by a different consideration. After all, Lacan was famous for his decidedly un-Romantic view of "the Subject," for his insistence on formalizing the "algorithm" of the linguistic sign, and for analyzing the "structures" in the patient's "discourse." Lacan claimed to be on the side of science and displayed his mechanistic credentials by dismissing humanism as "a bag of old corpses."[21] Lacan's objection to Chomsky could not possibly be founded on a hackneyed Romantic view of science!

Or could it? Perhaps Lacan's constant remarks about formalizing psychoanalysis and his claims to be on the side of science were mere lip service. Perhaps Lacan was a closet Romantic all along. This alternative view is not as unlikely as it may first appear. Some of Lacan's earliest publications were for the surrealist journal *Minotaure*—indeed, his interest in surrealism predates his interest in psychoanalysis. Perhaps Lacan never really abandoned his early sympathies for surrealism, with its neo-Romantic view of madness as "convulsive beauty," its celebration of irrationality, and its hostility to the scientist who murders nature by dissecting it.

Some support for this view can be found, paradoxically, in Lacan's attempts to develop a mathematical notation for psychoanalytic theory. His formulas and his diagrams give an initial impression of scientific rigor, at least to a nonscientifically trained eye, but on closer examination it becomes evident that they break even the most elementary rules of mathematics.[22] These equations are supposedly there to give substance to Lacan's avowed desire to formalize psychoanalysis. The fact that they are mathematically meaningless gives the lie to that claim. If Lacan was really concerned with formalizing his discipline, he would surely have taken more care to get his math right. The fact that he didn't suggests that he was more interested in the rhetoric of formalization than the reality. For Lacan, "formalization" and "mathematization" were just metaphors, mere sound bites for his neosurrealist technopoetry. No wonder, then, that when he saw Chomsky engaged in a truly rigorous attempt at genuine formalization, Lacan backed away in horror.

Conclusion

At the time of my initial encounter with Lacan, in 1992, I knew next to nothing about science. Like all British children, I had been given a smattering of physics, chemistry, and biology at school, but this consisted solely of isolated facts and figures without any overall view. Even worse, my high school science gave me no understanding of the process of scientific discovery, the dialectic of evidence and argument. I went on to study languages and linguistics at the university, but even there the emphasis was just as much on literature as on the scientific study of language. It is hardly surprising, then, that when I came across the ideas of Jacques Lacan, shortly after finishing my first degree, I was unable to spot their serious defects. Now that I understand more about how science works, those defects are so crashingly obvious that I sometimes feel ashamed of myself for being so naive.

Although it is several years now since I studied comparative literature in Buffalo, and I have rather lost touch with the world of literary criticism, I know there remain lots of literary scholars who still rely on Lacanian theory in their work. This strikes me as very sad. Perhaps their continuing reliance on Lacan is due to their poor understanding of science, just as mine was. I strongly suspect that if they devoted as much time to acquainting themselves with the principles of scientific discovery and the discoveries of modern biology and psychology, they would reach conclusions similar to mine. They would desuppose Lacan of the secret knowledge they seem to attribute to him today and see him for what he really was—sadly mistaken and perhaps even tragically deluded.

Notes

1. Evans 1996.
2. Evans 1999.
3. Evans 1996.

4. Evans 1996, ix.
5. Gallup 1970, 68.
6. Evans 1996, 115.
7. Lacan 1953b, 14.
8. Lacan 1949, 3.
9. Lacan 1953–54, 121.
10. Lacan 1953a, 102.
11. Lacan 1954–55, 75.
12. Lacan 1972–73, 145.
13. Tooby and Cosmides 1992, 23.
14. Newell and Simon 1956.
15. Dennett 1995, 384; Chomsky 1956.
16. Miller 1956.
17. Lacan 1954–55, 294–308.
18. This quotation is often attributed to Lacan. However, I have been unable to trace its source. It may well be apocryphal. I would be grateful to anyone who could supply me with information about its provenance. For "jouissance," see Evans 1998, 11.
19. Dennett 1995, 386.
20. Dennett 1995, 385–86, emphasis in original.
21. Lacan 1954–55, 208.
22. Sokal and Bricmont 1998.

What Happens in Hamlet? Exploring the Psychological Foundations of Drama

Daniel Nettle

Introduction

Performing the imaginary is big business. According to the British government's *Social Trends* survey, 23 percent of Britons over fifteen went to a play in 1999. No data are given on how often they went, but even assuming that the average was only twice, that would be 22 million visits, not counting children's theater. The cinema was even more popular, with 56 percent of adults visiting, and a total of 128 million visits. And this misses out the most significant source of drama in contemporary Britain. The average person watches 25.5 hours of television per week. A brief calculation using the television listings guide suggests that between 24 and 30 percent of the output time of the main channels is devoted to drama, depending on the day of the week. This amounts to an estimated 7 hours of drama per week from television for the average person, giving a yearly total of 364 hours. Adding theater, film, and television sources together, we can estimate that in 1999 the average Briton spent 369 hours immersed in some kind of dramatic performance. This is roughly 6 percent of all waking life.

The compelling popularity and widespread consumption of drama raises important questions. First, one might ask why so many people should be spending time engrossed in worlds of fiction performed in this way. This question is all the more compelling when raised from an evolutionary perspective. Hard-nosed Darwinism seems to suggest people should be ceaselessly preoccupied with the perpetuation of their genes. So is drama helping them to do this? Or is it like a virus, which creeps under their defenses and colonizes their attention? Second, it is clear that some dramas are more enduringly popular than others. Some plays have held the stage for many generations; some films are endlessly revived, while many others are instantly forgotten. So what features do dramas have that are found compelling and ensure their survival and reenactment? Are there features that make some stories adept at survival in the pool of stories?

It may be necessary to broach the first and second sets of questions together. After all, it is not nonveridical representations *in general* that humans appear predisposed to attend to but very specific classes of such representations which may, of course, vary across time and place but could turn out to have universal elements. We cannot, therefore, consider why drama in general captivates the human mind except by looking at particular successful examples of the genre. On the other hand, to understand why some particular stories have captivated humankind more than others, we will also need to consider the origins and functioning of drama in general. The two questions are two parts of the same problem. In this essay, then, I will discuss evolutionary foundations of the success of drama. By "drama," I will mean "the performance of fictional narratives in which actors personate individual protagonists from a first-person perspective." This covers all media—film, television, stage—and all genres—comedy, satire, action, and so on. Crucially, all dramas include some notion of mimesis—that is, imitation—however stylized, of human social behavior.

In sections two of this essay, I will consider what an evolutionary theory of the foundations of drama might look like. Known facts about the evolved mind lead to a certain number of general predictions about the dramatic form. Next, I set the evolutionary account against some more traditional notions about how drama works, finding considerable common ground between these two, independently derived bodies of knowledge. Following this discussion, I outline a typology of dramatic genres that draws both on literary analysis and evolutionary considerations. The dramatic mode actually shows remarkable continuity over more than 2000 years, and thus generalizations over its whole history appear possible. I do not here consider whether the same typology would be useful in dealing with non-Western dramatic traditions, though the logic of my claims is that it would. I conclude by stressing the potential consilience of traditional literary and cultural concerns and evolutionary psychology. Before launching into the account, though, I must set the theoretical context for the discussion by considering the relationship of Darwinian evolution to culture.

Theoretical Background

HAMLET: The purpose of playing . . . both at the first and now, was and
is as 'twere to hold the mirror up to nature.

William Shakespeare, *Hamlet*

CLOV: There's no more nature.
HAMM: No more nature! You exaggerate.

Samuel Beckett, *Endgame*

In common with the other contributions to this volume, I adopt an evolutionary perspective. This much is heretical and open to a prima facie objection that runs as follows: The dramatic mode of literature is obviously a cultural invention. While the production of narrative, poetry, and folklore are human universals,[1] they are not universally done in a dramatic mode. In the West at least, drama stems from specific, and historically contingent, developments in Greek epic poetry in the fifth and fourth centuries B.C. as described by Aristotle in the *Poetics*, chapter 4.[2] This is far too recent for biological change to be involved; the exploration of the radiation and transmutation of drama between then and now clearly belongs to the domain of the cultural, not the genetic, and thus evolutionary thinking is irrelevant.

This argument contains a truth—that drama is a product of a cultural not a genetic process—and a fallacy—which is that organic evolution is therefore irrelevant. Organic evolution produced the substrate, human minds, over which the flux of cultural evolution occurs. Let us consider a nonliterary example. Human kinship terminologies are dazzlingly variable. Every society has its own way of dividing up the semiotic space of family relations. In West Africa, for example, one would make a profound conceptual distinction between paternal and maternal uncles, the former being classified as a kind of father and the latter as something more than a nonrelative but less than family.[3] The basis of this difference is not a genetic difference between West Africans and Europeans, as the adoption of English-derived kin distinctions in West Africa under the influence of church and colony attest. A particular kin system is a *social construction*, a reification of collective semiotic and discursive practices carried out by a particular group of people at a particular point in history. Social constructions can clearly be made in myriad ways, as human cultural diversity so richly informs us. However, does it follow that they can be made in *any* way?

Here is where evolutionary theory becomes relevant. The theory of natural selection predicts that individuals will make preferential investment in their blood relatives, with the strength of the preference in proportion to the closeness of the genetic bond.[4] There is plenty of evidence that such effects do occur both in humans and other animals, and in order for them to do so, people must be predisposed to make the psychological distinction between different types of kin. It would be possible in principle for human beings to invent almost any kinship system. You could imagine one that resembled a short story by Borges, where a particular term was applied to all fathers of young children, left-handed people, and people who wear green hats, while another term included tall women and younger friends. Such a system could theoretically be invented, but would it persist? Of course, social constructions are not deliberate inventions but, rather, evolve gradually under the pressure of everyday use. This seems to put two kinds of constraints on the forms they will take. First, if our minds are set up by evolution to make us interested in discriminating our blood relatives, then we will tend to drop or transform kin terms that do not run along the right mental runnels. Thus all kin systems which are persistent will reflect in some way the mind's evolved structures. On top of this there will be locally specific pressures. In a society with matrilocal residence and transmission of land, the relationship between men and their sister's children will be especially important in terms of inheritance. Thus, that subset of kin systems from within all those generated by the human mind that gives special prominence to the maternal avuncular relation might be especially widespread in societies where inheritance is matrilineal.

Universal generalizations emerge from the study of kin systems; first, they do map onto genetic reality, albeit in variable and complex ways.[5] They all differentiate between different degrees of kinship, which are loosely coupled to the degree of genetic relatedness. Within these confines they have a large number of degrees of freedom, and which option evolves reflects local conditions and historical contingency. In West Africa, for example, the practice of conflating father and father's brother is useful given that the father's older brother would become the chief source of social support in the event of the father's death. Because of patrilocality, the link to the paternal uncle will involve physical proximity and cooperative work, whereas the maternal uncle will be in a different village. However, such cultural specifics notwithstanding, kin systems cannot vary arbitrarily or limitlessly. They are all ultimately constrained by the fact that evolution made the mind, and the mind makes culture; the mind generates it, the mind learns it, and the mind uses it. If it is unlearnable, unusable, or unmemorable, it changes or disappears. Thus, the structure of the mind is one arm of the explanation of why the cultural constructions that persist around us persist, the other arm being the environment or context. What explains the structure of the mind, above all, is the theory of evolution.[6] As Claude Lévi-Strauss once observed, when we set out to explain the cultural, the mind is the uninvited guest we tend not to mention but is unavoidably there.[7]

We can use similar reasoning in the dramatic case. The theater as an industry would simply have ceased if people did not achieve some return for patronizing it. Plays must compete for mental space against work, love, and field sports. Indeed, plays themselves are subject to a kind of Darwinian selection. Between 1585 and 1615, 765 new plays were first presented in England.[8] Many of these were never revived. Few have been performed in the last hundred years, and even fewer still outside England. Who remembers Chettle's *All Is Not Gold That Glisters*, Day and Houghton's three-part *The Blind Beggar of Bethnal Green*, or Boyle's *Jugurth, King of Numidia?* Yet from the same two years as these we have *Hamlet* and *Twelfth Night*. These have been ceaselessly reperformed, adapted, translated, and read all over the world for four hundred years. Most important, for every play that was performed at all, there is an infinite number of logically possible plays that no one deemed interesting enough to produce.

Some plays, like *Hamlet*, have gone on to proliferate in the cultural pool, while most others have gone extinct, either at the point of conception or, more rarely, after a brief hour upon the stage. Some factors have favored the repetition and reperformance of the successful ones at the expense of the other plays. Following the kinship example, we might investigate two kinds of factors that could be relevant, locally specific ones for the historical period in question and universal factors to do with the evolved structures of the mind. The former is a more familiar terrain for cultural and literary studies, but this essay argues for a consideration of the latter as well.

Contemporary literary scholarship has had little time for universalizing. Its commitments are generally historicist and particularist. The former commitment means that the evolution of a cultural form at a given moment is best understood with reference to other cultural elements at that time or immediately preceding it or to wider sociocultural conditions specific to that place and time. The latter commitment stresses the uniqueness of every cultural moment and the need for study on its own terms. In fact, these commitments extend not just to every cultural form but to every *reading* of every cultural form, since social constructivism in particular stresses that what an artistic form is used to mean itself changes with the circumstances of every group of interpreters.

Such historicism can be seen at work in accounts of the "Shakespeare effect," that is, the preeminent popularity of Shakespeare in world drama.[9] These accounts stress the way that Shakespeare came to be used and interpreted as part of a canon defining a cultural elite. The construct of the great dramatist and the tradition of his plays served to identify the club of the English ruling class and were interpreted as legitimizing continuity in sociopolitical arrangements. And of course, that Shakespeare, an Englishman, became the world's dramatist must be related to the fact that he became an establishment figure in London at the beginning of the colonial endeavor that led to English political dominance over much of the world.

Thus, the historicists stress the role of factors extraneous to the content of the plays themselves. Indeed, the inherent features of the plays are low in the list of explanatory possibilities. Thus, Hawkes states:

> No text offers values or meanings that exist as essential features of itself. Shakespeare's plays are not essentially this or essentially that, or essentially anything. They are, to take up Wittgenstein's metaphor, far more like natural phenomena, mountain ranges, pieces of scenery out of which we *make* truth, value, greatness, this or that, in accordance with our various purposes.[10]

While Hawkes's historicism and particularism must be right (if Shakespeare had been a Bengali fisherman, there would be no Royal Shakespeare Theatre), the question is whether it is a complete account. If a set of dramatic work was to be used as establishment propaganda and dispersed over the globe, why was it Shakespeare? Why not Ben Jonson, who held a more socially prestigious position in the seventeenth century?[11] Why, indeed, not any of the hundreds of other plays of the period available as material? Why not an Elizabethan shopping list or simply a dry recitation of the importance of obedience to the British empire? A dramatic genre of this kind would leave the playhouses empty, regardless of how firmly the cultural elite were behind it. Furthermore, why should Shakespeare go on to be performed in circumstances far removed from the Anglo-centric establishment, including as the voice for anticolonial sentiments?[12] It must be the case that the plays, for reasons that are more than accidents of their histories, grab the attention and afford possibilities of meaning.

Even Hawkes's own formulation seems to recognize this; Shakespeare has no intrinsic meaning, he says, but is like a natural feature of the landscape that we might choose to employ for some purpose. But not all natural features are the same; you simply couldn't successfully employ a swamp for the same things you could employ a mountain for. Thus, you still need a theory of what the geography of available natural features is and why some of these are good for some purposes, and some good for others. And this leads us back to questions about the intrinsic appeal of some dramatic forms. Certain forms or topics are inherently attention grabbing (as any newspaper headline writer knows), and thus certain genres afford richer possibilities for their own proliferation and reinterpretation.

In practice, in cultural evolution, the rise and fall of a particular genre must be some combination of direct factors (such as the universal psychological appeal of a particular form or story) and indirect ones (such as the prestige of the people who happen to champion it, and so on). The most sophisticated evolutionary-inspired models of cultural change incorporate both of these distinct forces.[13] It is doubtful that either direct or indirect forces alone can be a complete explanation of the Shakespeare effect or, indeed, the persistence of the dramatic mode in general. As long as some of the variation in the persistence of dramatic forms is directly related to psychology, then a universalist Darwinian theory of drama is possible. It is not an alternative to historicist studies; rather, it is a set of general principles and parameters within which historicist work should be nested.

Why Is Drama?

Shakespeare asks every spectator . . . to *sympathize* with his hero, to feel
with him, to put himself in his shoes, to understand his situation,
and to attempt, in imagination, a solution.
J. Dover Wilson, *What Happens in Hamlet*

Actors in long-running television serials report frequently being approached in the street and advised on what their on-screen characters should do next. Many receive letters not just of advice but of threat, and some actors playing malfeasant characters have been assaulted. People care about dramatic worlds, and, as we have seen, they will give up significant amounts of their time and money to enter them. On the face of it, this is extremely puzzling from a Darwinian perspective.

There has been a response to the evolutionary puzzle of the existence of art, and a number of possible alternative reasons for its persistence proposed.[14] Broadly speaking, the difference between them comes down to who benefits. On the one hand, there are approaches where human beings are thought of as gaining some direct fitness enhancement from participation in fictional cognition. Geoffrey Miller has suggested, for example, the ability to take part in fictional worlds is an honest indicator of high-level mental abilities such as counterfactual reasoning and empathy, abilities that are also useful in life and desirable in a mate.[15] Thus participation in the arts is a way of displaying mating potential, and being an audience a way of assessing it. David Sloan Wilson has suggested that stories serve the function of transmitting and coordinating local appropriate behavioral norms and, thus, are directly beneficial to the individuals (and groups) that participate in them.[16]

At the other end of the spectrum are approaches in which artistic forms are seen as "viruses of the mind."[17] That is, our capacity to transmit information socially, which presumably evolved to convey practical, useful information, unleashed a Darwinian evolutionary process among pieces of information, or "memes." Those memes that were best at sequestering mental space and communicative activity in human agents proliferated, while those less good at this faded away. Certain items—good stories, for example—would have been good at getting themselves transmitted because of their intrinsic attention-grabbing power and memorability. These would have then colonized minds regardless of their effect on the fitness of those that knew and told them (which was probably neutral at best).

While it is tempting to discuss the relative merits of these different positions, it is probably not possible to adjudicate between them at this point. The arts are no doubt exapted to fulfill the functions mentioned and many others at different times. On the other hand, there are certainly memelike effects at work in culture history. It is more important here to dwell on the common predictions that they all make. All approaches predict a process of cultural evolution in which fictional forms will adapt themselves to be optimally attention grabbing and memorable and, thus, sequester mental space for themselves.[18] Under the memetic account this is obviously true; however, it is also true under the others. If dramatic performances are about mate display, then the content of that display will be that which maximizes its psychological impact. If they are about the transmission of group norms, then those with maximal psychological appeal will be the best vehicles to fulfill this function. Thus, we can begin to theorize about the nature of "psychological impact" in advance of a single resolution of the question of the functions of art.

An example I find helpful is that of drugs.[19] We have an evolved motivational physiology that normally leads us to adaptive goals. Endogenous opioid chemical messengers are triggered by such fruitful activities as success in competition, social affiliation, and sex, and their phenomenology is one of pleasure, for very obvious evolutionary reasons. The addictive class of opiate drugs is able to sequester that pathway by a chemical mimesis of its key features; heroin for example, fits or even superfits the biochemical lock designed to accept endogenous opiates. This chemical mimesis unleashes two processes. First, people (some at least) will give up time and energy for drugs whether or not their personal fitness is directly enhanced by this. Second, an evolutionary process is unleashed among strains of opiates. A poppy whose psychoactive ingredient was more effective, more compelling, and brought people back for more would be sown and planted more. Thus the maker of chemical mimesis evolves by Darwinian selection to an ever more ingenious delighting of the host's physiology. Drugs, of course, are generally injurious to health, and this is certainly not my claim about art. But note that even the use of drugs can come to have important higher level social functions, for example in religious rituals that transmit group solidarity and group norms. Such functions are built upon the potential of drugs to sequester motivational systems.

The potential applicability of the drug idea to culture in general is obvious and has been explored elsewhere.[20] It also has suggestions for the dramatic case. Drama, Horace noted, "delights and instructs us." Aristotle added that "learning things is highly enjoyable," and drama is a process of learning things.[21] But drama isn't just any old thing to learn; it has a specific constellation of features. Before looking at what those features are, let us first try to derive what they might be from what we know about primate behavior in general.

If the Audience Is the Human Primate, What Should Drama Be Like?

He who understands baboon would do more toward metaphysics than
   Locke.

Charles Darwin, M Notebook, 1838

Human beings belong to the order of primates. Primates have relatively large brains. This tendency is increasingly marked from prosimians up through New and Old World monkeys to apes. We stand not as an exception but as the summit of the tree in this regard. Another essential characteristic of most primates is their sociality, with most species living almost all their lives in groups of a handful to a few dozen individuals.[22] Again, the tendency generally becomes more marked through the order and culminates in us.

Primate social groups have special characteristics that differ from, say, the social groups of bees and ants. Bees and ants are locked into hereditary castes dictated genetically and regulated physiologically. Primate groups, by contrast, are much more dynamic. Individual animals have places within a status hierarchy that determines mating and resource holding, but this hierarchy is constantly renegotiated through behavior. Status may be achieved by direct physical dominance, through the formation of coalitions based on reciprocity, or through piggybacking on the dominance of kin. To achieve status is desirable as it determines access to food and the likelihood of reproduction. Low-ranking individuals can suffer considerable physiological stress.[23]

Within primate societies, "cliques" and "groups" can be distinguished.[24] The group is the total number of individuals that travel, feed, or sleep together. Cliques are smaller sets of individuals within this who have stronger than average direct relationships with each other. The total group is tight; any two individuals in a group can usually be linked either directly or by one remove; either they are in a clique with each other or they are in a clique with someone who is in a clique with the other. The "social glue" that holds this intricate arrangement together is grooming. Wild primates spend up to 10 percent of their time going through each other's fur, removing parasites.[25] Subordinates groom superiors; alliance partners groom each other; kin are tended; potential mates flirt; and outcasts go ungroomed. The pygmy chimpanzee or bonobo has taken this to a new level by augmenting grooming with sex, but even in the unenhanced version, the group dynamics are impressively complex.

One consequence of the flexibility of primate social systems is that they need to keep track of a lot of social knowledge. A bee can *smell* who is a worker and who is a drone; a monkey has to *remember* who is dominant and who subordinate by close observation of who has been grooming whom. A bee knows who has the right to reproduce and who does not because only the queen has this right, and her physiology is an indelible mark; a monkey has to work out, negotiate, remember. Since primate rank is not entirely hereditary, life is a wheel of fire; with the possibility of rising to dominance and the risk of falling from it all contingent, all dependent on one's own behavioral decisions and the reading and remembering of the behavior of others. It follows from this that the larger the social group a primate lives in, the more complex the psychological task it needs to perform to behave in an adaptive way. This is because as the group size increases, the number of relationships one needs to observe and keep track of rises exponentially.

Across primate species, the larger the social group, the larger the relative size of the neocortex, the "higher cognitive" part of the brain.[26] More social information to track demands more computing power to do it, even at the evolutionary cost of laying down more cerebral tissue, one of the most metabolically expensive tissue types we have in our bodies.[27] And humans have the largest neocortexes of all, suggesting what common observation shows to be true, that our nature is to live in large and complex social formations. But, as Dunbar has argued, social groups as large and complex as ours would be very difficult to keep track of by grooming relationships alone. To directly observe all the pairwise grooming relationships amongst even a modest hunter-gatherer band would take a lot of time, and to groom or be groomed by every other individual even more so. But human beings have language. We can *share* social information. X is trying to curry favor with Y, so Y will cooperate in supplanting your father Z, we can say. This has the double advantage of quickly disseminating useful information and of creating a reciprocal bond between speaker and hearer, which is itself a kind of coalition that may come in handy later. Language binds us together as grooming binds monkeys and apes.[28]

Place a group of monkeys or apes in a room together, and if they do not fight or mate, they will groom each other. Repeat the same experiment with a group of people, and if they do not fight or mate, they will talk. And Dunbar's observational studies suggest that they will talk overwhelmingly about the social worlds they inhabit: people they know in common, the behavior of other individuals, and their own relationships.[29] Technological, institutional, philosophical, or aesthetic matters may intrude, but most natural conversations will soon return to the social network within which all of these other activities are embedded. For monkeys and apes, grooming releases the body's endogenous opiates, which is why they find it so rewarding.[30] In humans, it seems that language may have sequestered this mechanism; we like nothing better than a good conversation.

Conversations, then, are activities we are inherently motivated to seek for good reason to do with our evolutionary past. Any activity which could mimic the relevant features of a really good conversation would stand to natural conversation as the opiate drug to the endogenous opiate. It would delight us; some of us would become addicted; we would seek out the best variety. This, then, is a possible theory of the origin of the dramatic mode. It is a contrived conversation that stimulates the mechanisms of reward that evolved for natural conversation. This theory is only of use if it makes some more specific predictions.

It can be made to do so. I have argued that conversation is prototypically concerned with exchanging information about the vicissitudes of relationships within a small social group. The reason we have evolved to find conversation so enduringly interesting is that the group members around us are seeking to maximize their fitness, and the way they do so will have direct effects on our fitness prospects. For example, if another individual creates a coalition or carries out a deception to raise his status, then our relative status will probably decline (unless we are in his clique). If someone else wins the most attractive mate in the group, we cannot do so. Thus we need to know what others are doing, especially in regard to status strategies and mating. This may be why the newspapers are full of stories of shady political intrigues and sex or relationship gossip.

Drama exploits these informational biases. What does drama concern, if not, precisely, the fluctuating relationships between a small number of characters? Where scientific, political, aesthetic, or technical ideas impinge, they only become truly dramatic to the extent that they are made to live through the wants and relationships of the characters. And drama in particular tends to concern conflicts over love and status (see principle F below, pp. 71–72).

This analysis might seem to predict that the content of drama will simply mirror the content of ordinary conversations, which clearly is not quite correct. A drama consisting of a genuine slice of life, unedited, would be unlikely to be very interesting. The reason is that conversations are only interesting to the extent that you know about the individuals involved and your social world is bound into theirs; as their distance from you increases, the interest level declines. Given that dramatic characters are mostly strangers to us, then, the conversation will have to be unusually interesting to hold our attention. That is, the drama has to be an *intensified* version of the concerns of ordinary conversation. One is reminded of the "supernormal" stimulus effect in animal behavior. An egg elicits nesting behavior from a female gull; a football elicits an abnormally strong nesting reaction.[31]

What does this "supernormal conversation" hypothesis predict more particularly? We have stated that human beings evolved in small, tight-knit social groups in which one person's opportunity to maximize fitness was closely bound up with the attempts to do so by all the others, especially as regards love and status. Thus, a supernormal conversation would make the fitness stakes in these domains maximal. Thus, instead of Betty going shopping, dramas should concern Betty leaving one mate for another. Instead of Bill and Bob going fishing, dramas should concern Bill and Bob locked in conflict for control of country (kingdom, tribe, etc.). And the outcomes in terms of fitness changes should be the most extreme logically possible. The intricate amorous musical chairs of *A Midsummer Night's Dream* requires a final marriage to resolve it; left off as it begins, it would be much less interesting. A *Hedda Gabler* where Hedda reconciles herself to married life and takes up needlepoint will always be outcompeted in terms of psychological impact by the one where she shoots herself. And, in an interesting natural experiment, the bowdlerized *King Lear* produced in Victorian times, where Lear and Cordelia live, was chased off the stage by Shakespeare's original and horrific ending as soon as that sentimental era was over. This, then, is the reason why, in Byron's words, "All tragedies are finished with a death / All comedies are ended with a marriage." Those are the logically maximal fitness changes in the domains human beings are interested in, and, thus, dramatic genres will tend to evolve toward them.

What then emerges, from this discussion of our primate heritage, as principles that would reasonably characterize the types of drama likely to be high in psychological appeal? The following would seem reasonably clear:

A. Drama should prototypically involve the conveyance of social information about relationships within small, tight groups similar to those typical of our species' natural behavior.
B. These groups should interact in smaller units with especially strong relationships (cliques).
C. The protagonists should make attempts to maximize their biological fitness by, for example, protecting themselves, protecting kin, enhancing their own status, and seeking mates.
D. One determinant of how captivating the drama will be is the extremity of the fitness stakes and fitness changes; logically, the maximum extremes are mating and death.
E. The attempts by the protagonists to maximize their fitness will bring about conflict, either between different individuals or between different subgoals for one individual. The richer and more complex these conflicts, the more captivating the action will be.
F. Domains of special interest will be mate choice and status competition since those are domains where the behaviors of other group members in real life have strong effects on our own fitness.

Drama as we know it certainly conforms to these principles. Of course, discovering this to be the case hardly represents an objective test of an evolutionary prediction, since the evolutionary argumentation was informed by my prior understanding of drama. However, the principles are interesting and potentially useful. First, it is striking how easily many of the generalizations about drama made by practitioners and scholars over the years can be fit into the mold of this evolutionary perspective—a consilience ready to be made. Second, the principles can be made specific enough to inform close readings of individual plays,[32] explorations of dramatic form,[33] or proposals for cross-cultural work (see conclusion).

What Is Drama Like?

PRINCIPLES A AND B
"A man walks across [an] empty space while someone else is watching him, and this is all that is needed for an act of theatre to be engaged" writes Peter Brook.[34] Perhaps, but it wouldn't be a very good one, and I couldn't imagine it catching

on. However, Brook's formulation, designed as it was to unclutter a theater overly concerned with sets and settings, contains an important truth: someone has to walk across the empty space. All drama involves a social interaction between and among one or more characters and an audience. This interaction typically involves a conversation, as a result of which their social relationships are transformed. This minimal formulation seems to hold even for monologues; the premise of a monologue is that our *understanding* of the social relationships of the narrator has changed even if those relationships have not been directly presented. Group sizes vary from one to a few dozen. However, all characters in a play are rarely presented simultaneously, but, rather, they are presented operating in small cliques. The clique structure at the end of a play is generally different from that at the beginning; the action transforms the topography of the group.

James Stiller has recently shown, for ten Shakespearean plays, that the number of characters presented interacting in the same scene is comparable to the number who generally take part in a real human conversation—rarely more than four.[35] The total number in the play, however, averages around thirty, which is comparable to the mean size of a hunter-gatherer band. Stiller shows that characters are generally linked by no more than two degrees of separation; either they interact directly or they both interact with some third party. As the dramatis personae gets bigger, however, more and more of the characters have no direct relationship to each other. Thus, an upper limit on the number of characters is set by the fact that increasing them beyond a certain point would fragment the person-web into unlinked parts. In terms of the present argument, a drama that presented a single interconnected group would presumably sequester more attention than one that is fragmentary, with many unlinked threads.

The thirty-character finding is of course an upper limit; it is quite possible to construct dramas with fewer characters. Stiller's argument is about the fission that would be caused by attempting to have more. It remains to be investigated how group size in dramas has evolved over time. It could be the case that the limit comes not from audience psychology but from the economics of employing actors. However, this seems unlikely to be the case. A quick analysis of the dramatis personae of the ten most popular dramatic films of all time finds an average of 23.2 named characters per film (compared to 27.8 for Shakespeare; ranges: films 7–47, Shakespeare 18–47).[36] This is significant for several reasons. In the film industry, the budgetary constraints of the theater are essentially lifted in virtue of infinite reproducibility. Also, many films employ many hundreds of unnamed extras and bit players. Thus, the finding that the number of characters important enough to be named has remained constant or even decreased suggests that network size is a genuine factor in audience engagement in drama.

In fact, there seem impressionistically to be two main types of dramatic networks. The classical Shakespearean type involves around thirty individuals divided into vying cliques (for example, in *A Midsummer Night's Dream*, the court of Theseus, the young lovers, the Athenian workmen, the court of Oberon). The cliques then become embroiled in each others' concerns and may come into conflict. Each clique is linked to every other via some connection, but not everyone in the drama interacts directly with everyone else, hence an average of between one and two degrees of separation between characters. This is the structure of films like *The Godfather.*

The other type is what can be called a "clique drama." This is characterized by a much smaller network in which every character has a direct relationship to every other. Ibsen's *Hedda Gabler* (1890) is a classic example. There are seven characters, each multiply connected to all the others. For example, Lovborg is Hedda's husband's academic rival, but he also knew her separately in an earlier phase of life. Elvsted is married to Lovborg and thus relates to Hedda through him but also went to school with her. Almost all possible combinations of characters are seen interacting, and, thus, the modal degree of separation is one. Many modern dramas are of this type, hence the low character numbers in some films.

PRINCIPLES C, D, AND E

As Aristotle noted in chapter 6 of the *Poetics*, the aim or purpose of the protagonists is the most important aspect of a tragedy. A succession of well-composed speeches full of character is not dramatic if there is no objective: "tragedy is not an imitation of men, but of actions and of life." This idea resonates through the entire history of theoretical writing about drama. Stanislavsky's notion of objective underpins the theory of acting, which is why method actors ask not "What am I feeling?" but "What is my motivation?"[37] Alfred Hitchcock's idea that in a film, the protagonist is always in search of something (the MacGuffin).[38] That thing can be a secret code, world domination, or a beautiful woman, but the stakes for the protagonist must be high, and there must be obstacles along the way. If he gets the MacGuffin, his biological fitness or, at the very least, his social standing must be transformed.

The notion that the motivation of the characters is the essence of drama is a traditional one. For example, it was forcefully argued by the French critic Ferdinand Brunetière.[39] He argued that all "rules" for well-made plays that had been formulated over the years (unity of place, etc.) were only conventions that would necessarily vary and have exceptions. However, he retained one principle that he held to be universal and to represent the essence of drama: "What we ask of the theatre is the spectacle of a *will* striving towards a goal."

To convince ourselves of this fact, let us examine carefully two or three works whose dramatic value is universally recognized, and let us take them from species as different as *Le Cid*, *L'Ecole des Femmes*, and *Célimaire le Bien-Aimé*.

Chimène wants to avenge her brother; and the question is how she will succeed. Arnolphe *wants* to marry Agnès whose stupidity will guarantee her fidelity; and the question is whether he will succeed. Célimaire *wants* to get rid of the widowers of his former mistress; and the question is what means he will employ. But, Célimaire is hampered in the execution of his *will* by the fear of vengeance of his friends. Arnolphe is disturbed in the execution of his *will* by the young madcap Horace who arouses love, and with love a *will* in Agnès' heart. Chimène is betrayed in the execution of her *will* by the love she feels for Rodrigue. On the other hand, Chimène's *will* is checked and broken by the insurmountable obstacle which she encounters in a will superior to her own. Arnolphe, far from being a fool, sees all the plans of his will undone by the conspiracy of youth and love.[40]

Brunetière's argument is worth quoting at length for its isomorphism with the evolutionary considerations of the previous section. All that is missing is the additional specification that the acts of will are at root wills to increase fitness. All the volitions described by Brunetière are to do with biological fitness (Chimène: kin protection, Arnolphe: mating and paternity certainty, etc.). However, just as we predicted, these volitions cause conflict, either with others in the group (Arnolphe and Horace) or by different subgoals of the same individual (Chimène's protection of her kin versus her desire to mate with Rodrigue).

As Aristotle said, a drama must have a beginning, a middle, and an end. The beginning is the establishment of what all the different fitness volitions are. The middle section is the movement through behavior and transformation of social relationships toward a way that they may be resolved. In a complex plot, this phase may be characterized by reversals and recognitions. The ending is the denouement: the moment when fitness volitions are either satisfied or dashed (in Aristotelian terms, the change of fortune).

These general observations, and the examples that follow, seem to suggest that drama *does* function as a supernormal conversation. The action prototypically involves a fitness volition that brings about conflict with other fitness volitions either within the same individual or in other members of the group. There are, of course, myriad permutations and combinations, not to mention the culturally and individually specific layers of ramification that can be built on top of this, but this deep structure seems to work. Certainly it characterizes the tradition running from Greek theater through the early modern period in British and European drama (Shakespeare and Marlowe; Molière and Racine), right up into the nineteenth-century naturalism of Chekhov and Ibsen. It also characterizes the dominant dramatic genres of today: the romantic comedy, the thriller or action movie, even the realist "slice of life" television serial.

More avant-garde traditions are, at first glance, harder to fit into this frame-work. The plays of Beckett and Ionesco, for example, do not explicitly state fit-ness motivations and certainly do not end in death or marriage. There are two points here: First, none of these is a widespread vernacular form in the same way as are the action movie and the romantic tearjerker. Second, the framework also operates at a more implicit level: in *Waiting for Godot,* the characters can be under-stood as seeking social coalitions and status in a barren and alienated world. Thus, at the deepest level, the framework may still be useful. Superficial details of setting and construction, as Brunetière stated, are just "devices which may at any time give way to others"; fitness volitions and conflicts seem to endure.

PRINCIPLE F

There are conventionally held to be two main genres in the history of Western drama: tragedy—which concerns serious, often political, conflict and which gen-erally has a negative outcome for the protagonist, and comedy—where the con-flict is often amorous in nature, tends to the ridiculous, and resolves favorably. I have argued elsewhere that in fact, tragedy generally concerns status competi-tion, often the control of the kingdom in Shakespeare, for example.[41] Comedy, on the other hand, typically concerns the mating game, that is, the appropriate pairing off of the eligible mating-age individuals within a social network. This analysis applies equally well to *A Midsummer Night's Dream* and *Four Weddings and a Funeral.* Thus, these two enduring genres tap precisely into the domains I argued in section D that we should be especially predisposed to crave information about: status change and mate choice.

In fact, the typology should be a little more complex. On the one axis, drama plots can usually be identified as concerning either the status game (what Jan Kott called "the grand mechanism of history"),[42] or the mating game. On the other axis, the outcome can be either negative or positive for the individual or group that the audience has become most allied with. Thus, there are four cells. (See table 1.) Status game—negative outcome represents the quintessential tragedy ("all tragedies end with a death"); Hamlet not only loses his kingdom to his uncle but is killed too. Status game—positive outcome represents the heroic, whether it is Henry V successfully conquering France, or 007 saving the world from the schemes of his archenemy in the James Bond films. The mating game resolved positively is the great romantic comedy, and this endures unchanged except in details from Shakespeare and Beaumarchais to *When Harry Met Sally.* Finally, mating game—negative outcome represents the great tragedies of love gone wrong, such as *Romeo and Juliet* and *Hedda Gabler.*

The claim here is not that all dramatic works can be easily pigeonholed in this way, but an astonishing number of the most popular ones can. Many will

TABLE 1. A FOURFOLD CLASSIFICATION OF DRAMAS BY CENTRAL CONFLICT AND VALENCE OF OUTCOME FOR THE PROTAGONISTS

Central Conflict	Resolution	
	Negative	Positive
Status	Tragedy	Heroic
	Richard III	Henry V
	Taxi Driver	Die Hard
Mating	Love Tragedy	Comedy
	Romeo and Juliet	Twelfth Night
	Hedda Gabbler	When Harry Met Sally

involve elements of several, such as the status competition between Prospero and his brother with which the mating game of Ferdinand and Miranda is interlaced in *The Tempest*. Often, great plays and films morph and shimmer between several cells as we watch them. In *The Merchant of Venice*, are we watching the tragedy of Shylock or the marriage comedy of Bassanio? In *Richard III*, or *Taxi Driver*, do we sympathize or not with the protagonist, and, thus, are we in the heroic or the tragic cell? Part of the richness is the structural ambiguity that makes us linger longer, seek more information, to try and resolve the problem.

Conclusions: Overflowing, Reduction, Consilience

In this essay I have proposed some tentative suggestions about why the dramatic mode is so powerful, why it has some of the features that it does, and in particular why tragedy and comedy have endured so strikingly. On the basis of both the dramatic canon and my understanding of evolutionary psychology, I have proposed some generalizations and distinctions, such as group and clique plays, and the four-fold typology of plots, that could prove useful in doing empirical and comparative work. In particular, I would predict the appearance of essentially these archetypes in independent cultures.

There is no claim here that the dramatic mode is somehow innate, waiting to be evoked by appropriate environmental triggers. It is undoubtedly a social construction, and most of its particular evolution in the West can only be understood with reference to the historical and the particular. Thus, I see my claims as entirely compatible with most of the work of conventional literary and dramatic scholarship. However, there may be some general features canalizing cultural evolution, deep structures, as Joseph Carroll calls them.[43] I would hope that the enterprise of which this volume is representative begins a fruitful dialogue between cultural studies and evolutionary psychology, not with a view to the annexing of either one by the other but in the spirit of E. O. Wilson's "consilience."[44] The particulars of cultural evolution are—must be—nested or grounded within general knowledge about the natural history of human beings.

The meaning of a play is not set for all time by the evolved psychology of author, director, and audience. Onto layers of universal understanding will be grafted locally specific cultural understandings and preoccupations as well as individual learning. Thus a play will always change its meaning with new enactments. My point has been that it may not be able to change its meaning arbitrarily or without assignable limits. The human mind is structured in such a way that domain-specific schemata about kinship, love, competition, and cooperation are easily evoked, sometimes by a single word or image. Thus, certain stories or situations richly and intrinsically *afford* possibilities for dramatic meaning, even if that meaning varies in time to place.

In other words, there is no desire here to reduce the complexity and shifting nature of dramatic meaning. Just because *Othello* fits the cell of love tragedy doesn't mean it cannot become in the late twentieth century an examination of racism with the British police service. Just because *Troilus and Cressida* is in the cell of status competition, doesn't mean that in the aftermath of World War I it couldn't become a timely meditation on the weakness of military leadership. These plays can do all these things and more, but they can do so in part *because* they can tap into the biases and algorithms of the evolved mind. Once they have our attention, they afford limitless possibilities. In other words, to classify a drama as fitting one cell or the other is not a reduction of possibilities but a description of where it starts out from in fulfilling an equally important local or personal function.

One might be tempted to argue that mass-market, forgettable drama fits into the pigeonholes set up here, but great art transcends them. I find this formulation misleading. All art transcends the categories set up here, for they are not containers but foundational structures on which the richness and openness of meaning grows and ramifies. All great dramatic texts (and performances) are polysemous, ambiguous, defying generalization. Many great dramas are deeply ambiguous about who deserves sympathy, which desires predominate. However, this is not an alternative to the principles adumbrated here. Rather, dramas raise the psychological schemata described here and allow their inherent complexity and unsolvability to resonate. Thus, to the biases we have discussed so far—for small groups, mate choice information, and so on—we should add another that keeps the audience in the house: our bias toward attending to informational complexity. Great dramas are the kind we cannot look at and say, "I know what that is" but those to which we have to return for a second look and see something different.

Qualitative analyses of texts and performances will not be chased out by evolutionary typologies. But a qualitative analysis of drama not informed by what we know of the mind is pouring sand into a bottomless container. Whether we like it or not, the mind is present in culture, and the mind has intrinsic form and content. My hope is that we will see the two great bodies of knowledge—that of culture and that of human nature—move closer and bridge the artificial divides set up in the twentieth century. Drama holds the mirror up not just to culture but to nature.

Notes

1. D. E. Brown 1991.
2. Hutton 1982.
3. Labouet 1929; Nettle 1998.
4. Hamilton 1964.
5. Hughes 1993; Jones 2003a, 2003b.
6. Barkow, Cosmides, and Tooby 1992; Barrett, Dunbar, and Lycett 2002.
7. Gardner 1972.
8. Harbage 1964.
9. Taylor 1989; Hawkes 1992.
10. Hawkes 1992, 76.
11. Bate 1997.
12. Kott 1974; Loomba and Orkin 1998; Drakakis 2002.
13. Boyd and Richerson 1985.
14. See, for instance, Dissanayake 1992b; J. Carroll 1995; Storey 1996, as well as other essays in this volume.
15. Miller 2000b.
16. D. S. Wilson, this volume.
17. Aunger 2000.
18. Dennett 1990.
19. Nesse and Berridge 1997.
20. For example, by Dennett 1990.
21. Hutton 1982.
22. Smuts, et al., 1987; Dunbar 1988.
23. Keverne, Martensz, and Tuite 1989.
24. Kudo and Dunbar 2001.

25. Dunbar 1993.
26. Dunbar 1993; Kudo and Dunbar 2001.
27. Aiello and Wheeler 1995.
28. Dunbar 1993.
29. Dunbar, Marriott, and Duncan 1997.
30. Keverne, Martensz, and Tuite 1989.
31. Tinbergen 1951.
32. Nettle 2005.
33. Stiller, Nettle, and Dunbar 2003.
34. Brook 1968.
35. Stiller, Nettle, and Dunbar 2003.
36. Ten most popular dramatic films taken from the Internet Movie Database, http//imdb.com; Stiller, Nettle, and Dunbar 2003.
37. Stanislavsky 1948.
38. Mamet 1998.
39. Brunetière 1894/1914.
40. Brunetière 1894/1914.
41. Nettle 2005.
42. Kott 1974.
43. J. Carroll 1999b.
44. E. O. Wilson 1998.

Human Nature and Literary Meaning: A Theoretical Model Illustrated with a Critique of Pride and Prejudice

Joseph Carroll

The Challenge to a Darwinian Literary Criticism

The common notion of what Darwinian literary criticism could or should do is that Darwinian critics should, first, look into evolutionary psychology to identify universal, basic forms of human behavior—human universals—and that they should then examine this or that literary text to demonstrate that the characters in that text behave in precisely the way that evolutionary psychologists predict people will behave. The method involved in this common notion is naive and is vulnerable to obvious objections. People in reality do not simply exemplify common, universal patterns of behavior. They have individuality that is distinguished by the peculiarities of their individual temperaments, their cultural conditioning, and their individual experiences. Cultures vary widely in the ways they organize the common elements of the human motivational and cognitive system; even within any given culture many people deviate drastically both from the behavioral norms that characterize that culture and from the deeper underlying commonalities of human nature. Moreover, characters in literary representations are not real, living people. They are fictive fabrications that reflect the notions and beliefs and purposes of individual authors, and individual authors are themselves constrained by their larger cultural context and by the traditions and conventions of literary representation that are available to them. To treat characters as if they were actual people is to ignore the whole concept of "meaning" in literature, and to ignore meaning in literature is something like ignoring the concept of "energy" in physics or the concept of "life" in biology. It is simply to miss the point.

The deficiencies in the common notion of Darwinian literary study can easily be corrected. There is no necessity that Darwinian literary critics muddle along doing a bad job with a naive methodology simply because they have no notion of how to do a good job. The concepts necessary for integrating Darwinian psychology and literary criticism are neither hard to understand nor difficult to use. What I propose here is to lay out a necessary minimum of analytic concepts—five in all—that must enter into any reasonably competent literary analysis informed by a Darwinian understanding of human nature. The basic concepts are these: (1) human nature as a structured hierarchy of motives (within which the motive of constructing imaginative representations holds a prominent place); (2) "point of view," or the location of meaning within three distinct centers of consciousness—that of the author, the characters, and the implied or projected audience; (3) the use of human universals as a common frame of reference in relation to which authors identify their own individual identities and their own distinct structures of meaning; (4) a set of categories for analyzing individual differences in identity; and (5) the distribution of specifically literary meaning into three chief dimensions: theme (conceptual content), tone (emotional coloring), and formal organization (a concept that ranges all the way from macrostructures like plot and narrative sequencing to microstructures like phrasing, word choice, and sequences of sounds).

In the course of laying out these concepts and explaining their relations, I shall also make arguments that should be of some interest to Darwinian social scientists, whether or not they care much about literature and the other arts. I shall argue that Darwinian psychology is on the verge of achieving a paradigm—that is, a consensus about the necessary minimum of conceptual elements that enter into an understanding of "human nature." This emerging paradigm does not consist merely of a list of common basic motives or "universals." It consists both of universals, the common human elements, and of the variations among those elements that we describe as "individual differences." And the paradigm also includes an understanding of how the specifically human pattern of life-history—of birth, development, reproduction, and death—responds with flexible but integrated strategies to the wide range of physical and cultural conditions in which it is possible for people to subsist. Among Darwinian psychologists, there is still disagreement in all these areas, and the currently dominant school of Darwinian psychology, the school most readily identified as "evolutionary psychology," has committed itself to dead ends and fallacies in its deprecation of both individual differences and domain-general intelligence. But Darwinian social science as a whole has a diverse array of intellectually independent investigators from many convergent disciplines—paleoanthropology, life-history analysis, behavioral ecology, behavioral genetics, personality theory, and the study of intelligence, among others. Given this array of investigators eager to make advances in their own fields and to integrate those fields within the larger logic of evolutionary theory, claims that are motivated by ideology and that lack both empirical support and internal consistency are not likely to survive for long. The necessary elements for a paradigm in Darwinian psychology are already virtually in place, and I am fairly confident that the energy of active research will in the near future sweep away the obstructions that have temporarily arisen from the premature consolidation of certain orthodox doctrines.

To make an argument about the structure of Darwinian literary criticism, then, I shall first need to make an argument about the current condition and future prospects of Darwinian psychology. I shall sketch out what I take to be the emerging paradigm for human nature, and I shall introduce one concept—the concept of a "cognitive behavioral system"—that is relatively unfamiliar but that is, I shall argue, indispensable to the formation of an adequate paradigm both in psychology and in literary study. Most evolutionary psychologists have paid slight attention to literature and the other arts, and some have argued that the arts have no adaptive function central to human life-history goals.[1] Invoking the logic of the emerging paradigm in Darwinian psychology, I shall argue that literature and the other arts do indeed have an adaptive function and that understanding this adaptive function is a prerequisite to understanding our specifically *human* nature. The effort to construct a paradigm for Darwinian literary criticism and the effort to construct a paradigm for the broader field of Darwinian psychology are thus interdependent. They need each other. Fortunately, they are both within reach, and by reaching the one, we shall also reach the other.

The central challenge for a specifically Darwinian form of literary criticism is to connect the highest levels in the organization of human nature with the most detailed and subtle aspects of literary meaning. Can we connect the basic life-history goals—survival, growth, and reproduction—with the finest nuances of theme, tone, and style in the organization of literary meaning in specific works? The answer to this question will determine the success or failure of Darwinian literary criticism, and the answer is "yes, we can." The elementary principles of life-history analysis enter into the organization of all literary representations, and the manner in which any given author manages those principles is a defining feature in the character and quality of that author's work. To give a practical illustration of these claims, in the final section of this article I shall offer a Darwinian critical commentary on a single novel, *Pride and Prejudice.* I have selected this novel because it is one of the most familiar of all novels; it is relatively short and simple; and it is so finely realized, as an artistic construct, that it offers a good test case for the challenge of demonstrating the integral relation between life-history analysis and the finest components of literary meaning.

Let me emphasize that this choice of an illustrative text is in one sense arbitrary. Any work of literature, from any period or genre, could be chosen for illustrative purposes. Darwinists have written critiques of folktales, myths, plays, poems, romance novels, realist fiction, science fiction, operas, ballets, and movies. They have written interpretive studies of, among other writers, Homer, Shakespeare, Swift, Wordsworth, Pushkin, Tchaikovsky, Walter Scott, Charlotte Brontë, George Eliot, Hans Christian Andersen, Willa Cather, Walter Pater, Evgeny Zamyatin, and

Dr. Seuss. There is no work of literature written anywhere in the world, at any time, by any author, that is outside the scope of a Darwinian analysis. To be susceptible to a Darwinian analysis, an author does not have to be a Darwinian. An author can be a pagan Greek, a Christian, a Muslim, or a Zen Buddhist. He or she can be a Brazilian tribesman, a European lady, a medieval Japanese warrior, or a Tibetan monk. He or she can be heterosexual, homosexual, bisexual, or celibate. He or she need not be average or typical, and he or she need not personally embrace beliefs and attitudes that are similar to those of Darwinian psychologists or Darwinian literary critics. If Darwinism gives a true account of the human mind, and if the human mind produces all literary texts, all literary texts are susceptible to a Darwinian analysis. They are susceptible, that is, to an analysis of the constraining psychological structures that regulate the production of all imaginative artifacts.

Geneticists have often found fruit flies a convenient species for their experiments. But they do not believe or suggest that genetics applies only to fruit flies. I have written on *Pride and Prejudice* in various places, using it for various illustrative purposes. I want to be clear, then, that I do not consider *Pride and Prejudice* a particularly or specifically Darwinian text. I consider it the literary equivalent of a fruit fly. Various of my colleagues in Darwinian literary study are working on the literary equivalents of mice or nematode worms, but whatever the local subject of study, we are all contributing to the same larger field.

The Emerging Paradigm in Darwinian Psychology

The argument I shall make for what Darwinian literary critics can and should do will turn on the questions of individual differences and "domain-general" intelligence. The two main orthodox tenets of evolutionary psychology that have so far impeded the full development of a paradigm for Darwinian psychology are the repudiation or deprecation of the significance attaching to domain-general cognitive abilities and individual differences in personality and intelligence. "Evolutionary psychology" as a distinct school—and not just as a general term covering the whole field of Darwinian psychology—gives overwhelming, preponderating weight to "human universals," and it envisions the mind as consisting almost exclusively of "domain-specific" cognitive mechanisms, that is, "cognitive modules" that have evolved specifically for the purpose of solving adaptive problems within a Paleolithic environment. And that ancient environment is itself conceived as a set of statistically stable physical and social conditions, the environment of evolutionary adaptedness. The central tenets of evolutionary psychology as a distinct school, then, are these: (a) everyone has pretty much the same sort of mind and personality, not only in basic structures but in force or quality; (b) this one universal mind, the mind that is common to all people on earth, is "designed" (adapted) exclusively to deal with a statistically stable environment that lasted for perhaps two million years but that in good part no longer subsists; and (c) all the significant adaptive features of that mind are "cognitive modules" designed to solve adaptive problems specific to the statistical regularities of this ancient environment; domain-general intelligence is not one of these adaptive cognitive features.

This characterization of evolutionary psychology is stark, stripped of qualifications and equivocations, and it is thus far a "caricature," but the merit of a caricature is that it brings into sharp relief the signal, defining features of a physiognomy. The oddly misshapen countenance that emerges from these three starkly defined tenets is in its main outlines a true portrait.[2]

There are two reasons, I would suggest, that evolutionary psychologists have propounded this peculiarly distorted version of human cognitive evolution. The first reason is that they have been preoccupied with opposing the Standard Social Science Model of the mind as a blank slate or general, all-purpose computer in which all content is produced by external (social and cultural) influences.[3] Domain specificity offers an alternative to domain generality. The second reason is that they have been frightened by the association of Darwinian psychology with social Darwinism, eugenics, and the exploration of individual and group differences in behavior (the field known as "behavioral genetics"), and especially differences in intelligence. The radical environmentalism or blank-slate model that dominated the social sciences in the twentieth century was itself largely motivated by the fear or rejection of social Darwinism, eugenics, and racial theory. By emphasizing universals and domain-specific mechanisms the evolutionary psychologists have sought to effect a compromise between Darwinism and the Standard Social Science Model. They have reintroduced the notion of adaptive cognitive structure into psychology but have done so without violating the ideological taboos against acknowledging the significance of individual and group differences.

The appeal of these two advantages has been so strong that it has, since the early 1990s, blinded many Darwinian psychologists to the fundamental disadvantages of the concepts that enable the compromise. The disadvantages are that this whole complex of ideas runs counter to gross and obvious features of common experience—to the vital importance both of individual differences and of general intelligence in everyday life—and that it runs counter also to the elementary logic in the theory of natural selection. In that theory, "selection" can only work on variation, that is, "individual differences." No variation, no selection. No selection, no adaptation, and thus no evolution "by means of natural selection."[4]

Since the late 1990s, evolutionary psychology has achieved sufficient substance and stability to provide a big market for popular expositions and for textbooks—for summary expositions of common findings. In about the same period—in just the past few years—the psychological ideas that so quickly congealed into a premature orthodoxy have been under increasing pressure from new and genuinely innovative research into the most important event in human evolutionary history—the "cultural revolution" that took place some sixty to thirty thousand years ago and that produced the first evidence of complex technology, complex forms of socioeconomic organization, and sophisticated symbolic and artistic activity. This whole research area is fraught with controversy, but there is enough agreement about some basic facts so that a compelling new vision of human evolution has been emerging—a vision that contrasts sharply with the orthodox tenets of evolutionary psychology. In this new vision, the most distinctive feature of the specifically human mind—the feature that distinguishes it most from that of its primate cousins—is the emergence of a flexible general intelligence that enables humans to adapt to variations within an environment that is itself complex and unstable.[5]

It is a simple fact available to common observation that humans have evolved a truly extraordinary capacity to adapt to new and different environments—and to effect these adaptations while undergoing relatively little or no actual change in their anatomical or physiological characteristics. Humans can live everywhere from polar regions to deserts to tropical rain forests; they can organize themselves socially in groups that extend from small hunter-gatherer bands to tribes, hordes, nation states, empires, and new world orders; and they can adapt to socioeconomic ecologies that stretch from hunting and gathering to agriculture, market economies, industrial cities, and vast metropolitan regions linked digitally to a total world culture. The one crucial feature of human nature that underwrites this adaptability is domain-general intelligence, and that intelligence, along with all the distinctive features of human temperament and personal character, varies from person to person and group to group.[6]

In the new, emerging vision of human evolution and human nature, the idea of cognitive domains has not been discarded. It has been assimilated and integrated into the larger general structure of human cognition. Cognitive domains have their place and function; they subserve cognitive activities that track constant features of the environment. The eyesight that tracks the spatiophysical world is a prime example; and language aptitude that tracks the human physical and social environment is another. But these domain-specific aptitudes are only a part of the total human cognitive repertory. Another part is general intelligence, and general intelligence subserves the basic adaptive needs of human beings. The new vision does not fall back to the old blank-slate model. It does not assume that all human motives are simply fabricated by arbitrary cultural conventions. It identifies a distinct structure of human motives and cognitive dispositions that derives from the larger logic of inclusive fitness—the logic that regulates the adaptive structure of all life on earth. The distinct structure of human motives and cognitive dispositions is that which is appropriate to a primate species that is highly social and mildly polygynous; that displays concealed ovulation, continuous female receptivity, and postmenopausal life expectancy corresponding to a uniquely extended period of childhood development; that has extraordinary aptitudes for technology; that has developed language and the capacity for peering into the minds of its conspecifics; and that displays a unique disposition for fabricating and consuming aesthetic and imaginative artifacts. So long as we bear all this in mind, we need have no fear of falling back into the structural vacuum of the blank slate—a vacuum in which the mind evolved, the mind produced culture, and culture gave all content and structure to the mind.

In the 1990s, the most important theoretical conflict within Darwinian psychology itself was the conflict between "sociobiology" on the one side and "evolutionary psychology" on the other. In its simplest terms, this conflict turned on differing views of the human motivational system. Sociobiologists tended to regard humans as "fitness maximizers." As Irons formulates the idea, "Human beings tend to behave in such a way as to maximize their genetic representation in future generations."[7] In its most extreme form, as in the arguments produced by Betzig, fitness maximization is conceived simply in numerical terms as a matter of leaving the greatest possible number of progeny. Evolutionary psychologists, in contrast, committed themselves to the view that humans do not care particularly about reproductive success. In their view, humans are not "fitness maximizers" but rather "adaptation executors."[8] That is, humans are motivated exclusively by "proximal" motives such as the desire for food and sex. In the environment of evolutionary adaptedness, such motives operated reliably to maximize fitness but did not, supposedly, require that reproductive success be an active motive in its own right. In the modern world, the argument goes, birth control neatly severs the link between the proximal motive of sexual desire and the "ultimate" regulative principle of inclusive fitness. People are designed only to push the pleasure buttons in their proximal motives, not to worry about the ultimate evolutionary or adaptive rationale that produced those buttons.[9]

In the currently orthodox version of evolutionary psychology, the idea of humans as adaptation executors has gained a decisive victory. Insofar as this concept is set in contrast to the notion of counting offspring as a monolithic human motive, the victory has been legitimate, but the idea of pushing pleasure buttons is not in itself a satisfactory account of the human motivational system. We can formulate a better, more comprehensive account of the human motivational system by integrating two concepts: (a) the concept of human life history as a cycle organized around the distribution of effort between "somatic" and "reproductive" activities and (b) the concept of "behavioral systems."

The central categories of life-history analysis are birth, growth, death, and reproduction. The organisms of all species engage in two fundamental forms of effort—the acquisition of resources (somatic effort) and the expenditure of resources in reproduction. Birth, growth, and death are somatic activities. Mating and parenting are reproductive activities. (Not all individuals of all species engage in reproductive activity, but if reproductive effort were not part of the suite of characteristics in a species, that species would become extinct within a single generation.) All the main activities in the life history of an organism are integrated and interdependent. "What an organism spends in one endeavor cannot be spent in another. Life histories, the patterns of birth, growth, and death that we see, are thus the outcome of competing costs and benefits of different activities at any point in the life cycle."[10] Life-history analysis compares the different ways in which the logic of inclusive fitness—the maximization of reproductive success—has regulated the interplay of these large-scale principles in different species. The organization of life-history traits—of size, growth rate, life span, mating behavior, number and pacing of offspring, sex ratios of offspring, and parenting strategies—enters into every aspect of a species' characteristics: into its physiology, its anatomy, and its behavior. Life-history theory can thus be regarded as the overarching theory for both a macroeconomics and a microeconomics of biology.[11]

The human species has a distinct form for the organization of its life history, and the logic of this organization enters into every facet of the human behavioral and cognitive order. Humans are highly social animals with pair-bonded, semi-monogamous mating systems and extraordinarily high levels of parental investment. They have upright posture, narrowed birth canals, and large brains. As a result, their reproductive economy necessarily involves motivational systems geared toward male-female pair-bonding, sustained family structures, extended kinship systems, and complex social organization. Their large brains entail long development as children so that they can acquire the information and skills necessary for successful life effort. Their long childhood requires intense child-parent attachment, male-female cooperative parenting, and extended kin networks. Their large brains present them with unique adaptive opportunities, both technological and social, and also with challenges and problems other species do not face.

The idea of "behavioral systems" has been formulated as a concept in Darwinian psychiatry, and it has emerged also, implicitly, half-consciously, as an organizing principle in orthodox versions of evolutionary psychology. In *Darwinian Psychiatry*, McGuire and Troisi define behavioral systems as coordinated suites of behavior subserving specific life goals. "The term *behavior system* refers to *functionally and causally related behavior patterns and the systems responsible for them*."[12] McGuire and Troisi themselves identify four specific systems: survival, reproduction, kin assistance, and reciprocation—with reciprocation serving as a generalized term for social interaction beyond the kin group. In the now numerous textbooks devoted to evolutionary psychology, very similar terms typically serve as the chapter titles for the whole sequence of chapters. For instance, in the first of the textbooks, after introductory chapters on the history, theory, and methodology of evolutionary psychology, Buss (1999) has this sequence of main sections: "Problems of Survival," "Challenges of Sex and Mating," "Challenges of Parenting and Kinship," and "Problems of Group Living."[13] The organization of topics in Buss's textbook set the pattern for the subsequent textbooks, and the pattern itself tacitly underwrites the theory of behavioral systems. (Buss himself is alert to the importance of personality theory and to individual differences, and in a final section of his textbook he discusses this topic but also acknowledges that orthodox evolutionary psychologists have concentrated almost exclusively on human universals.)

Each behavioral system consists in a complex of motives that have a distinct object or set goal—to sustain life, find a mate, rear children, sustain kin networks, and function in a social order. Goals of this magnitude present themselves as fundamental motivating concerns in the organization of individual lives, and they thus also form the building blocks through which individual lives are organized within a cultural order. A motivational complex is not itself a simple "proximal" mechanism—the direct physiological trigger of a specific behavior; it is, rather, a cluster of interdependent and closely related mechanisms mediated by higher order thinking lodged in the cerebral cortex. Animals mate by instinct, through the direct action of proximal mechanisms. Human mating involves plans and long-term goals in which proximal mechanisms are integrated into functional sequences sustained over time. The symbolic dimension of culture—ritual, ceremony, narrative, and art—provides conscious and public images for these basic motivational complexes.[14]

By combining the idea of life-history analysis with the idea of behavioral systems, we can formulate an alternative to the opposing notions of fitness maximization and adaptation execution. Despite the evidence of a few great Sultans, humans are not typically motivated, in any very direct or active way, to maximize the number of their progeny. But neither are they merely puppets adequately fulfilled by the pushing of their pleasure buttons. People are neither fitness maximizers nor adaptation executors. They are highly integrated sets of behavioral systems that have been organized and directed by the logic of the human life-history cycle. Human nature is organized in structured sets of behavioral systems, and these systems subserve the goals that are distributed into the basic functions of somatic and reproductive life effort. Fitness maximization is not itself an active motive, but the fundamental somatic impulses (surviving and acquiring resources, both physical and social) and the fundamental reproductive impulses (acquiring mates, having sex, producing and tending children, helping kin) are in fact direct and active motives.

The behavioral systems identified by McGuire and Troisi and by the textbook writers—survival, mating, parenting, kin relations, and social interaction—are built into the human organism. They are mediated by innate structures in the genetically conditioned features of anatomy, physiology, hormones, and neuro-chemistry. All of these mediating forces manifest themselves psychologically as the "basic" emotions identified by Ekman and others as universal motivating forces in human psychology (joy, sadness, fear, anger, disgust, contempt, and surprise).[15] The main behavioral systems that subserve the largest life-history goals are sensitive to the appropriate stimuli, but they are latent in all conditions of life. Male sexual desire, for example, is activated by the sight of nubile females, but even a male raised in total isolation by machines would presumably have stirrings of confused sexual interest or sensation—a sense of vague, frustrated longing, accompanied by spontaneous erections and emissions, and I think it safe to predict that the first time any such hypothetically deprived male saw a nubile female, he would have a sudden and instantaneous conviction that *that* was what he had been wanting, had he only known. A woman raised in similar isolation would presumably not think to herself, "I wish to be inseminated, grow an embryo in my uterus, and produce a child, which I shall then suckle and nurture," but whatever her thoughts or longings might be, she would still grow breasts and undergo a menstrual cycle, and if she were inseminated by machines in her sleep, the growth and birth of a child, however terrifying to her ignorance, would have in it a certain natural, physical logic, and the effects would carry with them instinctive impulses and sensations. Language is an instinct, but feral children can never gain fluency in speech.[16] Maternity is an instinct, but female monkeys raised in isolation perform badly as mothers. Normal human development requires socialization, but socialization itself is channeled by innate dispositions. The behavior of a female raised in isolation is disorganized and dysfunctional, but it is not simply blank.

The anatomical and hormonal organization of women gives evidence of massive adaptive adjustments to the functional requirements of bearing and raising children. In the modern world, people can choose whether or not to reproduce, but the overwhelming majority do choose to reproduce. Many couples who for physical reasons cannot have children go to astonishing lengths, in expense and effort, to adopt children. Evolutionary psychologists emphasizing the activation of proximal mechanisms point to the fact that not everybody wants to have children. True enough, but most people are equipped by nature with the physical and psychological attributes that are necessary to the bearing and raising of children, and the majority of people feel at some point a powerful need to activate those attributes and to fulfill the behavioral capacities they feel latent within them. If this were not the case, we would have a hard time explaining adoption and the nearly universal human practice of treating pet animals as surrogate children.[17]

Child-bearing/rearing is only an instance, though an important one. The larger principle is that in most cases people accede to the psychological force of the total set of motivational systems that have been implanted in them by the logic of human life history. More often than not, people have a compelling need to give full and integrated play to the whole suite of their behavioral systems. Exceptions and special cases abound, but it is a broad general truth about human nature that people have a need to activate the latent capacities of the behavioral systems that have shaped the largest features of their bodies and their minds. For most people, achieving satisfaction in life depends on the fulfillment of the emotional needs built into those systems.

The Cognitive Behavioral System

The textbook versions of evolutionary psychology are a little uncertain about what, if anything, to make of the various specifically cognitive aspects of human nature. Language can usually be inserted somewhere in the sections on social interaction, but it is less clear where one is to locate aptitudes for tool use, cognitive biases for the acquisition of organized information about plants and animals, and the production of cultural artifacts of no apparent utility, especially if these artifacts do not push simple pleasure buttons in the way that pornography does for many people. If we combine the idea of behavioral systems with a recognition of the peculiarly human attribute of domain-general intelligence, we can solve this puzzle. The human mind is an extraordinary, complex organ. It is both highly structured and flexibly responsive to contingent inputs. It solves an immense array of adaptive problems. Some of its processes develop in predictably universal ways, as in the acquisition of language, of colors, or of botanical and zoological categories.[18] Other processes develop with the combinatorial fluidity that we designate as "creative" or "inventive," as in the invention of new technologies and new arts, but all new inventions and discoveries work by extending and combining the elemental cognitive components that develop spontaneously and universally in human minds, as the product of an adaptive evolutionary history, and all cultural artifacts, no matter how complex or seemingly arbitrary, are constrained by the limitations of physical nature and are both prompted and constrained by an evolved human psychology.[19]

The mind is a complex and integrated feature of human nature—sufficiently complex, structured, and integrated in its operations so that it answers to the criteria for what McGuire and Troisi identify as a "behavioral system." If we identify the mind in this way, we are adding it, as a specifically human characteristic, to the set of human behavioral systems. We identify it as having characteristic innate constraints and distinctive latent capacities elicited by appropriate releasers. The mate selection system arouses desire and fulfills it in successful coupling. The parenting system arouses concern for children and achieves fulfillment in the successful rearing of children. The social interaction system arouses desire for forming coalitions and finding a place within a status hierarchy, and achieving those goals offers pleasure and provides a sensation of satisfaction. The cognitive behavioral system arouses a need for conceptual and imaginative order, and that need fulfills itself and provides satisfaction to the mind through the formulation of concepts; the construction of religious, philosophical, or ideological beliefs; the development of scientific knowledge; and the fabrication of aesthetic and imaginative artifacts.

I have already argued that domain-general intelligence has an adaptive function; it facilitates a flexible response to a variable environment. That flexibility gives humans an advantage other animals do not have, and it presents them also with challenges and difficulties unique to the human species. Other species operate mainly by means of instinct, that is, by means of stereotyped behaviors that leave little room for conscious choice. Humans create elaborate mental models of the world and make decisions on the basis of alternative scenarios that present themselves within those models.[20] The materials available to the mind and imagination are vast, and the combination of those materials virtually infinite. The possibility for error, uncertainty, and confusion is an ever-present fact of human mental life. Because they have an irrepressibly active and unstable mental life, humans have a special need to fabricate mental maps or models that make sense of the world and provide behavioral directives that can take the place of instinctive behavioral patterns. For these mental maps or models to be effective in providing behavioral directives, they must be emotionally saturated, imaginatively vivid. Art and cultural artifacts like religion and ideology meet this demand. They fulfill a necessary adaptive function, that of regulating the human cognitive behavioral system. The arts provide emotionally saturated images and aesthetic constructs that produce a sense of total cognitive order and that help regulate the other behavioral systems. The arts make sense of human needs and motives. They simulate subjective experience, map out social relations, evoke sexual and social interactions, depict the intimate relations of kin, and locate the whole complex and interactive array of human behavioral systems within models of the total world order. Humans have a universal and irrepressible need to fabricate this sort of order, and satisfying that need provides a distinct form of pleasure and fulfillment.[21]

A Diagram of Human Nature

To clarify the hierarchical motivational structure of human nature I have been describing here, I shall put it into a diagram, with inclusive fitness at the top, as the ultimate regulative principle (but not as an active and direct motive). (See figure 1.) Active and direct motive begins at the next level down, with the organization of life effort into somatic and reproductive effort. Through this hierarchical structure, I am suggesting that over and above their specific goals and motives, many people have a generalized but distinct desire to acquire resources and also to achieve successful reproduction. Not all people have an active desire for reproductive success, but such a desire is nonetheless, I would argue, a characteristic of the species as a whole. Young men do not think only, I want to buy a red convertible so I can attract that girl there and have sex with her. They also often think, I'd like to become prosperous, and I'd like to get married and have a family. And young women do not think only, I'm impressed by that guy with the red convertible. I want to arouse his sexual interest and attach him to me. They also think, I'd like to find a prosperous, reliable man, marry him, have children, and raise a family. It is these latter, generalized inclinations that I am identifying as the somatic and reproductive motives in their own right.

Below the level of generalized desire to acquire resources and succeed in sexual reproduction, I shall place the various behavioral systems that subserve both those general motive dispositions. The specific subordinate systems identified here are systems dedicated to survival, technology, mating, parenting, kin relations, social relations, and cognitive activity. In a box under each behavioral system, I have placed a few motivational goals or directives characteristic of that system. Thus, under "survival," there is a directive "avoid predators." Under "mating," there is a directive "avoid incest." Under "social relations," a directive "build coalitions," and so on.

In the interest of completeness, I include one behavioral system—that of "technology"—that is not mentioned in the accounts by McGuire and Troisi and the textbook writers. The disposition to construct stone tools is one of the most ancient hominid adaptations, and our modern technology is continuous with the construction of complex, multipart tools that constitutes one of the distinguishing features of the "human revolution" from perhaps one hundred thousand to thirty thousand years ago. In one of the most elaborate efforts so far to mediate between evolutionary psychology and the idea of a domain-general intelligence, Mithen identifies technology as an integrated area of cognitive activity. He calls it a cognitive domain, but the concept as he describes it is on a structural level equivalent to what I have been calling a behavioral system.[22]

Specific cognitive modules would be activated within the relevant behavioral systems. For instance, the cognitive modules for vision—edge and motion detection, color, depth, etc.—would be activated within the technological behavioral system and the survival system. Kin-recognition modules would be activated within the kinship system. "Face recognition" modules would be activated within all interpersonal behavioral systems (mating, parenting, kin, social interaction). Modules for regulating social exchange or cheater detection would be activated in the mating system and in the social system, and so on. If, as seems likely, the brain has specific modules geared to the construction of narratives and

FIGURE 1. HIERARCHICAL MOTIVATIONAL STRUCTURE OF HUMAN NATURE

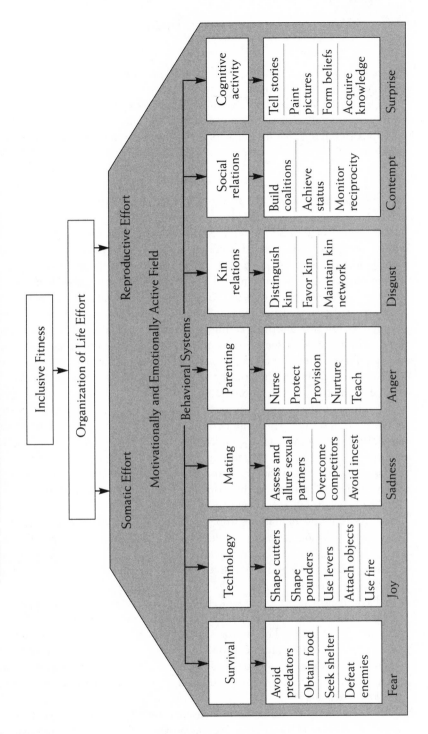

the recognition of aesthetically pleasing verbal patterns, those would be activated within the cognitive behavioral system.[23]

One final feature of the diagram is that the box in the diagram containing behavioral systems has a list of Ekman's seven basic emotions at the bottom of the box, thus signifying that all behavioral systems are activated and mediated by emotion.[24]

Meaning and Point of View in Literary Representations

Literary representation is first and foremost the representation of human behavior within some surrounding world. Creating such representations is itself a fundamental motive of human nature, and human nature is the fundamental subject of the representations. The "meaning" of a representation does not reside in the represented events. Meaning resides in the *interpretation* of events. And interpretation is always, necessarily, dependent on "point of view." "Point of view" in literary narrative is not just another technical feature in a catalog of formal literary devices. In its broadest sense, point of view is a term signifying *the locus of consciousness or experience within which any meaning takes place.* Point of view is thus the term we use to designate the primary components in the social interactions constituted in and by a literary representation.

There are three components in the social interactions of a literary representation: the author, the represented characters, and the audience.[25] The primary locus of meaning for all literary works is the mind of the author. Whether consciously or unconsciously, the author provides whatever determinate meaning resides in a work, but the author also negotiates among the competing points of view within the characters in the work and negotiates further with the point of view he or she attributes to an audience.

Authors are people talking to people about people. Most stories are about people seeking resources and reproductive success—fortune and love. But they are also about people seeking to perceive meaning in or impose meaning on the events of their own lives and the lives of every person they know. All authors seek to dominate the meaning of the story they tell, and all the characters in a story have their own version of what happens. As a rule, these versions partially overlap both with one another and with the version presented by the author, but they also often conflict. The author has final say among his or her own characters, but to control the interpretation of the story as it will be registered by the audience, the author can only persuade, manipulate, cajole, wheedle, intimidate, solicit, insult, flatter, bully, harangue, coax, shame, or otherwise appeal to or provoke the readers.[26]

It is important to grasp the foundational significance of this set of simple axioms about point of view. These axioms provide a distinct, finite, and manageable set of analytic categories for the analysis of meaning in a literary representation. There are *three specific components* in the social interactions of a literary representation. There are *always* three components. There are *only* three components. The members of each of these three categories organize the meaning of represented events in some distinct way. One of the chief analytic procedures a critic needs to perform in assessing any literary representation is to assess the relations between the author's point of view, the point of view of the characters, and the point of view in the audience that is implied or projected by the author. At the highest possible level, the meaning of a literary representation consists in the interaction among the points of view of author, characters, and implied audience. That interaction is largely controlled by one of those three distinct sets, the author.

Human Nature, Human Universals, Culture, and Individual Differences

Almost all authors explicitly invoke "human nature" as their ultimate referent and the source of their authority. The term "human nature" signifies a set of elemental motives and dispositions—what MacDonald calls "evolved motive dispositions."[27] The diagram of human nature sketched out previously suggests the sorts of motives that are usually contained in the common conception of human nature—motives like self-preservation, sexual desire, jealousy, maternal love, and the desire for social status—and these substantive motives are elaborated by the ideas that enter into the folk understanding of ego psychology: the primacy of self-interest and the prevalence of self-serving delusion, manipulative deceit, vanity, and hypocrisy. Authors understand that each elemental disposition varies in quality and degree from person to person; they know, for instance, that some people are more fearful of death, more sexually passionate, more maternal, or more ambitious than their neighbors. And they understand further that each of these dispositions, variable in itself, can be combined in different ways with the other dispositions so as to produce the distinct configurations of individual identity. A woman might be both terrified of death and intensely protective of her children but have little sexual desire and little social ambition—or be exactly the reverse, bold and fearless, coldly indifferent to her offspring, sexually ardent, and passionately determined to achieve high social rank. And yet again, she might be fairly bold, typically maternal, moderately amorous, and modestly ambitious.

Human universals or species-typical norms of behavior are merely behavioral patterns so firmly grounded in the logic of human life history that they are characteristic features of all known cultures. For instance, all cultures have marriage, rites of passage, social roles defined by age and sex, religious beliefs, public ceremonies, kin relations, sex taboos, medical practices, criminal codes, storytelling, jokes, and so on.[28] Universals are made up of motive dispositions that combine in relatively stable and consistent ways. The same motive dispositions can also be elaborated and organized, at higher levels of cultural complexity, in ways that vary widely from culture to culture. For instance, all cultures have marriage, but some cultures are polygynous and some monogamous; some allow divorce, and some do not. All cultures have games, but not all cultures play whist or football. All cultures have language, but not all cultures are literate; not all literate cultures have produced highly developed forms of prose fiction; and not all cultures with highly developed forms of prose fiction have produced stream-of-consciousness narrative styles.

No culture can deviate from human universals (by definition), but many individual people can and do deviate from species-typical norms of behavior. They murder their children, commit incest, fail to develop language, or otherwise behave in anomalous or dysfunctional ways. The behavior that is depicted in literary texts does not necessarily exemplify universal or species-typical behavioral patterns, but species-typical patterns form an indispensable frame of reference for the communication of meaning in literary representations. By appealing to this substratum of common human motives, authors activate a vein of common understanding in their readers. Consider maternal care and incest. Maternal care of infants is a "universal" feature of human nature, but all cultures make some provision for limiting reproduction, and in cultures that do not have access to birth control and abortion, reproductive limitation necessarily involves infanticide.[29] Literary authors can nonetheless depend on readers to feel the weight and value of maternal care. This is part of the common frame of reference, not just for any particular culture but for all cultures. Medea murders her own children, and Euripides can safely anticipate that the audience will react with instinctive shock and horror to the murder. So also, incest avoidance is a human universal. Different cultures define the details of incest in different ways, but certain kinds of incest are universally prohibited. No culture permits mother-son incest, and Sophocles can safely anticipate that his audience will instinctively sympathize with the revulsion of feeling that leads Oedipus to gouge out his own eyes.[30]

In the same way that each author has a unique fingerprint, he or she has also some unique configuration of identity—some individual variation of personality and experiential conditioning—and that identity defines itself in relation both to the cultural norms within which the author lives and also to the common elements of human nature. Individual identity is the basis for an author's point of view, and more often than not an author presents his or her own distinct point of view as a normative standard—as an ideal against which to judge other identities, other points of view. By appealing to "human nature," literary authors can ground their own values within what they take to be elemental realities. Sometimes, but not always, they contrast these elemental realities with the conventions of their own culture, suggesting that the conventions are shallow, perverse, artificial, unhealthy, or otherwise undesirable.[31]

Some distinctions of individual difference are obvious and available to untutored common sense—for instance, distinctions of age, sex, health, attractiveness, social affiliation, social status, vocational occupation, intelligence, and honesty. (The now pat triad of class, gender, and race—the standard topics of politicized literary criticism—is an arbitrary subset of these useful categories.) Such terms, available to common sense, are also necessary to a life-history analysis of the human species. The common understanding operates as an intuitive or "folk" version of life-history analysis. In addition to the distinctions from this range of analysis, all critics have access to the common vocabulary for assessing temperament and personality. Differences in personality are part of the adaptive environment among which individual humans make the choices that enable them to succeed in meeting the needs of their evolved motive dispositions. In traditional belle-lettristic or impressionistic literary criticism, differences in the quality of critical perceptions depend in good part on the acuity any given critic displays in accessing this common vocabulary. Modern personality theory has now distilled, codified, and elaborated the common vocabulary of temperament and personality, and it is very much in a literary critic's interest to become familiar with this body of empirical research. At present, the best available theory is that of the five-factor system (extraversion, neuroticism, conscientiousness, agreeableness, and imaginative and intellectual "openness"). Since this system was drawn in the first place from the common lexicon, it is not surprising that its categories correlate well, as a first approximation, to the depiction of characters in fiction. To identify the relations of authors to their own characters, the use of this common vocabulary provides an invaluable tool for a shared and delimited analytic vocabulary.[32]

The fifth factor in the five-factor personality system—imaginative or intellectual openness to experience—is the factor most closely associated with domain-general intelligence, and it is itself roughly concordant with the cognitive behavioral system. MacDonald explains, "The Openness to Experience factor taps variation in intelligence and what one might term optimal Piagetian learning—intrinsically motivated curiosity and interest in intellectual and aesthetic experience combined with imagination and creativity in these areas."[33] In virtually all literature, distinctions of wit or intelligence or imaginative vitality form a central distinguishing point of reference in the discrimination among characters and in the formation of a normative or dominant authorial point of view. Authors by nature have strong cognitive behavioral systems—they would be positioned at the far end of the right tail of the bell curve distribution measuring the fifth factor—and they tend strongly to value this same quality in their characters. They tend also to invite their audiences to share in their own normative approbation of this quality.

The primary purpose of literary criticism, as an objective pursuit of true knowledge about its subject, is to identify the specific configuration of meaning in any given text or set of texts. To make that identification, it is necessary for the critic to have three conceptual models or templates at his or her disposal: (a) a concept of human nature (like that in figure 1), (b) a concept of the cultural ecology within which any given text has been constructed, and (c) a set of categories for analyzing individual differences. To make analytic use of these three templates, the critic must also assess the author's own understanding of human nature, identify the author's own stance toward the cultural context, and identify the distinctive characteristics of the author's individual identity.

Life History Analysis and Cognitive Style in *Pride and Prejudice*

Before commenting on the relation of style to life-history analysis in *Pride and Prejudice*, I shall take a moment to summarize the novel, as concisely as possible, for the benefit of any reader who has not read it or who has not read it recently. The protagonist, Elizabeth Bennet, is twenty years old and the second of five daughters. Her father is a gentleman who married somewhat beneath his own social class and chose a wife for her physical charm. His wife's foolishness and vulgarity have alienated him, and he habitually engages in whimsical mockery of her. His estate is entailed to a cousin, a clergyman named Mr. Collins. When Mr. Bennet dies, Mr. Collins will inherit his estate, and Mr. Bennet's wife and five daughters will be left destitute. His wife is thus quite desperate to find rich husbands for her daughters. A wealthy and unmarried young man, Mr. Bingley, rents an estate in the Bennets' neighborhood, and his entourage includes two sisters and a friend, Mr. Darcy, who is also single and even more wealthy than Bingley. In short order, Bingley falls in love with Elizabeth Bennet's older sister, Jane, but Darcy discourages the match and persuades Bingley to leave the neighborhood. Darcy disapproves of the vulgarity of Elizabeth's mother and of her younger sisters, but he is himself nonetheless attracted to Elizabeth, whose wit and vivacity arouse his admiration. Mr. Collins, a monstrously foolish man, proposes to Elizabeth, and when she rejects him, he marries Elizabeth's best friend, Charlotte Lucas, who has little value on the marriage market and seeks only a comfortable establishment. Mr. Collins lives close to a wealthy, arrogant woman, Lady Catherine de Bourgh, who appointed him to his clerical living. Lady Catherine also happens to be Darcy's aunt, and when Elizabeth goes for an extended visit at Charlotte's new home, she again meets Darcy. He proposes to her but does so in an insulting way, expressing his vivid sense of her social inferiority, and she angrily rejects him. In explaining her rejection, she accuses him of interfering in her sister's marriage and accuses him also of failing to meet his obligation in providing support for the son of his father's steward, Mr. Wickham, a man who grew up with Darcy. Wickham had recently been stationed with his regiment near Elizabeth's home, had become friendly with her, and had divulged his supposed mistreatment at Darcy's hands. To vindicate himself, Darcy writes a letter in which he explains that his own conduct to Wickham has been honorable and that Wickham is in fact a scoundrel and a prevaricator. His evidence is compelling, and Elizabeth realizes she has misjudged him. Her aunt and uncle invite her to accompany them on a vacation tour that leads them into the vicinity of Darcy's estate. They meet Darcy by accident, and his manners undergo a major change. He ceases being haughty and reserved and seeks to ingratiate himself to Elizabeth and her relatives. Elizabeth's views have also changed, and she is receptive to his address, but then she gets a letter from her sister Jane telling her that a younger sister, Lydia, has run off with Wickham, thus bringing disgrace on the whole family. Elizabeth returns home, and unbeknownst to her, Darcy finds Wickham and Lydia and bribes Wickham to marry Lydia. Elizabeth discovers this secret and is duly grateful. When Bingley and Darcy return to Elizabeth's neighborhood, Bingley proposes to Jane, and Darcy proposes again to Elizabeth. Both women accept the proposals, and the epilogue informs us that these two main couples live happily ever after.

Pride and Prejudice is universally recognized as a classic, and specifically as a classic distinguished by the economy of its narrative and the elegance of its style. That economy and elegance depend in large part on one central tension in the narrator's own point of view, a tension between two poles: at one pole, the tough-minded recognition of the fundamental realities of human life history, the primacy of resource acquisition and reproductive activity; and at the other pole, the determination to value individual qualities of mind and character. Austen herself grasps with a singular acuity the governing power of the somatic and reproductive foundation of human action, but virtually every character in the novel is assessed also on the basis of the quality of his or her mind. If you will refer again to the diagram of human nature (figure 1), you can envision the novel as working itself out through a tension between the highest level of conscious human organization—the recognition of the primary need to acquire resources and to mate successfully—and the cognitive behavioral system. Everyone wants to marry well within the terms that are common knowledge among evolutionary sexual theorists—the women want wealth and status in their men, and the men want youth and beauty in their women. But the single most important criterion for registering personal quality in the novel is the degree to which both men and women rise above this basic standard and require also qualities of excellence in character and in mind.

The realization of character—and especially of conscientiousness—is best seen in action, in what the characters actually do. But the realization of mind is best revealed in their style—in what they say, and even more important, in how they say it. Austen's own style is "elegant" not in the sense of betraying effeminate delicacy or softness. It is elegant in the sense of being supple, sharp, quick, and crystal clear. It has less the quality of a brush held by a lady's gentle touch than of a finely tempered blade wielded by a hand that is strong, deft, and aggressive. The two chief characters, Elizabeth and Darcy, come to admire and love each other in good part because they share Austen's cognitive and stylistic powers. They select themselves out from amidst the babble of folly, nonsense, and polite fatuities that make up the stylistic world of their associates, and they come to admire one another for qualities of wit and judgment that unfold themselves in sharp and serious dialogue on subjects of character, tone, and point of view. Darcy first offends Elizabeth, when they meet, by uttering some arrogant and defensive rationalizations for his own stiff behavior at a ball. (He is introverted and not very likable, but he is ultra-high on conscientiousness. Wickham, his chief rival for Elizabeth's romantic interest, is extraverted and charming but deceitful and utterly unreliable. As in many novels, one main plot line involves the long-term discrimination among superficially attractive qualities and the qualities that will wear well—a difference relevant to the basic distinction between short-term and long-term mating strategies.) Darcy first fundamentally changes Elizabeth's view of him in the letter he writes to her, after she rejects his proposal, explaining his conduct with respect to her sister's marriage and his treatment of Wickham. Given the fact that he is an introvert and an intellectual, it is not surprising that he should present himself better in a letter than in a personal interview. The letter, which Austen transcribes in full, is the longest utterance he or anyone makes in the course of the novel, and if it does not display Austen's own humor—the subjects are somber, and Darcy is in no joking mood—it does display all of the precision, incisiveness, and acuity of her style. This style is itself a constant norm for the reader, and that same norm serves for all the main protagonistic characters as a measure of quality.

To take just one more of many possible examples for the signal importance of style as a measure of personal quality, Mr. Collins first introduces himself to the Bennet household in a letter that Mr. Bennet reads aloud to his family. The letter is an absolute marvel of fatuity and of pompous self-importance, and the way in which the individual family members respond to the letter reveals the quality of their own minds. Mary, the dull, plain younger sister who tries to build a niche for herself by diligent but uninspired study, thinks Mr. Collins's style rather good. Mrs. Bennet is as always simply indifferent to any quality of character or style and responds to all occasions solely on the basis of opportunistic interests. Elizabeth and her father alone register that the letter is a work of clownish absurdity. "'Can he be a sensible man, sir?' 'No, my dear; I think not.'"[34] In that exchange, Austen reveals the foundation of the singular affinity that Elizabeth and her father feel for one another, and the reason that they have formed an inner circle of companionship separated from all the rest of the family. Elizabeth is fond of her older sister Jane, and Jane is not vulgar, but she is so excessively sweet-tempered, so almost pathologically high on the scale of likableness, that she is incapable of any negative judgment, and thus fails to see at least half of what passes in front of her. She is, for instance, merely puzzled by the nonsense in Mr. Collins's letter but inclined to give him full credit for good intentions.

Elizabeth and her father form an inner circle of wit and judgment, and the central figure within that circle is Austen herself. She fashions the point of view as a field of intelligence, and within this field she creates a topography in which she locates all the characters and her audience. To get a sense for how this process works, consider the famous opening sentence of the novel: "It is a truth universally acknowledged, that a single man in possession of a good fortune, must be in want of a wife." There has been considerable difference of opinion over whether that sentence is meant to be taken ironically. The issue can be resolved by reference to the modifying effect of the sentence that follows the first sentence: "However little known the feelings or views of such a man may be on his first entering a neighborhood; this truth is so well fixed in the minds of the surrounding families, that he is considered as the rightful property of some one or other of their daughters." The first sentence is a good-humored affirmation of the rules of the game. Austen identifies the basic elements that are in play in social interactions (property and mating), and she acknowledges that the configuration of elements implied in her remarks constitutes a universal pattern of human behavior: men seek to acquire resources and to use them to acquire mates, and women seek mates who are in possession of resources. But the second sentence establishes a distance between the narrator and the common view she describes. She admits of anomalies, of individual differences. The "surrounding families" operate only on the basis of generalities, and they operate without regard to the inner lives of other people. They regard the man moving into the neighborhood not as a center of consciousness—a point of view—in his own right but rather as their own property. This is a simple and elementary failure in "theory of mind"— a failure to recognize that other people have inner lives of their own. Failures of this nature inform much of Austen's satire, and indeed of all satire. It is one of the central principles of satire. People are preoccupied with their own needs, and they treat other people as props or furniture in the self-absorbed narratives they construct about themselves. (Mrs. Bennet and Darcy's aunt Lady Catherine de Bourgh are signal cases in point and chief targets of the satire.)

As it happens, in this case, the common view holds good. Bingley is in fact in want of a wife. It is nonetheless the case that in the space of two sentences Austen has established a fundamental tension between her own perspective—a perspective that takes account both of point of view and of individual differences—and the common perspective of the neighborhood. That common perspective is also the perspective of the common world outside the novel. In the course of the novel, an inner core of protagonists, civilized, cultivated, and capable of making stylistic distinctions, will ultimately constitute a small in-group that distinguishes itself from the common world of their own community. Elizabeth's aunt and uncle Gardiner belong to this inner group, and it is one of the triumphs for the ethos advanced by the novel that their cultivation and gentility of manner take precedence over their lower socioeconomic status (Mr. Gardiner is "in trade"). Austen's own point of view defines and dominates this inner group—she is its normative mind—and she tacitly invites receptive readers also to join this group. The criterion that permits a reader to join the group is the ability to read and judge the letters and conversational style of Darcy, Mr. Collins, Lady Catherine, and all the rest. Readers who pass this test of literacy succeed in segregating themselves from the common world that operates exclusively at the level of the lowest common denominators of life-history analysis—the reduction of other people to general cases—and the identification of people exclusively in terms of "property."

Note that what has happened in the course of two sentences is that the author has established a set of relations among three points of view: her own, that of her characters, and that of her audience. This set of relations is not peripheral to the "meaning" of the story. By creating these relations, Austen creates an active field of communicative interaction. That is what hooks the reader, brings the reader in, rivets the reader's attention. All this happens before a single event has transpired and before a single specific character has been introduced. To notice this is to realize that we cannot reduce the "meaning" of a story to the represented events. And even the very content of the two sentences admonishes us that if we reduce the events of the story to an exemplification of "human universals" or "species-typical behaviors," we shall have missed at least half the story. We shall in fact be on precisely the same level as the "surrounding families" personified for us, in the subsequent scene, by Mrs. Bennet. We shall be among the dullards and vulgarians who operate only on general rules and neglect to notice that every single character has a distinct center of consciousness.

Mrs. Bennet has access to a big chunk of the truth. Resources and mating do in fact form elementary building blocks in the human relations that provide the basis for stories. But in grasping this elemental reality, Mrs. Bennet neglects all other considerations of mind and character. She neglects the minds of other people, and she thus demonstrates the poverty of her own mind. The successful protagonists fully acknowledge the hard and sometimes harsh logic in the human reproductive economy, but they do so without neglecting the significance of the human mind and individual differences in identity.

Mate selection is the central behavioral system activated in this novel. That is a distinguishing, defining feature of the literary genre it exemplifies, the genre of "romantic comedy." (This genre probably provides at least half the literary biomass for the sum total of narratives in the world.) In its simplest designation, a romantic comedy is a love story that concludes in a happy marriage. Usually such stories are light in tone or enlivened with humor. But as it applies to Austen, the connotation of the words "romantic" and "comedy" could be a little misleading.

There are many comical scenes, but the humor of the novel is often harsh, and the mating game is fierce and determined. Mr. Bingley's sister wants Darcy for herself and snipes incessantly, cattily, ineffectually at Elizabeth, denigrating her appearance, her temperament, her mind, and most of all her family and her social status. Miss Bingley also wants Darcy's younger sister, Georgiana, for her own brother—a liaison that would enhance her own social standing—and she thus conspires with Darcy to detach Bingley from Jane Bennet. She at first expresses the warmest friendship to Jane, activating Jane's own affectionate disposition and then coldly cuts her. Lady Catherine wants Darcy to marry her own daughter, his cousin, but her daughter is sickly and peevish, and no one but her own mother and her governess pays her any regard at all. Austen's treatment of this girl betrays a certain streak of brutality. She sacrifices Miss de Bourgh on the altar of a ruthless principle of fitness, and the only sensation Elizabeth or Austen herself express toward this poor sick girl is that of vindictive contempt; there is no hint of pity. (To get an even better feel for this streak of brutality, one should read Austen's "juvenilia," the stories she wrote as a teenager. The stories consist of a rapid series of violent and grotesque events, many of them involving characters of certifiably psychopathic disposition.) Elizabeth's own chances of successful mating are seriously endangered when her sister Lydia runs off with Wickham, thus lowering the social standing of the whole family even further. There is a real possibility that by an inevitable progression Lydia would eventually be abandoned by Wickham and would "come on the town," living as a prostitute and in all likelihood dying early of disease and abuse. This doesn't happen because Darcy is determined in his choice of Elizabeth as a mate, and he exploits for his own purposes the opportunity Lydia's folly presents to him. By bribing Wickham to marry Lydia, Darcy does Elizabeth the greatest and most intimate service he could possibly do for her, and at the same time he decisively demonstrates the firmness of his commitment to her. He demonstrates that his preference for her outweighs even the disgrace of a marital association with a sluttish sister married to a reprobate of inferior birth.

The very nature of Wickham's disrepute signals the way in which resources and reproduction constitute the fundamental categories of human behavior in the novel—as they do in actual life. Wickham's evildoing consists in two main forms of malfeasance: he leaves unpaid debts behind him, and he engages in illicit sexual liaisons with the daughters of the tradesmen and farmers in the neighborhoods he frequents. Before arriving in Elizabeth's neighborhood, he had even had the audacity to try running off with Darcy's sister. If he had succeeded, he would have damaged Darcy in his family pride and in his tenderest family feeling. He would have gained a fortune, advanced in status, and triumphed over a rival male. Darcy has good reason to resent Wickham, and this resentment renders his act of conciliation with Wickham all the more signal an instance of the self-sacrificing chivalry he displays in his commitment to Elizabeth.

Property and rank for men and youth and beauty for women count for much. They count almost more than anything, but within the normative perspective of the novel, they must, at every point along the way, be weighed in the balance of the total set of values that can be integrated within a well-proportioned economy of human life—the kind of economy that leads to the "rational" sort of happiness that Austen and Elizabeth both identify as their own central criterion of value. The total set of values that have to be given their due proportions to bring about rational happiness is not amorphous and unbounded. Sex and property, family or kin relations, parenting, social relations, and cognitive power—those are the central concerns of the book.

Next to sex and property, fidelity to kin presents itself as an urgent motivational force. Within the normative structure of values constituted by Austen's own point of view, even when family members are disgraceful and ridiculous, remaining loyal to them is a fundamental criterion of personal merit. Mr. Collins's baseness displays itself when he advises Mr. Bennet to abandon Lydia altogether after she runs off with Wickham, and Elizabeth displays her strength of character, in the epilogue, by effecting a rapprochement between Darcy and the alienated Lady Catherine, despite the insults Lady Catherine has heaped on Elizabeth herself.

The issue of parenting bulks large in the concerns of the book. The main background marriages—the marriages that serve as models or as warnings for the protagonists—are bad, either in their personal relations (as with Mr. and Mrs. Bennet) or in their parenting functions—as with both Darcy's and Elizabeth's parents. Elizabeth's mother is coarse, stupid, and frivolous, and her father is remote and detached. The situation of the family is bad, not just because of the entail but because he made a bad marriage, neglected to make the economies necessary to provide for his family after his death, neglected the discipline and education of his daughters, and failed to maintain the decorum of marital civility. (Jane and Elizabeth have educated themselves, but one chief attraction that Darcy holds for Elizabeth is that he is himself educated and holds out the promise for her of helping her to continue cultivating her own mind. Much is made of the magnificent library in his possession at his family estate.) Darcy's own parents, he says, were excellent people, but they neglected to form his temper, and they get the blame for the arrogance that first offends Elizabeth and that comes close to spoiling Darcy's ability to attract her to him, despite his wealth and rank. Mr. Collins is an oddity in part because he is a fool, a man of weak understanding, but the other half of the causal explanation is that he was raised by "an illiterate and miserly father."[35]

All the most intimate relations of sex, marriage, and family embed themselves within a larger social context. For this novel, one central plot question is whether Elizabeth will be accepted into the dominant social group. Her rivals hope she will not. Austen herself disparages their brittle snobbery (they laugh witlessly over the fact that she has an uncle in trade and another uncle who is a country attorney), but she also wishes for Elizabeth to gain access to the highest social level. She defines that level not only by wealth and status but by dignity and authority. One can be born into wealth and rank, but dignity and authority have to be earned by personal merit. Lady Catherine offers a self-parody of upper-class authority. Darcy is the real thing. When Elizabeth first sees Darcy's great estate and hears his housekeeper praise his integrity and beneficence, she thinks to herself, "What praise is more valuable than the praise of an intelligent servant? As a brother, a landlord, a master, she considered how many people's happiness were in his guardianship!—How much of pleasure or pain it was in his power to bestow!—How much of good or evil must be done by him!"[36] Austen mocks false status—rank and wealth unsupported by education, wit, manners, and character—but she ultimately affirms the authority of legitimate social status as represented by the normative couple, Elizabeth and Darcy.

The chief social dynamic in the novel, the underlying social narrative, is that of a process in which dominant males marry down, selecting women of lower social rank but of superior personal quality. Conversely, women of high quality from a lower rank marry up into the higher gentry and thus integrate the standard of personal quality with the values of wealth and rank. Even Mr. Bennet, unhappily married though he is, has contributed to this process. He married a beautiful though silly woman from a social rank lower than his own. Two of his daughters are both beautiful and intelligent, and one (Elizabeth) is genuinely clever. And the two beautiful, intelligent girls both marry well, extremely well. Even Mrs. Bennet must be gratified with the results, though she understands so little of the process that produces those results.

And finally, again, in all the behavioral systems that have to be balanced in the economy of values in the novel, the cognitive system holds a place of predominating value. Mrs. Bennet contributes some heritable physical attractiveness, a matter not negligible in the total mix, but she contributes nothing of wit, and she is left almost wholly outside the scope of the inner social circle that constitutes the normative group at the end of the novel. "I wish I could say, for the sake of her family, that the accomplishment of her earnest desire in the establishment of so many of her children, produced so happy an effect as to make her a sensible, amiable, well-informed woman for the rest of her life; though perhaps it was lucky for her husband, who might not have relished domestic felicity in so unusual a form, that she was still occasionally nervous and invariably silly."[37]

The Value of a Darwinian Literary Criticism

Previous criticism of Austen can be divided roughly into two bodies of work: (a) the traditional, common-language criticism that dominated academic literary study until the middle of the 1970s and (b) the various forms of theory-driven criticism that emerged under the umbrella of postmodernism in the past three decades or so. The traditional criticism operates at the level of Austen's own lexicon. At its best, it makes alert observations about theme, tone, and formal organization, but its insights are impressionistic, opportunistic, and adventitious; it seeks no systematic reduction to simple principles that have large general validity.[38] At less than its best, traditional criticism consists only in otiose summary and formalistic elaboration punctuated by the occasional exercise in cranky emotional posturing.[39] The positive rationale behind the revolution in theory-driven criticism is the recognition that all narratives have a surface-depth structure. Beneath the surface of local incident and occasional commentary in a narrative, there is a simpler, more basic structure of elemental motives and organizing principles. These motives and principles are the skeletal structure of the work. The business of interpretive criticism is to probe beneath the surface of common-language exposition and to find the skeletal structure. Theory-driven interpretation seeks to cut literary meaning at its joints.

The turn to theory-driven criticism answered to a manifest need, but the theoretical models that have been used, up to now, have been painfully inadequate. Deconstruction, Marxism, Freudianism, and Foucauldian political criticism have all presupposed ideas about human nature that conflict sharply with the Darwinian conception. The other main school, feminism, is less a single, coherent theory than a preoccupation about a specific subject matter—the condition of women—but the notions that cluster around this preoccupation often entail false ideas about human nature, and most feminist critics over the past thirty years have affiliated themselves with one or another of the dominant theoretical schools. All of the schools, as subsidiaries of postmodern theory, have fundamentally repudiated the idea of an innate, biologically constrained structure in the human motivational and cognitive system. Postmodern critics have sought the elemental forces of human experience in terms such as "semiosis," "textuality," "class struggle," "the phallus," "bourgeois ideology," "desire," "discourse," "power," "gender," "dialogism," "heterosexism," "the Other," and "patriarchy," and they have contended that such terms reveal the underlying, governing forces in all literary production. In the degree to which they have succeeded in avoiding the passively reflexive character of traditional criticism, theory-driven criticism has offered distorted, skewed, and strained accounts of the elemental motives and governing principles in literary texts.

Literary criticism is both analytical and evaluative. Literary critics commit themselves to distinct concepts and to definite values. The values that animate postmodern theoretical criticism are emphatically radical, and the political critics incline either to disparage authors for their putative complicity with oppressive epistemes or, more frequently, to invest authors with their own characteristic attitudes of resentment, ideological indignation, and subversive animosity. Both the conceptual content and the political attitudes of the radical criticism are deeply alien to Austen. The conceptual content is alien to the elemental simplicity of her good sense, and the political attitudes are alien to the conservative temper of her wisdom. Many of the postmodern critics have nonetheless made some effort to assimilate Austen to an ethos of epistemological indeterminacy and political radicalism. They have sought to identify various "gaps" or "contradictions" between her overt meanings and this or that supposedly subversive implication in her style or tone. In Austen's case, particularly, these routine invocations of deconstructive formulas often appear half-hearted. The more sensitive postmodern critics evidently feel a certain queasy diffidence about pressing a case that can be made only by fabricating interpretive theses that run so clearly counter to Austen's own determinate meanings. Despite the obligatory invocation of deconstructive formulas, the bulk of commentary in the postmodern critiques blends insensibly into the thematic, tonal, and formal analyses of the traditional criticism.[40]

Darwinian literary criticism is grounded in the large facts of human evolution and human biology, facts much larger and more robust than the conceptions that characterize the various branches of postmodern theory.[41] Darwinian psychology provides a scientifically grounded and systematic account of human nature. This is the first time in our intellectual history that we have had such a theory, but the subject of this theory—human nature itself—is the very same nature that has always animated writers and readers. Most writers historically have not had access to the evolutionary explanation for how human nature came to be what it is, but they have nonetheless had a deep intuitive understanding of human motives and human feelings. What a Darwinian social science can now do for literary criticism is to give us conscious theoretical access to the elemental forces that have impelled all human beings throughout time and that have fundamentally informed the observations and reflections of all writers and all readers. Darwinian criticism can lift us above the superficial paraphrases of traditional criticism without forcing us into the often false reductions in the postmodern conceptions of human nature. It can help us to understand the source and subject of all literary representation, and it can help us to identify the sources of exceptional power in great literary works like *Pride and Prejudice*.

The Whole Story

More could be said, in detail, about *Pride and Prejudice*, much more. I hope I have said enough to give some indication of what I have in mind when I affirm that to construct an even minimally adequate account of any literary representation, we have to set up a polar tension between the highest level of reduction in life-history analysis—the level of the somatic and reproductive organization of life effort—and the most fine-grained analysis of formal organization: of theme, tone, and style. I hope to have convinced you that point of view is the central locus of literary meaning because it is the dimension within which people have mental experiences. The only people who can be involved in a literary social interaction are the author, the characters, and the audience, and those three sets of people *are* involved—all three sets, always. Delineating the dynamics of that specific set of social interactions—dynamics that vary from author to author and book to book—is a fundamental and indispensable procedure in literary criticism. Darwinian literary critics who ignore this dimension of analysis might be Darwinians, but they are not literary critics, and even as Darwinians, they are missing a major part of the story.

Many Darwinian psychologists and anthropologists have been missing a major part of the larger human story—that whole part of the story that concerns itself with the evolution of the cognitive behavioral system: the fifth personality factor, "g," domain-general intelligence. They have told us a good deal about life in a supposedly stable and homogeneous environment of evolutionary adaptedness, but they have neglected to tell us much about the evolution and adaptive functions of the distinctively human mind. A number of Darwinian anthropologists and psychologists are now correcting that signal omission, and Darwinian literary critics should rejoice that the development of the whole field is now producing a model of human nature that converges with their needs and interests as literary critics. The benefits can be reciprocal. Darwinian psychologists and Darwinian anthropologists take human nature as their field of study. Literature can provide important information on that topic, and Darwinian literary critics can help them to gain access to that information. Practitioners on both sides will need to make some allowances for differences of idiom and method. If they make these allowances, they will benefit not just in the gain of needful information but also in a closer acquaintance with the skills and cognitive habits that constitute the characteristic strengths in each discipline.

Notes

1. See Miller 2000b; Pinker 1997, 2002.
2. See Cosmides and Tooby 1994; Pinker 1994, 1995, 1997, 2002; Symons, 1992; Tooby and Cosmides 1992, 25, 35, 38, 79, 80. Also see the textbooks by Barrett, Dunbar, and Lycett 2002; Bridgeman 2003; Buss 1999; Gaulin and McBurney 2001; Palmer and Palmer 2002; Rossano 2003.
3. See Tooby and Cosmides 1992.
4. Darwin 1859.

5. See Chiappe 2000; Chiappe and MacDonald under submission; Crawford 1998; Foley 1996; Geary 1998; Geary and Huffman 2002; Irons 1998; MacDonald 1990, 1995b, 1997, 1998a, 1998b; Mithen 1996, 2001; Potts 1998; Richerson and Boyd 2000; D. S. Wilson 1999; E. O. Wilson 1998.

6. See Bailey 1997, 1998; Barash 1997; Bouchard 1994, 1997; Buss 1990, 1995; Eaves, Eysenck, and Martin 1989; Eysenck 1979, 1980, 1995; Herrnstein and Murray 1994; Jensen 1998; MacDonald 1990, 1995b, 1997, 1998a; Rushton 1995; Sarich and Miele 2004; Segal 1997, 1999; Segal and MacDonald 1998; Seligman 1992; D. S. Wilson 1994, 1999.

7. Irons 1979, 257.

8. Tooby and Cosmides 1992, 54.

9. See Alexander 1990; Barkow 1990; Betzig 1986, 1998; Chagnon 1979; Chagnon and Irons 1979; Irons 1990, 1998; MacDonald 1995a; Symons 1989, 1992; Turke 1990.

10. Low 1998, 131.

11. See Alexander 1979, 25; Alexander 1987, 40–41; Geary 1998, 11, 199; Low 1998, 138–40; Low 2000, 92; MacDonald 1997, 328; McGuire and Troisi 1998, 58–59; Ridley 1999, 12, 127–28; Trivers 1972, 168–74; Trivers 1985, 311–14.

12. McGuire and Troisi 1998, 60.

13. Buss 1999.

14. On the ontogenetic and phylogenetic development of human behavioral systems, as consciously mediated set goals emerging out of lower-order proximal mechanisms, see Bowlby 1982, 153–57, 160, 172, 237–38; Shaver, Hazan, and Bradshaw 1988.

15. See Damasio 1994; Ekman 2003; Ekman and Davidson 1994; LeDoux 1996; Lewis and Haviland 2000; MacDonald 1995b; Panksepp 1998.

16. See Bickerton 1990; Pinker 1994.

17. See Alcock 2001b, 35–40.

18. See Atran 1990; Brown 1991; Geary 1998; Pinker 1994, 1995, 1997, 2002; Tooby and Cosmides 1992.

19. See Barrow 1995; J. Carroll 1995, 1998, 1999a, 2001c; Chiappe 2000; Chiappe and MacDonald under submission; Darwin 1871a, vol. 1, 42–46; Geary 1998, 176–99; Geary and Huffman 2002; Mithen 1996; D. S. Wilson, this volume; E. O. Wilson 1998, chap. 10.

20. See J. Carroll 1999c; E. O. Wilson 1998.

21. See Boyd 1998, 2001; D. E. Brown 1991; J. Carroll 1995; Cooke 1999, 2002; Dissanayake 1992b, 2000, 2003; Fromm 2003; Love 2003; Scalise Sugiyama 2001b; Storey 1996; E. O. Wilson 1998.

22. See Mithen 1996.

23. For lists of domain-specific cognitive modules, see Carey and Spelke

1994, 171; Cosmides and Tooby 1994, 103; Mithen 1996; Pinker 1994, 420; Pinker 1995, 236; Pinker 1997, 128, 315; Sperber 1994, 42; Tooby and Cosmides 1992, 113. For suggestions about cognitive predispositions to certain kinds of aesthetic order, see Barrow 1995; Eibl-Eibesfeldt 1989; F. Turner 1992; M. Turner 1996.

24. Ekman 2003.

25. See Abrams 1986.

26. See Booth 1996; J. Carroll 2001a; Leaska 1996, Scalise Sugiyama 1996.

27. MacDonald 1990.

28. See D. E. Brown 1991, 2000; J. Carroll 2001c.

29. See Daly and Wilson 1988; Low 2000; Symons 1979.

30. See Daly and Wilson 1990; Low 2000; Scalise Sugiyama 2001b.

31. See J. Carroll 1995, 2001a; Jobling 2001a, 2001b; Nesse 1995; Nordlund 2002; Scalise Sugiyama 2003.

32. See Bouchard 1994; 1997; Buss 1990, 1995; Costa and Widiger 2002; Digman 1990; Eysenck and Eysenck 1985; Hogan, Johnson, and Briggs 1997; MacDonald 1995b, 1998b; McCrae 1992; Pervin 1990, 2003; Pervin and John 1999; Segal and MacDonald 1998; Wiggins 1996.

33. MacDonald 1998b, 126. Also see McCrae and Costa 1997, 831.

34. Austen 2004, 44.

35. Austen 2004, 48.

36. Austen 2004, 162.

37. Austen 2004, 251.

38. See Bradley 1929, 32–72; C. L. Johnson 1988; Lewes 1859; Litz 1965; Tanner 1986; Van Ghent 1953; Woolf 1925, 137–49.

39. See Butler 1975; Duckworth 1971; Halliday 1960; Harding 1940; Langland 1984; S. Morgan 1980; Mudrick 1952; Phelan, 1989.

40. See Ahearn 1987; I. Armstrong 1990; N. Armstrong 1981, 1987; Auerbach 1978; Belsey 2002; Brownstein 1988; Fraiman 1989; Handler and Segal 1990; Litvak 1992; Newman 1983; Newton 1981; Poovey 1984; J. M. Smith 1993, 2000; Wylie 2000.

41. See B. Boyd 1998; J. Carroll 1995; Dissanayake 1992b; Storey 1996.

The Problem of Romantic Love: Shakespeare and Evolutionary Psychology

Marcus Nordlund

What is the nature of love? This is an ambitious question, and one that has inspired innumerable literary works. Perhaps for this reason the philosopher Jon Elster thinks we can learn more about an emotion like romantic love "from moralists, novelists, and playwrights than from the cumulative findings of scientific psychology."[1] But here we encounter a major obstacle since most of the academic experts on literature that might elucidate these insights have so far lacked a theoretical framework of corresponding dignity. For example, the otherwise eminent Shakespearean critic Richard Levin gives voice to a broad consensus among literary critics with his assertion that "what is called romantic love cannot be universal, natural, or essential because it is socially constructed, and we know this because it is constructed differently in different societies."[2] To someone who is versed in modern evolutionary theory, this position is bound to appear misguided since it revives an obsolete dichotomy between nature and culture and assumes that cultural variation in a trait or behavior is sufficient evidence that it is "cultural" rather than "natural." So whether or not we can learn "more" from literary works than from scientific psychology, it seems likely that our analysis of the former will benefit from some awareness of the latter.

In what follows, I will be making two claims. First, I will suggest that love, and more specifically romantic love, is not a social construction in any useful or meaningful sense of the word. This assumption will be supported with evidence from a wide range of disciplines, including neuroscience, psychology, history, philosophy, and anthropology. Together with modern research into psychosexual dimorphism, the proposed universality of love will then underpin my second objective, which is to give a very brief example of the interaction between an evolved human nature, a specific historical environment, and literary genre in two plays by William Shakespeare: *Troilus and Cressida* and *All's Well that Ends Well*.[3]

Is Love a Social Construction?

In 1995, Anne Beall and Robert Sternberg argued in the *Journal of Social and Personal Relationships* that love is a "social construction that reflects its time period because it serves an important function in a culture." The authors address the question of love's potential universality by means of four theoretical hypotheses, choosing to side with the following view: "Love is not a universal experience. It changes according to its cultural milieu and is viewed differently in numerous cultures." This claim is based on a broad, but necessarily rhapsodic, account of historical and cultural differences. They show how love can vary in terms of its object as well as function in a society, and they rightly point out that "an essential part of one's experience of love is one's conceptualization of it."[4] The latter point is also supported by means of a brief but exemplary discussion of the cognitive component in love; that is, how our beliefs and expectations affect our experience.

Let me first outline some points of agreement between Beall and Sternberg's argument and the Darwinian perspective I adopt here. Human beings are cultural beings whose emotional experience is at least partly shaped and channeled by the governing assumptions of their societies. Beall and Sternberg also respect the fact that it is difficult to understand human beings or societies merely "from outside" since we must also take their own self-understanding and governing beliefs into account.

But then we get to the central premise that "love is a social construction" because it is not everywhere the same. In itself, the perception of cultural and historical variation is a truism that can, at best, serve as the starting point for a deeper and more sophisticated analysis. Indeed, Beall and Sternberg do not appear to consider a rather obvious rejoinder to their argument: that the very notion of love as something that is experienced and conceptualized differently in various cultures necessarily presupposes that it is precisely a *single* phenomenon (rather than a random set of phenomena that happen to have been grouped together).

This is not a mere play on words. So far as I can tell, Beall and Sternberg can respond to this complaint in two different ways. One is to emphasize the aspect of difference even further, so that different cultures and forms of love are seen as truly incommensurate. But in that case they should really stop talking about "love" altogether and write it off as an unfortunate remnant of folk psychology. A similar case has been made by Paul Griffiths regarding the concept of emotion, which he deems too imprecise to be of any academic use.[5] But at least in their present form, Beall and Sternberg's repeated references to love in the singular seem to preclude such an option: "Although we believe that love is an idea that reflects its culture, we believe that it has an enormous impact on how people think and feel about themselves and others."[6]

The other alternative is, of course, to attempt to reconcile the idea of love as a single, universal phenomenon with the evidence for its cultural and historical variation. To venture a potentially misleading but hopefully illustrative analogy, we can consider the much simpler universal act of *eating*, which varies substantially between different cultures. People eat different things, they eat in different ways, at different times, using different utensils; some cultures eat more than others; some make a virtue of not eating at certain times; and eating has different social functions in different places. But we all recognize that these are cultural variations on a single universal theme, and that this theme, in turn, answers to a basic human need.

Beall and Sternberg's dismissal of a similar universality in the case of love seems to derive primarily from the absence of a single "definition that describes love throughout the ages or across cultures."[7] But if they ever hoped to find such a universal definition—one that would be mirrored by the official concepts of ancient Greeks, Aztecs, Kalahari bushmen, and modern Westerners alike—then this hope must have been optimistic on the verge of misguided. There is a plethora of human phenomena that can safely be termed universal to human cultures—such as religion, or culture itself for that matter—in spite of our demonstrable incapacity to arrive at neat and unshakeable definitions of their exact nature.

What is more, a culture's dominant "definition" or attitude toward love (to the extent that the latter is even recognized officially) is not always representative of its actual experience or practice. For example, how can we ever hope to find an adequate definition of romantic love in a culture that regards individual passion as a social evil and therefore refuses to talk about it? For this reason, we also need an empirical approach that is not entirely dependent on a culture's dominant conception of itself. We will see further on that in one study of the ethnographic record, romantic passion turned out to be *at least* a near universal element found in almost 90 percent of the 166 societies studied.

Sooner or later, the question of love's universality will need to be restated below the proximate level of cultural differences and similarities. We must also consider the biological dispositions that enable people to feel for each other in the first place. Like most social constructivists, Beall and Sternberg do not actively dispute the idea of a biological foundation for love, they just deem it irrelevant: "We can presume that love includes such a component."[8] End of story? No, only the beginning.

Is Romantic Love a Social Construction?

But let us not get ahead of ourselves. Even if we should assume that love is a universal aspect of human nature that will not be properly understood until we have also explored its biological roots, then it is still possible to argue that more specific forms of love are socially constructed (in the more limited sense that they constitute unique cultural modulations of the same basic emotion). The assumption that romantic love is a uniquely Western phenomenon is, as we have seen, still widespread among literary scholars and social scientists. In *Medieval Misogyny and the Invention of Western Romantic Love*, Howard Bloch puts forward a representative version that traces its roots back to the twelfth century:

> If the expression "invention of Western romantic love" seems like a contradiction, it is because we so often assume love as we know it to be natural, to exist in some essential sense, that is, always to have existed. Nothing, however, could be further from the truth. . . . The terms that serve to define, or mediate, what we consider to this day to constitute romantic involvement were put into place definitively—at least for the time being—sometime between the beginning and the middle of the twelfth century, first in southern and then in northern France.[9]

In my view, there is good reason to suppose that this assumption is incorrect. First of all, it confuses the historical emergence of certain "terms" with the appearance of a new emotion, and the "terms" are seldom (if ever) defined properly so that the constructivist argument can be assessed. Second, it is true that something important did happen in France in the twelfth century that would have great consequences for our Western conception of love, but Irving Singer's monumental study of the Western love tradition reminds us that we must not confuse the emotion with the ideal. In his definition, the tradition of courtly love assumed that sexual love between men and women is *in itself* something splendid, an ideal worth striving for; love ennobles both the lover and the beloved; being an ethical and aesthetic attainment, sexual love cannot be reduced to a mere libidinal impulse; love pertains to courtesy but is not necessarily related to the institution of marriage; and love is an intense, passionate relationship that establishes a holy oneness between man and woman.[10]

What the tradition of courtly love affirmed was that sexual love is both authentic and valuable and that it has an aesthetic or even religious value. It was first and foremost the valorization of a human need in a cultural milieu that seemed diametrically opposed to its very existence. Originally a response among the ruling elite to the political reality of arranged marriages, it gradually freed the amorous passion from its denigrated role in Christian culture and became "Western man's first great effort to demonstrate that the noble aspirations of idealism need not be incompatible with a joyful acceptance of sexual reality."[11]

What was culturally specific about courtly love and its later offshoots was that romantic passion, understood as a spiritual phenomenon, was fused with a central aspect of Judeo-Christian religion: "In general, courtly love attacked promiscuity as the church also attacked polytheism. As there was only one God, so was there only one man and one woman who could satisfy the ideal longings of the other."[12] If we want, we can perhaps describe this institutionalized version of the exclusivity that modern researchers associate with passionate or romantic love (that people generally do not feel it for more than one person at a time, and that they will normally want to reserve that person for themselves) as a historical "construction." But this is a far cry from saying that the basic emotion was a new-fangled historical invention, and that Sappho gave expression to something entirely different on Lesbos in the sixth century B.C. What courtly love did was to seize upon a universal human potential, invest it with social significance, and place it within a normative framework where authentic love was a laudable spiritual connection between two unique souls. As such it also had to be unchanging, as Shakespeare suggests in his famous sonnet: "Love is not love / Which alters when it alteration finds."

As an institutionalized tradition, courtly love and its later offshoots would exert a powerful influence on Western styles of loving to the point where many people today regard the absence of passionate love in their lives as a social or personal failure.[13] By the fifteenth century, much of the original sexual dimension in the courtly love tradition had been downplayed as the church renewed its onslaught on sexual passion, and Petrarch's poetry in particular would immortalize the conflict between spiritual and sexual passion. From there, the road of literary influence leads directly to Shakespeare, who satirized Petrarch and yet shared a good deal of his ambivalence. Like his literary predecessor, Shakespeare shows us a perspective on human affection that is alternatively detached and conflicted, idealistic and realistic. He also adds an important component that is absent in Petrarch: a sense of humor.

Seen in this way, the story of courtly love is the story of a tug-of-war between evolved needs and cultural constraints that eventually produced an ideal that had been harmonized with a culture's official system of belief. This is a good example of how a modern Darwinian perspective on human nature or love enables us to explore the adaptive dimensions of genetic as well as cultural evolution. Nature presupposes nurture. All humans are the inheritors of innate needs and dispositions that have been tailored by an evolutionary process to interact with specific environments. In some situations, such as social deprivation, the innate disposition for love may be totally suppressed. But there will also be constraints on the capacity of any culture to regulate or vanquish those rudimentary needs and desires whose history lies buried deep inside the human genome.

The Evolution of Love

A good place to start a closer inquiry into these emotional substrates of romantic love is John Bowlby's attachment theory. In the 1950s, Bowlby rejected the contemporary emphasis on interior fantasy worlds in psychoanalytic and object-relations theory and emphasized a very concrete problem that faces all primate infants: that their slow maturation process makes them totally dependent on the presence of a dependable caretaker with whom they can form a strong personal bond. Linking Freud's original emphasis on the formative nature of childhood experience with the concrete problem of survival, Bowlby pointed to strong similarities in behavior between human infants and their primate relatives: "That the child's tie to his mother is the human version of behaviour seen commonly in many other species of animal now seems indisputable; and it is in this perspective that the nature of the tie is examined."[14]

In the 1980s, Cindy Hazan and Philip Shaver developed Bowlby's intuitions about the lasting effects of childhood attachment into a theory of adult love. In their view, romantic love "has always and everywhere existed as a biological potential."[15] This would make it akin to most human traits that can be explained in evolutionary terms; that is, a *disposition* that is attributable to an evolved genotype but that also requires favorable ecological conditions in order to emerge. They have also proposed that adult love involves three biologically based behavioral systems: attachment, caregiving, and sexuality.[16]

Although the claim for a strong causal relationship between childhood attachment and adult love is still debated (will, for example, insecurely attached children tend to become jealous adults), it is difficult to dispute that the two are intimately connected.[17] As Lisa Diamond points out, there is "increasing (albeit not universal) consensus and voluminous evidence from human and animal research that adult pair-bonds and infant-caregiver attachment involve the same basic emotions and behaviors."[18] To take just one simple example, it will hardly have escaped anyone's attention that there is a considerable similarity in the expression and experience of intimacy, since both types of relation involve caressing, kissing, smiling, and so forth.[19]

This connection between infant and adult attachment can be understood in different (but potentially complementary) ways. One approach is to side with the Freudians, who see adult romantic attachments more or less as outgrowths of the mother-infant interaction in infancy.[20] As we have seen, this view is also present in Bowlby's heritage, albeit in modified form. But the link between infant and adult love need not be as rigidly causal as the Freudians would have it: it could be that both infantile and adult attachment are individual outgrowths of the same functional system, stemming from the same limbic blueprint, quite apart from the question of how far-reaching the effects of an individual's childhood experiences might be on adult love. "The evolution of the brain would have to be considered unparsimonious if it were not able to draw upon the same basic capacities of emotion and action in the various settings where strong attachment is called for."[21]

What the traditional psychoanalytic perspective overlooked, however, was the need to distinguish between sexuality and attachment. Lisa Diamond has marshaled considerable empirical evidence to suggest that "the evolved processes underlying sexual desire and affectional bonding are functionally independent," even if they tend to overlap in the case of adult sexual love.[22] In this essay I will assume, in keeping with traditional assumptions, that romantic love has a sexual component, but it is quite possible that future researchers will revise the concept so that this is no longer a necessary criterion. The desire for emotional and physical "union" it involves could be merely a matter of proximity or touch, and it may be possible to feel romantic love for someone without wanting to have sex with him or her.

Regardless of how we define romantic love, the "functionally independent" view of sexuality and attachment/caregiving is promising. For one thing, it may explain why people sometimes fall in love with members of their own sex in spite of having a strictly heterosexual orientation. It could also tell us why children are capable of "maximally intense infatuations" long before they reach puberty and sexual maturation.[23] While Diamond does not draw this conclusion, the theory could also explain why people in some cultures have invested same-sex friendship with much of the same emotional intensity that other cultures reserve for sexual relationships.

Consider, as an example, the nature of adolescence in Shakespeare's England: "It was one of the peculiarities of Britain (and northwestern Europe generally) that young people initially experienced love as a form of polygamous play. . . . They spread their affections broadly, preferring to invest friendship with members of the same and opposite sex with the emotional intensity that we would reserve to our heterosexual relationships."[24] It seems plausible that this historical phenomenon will eventually be understood in terms of a complex interaction between the functional systems of sexuality and attachment and a culture that reserved sexual activity for a marital union that most people did not enter until their mid-twenties. Such a system is bound to make young people emotionally inventive.

For the sake of clarity, I want to stress once more that this functional independence does not add up to a sharp distinction between love and sex. A pair-bond based on romantic love usually includes both sexuality and attachment/caregiving, and it is more than likely that many sexual acts draw heavily on formative childhood experience. But in both cases, sexuality and attachment are best understood as overlapping systems.

In *Mother Nature*, Sarah Hrdy gives a beautiful example of how closely related these systems can be without really being one self-same drive. Some people, she writes, "are unnerved by what they perceive as the 'sexual' sensations mothers experience during breast-feeding." Since oxytocin levels spike during nipple stimulation as well as during orgasm, there is a good deal of truth to this observation—provided that we reverse it completely. In evolutionary terms, maternal behavior has not coopted sexual behavior but the other way around.[25] Similarly, the warm eroticism of feeling your child's skin against your cheek— which again involves a boost of oxytocin—is a question of powerful attachment rather than sexuality in any meaningful sense of the word.[26]

If Hazan and Shaver are right about a more specific universal disposition for romantic love, then we would expect this fusion of intense attraction and a desire for commitment to be a fairly widespread phenomenon in human cultures (and not merely a Western construct). In 1992, the anthropologists William Jankowiak and Ted Fischer tested this idea by examining a sample of 166 societies in the ethnographic record. They found evidence of romantic love (defined as "any intense attraction that involves the idealisation of the other, within an erotic context, with the expectation of enduring for some time in the future") in no less than 147, or 88.5 percent, of these societies. They added that this was a conservative estimate that probably masked a much higher figure. Romantic love was in all likelihood a human universal, or at the very least a near-universal.[27] This claim has since been given further corroboration by a number of field studies across the planet, and to my knowledge, no evidence has come forward that challenges it directly.[28] What is more, Patrick Hogan's recent empirical study of world literature has also identified "romantic union" as a universal prototype that suggests cross-cultural constants in emotional experience.[29]

I will assume here that this account of the human affections—rooted in evolved dispositions with sexuality and attachment as separate but overlapping systems, with important connections between adulthood and childhood, and with romantic love as a universal human disposition—is correct in its broad outlines. It also enables us to piece together two different explanations for romantic love, which I will call the "weak" and the "strong" version.

According to the weak version, most humans are capable of sexual desire as well as long-term attachment, and romantic love is simply what happens when these systems converge intensely upon the same love object. To disprove this version one would have to show either that *some cultures have no romantic love* because they are capable of *preventing* their members from feeling both things for the same person or that *some cultures have romantic love* only because they *instruct* their members to feel both things for the same person. I suspect that both of these hypothetical research projects would collapse before they even got off the ground.

The strong version is more speculative: it regards romantic love as a specific emotional adaptation, which leads us directly to a second question about its precise evolutionary function. One popular view is that romantic love has served as an emotional incentive for pair formation, keeping sexual partners together and thus securing parental investment for their children.

At first sight, this idea seems questionable since romantic love is often adulterous,[30] and in many cultures where marriage is not based on love it might even be the chief nemesis of any lasting pair-bond. But this is really only a theoretical problem so long as we assume that the "commitment" component in romantic love is synonymous with lifelong monogamy and that arranged marriages were also the rule in those ancestral environments where our current emotional dispositions were calibrated. It is quite conceivable that a tendency for serial relationships—where people get together, have children, break up, and then form new relationships—would have contributed much more effectively to the evolutionary fitness of our ancestors.

In 1992, the anthropologist Helen Fisher argued eloquently (if somewhat speculatively) for this view with her hypothesis of the "four-year itch." She pointed out that in those contemporary societies where divorce is permitted, marriage appears to have a "cross-cultural pattern of decay" that corresponds to the time it takes to raise a child to some independence.[31] This might suggest that humans are indeed naturally disposed to commit to each other but not necessarily for life.

Since Western culture currently appears to be shifting from lifelong monogamy to serial monogamy, it may be tempting to write this off as sheer ethnocentrism. What a singularly convoluted way to convince ourselves that our own way of life is both natural and just! But this convergence between the hypothesized four-year itch and Western social arrangements can be understood very differently. As modern evolutionists are well aware, there is a fundamental conflict at work in human nature: we are individual organisms as well as social animals, and we are constantly seeking to reconcile these two demands by means of conflict and cooperation. It could well be that Western culture is currently engaged in a social experiment where individual desires—including the desire to leave your partner and start afresh—are given relatively free rein because our social organization permits this. From this perspective, Western culture is not being true to human nature: it is being true to the individual, and that is clearly not the same thing.

The view of sexuality and attachment as functionally independent systems leads me to a final aspect of the human affections: the question of psychosexual dimorphism. Since the evolutionary perspective raises strong doubts about the dualistic division between biological sex and cultural gender that still predominates in the humanities and social sciences,[32] there are few issues that are more controversial today. But as long as we respect the analytical gap between what is natural and what is right, and as long as we do not reduce our complex biology or statistical patterns across populations to a set of reified sex roles, it is possible that future generations will look back on our bitter gender debates and wonder what all the fuss was about: "That individuals and groups must be identical in order to be equal is surely one of the most pernicious dogmas of our time, and the fact that, ironically enough, it has become a liberal dogma does not make it any less so."[33]

The aspect of sexual dimorphism that will be relevant here concerns the probable effects of sexual differences in parental investment: that sexual selection will produce at least small statistical differences in reproductive strategies between men and women.[34] While both sexes come equipped with the same systems of sexuality and attachment, men will find it more difficult to extract all the sex they want from women while women will find it correspondingly harder to extract commitment from their sexual partners. What I propose to do in the final section is to briefly explore the interaction in Shakespeare's *Troilus and Cressida* (c. 1602) and *All's Well that Ends Well* (c. 1604) between four different factors: evolved dispositions, cultural strictures, literary genre, and a literary intellect that is still unrivaled in world literature.

Romantic Love as a Literary Problem

A good way to approach the nature of romantic choice in these Shakespearean problem plays is to make a brief detour to the romantic comedies. Numerous critics have remarked over the years that the young women in these plays seem to enjoy a good deal of self-confidence and power, while the men often look like blundering amateurs who are typically one step behind in the amorous repartee. Most recently, Maurice Charney has observed that "in the comedies, the women lead the love game. They are strikingly intelligent and witty and enjoy role-playing, especially when they are disguised as boys."[35] How can we explain this considerable latitude and self-confidence of women in the comedies who stand out so markedly against the demure, self-effacing virgins and destructive mothers that stalk the tragedies?

There is more than one way to answer this question. First, it is in the nature of a romantic comedy to "lick the icing off the cake," so to speak. The social pressures that confront the lovers are there mainly to create the dramatic tension required for comic release, and we know more or less from the start that any hindrances will eventually be overcome. Even more crucially, a romantic comedy deals with the most emotionally intense phase of a relationship—that of courtship or mate choice—and then discretely closes the curtain before we have time to worry about things like spousal compatibility, marital boredom, or potential infidelities. (This is a simplification on my part; the endings of Shakespeare's comedies are not always free of doubts about future happiness, and one critic even goes so far as to declare that "the makings of marriage in Shakespearean comedy are not promising ones.")[36] In such a dramatic world, where the stress lies on human inventiveness, the power of love, and our triumph over adversity, it is not unreasonable to expect that women will be depicted as more resourceful and in control of their destinies in the comedies than in, say, the tragedies.

Of course, this still fails to explain why Shakespeare's comic heroines seem *more* resourceful than the men. There must be a more specific connection between gender identity and genre. Maurice Charney does not seek to answer this difficult question, but he does embrace the currently orthodox view among literature professors that "the characteristics of gender are constructed socially and historically rather than physiologically. . . . What it means to be a man or a woman is a social and historical construction rather than an innate set of masculine or feminine traits."[37]

I have already raised substantial objections to such dichotomies—where nature is first opposed to culture and then neatly removed from the equation, leaving only cultural stereotypes as the sole determinants of human identity. From such a perspective, Shakespeare's comic heroines will be understood as carnivalesque role reversals, as subversive inversions of everything that women were expected to be in a patriarchal culture. Charney writes: "What is interesting in Shakespeare is how male and female characters seem to play against conventional expectations. It is as if Shakespeare is determined to set up a counterpoint between what is expected and what actually occurs, so that characters have latitude to move in and out of preconceived stereotypes."[38]

The inversion of expectations that Charney touches on here is indeed a frequent dramatic strategy in Shakespeare, but his comic heroines are probably more than just reversals of cultural stereotypes. In contrast to the broad constructivist perspective, I suggest that the relative freedom of these literary characters may reflect the interaction of broader tendencies in human nature with Shakespeare's specific historical environment. While a more complete interpretation would also incorporate sex differences in verbal skills (the stuff of comic repartee) as well as temperamental dispositions for harm avoidance,[39] this reading will focus more narrowly on specific tendencies in mate selection.

According to the theory of parental investment, sex differences in parental contributions to offspring will also have consequences for the reproductive strategies of either sex. Given the relative differences in reproductive conditions for men and women, it seems likely that the traditional stereotype of ardent males and choosy females did not simply fall out of the sky. At least until the modern age of contraception, women have always had more to gain from carefully scrutinizing the commitment and quality of a sexual partner, while men have not had a comparable evolutionary incentive for short-term discrimination.

There is nothing ideologically suspect about this idea as long as we avoid confusing it with normative assumptions that *all* women *should* be this or that—coy, sexually passive, and so forth. What is more, being choosy is not the same thing as being coy, and it is quite possible to be a choosy sexual predator. There is no reason to confuse this account with a reductive picture of men as desiring "subjects" and women as passive "objects." Female choice and female objecthood are not easily compatible since an object has no agency and so is inherently incapable of choice. Finally, it must be remembered that the patterns predicted by parental investment must be understood in proximate as well as ultimate terms: "Even if women enjoy sexual variety as much or more than men, for thousands of years they have not needed to be rocket scientists to understand that they make a greater potential commitment per copulation than do men."[40]

For young women in Shakespeare's England, this tendency toward female choice was often curtailed, or at least partially circumscribed, because the patriarchal society they lived in defined them either as dutiful daughters, dutiful servants, or dutiful wives. But there were at least two phases in women's lives when they could enjoy an unparalleled degree of freedom and power. One was widowhood, which meant that a woman might finally be in legal control of her own property, and the other was the period of courtship and betrothal, which "could obliterate differences in rank and alter the relationship between the sexes. It gave females a measure of choice and a degree of power more equal to that of men."[41]

As long as the betrothal had not been consummated sexually, it could be broken off if conditions were not satisfactory. Even if some parents expressed strong views on the choice of partner, marriage was always legally a matter of individual consent. It is not unreasonable to suggest, therefore, that Shakespeare's comic heroines "lead the love game" because the dramatist understood the uniqueness of this phase in the life of the average English woman. In this significant phase between the cultural roles of obedient daughter and obedient wife, many women were able to embrace more fully the ecological niche carved out by sexual selection. What Shakespeare's romantic comedies appear to stage, in other words, is not an inversion of patriarchy but an affirmation of female choice.

It is a defining trait of Shakespeare's problem plays (or problem comedies, as they are sometimes called) that they present their audience with an essentially comic plot but hold back the expected comic release. In this way, they breed ambivalence and doubt rather than just a pleasurable sense of resolution and wish fulfilment.[42] While the comic element is much more subdued in *Troilus and Cressida* than in the other problem plays, its female protagonist can be described as a disillusioned cousin of the comic heroines. When we first encounter Cressida in act 1, scene 2, she displays a razor-sharp wit, cool mastery of the situation, and a marked predilection for bawdy jokes as she banters with her uncle Pandarus.[43] A little further on in the same scene, however, she reveals a darker side when she explains her reluctance to admit her love for Troilus:

Women are angels, wooing:
Things won are done; joy's soul lies in the doing.
That she belov'd knows nought that knows not this:
Men prize the thing ungain'd more than it is. (1.2.286–89)

This passage has attracted much critical attention. As Lu Emily Pearson points out, Shakespeare takes over the idea that "love too easily attained is not prized" from Chaucer's version of the story.[44] Charles Lyons reads the passage with a slightly different emphasis, as a comment on love's finitude in which Cressida is "acutely aware of the disintegration of love in the flux of Time."[45] This is an apt formulation, but we must not forget that Cressida defines the problem explicitly in gender terms: it is *women* who are temporary angels and *men* who do the prizing. Compared to Troilus she "displays a good deal more apprehension over the dangers of romantic idealization; she speaks in a vocabulary of fear and Troilus in a vocabulary of hope."[46] Carol Thomas Neely, finally, sees *Troilus and Cressida* as an instance of a common tendency in several Shakespearean plays where the men "idealize their beloveds, and the women deny, mock, and qualify their lovers' protestations of commonplaces." The women in these plays attain "verbal superiority" and "seize control of courtship" before they pay the price of subordination within marriage.[47]

True to the current ideological fashion that privileges abstract systemic explanations over individual or psychological explanations, many critics actively deny that this tension can have anything to do with Troilus and Cressida as individual characters or human beings. It must be a stereotype produced by their oppressive patriarchal culture. O'Rourke's comment is representative: "If her idealization of him is less firm than his of her, this is not the revelation of individual character but the result of the different promises made to men and women in a patriarchal culture."[48] As intimated previously, such an approach will find it difficult to explain how Cressida and her comic colleagues manage to "lead the love game" (Charney) or "seize control of courtship" (Neely) when Shakespeare's patriarchal culture is meant to push them in the opposite direction. At first sight, it may seem like a solution to argue that they take control by *reversing* or *subverting* the dominant assumptions of their culture, but that would contradict the original idea that individual agency is irrelevant. In this way, the systematic reading becomes caught in a double bind of its own making.

A better approach is to acknowledge that this tension between male idealization and female choice has deeper roots than arbitrary cultural strictures. From the perspective of parental investment theory, it is only to be expected that the average man will be slightly more prone to "idealize" a prospective sexual partner, at least in the sexual short term, while the average woman will have a greater incentive to prolong the courtship (which means more time for assessment and choice). No wonder, then, if women are "angels, wooing" and the average man proves a little more trigger-happy. As Jane Campbell points out, there may even be a connection here between sexual behavior and a general male proclivity for risk taking, since men have "lower levels of serotonin and consequently a weaker ability to inhibit their behaviour."[49] When Shakespeare browsed through book 3 of Ovid's *The Art of Love*, he could even find detailed instructions for women on

how to capitalize on this difference by keeping men on their toes: "Neither promise yourself too easily to him who entreats you, nor yet deny what he asks too
stubbornly. Cause him to hope and fear together. . . ."[50]

This is, of course, exactly what Cressida does, like many other Shakespearean women. In act 2, when she has finally revealed her love, she repeats her
earlier fear that this admission will alter the balance of power between them:

> TROILUS: Why was my Cressid then so hard to win?
> CRESSIDA: Hard to seem won; but I was won, my lord,
>   With the first glance that ever—Pardon me:
>   If I confess much you will play the tyrant. (3.2.114–17)

Cressida's fear that Troilus may become a "tyrant" can be read on several complementary levels. As we all know, strong emotions of this kind are difficult to express
because they acknowledge our dependence upon another person, which leaves us
vulnerable and weak. For Cressida, allowing herself to be "won" also means relinquishing the more specific power afforded her by female choice. But Shakespeare
was far too aware of the shaping force of human culture to depict human relationships as purely "natural" in the sense of arising only from innate mechanisms or universal needs. A little further on, Cressida laments her own position in a society that
reserves the romantic initiative for men: "And yet, good faith, I wish'd myself a man,
/ Or that we women had men's privilege / Of speaking first" (3.2.125–27). This
complaint may in fact be slightly beside the point, since taking the first step would
not have insured her against the brevity of male idealization. But her words are still
a lucid example of how human culture can pick up on a broad pattern in human
nature and turn it into an oppressive normative rule.

In all likelihood, Shakespeare composed *All's Well that Ends Well* a few years
into the seventeenth century, soon after his searching excursion into Troy.
According to David Hoeniger, "the story of *Troilus and Cressida* was obviously on
Shakespeare's mind while he was composing *All's Well*."[51] There are several points
of tangency between the two plays, including two references in *All's Well* to characters used in the earlier play. When Lafew leaves Helena alone with the King, he
refers to himself as "Cressid's uncle / That dare leave two together" (2.1.96–97).
More significantly, it does not seem to have escaped Shakespeare's highly associative mind that he was now writing a second play involving a woman called
Helen:

> COUNTESS: Sirrah, tell my gentlewoman I would speak
>   with her—Helen I mean.
> CLOWN: Was this fair face the cause, quoth she,
>   Why the Grecians sacked Troy?

> Fond done, done fond,
> Was this King Priam's joy? (1.3.68–72)

In *All's Well*, Shakespeare set out to retell a very different story, a folkloric piece derived from William Painter's English translation of Boccaccio. In Shakespeare's version, the young Helena heals the French king's fistula in exchange for the right to choose any husband she wants. When she chooses the unwilling Bertram, the latter refuses to consummate the marriage and escapes to the Florentine wars, whereupon Helena follows him and ingeniously gets him between the sheets (and thus into the marital fold). But while the plot similarities between *Troilus* and *All's Well* may not be very striking, the Clown's song returns us to the problem of value—and more specifically, the risk of overvaluation—that seems to have pre-occupied Shakespeare in the earlier play. How could the Trojans and the Greeks have deemed this woman so important that they embraced this horribly pro-tracted bloodshed for her sake?

What the story of Helena and Bertram enables Shakespeare to explore, among other things, is the other side of this coin: the problem of underestima-tion. Almost all characters in *All's Well* are convinced that Bertram has seriously underrated the beautiful, intelligent, and virtuous Helena, and this opens up a thought-provoking tension between social consensus and individual appraisal. As a consequence, *All's Well* approaches the relation between value and choice from a new (and fully complementary) direction compared to *Troilus*. In his Trojan play, Shakespeare emphasizes the relational aspect of desire and anatomizes the dependence of individual appraisal on social appraisal, with all the endless com-parisons and reappraisals that this gives rise to. In *All's Well* it is instead the limits of the relational aspect and the ultimate incongruity between individual desire and social appraisal that come into focus. In *Troilus*, fifty thousand flies can't be wrong; in *All's Well*, one of the flies simply won't hear reason.

Let us turn to act 3, scene 5, where Shakespeare returns us to the question of love's choice. At this point in the play Bertram has left both court and wife behind and woos a chaste Florentine woman by the appropriate name of Diana. His insistent and unsuccessful advances are related by different characters to a recognizable pattern where men promise women everything between heaven and earth to procure casual sex from them and women try their best to extract signals of genuine commitment from their suitors:

> Beware of them, Diana: their promises,
> enticements, oaths, tokens, and all these engines of
> lust, are not the things they go under; many a maid
> hath been seduced by them; and the misery is,
> example, that so terrible shows in the wrack of

> maidenhood, cannot for all that dissuade succession,
> but that they are limed with the twigs that threatens
> them. (3.5.18–25)

Like Cressida in Troy, this Florentine woman also confronts her impatient suitor with the undependable and fleeting nature of men's desires:

> DIANA: Ay, so you serve us
>   Till we serve you; but when you have our roses,
>   You barely leave our thorns to prick ourselves,
>   And mock us with our bareness. (4.2.17–20)

Although Diana is young and inexperienced in the ways of the world, she can safely fall back on her mother's advice since men are predictable beings: "My mother told me just how he would woo / As if she sat in's heart. She says all men / Have the like oaths" (4.2.69–71). When Helena later learns of Bertram's attempts to get Diana into bed, she completes the picture by describing men as alien creatures who will happily jump into bed with women they do not even *like*, with no thoughts about prior commitments:

> But O, strange men!
> That can such sweet use make of what they hate,
> When saucy trusting of the cozen'd thoughts
> Defiles the pitchy night; so lust doth play
> With what it loathes for that which is away. (4.5.21–25)

Shakespeare is obviously repeating the pattern from *Troilus and Cressida* where an ardent male, beside himself with sexual desire, is held at bay by a woman who seeks to assess his real intentions because she suspects that his oaths may not be entirely ague-proof. Readers and audiences of all conflicting creeds and convictions—from neo-Victorians to literary queer theorists—will agree about one thing: these are instantly recognizable stereotypes about male sexual behavior (and, by extension, differences between men and women).

What kind of substance and how *much* of it we attribute to these stereotypes is a different matter. When Diana's mother warns her above about the "wrack of maidenhood," it is obvious that her fears are largely inspired by cultural ideals and strictures. Although early modern English women enjoyed a relative freedom compared with women in other European countries, the nation was also characterized by a rigid sexual double standard that matched the cross-cultural tendency described by evolutionary psychologists.[52] Whenever men broke the marriage vows, the act was defined legally as fornication, while women were guilty of the more serious crime of adultery. The double standard was actively justified with reference to the risk of illegitimacy,[53] but it was also criticized by contemporary moralists (as well as literary characters like Shakespeare's Emilia in *Othello*). In other words, the insights offered by parental investment theory may be essential for a deeper understanding of the passages discussed, but they are hardly sufficient in themselves.

I would now like to sum up my findings as follows: First, I hope to have shown that a Darwinian perspective that fuses ultimate and proximate explanation outshines the traditional constructivist perspective on love. Second, it seems clear that my brief examples from two problem plays are fully compatible with Maurice Charney's observation about gender and genre in Shakespeare: compared to the comedies, the women in the problem plays are certainly moving into a more constricted role. But to understand this phenomenon as fully as possible, we must combine ultimate explanation with an attention to the proximate conditions of Shakespeare's society (or, in relevant cases, what he knew about the societies he depicted). In both cases, the female distrust of male idealization is at once biological and cultural, in keeping with the interactionist orientation of modern Darwinian theory.

My third and final conclusion is a counterpoint to the other two. Another crucial similarity between *All's Well* and *Troilus* that I have so far passed over is that both plays make much of the sexual stereotype but work against it actively in their main plots. In *All's Well*, Helena takes the sexual offensive, courts Bertram aggressively, and even marries him against his will. In *Troilus*, Cressida's fears about male idealization are given a very ironic twist since it is *she* who betrays Troilus only a day after they have promised each other undying love. This illustrates another important aspect of the relationship between human nature and literary figuration—that literary texts are often at cross-purposes with our stereotyped or generalized assumptions about human nature. Like most writers, Shakespeare plays a delicate cat-and-mouse game with his audience, alternately gratifying and frustrating our expectations. We are not likely to give a particularly accurate account of his plays unless we come prepared with a theoretical perspective that does justice to such complexities.

Notes

1. Elster 1999, 48.
2. Levin 1993, 52.
3. Shakespeare 1998. All quotations are from this edition.
4. Beall and Sternberg 1995, 418, 419.
5. Griffiths 1997.

6. Beall and Sternberg 1995, 434.
7. Beall and Sternberg 1995, 433.
8. Beall and Sternberg 1995, 436.
9. Bloch 1991, 8.
10. I. Singer 1984, 22–23.
11. Singer 1984, 35.
12. Singer 1984, 70.

13. In spite of his questionable equation of passion with adultery, Denis de Rougemont's views on the narcotic ideal of romantic passion in Western culture strike me as ruthlessly to the point. See Rougemont 1939.

14. Bowlby 1997, 183.
15. Cited in Cornelius 1996, 198.
16. See Shaver, Hazan, and Bradshaw 1988.
17. See, for example, Hinton 1999, 312.
18. L. Diamond 2003, 179–80.

19. For what appears to be an exhaustive list of common denominators, see Shaver, Hazan, and Bradshaw, 74–75, table 4.

20. See, for example, Bristol 2001.
21. Konner 1982, 298.
22. L. Diamond 2003, 173.
23. L. Diamond 2003, 176.
24. Gillis 1985, 37.
25. Hrdy 1999, 139.

26. For further perspectives on the biochemistry and neurophysiological substrates of love, see Fisher 1995; Bartels and Zeki 2000. Most recently, Helen Fisher, Arthur Aron, and Lucy Brown have proposed a model that involves three biological drives with corresponding neurophysiological centers: sexuality, attraction, and attachment. See Fisher 2004.

27. Jankowiak and Fischer 1998.
28. Jankowiak 1995.
29. Hogan 2003.
30. This objection is raised in Griffiths 1997 with reference to Konner 1982.
31. Fisher 1994, 109–12.
32. See A. Campbell 2002; Geary 1998; Low 2000.
33. Spiro 1987, 70.
34. For example, see Kendrick, Sadalla, and Trost 1997; Trivers 1972.
35. Charney 2000, 209–10.
36. Hopkins 1998, 33.
37. Charney 2000, 6, 133.
38. Charney 2000, 150.

39. On neurophysiological gender differences in harm avoidance, see Pujol, López, Deus, et al. 2002.

40. Ehrlich 2000, 194.

41. Gillis 1985, 52.

42. For a thorough discussion see Thomas 1987, chapter 1.

43. Text references are to act, scene, and line in the 1998 Arden edition.

44. Pearson 1966, 20.

45. Lyons 1971, 83.

46. O'Rourke 1992, 149.

47. Neely 1985, 6.

48. O'Rourke 1992, 155.

49. A. Campbell 2002, 86–87.

50. Ovid 1947, 153.

51. Hoeniger 1992, 293.

52. See Wilson and Daly 1992.

53. Gowing 1996; Foyster 1999.

Male Bonding in the Epics and Romances

Robin Fox

From Gilgamesh and Enkidu, through David and Jonathan, up to Holmes and Watson, Aubrey and Maturin, or Butch and Sundance, the male bond has been celebrated in literature, song, and drama. The combative male group from Jason and the Argonauts through the Knights of the Round Table and Robin Hood and his Merry Men to the Seven Samurai/Magnificent Seven exercises a constant fascination. This holds whether the male group is noble in its purpose like Hawkeye and his Mohicans, or downright nasty like the Dirty Dozen. The Western outlaw band (the James Gang, the Daltons) draws us as surely as the Pre-Raphaelite Brotherhood. There is a continuing appetite for World War II "buddy" movies (*Saving Private Ryan, Band of Brothers*), where men die for each other as surely as Romeo died for Juliet in the world's most famous heterosexual tragedy. (Although Romeo's death could also be seen as a result of his devotion to Mercutio.)

The theory of male bonding as a special instance of bonding in general, was first formulated by Lionel Tiger in his *Men in Groups*. Tiger saw intense emotional attachment between males as having its roots in the prehuman group-living primates but coming to full flower in hominid evolution (particularly in the Upper Paleolithic when modern humans were formed) with the development of hunting and warfare. Males hunting or fighting together had to develop a special kind of trust that went beyond simple friendship as might be expressed in grooming or proximity. This kind of dependence involved, first, a selection among young males for those with the right qualities (for males will differ in their bonding capacities) and led to elaborate recruitment systems of trial and initiation. The second element was "female exclusion," in which the heterosexual bond was ritually downgraded and exclusive male groups were formed with their secret ceremonies, oaths, and sanctions.

The heterosexual bond was necessary for reproduction but was seen also as inimical to the male bond, necessary for predation and protection. There was in consequence a constant tension between the demands of the reproductive bond and those of the male bond. Men would be ambivalent about the heterosexual bond insofar as it threatened the male association; women would find the demands of the male group equally threatening to the needs of the family.

This whole evolutionary scenario later came to be seen in light of the differential reproductive strategies of males and females, and of hominid males and females in particular. In the prehunting stage of hominid development, males had not been responsible for the provisioning of females and young. Male chimpanzees occasionally hunt, but the meat is not part of the steady food supply. They do, however, form cooperative male bands, which operate exclusive of females for a good part of the year and which carry out lethal raids on other such bands.

With the transition to hunting/scavenging, and the incorporation of meat into the regular diet, the evolving hominid infant, with its ever-increasing demands for fuel for its growing brain, required what Trivers came to call a "high male parental investment."[1] This mitigated the totally selfish behavior of the males and required them to divert energy and resources to the women and children. It would always be in the female interest to garner male support for herself and her offspring. This would be largely in the form of high-energy protein from meat—the females provided the bulk of the carbohydrate themselves. The males would still be inclined to promiscuity, or at least polygamous mating, to maximize their own reproductive success.

Male and female reproductive strategies were thus always asymmetrical, and this asymmetry was, if anything, intensified during the course of hominid development. Looked at from the point of view of "survival of the group," of course, both male protection and provision and female reproduction and nurturing of infants were equally required. But from the perspective of individual reproductive success, these two forms of bonding would be at odds. It could be argued that the most successful males would be those that balanced male bonding for the protection and provisioning of the whole group, with the particular care and provisioning of their own mates and young. The alternative strategy of random promiscuity would probably have less chance of success unless it was totally concealed, something not easy to achieve in a small hunting group. Nineteenth-century anthropology suggested the alternative of "group marriage," in which mates were held in common. While theoretically possible, this has not been found to occur in actuality, and the concept arose from a misunderstanding of cousin-marriage rules and terminologies.[2] Even in societies where the ideology of procreation excludes the father as progenitor of his children, individual rights to mates are recognized, and these include rights of sexual access. Regardless of the theory of procreation, sexual jealousy appears to be universal, although there are exceptions for ritual orgies and wife lending. With the latter, however, the males are still in control of sexual access.[3]

The strength of the Tiger-Trivers thesis is that it forces us to recognize the male-male bond as equal to, and in many ways inimical to, the male-female bond, serving its own important evolutionary functions. We can expect, therefore, that once symbolic capacity was developed, this emotionally charged relationship would receive attention in ritual, art, music, and story. In the same way that sexual competition between dominant and subordinate males for fertile females would dominate the earliest narratives, as I have tried to demonstrate elsewhere,[4] so we would expect to find the male-male bond and its vicissitudes as a theme around which oral narratives, and then written epics, arranged themselves.

An evolutionary analysis of the literature of male bonding requires a simple switch of focus, in which the male bond is put to the forefront of the narrative and the rest of the action is seen as affecting the bond, for better or for worse. In particular, it requires us to examine afresh the role of the females in the plot to see how their actions affect the creation and stability of the bond (for women often have an interest in the support they may receive from the bonded males), but more often in its dissolution. And we should always remember that the making of epic narrative was itself a male activity, and thus should indeed reflect basic male concerns and prejudices. I do not therefore intend to argue that male-female relationships must always, in reality, take exactly the form we find in the epics; fortunately, this is not the case. But it might be instructive to look at these powerful writers as narrators of a particularly intense version of the universal theme.

Gilgamesh

The earliest known written epic (that is, *preserved* by writing, whatever the method of initial composition) is the Babylonian story of Gilgamesh. Gilgamesh was ruler of the Sumerian city of Uruk around 2700 B.C. In Assyro-Babylonian society he was worshiped as a god and celebrated in verse, which was standardized by 1300 B.C. David Ferry, in the translation we use here, used the Babylonian text, some three thousand lines dating from the seventh century B.C.

The Goddess Aruru, at the request of the gods, created the wild man Enkidu as the double of Gilgamesh. He was to be a counterweight to the growing power of Gilgamesh, which was threatening to the gods. Enkidu ran wild, and Gilgamesh went after him, accompanied by a "temple prostitute" who was to "tame" the wild man to "show him the things a woman knows how to do." Enkidu lost his wildness; the beasts fled from him. Gilgamesh has a dream, and his mother, Rimat-Ninsu, interprets it. The meteorite of the dream "is the strong companion, powerful as a star, / the meteorite of the heavens, a gift of the gods. / That you were drawn to it as if drawn to a woman / means that this companion will not forsake you. / He will protect and guard you with his life."

Shamhat, usually described as a "temple prostitute," is actually a priestess of the goddess Ishtar. These priestesses, representing the goddess, had intercourse with men who gave gifts to the temple, much as still happens in parts of southern India, where the practice is known as *devadasi*.[5] Shamhat divides her clothes to dress Enkidu "as a bridegroom." Meanwhile Gilgamesh, as king, is asserting his right over a new bride. This enrages Enkidu who challenges him. They fight, but neither can prevail. Finally, they embrace, kiss, and take each other by their hands, with Enkidu saying: "You are the strongest of all, the perfect, the terror."

Gilgamesh and Enkidu then take on the great demon Huwaw and defeat him. After this victory the goddess Ishtar falls in love with Gilgamesh, pleads for his semen, and offers him "riches beyond the telling." Gilgamesh repulses Ishtar, claiming that her lovers, like Tammuz, all came to a bad end. Ishtar then begs her father, Anu, to give her The Bull of Heaven to attack Gilgamesh. But Gilgamesh and Enkidu together kill the bull and tear out its heart. Enkidu rages against Ishtar, and the gods decide that Enkidu must die. He falls sick and dies, and Gilgamesh mourns movingly and elaborately over more than seventy lines: "Gilgamesh touched the heart of the companion. / There was nothing at all. Gilgamesh covered / Enkidu's face with a veil like the veil of a bride. / He hovered like an eagle over the body." Gilgamesh, in his grief, tries even to become Enkidu: "Now you are gone, and Gilgamesh will wear / the skins of beasts, and wander hairy-bodied / grieving in the wilderness for you." The rest of the epic deals with Gilgamesh's quest for immortality and his search for Utnapishtin, the earliest Noah-like flood survivor, who holds the secret.

There is no question that the world's first great epic poem is a long hymn to the bond between the two heroes. Looked at from this angle, the role of the women can be seen as either promoting or undermining the male bond. The goddess Aruru creates the bond by creating the heroes in the first place. The temple priestess/prostitute, Shamhat, is crucial in taming Enkidu and then introducing him to Gilgamesh. Gilgamesh's mother then adopts Enkidu, thus further cementing the bond, whose stability she predicted. These can be termed *enabling* females: those who have something to gain from the male bond (protection for a son, for example) and, hence, support it. The goddess Ishtar, on the other hand, by her desire for Gilgamesh, threatens the bond, and after Enkidu has raged at her, destroys it. She then is a *disabling* female.

Many of the basic themes are then established in this powerful poem. We shall forego further discussion of them here and pick up the topic as we proceed through the later epics.

Táin Bó Cualinge

The *Táin Bó Cualinge* (*The Cattle Raid of Cooley*) refers to events traditionally happening in Ireland around the time of Christ at the height of barbaric Iron Age society.

The language of the mixed verse-prose epic is that of eighth-century Irish Gaelic, but the completion of the stories dates to the twelfth-century *Lebor na hUidre* (*Book of the Dun Cow*). In the fourteenth century a version was written known as *The Yellow Book of Lecan*. Both versions, compiled in monasteries, show heavy Christian interpolations from the monkish authors, but the essence of the pagan story comes through clearly.

The cattle raid in question was instigated by Queen Medh (Maeve) of Connaught to capture the brown bull owned by Dáire, one of the chieftains of Ulster. The army of Ulster is immobilized by a spell, and the hero Cúchulainn has to meet the invaders alone. He delays them by challenging their best warriors to single combat, which they cannot refuse but always lose. The bulk of the story concerns these combats and battles, but the central event is the combat of Cúchulainn and Ferdia. This is particularly poignant since they had been lifelong friends, fostered together as children with Scáthach, an Amazon queen who taught them the arts of war and who is thus the enabling female of the story. Cúchulainn frequently refers to them as "Scáthac's foster-sons." Fostering was a sacred duty in ancient Ireland, and the bond of foster brothers was likewise sacralized.

The bond is, however, threatened by the manipulations of Medh, who is variously treated as completely mythological or as representative of the high status of women in Celtic society, and north European society generally, at this time. Determined to sabotage Cúchulainn, she decided to suborn the loyalty of Ferdia. She thus becomes the major disabling female of the story. She tempts Ferdia with an offering remarkably like that of Ishtar to Gilgamesh, including "a chariot worth three-times seven bondmaids," a tax break for his kith and kin, fine jewelry, and her daughter, Finnabair, for wife. Finnabair has already been provocatively dangled before him as bait; Medh then adds, "and my own friendly thighs on top of that if need be." She offered the same prize to Dáire in return for the bull. Since the Irish did not have ruling queens, Medh's queenship was, according to Thomas Kinsella, a mistake of the scribes, since she was in fact the goddess of Tara. The parallel with Ishtar probably reflects a theme deep in Indo-European–Semitic myth. But in both cases, the purpose of the fertility goddess, as is appropriate, is to disrupt the male bond with heterosexual temptations.

At first Ferdia is not tempted, but Medh appeals to his pride through a false statement impugning his honor, attributed to Cúchulainn. Ferdia ("the fiery") is quick tempered and agrees to the fight but demands six hostages to make sure she keeps her word.

We thus move to the tragic single combat. During the fight, both heroes have antiphonal verse debates with their charioteers, reflecting the same dialogue Krishna has with Arjuna in the Bhagavad-Gîtâ. This bond with the wise charioteer is a kind of grace note on the theme. The two combatants engage in a lot of prefight banter, and while Ferdia, perhaps a little guilty, is truculent, Cúchulainn often laments the breaking of the bond and invokes their common fosterage. In Kinsella's translation: "While we stayed with Scáthac / we went as one / with a common courage / into the fight. / My bosom friend / and heart's blood, / dear above all. / I am going to miss you."[6] He chides Ferdia for imagining that Finnabair will ever be his. Medh has used the same trick on fifty men before, he says. He is particularly bitter that Ferdia should let a woman come between them. "If they had offered her to me, / if I were the one Medh smiled at, / I wouldn't think to do you harm / or touch the least part of your flesh." They alternately fight and banter, and Cúchulainn returns again and again to the theme: "Now I know it was your doom / when a woman sent you here / to fight against your foster brother."

The combat is described in heroic detail, but finally, by using the super weapon, the *gae bolga* (a kind of sling thrown with the foot), Cúchulainn mortally wounds Ferdia. He carries the body from the ford where the fight took place and faints beside it. Loeg, his charioteer, rouses him, and the victor breaks into a series of laments (interspersed with prose conversations) that match in emotion and beauty those of Gilgamesh for Enkidu: "When we were with Scáthac / learning victory overseas, / it seemed our friendship would remain / unbroken till the day of doom. / I loved the noble way you blushed, / and loved your fine form. I loved your blue clear eye, / your way of speech, your skillfulness." He returns again to his main complaint: "Medh's daughter Finnabair, / whatever beauty she may have, / was an empty offering, / a string to hold the sand, Ferdia." He remembers his dead friend tenderly: "You have fallen to the Hound [i.e., Cúchulainn], / I cry for it, little calf." They cut the *gae bolga* from his body, and Cúchulainn ends in a fury of grief with the same two lines repeated in each stanza: "It was all play, all sport / until Ferdia came to the ford. / Misery! A pillar of gold / I have leveled in the ford, / the bull of the tribe-herd, / braver than any man."

Thus we can see that the heart of this great epic is another hymn to the male bond, and the most obvious of the complaints against the disabling role of the female. Heterosexuality is seen largely as a threat to the sacred bond, or, insofar as the heroes have their heterosexual partners, subordinate to it. Cúchulainn's sexual escapades are little above rape and rarely rise above friendly teasing. In the whole of "The Wooing of Emer" where Cúchulainn gains his bride, there is no love poetry remotely matching his threnody for Ferdia.

Beowulf

Beowulf is a seventh- to tenth-century Anglo-Saxon poem written in England but about events taking place in Denmark and southern Sweden. More so than the

Táin, it is filled with Christian interpolations, but they do nothing to hide the intensely pagan nature of the values and mores of the warrior age. The hero, Beowulf, a prince of the Swedish Geats, hears of the plight of the Danes, who are beset by a monster, Grendel. Beowulf sets sail with a picked band of followers for the land of the "Spear-Danes" and the hall Heorot, home of the Danish king Hrothgar. Here they await the attack of Grendel.

The foremost male bond of the poem is that between Beowulf and Hrothgar. The bond between Beowulf and his band is certainly there and very real, in the tradition of Jason and his Argonauts. But the specific bond is that between the hero and the king. We are introduced early to Hrothgar's queen, Wealhtheow, who takes mead to all the warriors. She is especially gracious to Beowulf, who makes a formal boast to protect her people.

Grendel attacks; there is a huge fight, and Beowulf tears off the monster's arm. Grendel retreats to his lake home to die, and Hrothgar sings the praises of Beowulf, adopting him as his son "in his heart." The queen praises Beowulf and stresses how she trusts him to be "strong and kind" to her sons. Wealhtheow does not figure prominently in the poem, but she does fill the role of enabling female in her endorsement of Beowulf. She can be seen as being balanced against the next major player to appear. The night after the fight, Grendel's mother, bent on revenge, attacks Heorot and carries off one of Hrothgar's warriors. Beowulf dives to the bottom of the mere and overcomes Grendel's mother in a furious fight. He brings back her head to Heorot, where there is much mutual praising as the Geats prepare to depart. At one point Hrothgar is overcome with emotion:

> And so the good and grey-haired Dane,
> that high-born king, kissed Beowulf
> and embraced his neck, then broke down
> in sudden tears. Two forebodings
> disturbed him in his wisdom, but one was stronger:
> never more would they meet each other
> face to face. And such was his affection
> that he could not help being overcome:
> his fondness for the man was so deep founded
> it warmed his heart and wound the heartstrings
> tight in his breast.[7]

Beowulf returns home, where he succeeds to the throne of the Geats. A dragon ravages the country, and again Beowulf leads a band to fight it. This time, however, the men desert him, except for Wiglaf, who rebukes the others and tells them they must defend their prince. Wiglaf and Beowulf slay the dragon together, but Beowulf is mortally wounded. The shirkers, ashamed, come back and find Wiglaf supporting the dying hero, like Bedevere with Arthur. The episode ends with "the living warrior watching by the dead, / keeping weary vigil, holding a wake / for the loved and the loathed."

This great poem of warrior virtues shows again the male bond as central. Beowulf and Hrothgar dominate the body of the text, and the hero and Wiglaf end the tale. We have already noted Wealtheow as the rather shadowy enabling female, but the critic might hold that there is no balancing disabling female who threatens the bond. But this would be to miss the point that Beowulf comes nearest to death, not from the male monster Grendel, but from Grendel's unnamed *mother*. Yet again, there have been numerous interpretations of her symbolic value: psychoanalysts have a fine old time with her, and structuralists see her, like Enkidu, as Nature as opposed to the heroes' Culture. But from our perspective, she is a female, like Ishtar and Medh, of superhuman powers, who is the most direct threat to the male heroes.

The disabling female need not always be so monstrously threatening. She can threaten more by simply diverting a hero from his primary allegiance by her feminine attraction. We shall look now at examples of where this passive attractiveness is fatal to the bond between heroes.

The *Iliad*

The *Iliad* is attributed to the poet Homer, and although composed in about 750 to 725 B.C. it concerns an earlier Mycenaean society of the Greek Bronze Age and was derived from earlier oral poems. The preeminent male bond in Homer's story is that between the Greek hero Achilles and his companion Patroclus. Indeed, we can see that this bond and its vicissitudes are what the story is *about*. The plot is too well known to need much recitation. Menelaus's wife, Helen, elopes with Paris and is taken to Troy on the coast of what is now Turkey. The Greek principalities combine to attack Troy, and the poem covers an episode at the end of the ten-year siege.

Agamemnon, as commander in chief of the Greeks, has appropriated Briseis, a captive girl belonging to Achilles, the greatest of the Greek warriors. Achilles then refuses to fight. Patroclus, Achilles' constant companion, prevails on him to lend his armor and chariot so that the Trojans might mistake Patroclus for Achilles. Thus Patroclus hopes to aid the Greeks, who are losing badly and are driven back to their ships. Hector, the Trojan hero, kills Patroclus, then Achilles in turn kills Hector and mutilates his body in fury. Achilles in turn is killed, as is reported when the *Odyssey* picks up the story.

Our interest is in the nature of the bond between the two heroes and the relationships between the women and the heroes. Helen could be seen as a disabling female, except that she does not directly affect any particular male bond. She is, however, ultimately the "cause" of the terrible conflict—or at least the excuse for it on the part of the Greeks. Briseis, on the other hand, while completely passive, is the direct cause of the breach between Agamemnon and Achilles, and thus sets in motion the death of the heroes. The disabling female does not have to attack the bond to threaten it. Her role is often merely to act as a serious distraction: she is the agent of the heterosexual bond in its constant battle for attention with the male bond.

Achilles, then, is the son of the goddess Thetis and the leader of the Myrmidons. But who is Patroclus? He is described as the "dear companion" of Achilles. They were raised together in the house of Patroclus's father Menoetius. Patroclus is in fact the "older brother" of the pair. They were thus, like Cúchulainn and Ferdia, virtual foster brothers. Patroclus seems always to be there with Achilles in any crisis. He is there during the quarrel with Agamemnon, and it is he whom Achilles asks to handle the delicate matter of handing Briseis over to the heralds. Achilles addresses him on this occasion, and often later, as *diogenes Patroklus.* Fagles gives this simply as "Prince," while Fitzgerald has "my Lord." The Loeb Classical Edition has "sprung from Zeus." The latter is the most literally correct, although it could be "god-born" (i.e., "divine"). He has other epithets, including *megathumon,* "great-hearted," and *isotheos,* "godlike," but the point is that Achilles never treats him as anything less than his equal.

When the delegation from Agamemnon visits Achilles, Patroclus is again always there too. Together the two cook for and serve the ambassadors, and Patroclus appears "like a god in the firelight." In a defining episode, Patroclus, carrying a message from Nestor to Achilles, meets the wounded Eurypylus, who bemoans at length the condition of the Greeks and asks how Achilles can ignore their plight. Patroclus (again called *diogenes*) helps Eurypylus, then goes on to rebuke Achilles, essentially as an equal: "Have you no pity? / Peleus, master of horse, was not your father, / Thetis was not your mother! Cold grey sea / and sea-cliffs bore you, making a mind so harsh."[8]

Achilles accepts the rebuke and gives his armor to his friend, with strict instructions not to pursue the Trojans once the Greek ships are safe. Once Patroclus is gone, Achilles prays long and hard to Zeus to keep Patroclus safe. Zeus is torn. Then Patroclus kills the high-god's favorite mortal son, Sarpedon, and Zeus allows Apollo, patron of the Trojans, to aid Hector and the Trojans in killing Patroclus.

Nestor brings the news, and Achilles is distraught: "Then in the dust he stretched his giant length / and tore his hair with both hands." Thetis hears her son's "terrible, wrenching cry" and comes to him. He pours out his grief to her. Thetis persuades Achilles to reconcile with Agamemnon, and Briseis is returned. She sees Patroclus's body and is deeply moved. She recounts how, when she was captured, Patroclus protected her and agreed to arrange her marriage to Achilles. She is wracked with grief for him. Nothing, however, compares with the grief of Achilles. After he has his revenge on Hector and Hector's corpse, Achilles holds funeral games for his friend as for a king. The ghost of Patroclus visits him, prophesies Achilles' death beneath the walls of Troy, and asks that they be buried together in the same barrow. Achilles begs the vanishing shade to stay and weep with him, but he arranges the burial as requested. He causes a great funeral pyre to be built and sacrifices twelve noble Trojan captives on it to appease his friend's shade: "Achilles mourned his friend and gave his bones / to the great flames to be devoured; with dragging / steps and groans he moved about the pyre."

Comment would be almost indecent. So let us move on to a truly Christian version of the theme but still in a warrior setting full of pagan overtones and derivations.

Morte d'Arthur

Sir Thomas Malory's *Morte d'Arthur* (published by Caxton in 1485) is the best known of the medieval romances and was indeed a melange of material from the French romance writers recreated by Malory. The material circulated freely among medieval authors. Geoffrey of Monmouth took generously from the Welsh *Mabinogion* (with its tales of "Gwenhwyvar") for his Latin *History of Britain*, which in turn was used by the French (de Borron, de Troyes), who in turn supplied the basis for Malory's exquisite recreation. Our own age remembers it best for the themes of the Holy Grail, particularly as in Wagner's *Parsifal*, and more popularly for the love triangle of Arthur-Launcelot-Guinever (or Guinevere as she is now rendered) with the Lerner and Loew *Camelot* as perhaps its best vernacular rendition.

We, however, must look at another triangle—that of Arthur-Gawaine-Launcelot—in the setting of the quintessential male band: the Knights of the Round Table. In the modern retellings Gawaine tends to get lost, yet he is from the start Arthur's most constant companion and is with him to the end. He is, of course, Arthur's nephew, the son of Arthur's sister Morguese, Queen of Orkney. By an irony that haunts the tale, Arthur has slept with Morguese without knowing she is his sister, thus begetting Mordred. The same woman gives birth both to Arthur's boon companion, his most loyal friend, and the half-brother who is to bring about Arthur's ruin and who is Arthur's son.

Morguese, except in some modern feminist versions, also tends to get lost in the retellings. But she is crucial: she is at once enabling in supplying nephews who aid Arthur and, at the same time, ultimately disabling in supplying both a nephew/son who is Arthur's nemesis and another nephew, Agravaine, who aids and abets Mordred in his plotting. Indeed, insofar as Gawaine's intransigence toward Launcelot prolongs the civil war and prevents reconciliation between the parties, the sons of Morguese can be seen as centrally effective in the doom of Camelot. Add that Gawaine's ultimate hatred of Launcelot stems from the latter's unwitting killing of two other brothers, sons of Morguese, Gareth and Gaheris, when rescuing Guinevere. Morguese herself actively pursues a hatred of Arthur, as does his other sister, Morgan le Fay, who at various points in the plot betrays almost everyone. (She is instrumental in first causing the quarrel and then thwarting the bond between Gawain and Benlake in *Sir Gawain and the Green Knight*.)

The women mostly, wittingly or unwittingly, serve to disable the bonds between the knights. The Lady Ettarde betrays Gawaine and Pelleas, who had "plighted their troth" to each other. Pelleas leaves her for Nimue, the Lady of the Lake who had previously been the cause of Merlin's desertion of Arthur, which ended with Merlin being tricked and imprisoned in a rock. But in *The Book of Sir Gareth*, Dames Linet and Lyones are both directly enabling, succoring Gareth and helping to establish him as one of the knightly company. Linet prevents Gareth and Gawaine from unwittingly killing each other. These women stand in sharp contrast to Morgan and Morguese. Others, like Elaine and Guinever, do not actively seek to disrupt the male bonds but become the cause of the dissolution because of their drawing power. One way or another the band of knights, bonded through battle and ritual, is threatened by either female attractiveness or female manipulation.

While Gawaine dominates the early books, he is replaced by Launcelot du Lake, who becomes the focus of male and female attraction and is especially close to both Arthur and Gawaine. He pledges devotion to Guinever, but then so have all the knights, and it is not at this point an obvious problem but part of the chivalric devotion to the married "lady."

The relationships become dense and complicated, particularly with the advent of Tristram, but crucial as he is in understanding the bonds between the knights, we must move on with the main theme. Enough to say that Tristram becomes the foil by which Morgan le Fay plots to destroy Arthur.

The general theme here is that the knights recruit new members to the band, usually through a fight or a trial of adventures. They swear eternal loyalty and watch each other's backs, but at some point a woman actively or passively breaks up the bond, and there is disaster for the male group.

Both Tristram and Launcelot are driven mad by their conflicts over women. Tristram wanders in the woods, and the other knights go after him to bring him back to sanity. The conflict between Guinever and Elaine (the first Elaine, mother of Galahad) drives Launcelot into the same predicament, and Ector and Percival go to the rescue. The men are relentless in their efforts to save one another from the results of breakdowns induced by heterosexual feelings.

The "Book of Galahad" is very much a father-son story, in which he and Launcelot, like Sohrab and Rustum, fight each other without knowing they are father and son. Percivale is very much a loner on his Grail quest. In fact, after the Grail vision and Arthur's pledge to search for the holy vessel, the knights go off on their almost wholly individual quests. It is as if the Christian idea of individual salvation is inimical to the pagan ideal of the male bond. With the continuing stories of Galahad, Percivale, and Bors, Malory carefully sets up the male alliances that are to be sundered.

Malory has equally carefully held the issue of Guinever and Launcelot in suspense since, several books ago, King Marke and Morgan le Fay sent their accusatory letters. Now it all starts to come apart. The nephews of Arthur divide over the issue. Agravaine and Mordred are for action against the lovers, while Gawaine and Gareth swear loyalty to Launcelot. Agravaine and Mordred persuade Arthur to agree to trap Launcelot into going to the queen's chamber, and there they surprise him. While making his escape, Launcelot kills Agravaine and twelve knights.

Arthur demands Guinever's death by fire for treason. Gawaine, still bound in friendship to Launcelot at this point, pleads the innocence of the lovers and refuses to be Guiniver's executioner. Launcelot with his partisans rides to Guinever's rescue, and, without recognizing them, kills the unarmed Gareth and Gaheris. Launcelot takes Guinever to his castle of Joyous Gard, where, in the preview of this episode, Tristram had taken Isoude.

The band of knights is thoroughly severed now between Arthur and Gawaine and their supporters on the one side and Launcelot and Bors and their kin on the other. The killing of his brothers has rendered Gawaine cold with fury against Launcelot. Launcelot is devastated that he has killed Gareth in particular and protests his innocence of intent but to no avail. Arthur wavers and is always ready to find some compromise, but Gawaine is adamant. In the battle, Bors wounds Arthur, but Launcelot will not let his nephew kill the king. Arthur weeps with misery that he must fight Launcelot. At the Pope's intervention (not usually mentioned in modern versions) Launcelot gives up Guinever, but at Gawaine's insistence the war continues. The loyalists leave off fighting Launcelot to take on the traitor Mordred, who has imprisoned the queen and threatened to marry her. In this battle, Gawaine himself is mortally wounded. Arthur holds his dying friend and laments:

> Alas, my sister's son, here now thou liest, the man in the world that I loved the most; and now is my joy gone. For now, my nephew, Sir Gawaine, I will discover me unto your person: in Sir Launcelot and you I most had my joy and mine affiance, and now I have lost my joy of you both, wherefore all my earthly joy is gone from me.

Gawaine, on his deathbed, writes an eloquent letter of reconciliation to Launcelot, who comes over to try to save Arthur. But he is too late to stop Mordred and Arthur from killing each other. In the boat with three queens, including his now mourning sister Morgan le Fay, and with Nimue, the Lady of Lake, the nemesis of Merlin, Arthur is borne away to Avilion. Thus in the end the women are there to tend to the man they harmed so much and to bear him away from Camelot and his knights forever.

We still see Malory through the spectacles of romanticism and see the main issue as the "love interest"—with all the stuff about chivalry and knights and adventures and quests and battles as somehow secondary. But if we shake off this miasma and take a fresh look, what we see is the chivalry as central and as being about the deep emotional, even spiritual, bonds between the knights. The romantic love interest is intrusive and destructive of this sacred bond. It is not clear that Arthur loves Guinever nearly as much as he loves Gawaine and Launcelot. He would have burned Guinever (and certainly without any trial) for causing the destruction of the Round Table, but he could not kill Launcelot, and Launcelot could not kill him. Arthur-Gawaine-Launcelot is the bonded triad around which the story moves, and the destruction of this basic male bond by the power of heterosexual attraction is the heart of the tragedy.

Chanson de Roland

The continental romances from the twelfth to the fourteenth century, some preceding Malory, some deriving from him, are replete with the same themes.

The best known romance is certainly the *Chanson de Roland,* and again the theme is the friendship unto death of Roland and Oliver. Roland probably was a historical warrior in the retinue of Charlemagne. He is mentioned briefly in a history as "Hruodlandus," and his death at Roncesvaux in A.D. 778 is noted. He was killed by Basques, not Saracens as in the *Chanson,* and Basque ballads sung to this day celebrate his death as the "the darling of king Karloman." In the romances he is, as we have come to expect, the sister's son of Charlemagne. There are many versions of his youth, told in *Chansons de Geste* other than *Roland,*[9] but all agree that Bertha, the sister, was estranged from her brother and that Roland had to win his way back into his uncle's favor. Like Cúchulainn, Roland has a precocious childhood, then he performs mighty deeds to impress his uncle and is returned to favor.

Roland meets Oliver in the traditional way, through combat. Oliver's uncle, Duke Girard, is in contention with the emperor, and they agree to fight in a championship. Charlemagne nominates Roland, who has fallen in love with Oliver's sister, Alda. They fight until exhausted, then they embrace and swear undying friendship. The quarrel between their uncles is resolved, and Roland marries Alda, who was much mentioned between them during the fight. Since love of her has softened Roland's heart toward his opponent, she can be seen as the enabling female in the relationship.

The pair have, however, made a great enemy in Ganelon, Roland's stepfather. He is the Mordred of the tale and works for everyone's destruction. He was at the time the most hated figure in Europe for his treachery: Dante places him in the lowest depths of the inferno. In the end his treachery brings about their deaths in the famous episode of the Pass of Roncesvaux/Roncesvalles.

Charlemagne is withdrawing from his war with the Moors in Spain since the Saracen king Marsilius had promised submission. Through the treachery of Ganelon, Roland and the flower of French chivalry are delivered to Moorish vengeance. Caught in an ambush, outnumbered twenty to one, they fight to the death. Oliver begs Roland to sound his horn to summon the main army, but Roland is too proud. Oliver, like Patroclus with Achilles, hotly rebukes him for sacrificing so many to his pride, and Roland relents and, when it is too late, finally sounds it, "not for succor, but for vengeance." Charles hears the horn, but Ganelon insists that Roland is hunting. Finally they go back to the pass and find Roland, Oliver, and all the French knights dead.

In the manner of the great epics, the heroes are dramatic in their grief for the loss of a "companion." In the poignant lines of the original (Bédier's edition): "*Rollant li ber a pluret, sil duleset; / Jamais en tere n'orrez plus dolent hume.*" ("The brave Roland wept and lamented / never has the world known a more sorrowful man.") In what is perhaps the best English translation, Dorothy L. Sayers renders Roland's grief: "Sir, my companion, woe worth your valiant might! / Long years and days have we lived side by side, / Ne'er didst thou wrong me nor suffer wrong of mine. / Now thou art dead I grieve to be alive." Charlemagne's grief is even more ecstatic. He swoons and falls, weeps and tears out his white hair: "All my life in sorrow I must reign, / nor any day cease grieving and complaint."

There is no directly disabling female in the story, but the evil Ganelon comes into it through his relationship to Roland's mother, who thus passively introduces the traitor.

In her incisive commentary, Dorothy Sayers offers us a picture of "Nurture and Companionage" in the poem. The first we have already come across in the fostering of Achilles and Patroclus, and Cúchullain and Ferdia. Boys thus fostered together became "companions." This relationship was very strong, often overshadowing blood relationship. The Twelve Peers who accompanied Roland and Oliver and died with them, Sayers notes, are always given in pairs: Gerin and Gerier, Ives and Ivor, Orthon and Berenger, etc. "Intimacy and friendly rivalry" she says, prevailed through life, and, as the poem's great moments show, led to massive grief after death: grief of one companion for another and of the foster-father for them both.

Volsung Saga

In the interests of fairness, I am including a few words here on an epic that is low on male bonding. All the epics celebrate the individual deeds of the heroes, but some, like the Nordic tales of the Volsungs and Niblungs given to us in English by the great work of William Morris and his collaborator Eiríkr Magnússon, stand out in their individualism. They also, like the Irish epics, have strong, even dominant, female characters. The twelfth-century saga of the Volsungs, in both its prose and verse versions (the *Eddas*), is usually taken to be "about" the hero Sigurd (Wagner's Siegfried). Yet it perhaps could more easily be seen to be the story of his second wife Gudrun, and her fatal relationships with her mother Grimhild and the warrior maiden Brynhild. As in all the epics, there is no female bonding in evidence. The women are either passively attached to their males or fiendishly plotting to destroy them.

The story of the Volsungs is "about" male bonding that never gets off the ground. Sigurd, the son of Sigmund, has his whole future told to him by his mother's brother Grifir. Fortunately, the author does not tell us what this is, although throughout the tale various people, usually the wives, foretell the future, which is, of course, fixed by fate. Sigurd forms an early alliance with Regin the smith. But Regin is using Sigurd to kill his brother Fafnir, turned into a dragon to guard a treasure horde. After killing Fafner, Sigurd kills Regin. He then braves the Ring of Fire to find Brynhild, who gives him a love potion, and they swear eternal love. The poet of the *Edda* gives the women by far the best verse, and Brynhild sings to Sigurd of the power of words, of runes—sea-runes, ale-runes, help-runes, bough-runes, thought-runes.

The plot thickens as Sigurd finds his way to the Giukings (or Niblungs). King Giuki and Queen Grimhild have three sons, Gunnar, Hogni, and Guttorm, and a daughter, Gudrun. As the poet puts it: " Sigurd of yore / Sought the dwelling of Giuki, / As he fared, the young Volsung, / After fight won; / Troth he took, / From the two brethren; / Oath swore they betwixt them, / Those bold ones of deed." Note that the oath was sworn with only two of the brothers, Gunnar and Hogni; Guttorm must have been thought too young. Grimhild wants to have Sigurd for her daughter Gudrun, so she gives him yet another potion, which makes him forget Brynhild, and the two are married. Then, true to his oath, Sigurd sets out to help his blood-brother Gunnar find a bride, who is of course Brynhild. Using his magic helmet, Sigurd takes the form of Gunnar, rides through the fire, and wins Brynhild, who has sworn to marry the man that did so. Thus is the recipe for disaster set, for once Brynhild and Gunnar are married, Sigurd's memory returns.

Gudrun is disturbed by Sigurd's love for Brynhild and reveals to her the truth about her wooing. Brynhild is furious and distraught. She wants revenge and persuades Gunnar to break his oath and, with Hogni, kill Sigurd. But the henpecked brothers find a way out: Guttorm has not sworn the oath, so he can creep up in the night and kill Sigurd, who in turn kills him before dying. The first lay of Gudrun—her lamentation over the body of Sigurd—is interesting in that her female relatives gather to give her support and rebuke Brynhild, who, at the top of her voice, commits suicide, foretelling the rest of the tale with her dying words. She demands to be burnt on a pyre with Sigurd, which is done.

There Sigurd's story ends. His promising bond with the Giukings is brought to nothing by the machinations of Grimhild and the fury of Brynhild. But Grimhild is not done. She engineers the marriage of Gudrun to Brynhild's brother Atli, who covets the horde of gold. Atli tricks Gudrun's brothers to come to his hall and, after a furious fight, captures and kills them horribly: Hogni's heart is torn out while he lives, and Gunnar is fed to snakes, in the original "worm-hole." (Gudrun smuggles a harp to him, and playing it with his toes, he charms all the snakes but the fatal one.) Gudrun fights with her brothers but cannot save them, and she vows vengeance on Atli. She has two sons by him, whom she kills and feeds to him. Along with Hogni's son Niblung, she kills Atli. Her story ends the book, as with the sons of a third marriage she avenges the death of Swanhild, her daughter with Sigurd, trampled to death by horses. Finally, Odin, who had started the saga, ends it by ordering the death of the last of the Giukings.

These are the barest bones of the plot of this primaeval soap opera. I left out the incest of Sigmund and Signy, for example. But the themes we have been exploring are all there. Sigurd tries to form a "normal" male bond with the Giuking brothers. They swear their oaths and go through the by-now familiar routines. But the women sabotage the bond. Grimhild and Brynhild are the archetypes of disabling females. The mother seeks to advance the reproductive interests of her daughter, and Brynhild is thwarted in pursuit of her own. Gudrun, on the other hand, even though manipulated by her mother, is loyal to Sigurd and even to her treacherous brothers. She is effective in organizing her kinsmen for revenge against Atli and the killers of Sigurd's daughter. Gudrun sacrifices her own reproductive interests by killing her sons by Atli. In however convoluted a way—and this is a splendidly convoluted plot—the valiant Gudrun has to be counted an enabling female, and her selfless devotion contrasts dramatically with Brynhild's egregious self-concern.

But for a student of male bonding, this is a disappointing saga. The great lays of lamentation, the fine poetry (like the Hell Ride of Brynhild), and the massive grief and furious verse of deprivation belong to the women. The men, while brave warriors, are dim and malleable. Gunnar and Hogni die bravely, but their spineless treason of their blood brother, at a woman's instigation, leaves the male bond in tatters.

Conclusion

If Tiger is correct about the adaptational significance of the male bond, we are dealing with something other than just male friendship. For what is being argued is that the strength of feeling men have for each other is the equivalent in intensity and specificity of the sexual feeling men have for women or of the feelings parents have for their children. That is to say, this *menschkeit*, these "male sympathies" as we used to say in college brochures, are a genuine, specific human need. What we see in the epics and romances is that in a warrior society these emotions will be particularly favored and reinforced because of the warrior's crucial need for dependable male support. It is literally a matter of life and death: males who bond will have allies they can trust; it is that simple.

What comes through from these examples, perhaps more than anything else, is the intensity of emotional attachment and the terrible grief engendered by the death of a companion. The cultural situations are completely different from Sumer to Camelot, but they have this in common. Also in common is the subordinate, but often fatal, role of the female and the strife between the needs of the heterosexual and homosexual bond.

This raises the question of whether the male bond in these cases involves physical homosexuality. The answer is that it may or may not. Certainly it did among the classical Greeks and among the Romans, with the qualification noted by Paul Veyne, that the passive position in the partnership could only be assumed by an inferior (1982). We are well aware that in Greece, marriage, while a duty and often a pleasure, often took second place to the physical love between men. But Socrates and his friends, taking the middle ground, poked fun equally at men who were totally uxorious and those who were preoccupied solely with boys. There is certainly no evidence in the *Iliad* that Achilles and Patroclus were lovers. There does not seem to be any suggestion that Malory meant us to see the Arthurian knights as homosexual. Indeed, a major part of their problem was the strength of their heterosexual attachments, which were fatal to the male group, as was also the case with the Volsungs. Those contemporary critics who see all literary instances of male affection for males as proof of "repressed homosexuality" have the same problem as other conspiracy theorists: their hypothesis is invulnerable to disproof; we have no way of knowing if they are wrong. The safer view surely is that the male bond could *involve* sex, but it was not *about* sex, as the bond with the female was. Without sex between male and female there could be no reproduction, but the male group reproduces first by recruitment (knighthood is a kind of cloning)—only secondarily by sex.

Sons, for example, are rare in these stories. Galahad is an interesting exception, but even there, Launcelot's bonds with Arthur, Tristram, Gareth, and Gawaine are stronger than the bonds with his son. The typical relationship between males of different generations is between a man and his foster father, and a man and his mother's brother—who can be one and the same. A son, particularly one like Mordred who can pass as a maternal nephew, is a dubious blessing. Foster-brothers often are preferred to real brothers, and most often the bonds are between two strangers who fight and then embrace each other for life. Someone you have tested is a known quantity. Insofar as this binds males who are not related, it cannot be explained by inclusive fitness theory alone. This would handle the maternal uncle, perhaps, but not the "companions." It is rather perhaps an elementary instance of what Trivers called "reciprocal altruism," in which genetic strangers are assimilated to kinship roles, typically through the device of fostering. Fostering might seem at first to pose the same problem as sterile castes in insects. Why should anyone invest in someone else's genes? It works, however, as long as everyone does it: I raise your sons; you raise mine.

The women, as we have seen, play either beneficial roles, like Shamhat, Wealhtheow, Thetis, and Gudrun; passively destructive roles, like Helen, Briseis or Guinever; or positively disabling roles like Ishtar, Medh, Morgan le Fay, Grimhild, Brynhild, and Grendel's mother. The women's complex qualities and characters are certainly not exhausted by the distinctions that lie along the enabling-disabling continuum. But we are looking rather narrowly at their function vis-à-vis the male bond. For the epic poets, the women revolve around the male bond, and the women only make sense to the structure of the epic if we see them as creating situations that affect the bond for good or evil.

In contrast to the men, the women do not bond with each other. On the contrary, they are either passively attached to a male or, more usually, locked in conflict over a male or seeking to advance the interests of their offspring at the expense of males. It is not that women cannot appear as towering figures in these stories; they do so, in all their wonder, from Ishtar, through Medh, to Brynhild. But they do not appear as female bands, and they do not form female-bonded groups. The earls' wives who gather to support Gudrun and rebuke Brynhild are the nearest thing we get, however transient, to an active female group. If the men in these epics fear the women, it is as they love them: as individuals, not as cabals or as female conspiracies.

The need for males to bond may be part of the hard-wiring of behavior, but this should not be confused with "determinism." Only the need is programmed; the form that the bonding will take will vary with the external circumstances, as is the case with the heterosexual bond and as is, indeed, the case with all genotypes in nature: the phenotype is always problematical. Thus, the need for males to bond with each other as strongly as they bond with females, if not more so, is clearly most obvious in warrior societies like those of the epics. But is it simply an artifact of those societies, disappearing under conditions of trade and peace? Would the literature of less warlike societies reflect the same themes? I think the answer is that it would, but of course the emphases and outcomes will be differ-ent. This is the subject of another investigation.

I have committed myself to the view that the bond, being a genuine need, will persist. While the details may differ, it will continue to find its place, often through comedy and gentle satire (see the quite perfect contemporary sitcom *Two and a Half Men*) in the literature and drama of societies far removed from the war-rior ideal. And even in these increasingly androgynous societies, the warrior virtues, and the male bonding that goes with them, often continue to get a lively representation in literature and the arts, the popular media, and even (or espe-cially) in sports. It is at the heart of the success of the *Godfather* novels and movies and Patrick O'Brian's *Master and Commander* series. It received eloquent treatment in the superb but underappreciated remake of the bible of aristocratic male honor, *The Four Feathers*. In *The Man Who Would Be King*, Sean Connery and Michael Caine gave perhaps the most perfect rendition of the theme, in Kipling's story of two ordinary British soldiers bonded through Freemasonry and vaunting ambition. To reinforce the bond, they foreswear women until such time as they conquer a trans-Himalayan nation only to have the desire for a woman (a passively dis-abling woman) bring them down and lose them their hard-won kingdom. The reader will no doubt be thinking of many other examples.

A good evolutionary prediction would be: while social conditions may cause the male bond to be muted, they will never extinguish it. As the current saying goes: "It's a guy thing."

Notes

1. Trivers 1972.
2. See Fox 2000.
3. Fox 1983.
4. Fox 1997.
5. N. Singh 1997.
6. Kinsella 1969. It is worth noting that Kinsella's translation makes beauti-ful reading in English, but perhaps smooths over some of the roughness of the Old Irish. For a more literal rendition, see the versions in Cross and Slover, *Ancient Irish Tales* (1936).
7. *Beowulf*. All *Beowulf* quotes are from Heaney's translation (2000).
8. All *Iliad* quotes are from Fitzgerald's translation (2004).
9. These are summarized in Moncrieff 1978.

PART II

The Evolutionary Riddle of Art

The two articles in this section propose different solutions to the evolutionary riddle of art, especially narrative art. (For different perspectives see Carroll, D. S. Wilson, part 1.) The puzzle is roughly this: in ancestral environments characterized by intense competition for survival and reproduction, how could the evolutionary process "allow" any animal to spend (waste?) so much time producing, elaborating, and consuming art—time that could be spent pursuing mates and other quarry? This puzzle is akin to the evolutionary problem of altruism, which has dominated so much of evolutionary thinking over the last several decades. The core problem posed by art and altruism is the same: How do we explain behavior that produces such ostensibly unfavorable cost-benefit ratios? How can self-sacrifice evolve if the sacrificer is, by definition, disadvantaged relative to selfish competitors? How could the artist or aficionado successfully compete with individuals who eschewed cave painting, axe-handle elaboration, and storytelling in favor of hunting, gathering, pursuing mates, lavishing investment on offspring, cultivating allies, and other behaviors that directly augment survival and reproduction?

Evolutionists have been increasingly attracted to this quandary, and debates over the evolutionary role (or lack thereof) of literature and other forms of art will figure still more prominently in coming years. So far, evolutionists have argued that art "behaviors" are the result of direct adaptation (that is, they emerged because they promoted the survival and reproduction of our ancestors) or that they are evolutionary side effects that do not themselves promote survival and reproduction. The articles in this section provide overviews of the existing literature on the subject and propose two different solutions to the problem of art. While both of these authors may have hit upon part of the correct answer, their answers are quite different and, therefore, cannot both be correct. This is not inappropriate. The thinking on this subject remains at a relatively early stage, where the problems are being defined and potential solutions proposed and weighed. To bring this work fully into the scientific realm, the next wave of research must begin to devise and conduct empirical tests of the competing hypotheses.

Evolutionary Theories of Art

Brian Boyd

The Enigma of Art

Although discussing religion, Daniel Dennett could easily have had art in mind when he wrote: "Any phenomenon that apparently exceeds the functional cries out for an explanation. We don't marvel at a creature doggedly grubbing in the earth with its nose, for we figure it is seeking its food; if, however, it regularly interrupts its rooting with somersaults, we want to know why. What benefits are presumed (rightly or wrongly) to accrue to this excess activity?"[1] Nor do we marvel too much at the bone spear-throwers that helped Paleolithic hunters fell prey at greater distances, but when we see that the handle of a spear-thrower has been exquisitely carved to represent a leaping horse or an ibex turning to watch herself give birth, we want to know why.[2] How can a species as successful as Homo sapiens have evolved to devote so much time and energy to "somersaults" like sculpture, song, and story, rather than stalking steadily after food or mates?

In trying to explain fiction, John Tooby and Leda Cosmides note that the "appetite for the true" that we could expect in any natural data-gathering system like the human mind "fails to predict a large part of the human appetite for information": most people prefer novels to textbooks, fiction film to documentary.[3] In explaining art in general, and our intense pleasure in engaging with art, we need to explain why an "appetite for the useful" fails to predict so much of human activity, from a tribeswoman weaving designs on a basket to a townswoman watching a TV soap opera.

Unless we revert to myths of divine creation, evolution must be part of any complete account of the human, including human art. Many needlessly fear that evolutionary explanations of the human imply "genetic determinism" and the end to hopes of transforming human lives for the better. If evolution can help explain art—human behavior at its freest and most creative—any fears that it implies determinism or denies culture should be dispelled once and for all. No one was ever "genetically determined" to write or read something as unprecedented as *Ulysses*.

Defining Art

But what do we mean by art? What do we include as art? Modern aesthetics argues about what human products count as works of art in response to the challenges to the boundaries and definitions of art posed by modern artists—like Andy Warhol with his Brillo boxes, to cite a much-discussed example. An evolutionary approach tends to see art not primarily in terms of works worth gallery display or literary awards but as a widespread human behavior stretching from ocher body-painting to O'Keeffe.

In this sense, art covers a huge range of activities, from a child making up stories, humming, or drawing in the sand to Tolstoy, Mahler, or Zeng Jing. Let me suggest what they have in common: Art is the attempt to engage attention *by transforming objects and/or actions in order to appeal to species-wide cognitive preferences for the sake of the response this evokes. The more (1) the appeal is purely to these preferences, and the more (2) it operates within some tradition of appealing to (and, hence, elaborating and refining) such preferences, and (3) the more skilled and successful is the attempt to engage attention and evoke a rich response, the more centrally it will be art.*

We engage each other's attention, of course, in casual conversation or in information exchange, but even here there may be elements of artfulness to the degree that we use images, allusions, jokes, mimicked intonations, or ironic deflations as we vivify gossip through selecting, highlighting, animating, reenacting, or stretching the truth toward fiction for the sake of holding an audience. In the metaphors and metonymies and pungent apothegms of Johnson's conversation or the freewheeling amplitude of Coleridge's, or in the dense imagery of Keats's letters or Flaubert's, social exchange shades toward pure art, but not as close as a Keats ode or a Flaubert fiction. For the poem or the fiction has been designed to appeal to still more of our preferences for pattern, situation, character, or story and thereby to catch and hold the attention of any audience, far beyond the naturally shared focus of a moment, a situation, a friendship.

Art, Nature, and Culture

Traditional views of art have tended to see art as reflecting nature, especially human nature, all the way from Plato's discomfort with, or Aristotle's admiration for, mimesis to Shakespeare's or Stendhal's images of art as holding the mirror up to nature. Common-sense traditional views have easily shaded into transcendental views of art, widespread because religious beliefs have been so pervasive and because both artists and their patrons in state or church benefit by nurturing a sense of awe at art's putatively divine origins and power.

The pervasive contemporary critical inclination often known as Theory, but recently labeled more meaningfully Cultural Critique,[4] rightly critiques traditional common-sense and transcendental views, pointing out that the nature, human nature, or supernature that art was supposed to reflect was often merely what was assumed of these things from within a local cultural perspective. Roland Barthes, for example, criticizes "the mystification which transforms petit-bourgeois culture into universal nature."[5] But such critics' critiques also mislead, since they jump to the conclusion that human nature is either nonexistent or is to be explained by culture alone, which they assume detaches human nature from biology. If cultural anthropology has shown that human nature is much more diverse than any one society had assumed, evolutionary biology and anthropology have also begun to discover that culture exists in many animal species (dialects and fashions in bird and whale song, for instance, or in chimpanzee traditions of toolmaking), that there is a universal human nature, and that in humans, too, culture is not *apart from* nature but *a part of* nature. And as many have noted, "explaining" human cultural variation by the power of culture is too circular to be an explanation at all.[6]

In the study of art, stress on cultural difference has even led to the denial that those in other cultures, or in Western culture before, say, the eighteenth century, have such a notion as art. But as Stephen Davies observes, the very concept that there is no non-Western art is a Western one; as Denis Dutton argues, neither the ancient Greeks nor Sepik carvers in Papua New Guinea have a single word to match modern Western "art," but both peoples practice and have concepts of art akin to some of the *many* notions of art currently available in the West.[7] It takes considerable effort to decipher another language, but art can be appreciated and appropriated rapidly across cultures, from Dürer in the 1520s encountering treasures from Mexico and commenting that he had "never seen in all my life anything that has moved my heart so much" or Goethe reading Chinese novels and observing that "These people think and feel much as we do" to Japanese audiences enraptured by Shakespeare and Beethoven.[8] In the nineteenth and twentieth centuries Maori and Sepik carvers picked up Western tools and techniques as keenly as Gauguin or Picasso borrowed from non-Western cultures.

Evolution and Art

Evolutionary theories of art consider art in the light of the first fully scientific attempt to understand human nature. They can ask why art exists at all, how it relates to precursors of art in other species, why it is so prevalent in human behavior. Why *do* we spend so much of our time in sensory somersaults?

There are many evolutionary accounts of art. I will focus on four of the fore-most theories of art as possibly a biological adaptation and their most prominent proponents: (1) art is not an adaptation but a *byproduct* of the evolution of human brains by natural selection (Steven Pinker); (2) art is a product not of natural selection but of *sexual selection* (Geoffrey Miller); (3–4) art is an *adaptation*, its chief function *social cohesion* (Ellen Dissanayake) or individual mental *organization* (John Tooby and Leda Cosmides).

In evolutionary theory, an "adaptation" is a biological trait, physiological, psychological or behavioral, shaped by natural selection to enhance the fitness of members of a species.[9] For a trait to constitute an adaptation there must be clear evidence of a fitness-enhancing *function* and of complex *design* toward achieving it.

Many functions of all sorts have been proposed for art over the years by artists, philosophers, and anthropologists puzzled and impressed by the human drive to produce and consume art.[10] But in evolutionary theory, the notion is distinct and strict: "function" means *design* that increases reproductive or survival advantage.

Those who study the human in the light of evolution do so from a wide range of backgrounds. At one end of the spectrum are those close to artificial intelligence and cognitive psychology, who see minds as designed to solve information-processing problems and, hence, in evolutionary psychology, who see aspects of the human mind as having evolved to solve particular problems our forebears had to face in the Pleistocene era. How can we reverse engineer this or that aspect of the mind, they ask, to discover the function it would have served under ancestral conditions?

But others interested in the evolution of the human who come from back-grounds in biology such as animal psychology or primatology often prefer not a single-minded concentration on function but answers to the four questions that ethologist Niko Tinbergen felt necessary to explain an adaptation: Why? (What *function* does it have; how does it help the species survive or reproduce?); How? (What *mechanism* does it operate by?); Whence? (What is its *origin* in the evolutionary history of the species?); and When? (When does it *develop* in the individual?).[11] To be comprehensive on evolutionary grounds, an adaptive explanation of art needs to consider all these criteria.

Evolutionary explanations of art, however, need not claim that art is itself an adaptation. Steven Pinker issues this crisp caveat: "For the same reason it is wrong to write off language, stereo vision, and the emotions as evolutionary accidents—namely their universal, complex, reliably developing, well-engineered, reproduction-promoting design—it is wrong to invent functions for activities that lack design merely because we want to ennoble them with the imprimatur of biological adaptiveness."[12] Art may be explained as a product of the evolved human mind without the further claim that art is itself an adaptation.

Adaptationist or not, a worthwhile evolutionary explanation of art needs not only to account for the biological, psychological, and behavioral evidence but also to add both depth and detail to our engagement with art. It should be able to explain not only how and why art in general exists but also why particular modes, traditions, and works take the form and have the impact that they do.

Art as Adaptation: Attention

"Your brief, should you decide to accept it," my editors wrote me, "is to sum up existing evolutionary theories of art. Because you favor no particular theory, we can trust you to be neutral and objective." After warning them that I was developing my own theory, I accepted the brief. But after trying to present only the theories of others, I found that aspects of my assessments so presupposed my theory that I had no choice but to outline it first. To summarize it as I have the others, it is this: art is an adaptation whose functions are *shaping and sharing attention*, and, arising from that, fostering *social cohesion* and *creativity*.

Although much evolutionary psychology stresses a single function for a single adaptation, there is no reason to exclude multiple functions. An elephant's trunk evolved so that it could sniff, dislodge, grasp, pull, deliver, push, twist, caress, trumpet, siphon, and squirt.[13] Although much evolutionary psychology settles on adaptations at a single level, the individual or the group, there is also no reason not to accept the multilevel selection that David Sloan Wilson has argued so persuasively for.[14] The explanation I propose is both multifunctional and multilevel.

To explain art we have to attend to attention. Art dies without attention, as has often been seen both without and within evolutionary explanation.[15] But except for Ellen Dissanayake's *Art and Intimacy*, even evolutionary studies of art have not investigated the special role shared attention plays in human lives from infancy onward.[16] All organisms must attend to the opportunities and threats that matter to them, as far as their minds and senses allow. But something peculiar happened to attention in humans.

In chimpanzees and bonobos, the color contrast in the eye between sclera and pupil is greater than in other apes and monkeys, and in humans the contrast is still greater, a sign that the ability to monitor the direction of others' attention has mattered more to humans than even to our nearest relatives.[17] Monkey babies lack the stimulus tools to capture and hold their mothers' attention. Chimpanzee mothers rarely gaze at their babies or communicate with them, though they will respond when babies initiate play by biting, and will tickle and laugh in tender reply.[18] But human mothers and infants attend to one another from the first. Infants' eyes after birth can focus only about eight inches away, the distance between the mother's breast and her face, and unlike infants in other species they maintain eye contact while suckling. Newborns preferentially attend to faces and under laboratory conditions have been shown to be capable of imitating humans, but not animated models, within an hour of birth.[19]

So it continues, in infant and adult. Out of the early features of human attention, especially the capacity for shared attention, humans, uniquely, develop a full theory of mind, a capacity that by the fifth year allows children to appreciate what others can infer from their situation. The unique sharing of precise attention among humans ultimately leads to language and the capacity to pinpoint attention even to the extent of directing others to something absent and perhaps unreal, impossible, or unprecedented and to an ability to understand multiple-order intentionality, to conceive what A thinks of B's thoughts of C's thoughts of D's.[20]

All intelligent animals can focus on the immediate present, expectations of the immediate future, and perhaps some recollections of their personal past. But we alone, because of our special capacity to share and sharpen attention, can focus our minds together on particular events of the past as experienced or witnessed by ourselves or others, living or dead, on possibilities and impossibilities, and on events hypothetical, counterfactual, and fictional. Most animals cannot afford *not* to attend to their immediate environment and cannot easily reason beyond it. But the human capacity to think beyond the immediate allows us an extraordinary power to test ideas and to turn them through the vast space of possibility.

Evolution could not build into even an intelligent animal either an organ of truth, to soak up the discoveries of science, or an organ of useful design, to produce the tools of technology. It has no foresight; it can select only on the basis of current variation, and it can construct cognition only using input from each species' immediate environment. But by slowly expanding the human capacity for sharing attention, and by making it pleasurable for us to explore possibilities *not* limited by the here and now, evolution has gradually lured us into finding ways to search more and more widely for truth and design.

My evolutionary theory of art, then, is this. In humans, social attention, which had been developing in importance in the primate line, especially among the apes, became still more important: earlier, more intense, more interactive, more flexible, more precise, more powerful.[21] Because shared attention had come to matter so much, especially as infants were born less fully developed and remained longer in childhood, the ability to share and shape the attention of others by appeals to common cognitive preferences led to the development of art: to behaviors that focus not on the immediate needs of the here and now but on directing attention and engaging emotion for its own sake, even toward distant realities and new possibilities.

Art therefore has an immediate *individual* function, since keeping up with attention is essential to us (the threat of cutting off attention is a human universal, and the risks of exclusion severe)[22] and since commanding attention is an advantage (it correlates closely with status).[23] It also has a *social* function, in increasing social attunement and social cohesion. Societies that could coordinate more closely could outcompete those with less coordination or more internal competition, and there is good reason to think that on average societies with shared costume, song, dance, and heroic or admonitory story could coordinate better than those without. And art has a further individual *and* social function in creativity, which leads not only to the triumphs of tribal art or the flourishing of Florence but also to the emergence of religion and, eventually, the invention of science.

But this is not the place to elaborate. What of other evolutionary accounts of art?

Art as By-Product

Even those who accept that evolution has adapted the human mind in highly specific ways can argue that art is no adaptation but only a by-product of the brain's complexity. Steven Pinker has famously explained "how the mind works," how it has been adapted by evolution rather than left a "blank slate." Once on the verge of choosing an engineering career, he sees evolutionary psychology as "reverse engineering" the mind, taking apart its components to determine their function, but he finds no evidence that the mind has any specific design for art. He therefore rates art as not an adaptation but an evolutionary by-product.[24]

For Pinker we have not only, like other species, our own special suite of evolved cognitive preferences but also an evolved capacity to design artifacts to ends we desire. Narrative, he concedes, may serve an adaptive function in enabling us to develop scenarios to test possible courses of action and their consequences without risking real-world harm.[25] Otherwise, he considers art a by-product, in which we deploy our capacity for design to deliver high-energy treats to our cognitive tastes, to concoct "cheesecake" for the mind, or to develop "a useless technology for pressing our pleasure buttons" by "defeat[ing] the locks that safeguard" them.[26]

Pinker rightly stresses the role of our cognitive preferences, which did not evolve *for* but are appealed *to* in art. Here, indeed, lies a rich research program for the new sciences of the mind: just what are the preferences that music, visual art, and literature appeal to, how and why have they evolved, and how are they traded off against one another in art?[27] In his most in-depth examination of a single art, Pinker summarizes the work of other psychologists and offers additional suggestions about the mental mechanisms behind the pleasures of music.[28]

When Pinker calls art "a cheesecake for the mind," he implies that just as we have developed technologies to satisfy our evolved taste preference for sweetness—valuable at a time when high-calorie foods had to be actively sought out—so in art we have developed technologies to satisfy other cognitive preferences for rich aural or visual or social information. His metaphor becomes a motif throughout his major examination of the arts and is meant to provoke. But as he often does, Pinker rhetorically substitutes a particular preference which evolution could never have selected for, for a general one which it could. A Porsche or a linen suit may help to secure a partner, he remarks elsewhere, but is not an adaptation. No, but capacities to display and assess signs of status have evolved in many species, as in humans.[29] And if we compare our taste for art in general with our taste not for cheesecake but for sweetness in general, art may seem much less improbable as an adaptation.

Pinker's metaphors—cheesecake, pleasure-buttons, or music as "a cocktail of recreational drugs that we ingest through the ear"[30]—foreground art as consumption. But before we respond to art, we first have to generate it. In modern society ready-made art is as available as ready-made cheesecake, but for most of human history and in most societies, art results from the efforts of all, as people weave and carve, sing and dance, tell and reenact stories. The compulsion to engage in art needs to explain the compulsion to *make* art as well as to enjoy it. Art has usually involved intense effort, and the cheesecake metaphor fails to explain why in every society that effort has seemed worthwhile.

Art as cheesecake seems an indulgent extra. But if art were so superfluous, how could it not have been selected against? Why would groups without art, and therefore with much more time and energy for practical purposes, not have outcompeted, outbred, and ultimately outlasted their more self-indulgent neighbors? The fact that all known societies engage in art[31] suggests that it has advantages strong enough for a predisposition to art to have become part of the design of the human mind.

The cheesecake metaphor has a specific evolutionary overtone: that art might even be maladaptive, just as our once adaptive appetite for sweet and fat now threatens us with an epidemic of obesity. Paul Hernadi replies to Pinker's implication by suggesting that it explains only "why too many literary calories may clog our mental arteries" *today*, when we can buy novels and videos a few supermarket aisles past the cheesecakes. But turned around the other way, Hernadi notes, the metaphor might suggest that "well-adapted early humans were pursuing scarce mind-sharpening opportunities for protoliterary experience with almost as much gusto as they pursued meals rich in fats and sugars": the arts *were* adaptive.[32] In fact, they seem to remain so. Despite the increasing abundance of art, despite complaints about the dumbing down of culture, despite children having ever more music, story, and art available in print, on screen, on disc, no epidemic of intellectual obesity threatens us, and as the Flynn effect notes, IQ levels have risen with each decade since they were first measured.[33]

Pinker explains art as our applying our design ability to feed our inbuilt preferences. But why does he assume that our ability to design developed only in purely instrumental modes? The ibex on the spear-thrower found at Mas d'Azil in France required far more design skill than the spear-thrower itself. It seems at least arguable, and in fact highly likely, that art has helped ratchet up our interest in, capacity for, and confidence in design as it has helped us to think beyond the given and to generate the new. A society whose members wove elaborate and superfluous designs because they were pleasing was in a better position to think up a woven eel-trap than a putative society focused exclusively on utilitarian technological solutions could think up decoration for clothing, containers, or coverings.

In *How the Mind Works* Pinker challenged those who might argue that art is an adaptation. Five years later, in *The Blank Slate*, he reaffirmed his position but stressed that "Whether art is an adaptation or a by-product or a mixture of the two, it is deeply rooted in our mental faculties."[34] The limitation of Pinker's treatment of art lies not in his treating art as a by-product but in an insouciance that results from his ignoring the link between artist and audience, his overlooking the role of shared attention in human life. By detaching seemingly pointless design from seemingly indulgent delight, he fails to explain why anyone should have ever wanted to make prodigious efforts to move others, or why we should all care so much about being so moved.

Art as Sexually Selected

Art can seem as showy and superfluous as a peacock's tail. That amazing appendage costs its bearer energy to produce and maintain and makes the peacock both more conspicuous to enemies and less able to elude them. How could ornaments like that have evolved in a competitive world? Charles Darwin realized that such extravagant caprices, such somatic "somersaults," appeared to challenge his theory of natural selection, but he explained them through his additional theory of *sexual selection*.[35] Males can fight each other for access to females, developing in size (like a bull elephant seal) or armaments (like the horns of a stag or a stag beetle), or they can compete to attract females. In the latter case the mere *sensory biases* of the female could, over many generations, shape the appearance or actions of the male, producing striking colors or forms (like the peacock's tail) or behaviors like song (in many songbirds), dance (in lekking birds) and bower-making (in bowerbirds).

Sexual selection theory has been extended and clarified in the twentieth century.[36] The theory of *runaway sexual selection* explains that if peahens, say, preferred to mate with peacocks with showier tails, the male tendency to produce *and* the female tendency to prefer elaborate tails would both be passed on and would compound one another until survival pressures set a limit. The concept of *fitness indicators* suggests that sexual selection might often reflect not arbitrary biases but factors that outwardly manifest some inner advantage. As recent findings suggest, only the healthiest of animals, such as those freest of parasites or commanding the richest territories, can display the brightest colors or sing the loudest songs.

Robert Trivers's theory of *parental investment* further explains why it is usually the female, not the male, which is the choosier sex. Whichever sex invests more time and energy in producing offspring (usually the female, since by definition the female is the sex with the larger gamete) has more to lose in producing offspring with a partner with poor genes; whichever sex has the lesser investment (usually the male) has more to gain by being chosen by as many partners as possible. Males chosen by many females can have huge reproductive success, since their investment in any partner can be brief and they can move on to others; but males chosen by none may fail to produce offspring at all. Because of the great variance in male success, there is intense pressure on males for access to females, whether by fighting other males or by attracting females.[37]

Darwin himself had little to say about the origins of human art, but he thought that in humans as in other species "high cost, apparent uselessness, and manifest beauty usually indicated that a behavior had a hidden courtship function."[38] He ventured ("not too plausibly," comments Pinker) that music developed "for the sake of charming the opposite sex" and that body adornments formed a beginning of human visual art.[39] Although others have suggested in passing that art may owe something to sexual selection,[40] Geoffrey Miller is the first to propose on a major scale that sexual selection has been the driving force behind the expansion of the human mind and higher human behavior: intelligence, inventiveness, art, humor, kindness.

Miller presents himself as an evolutionary hard man: "Adaptation can arise through natural selection for survival advantage, or sexual selection for reproductive advantage. Basically, that's it."[41] He notes that evolutionary psychology has almost always searched for the former and overlooked the latter, and he seeks to redress the balance. He rejects other approaches as being insufficiently rigorous. Identifying a plausible origin of, say, music, is insufficient to explain an adaptation: "Evolution just does not work like that. Instead of speculating about precursors, the adaptationist approach puts music in a functional, cost-benefit framework and asks theories for just one thing: *show me the fitness!*"[42]

Hard on others, Miller proves soft on the sexual selection he so favors. So convinced is he of its power that he thinks it can explain almost anything about us: "any feature one is even capable of noticing about somebody else . . . could have been sexually selected."[43] *Could* have been. But to demonstrate that this or that feature actually *has* been sexually selected requires more than quickly dismissing other alternatives such as natural or social selection.

Miller suggests that among the higher apes, one species could have been sexually selected for muscle mass, becoming gorillas, another for constant sex, becoming bonobos, a third for creative intelligence, becoming humans.[44] He does not note that ecology and diet can explain the large size and the harem-guarding sexual system of gorillas or the open sexual and social system of bonobos.[45] When he claims that human minds "are entertaining, intelligent, creative, and articulate far beyond the demands of surviving on the plains of Pleistocene Africa" and that psychology has been wrong to view them as computers that learn to solve problems rather than "entertainment system[s] that evolved to attract sexual partners," he neither explains why creatures in the plains of Pleistocene Africa would suddenly develop such odd preferences nor considers the huge energy costs of a larger brain.[46] Intelligence would help *any* species respond to its environment more flexibly, but few lineages have evolved it to an advanced degree because of the steep cost and the lack of intense selection pressure—which is exactly what hominids were under on the African plains, being so much slower on two legs than the four-legged prey that speedy predators could already catch. *Preference* for intelligence would come only when intelligence had already become central to a species' mode of existence.

Miller impatiently dismisses the power of *social* as compared to sexual selection in human evolution. Sexual selection indeed has an immediate bearing on whose genes are recombined with whose; but in a species as highly social as humans, social selection affects us throughout life, impacting on our survival to reproductive age, our chances during sexual selection (on average a male achieving higher status through social selection by other males has better sexual prospects than one with lower status), and our chances of supporting children to *their* reproductive success. Miller can write almost as if we did not engage with one another except to mate. After arguing, not implausibly, that the size and shape of the human penis and breasts are sexually selected, he observes that we stare at faces instead of the penis or breasts because these are the most complex and richest indicators of possible mutations: "We pick the one part of the body where fitness differences are most manifest, and regard that as the seat of personhood"[47]—as if we did not have to watch the faces of others to predict their intentions, moment by moment, from infancy to old age, to select whom to engage with and on what terms.

As parental investment theory explains, males can compete over anything: even, as Dissanayake notes, who can pee the highest.[48] With so many potential means of display at hand, males' capacity for competitive display explains little about behavior as biologically improbable as carving likenesses or composing epics.

Miller notes that "male pigeons harass female pigeons with relentless cooing and strutting. If the females go away, the male displays stop. If the female comes back, the males start again."[49] The very difference between pigeon pouting and human art should give him pause. If art were sexually selected, this would predict that it is overwhelmingly male and directed to females, it begins only with puberty, it peaks just before mate selection, and it diminishes drastically afterward. Miller does adduce statistics to show that rock and jazz musicians produce most records in early maturity,[50] but mothers of all cultures sing to infants; infants prefer their mother's singing to their father's; infants of both sexes engage in cooing and singing, clapping, and dancing as soon as they can; adolescent girls go wild over all-female bands like the Spice Girls or Destiny's Child; Hokusai, who in his seventies and eighties adopted the nom de plume Gakyô-rôjin, Old Man Mad with Painting, was still producing masterpieces in his ninetieth year and pleaded on his deathbed for more time: "With even five more years . . . I could become a true artist."[51]

While males strut, females select. If they select according to sensory biases on the basis of caprice and chance initial conditions, as sexual selection theory allows, this would offer little opportunity to *explain* the particular features of forms and works of art except to record a succession of arbitrary inclinations. If, on the other hand (Miller hesitates to choose between alternatives, so long as they support sexual selection), females select according to fitness indicators, can *this* explain art? Miller hopefully proposes that artistic talent might be a reliable fitness indicator. Blind Homer, castrated Farinelli, deaf Beethoven, syphilitic Schubert, manic Schumann, epileptic Dostoyevsky, neurotic Proust, psychotic Woolf?[52] "Imagine a tribe of hominids," writes Miller, "half of them male and half female, all single, all just reaching sexual maturity at the same time. Some males have higher fitness than other males, and they advertise their fitness using fitness indicators such as vigorous dancing, intelligent conversing, or realistic cave-painting."[53] Miller here shows little sense of either hominid social life or of art—of what it might actually take for a species to develop the capacity, taste, traditions, means, and occasions for realistic cave painting.

In insisting on fitness, Miller rejects questions of origins. In fact the identification of a pathway is a necessary part of any complete evolutionary explanation, and in the case of music, Steven Brown shows that the most complex song outside humans, both in songbirds and in other primates, arises not from courtship but in the maintenance of territory and relationships by several species of monogamous duetting tropical songbirds and by gibbons. He notes that duetting resembles human music in several ways that "cannot be accounted for by a courtship hypothesis of music": first, "responsorial, antiphonal, polyphonic and homophonic singing. . . . [which] greatly increases the potential complexity of acoustic signals"; second, both sexes are singers and "make more or less equivalent contributions to the song"; third, "duetting is cooperative and coordinated, rather than competitive or disjoint. Gibbon couples place a high premium on maintaining tight coordination and restart a duet if the appropriate level of coordination is not achieved. . . . Duetting is not a contest but a display of cooperative strength"; fourth, duetting "is involved in defending year-round territories . . . , just as in many human tribes and bands," and serves as "a highly ritualized 'keep out' signal accompanied by exaggerated physical displays"; and fifth, it plays "a significant role not only in defending territories but in maintaining social bonds." Brown adds that "none of the known primate calls is thought to be directly involved in courtship. Primates do not seem to exploit vocalization for courtship purposes, but instead rely on visual, olfactory and kinetic cues. Courtship calls are rare to nonexistent in hominoids, whereas territorial calls are ancestral to the entire group of species."[54]

Brown's examination of analogies (functional equivalents in other taxa) and homologies (structural similarities in closely related taxa) offers a very different approach from the strict adaptationist line that Miller advocates. Not only does Brown's ethological approach respect biological detail and analogues to precursors of human behaviors in other animals, it also respects the peculiarities of a human art.[55] Brown can show that qualities like pitch blending and isometric rhythms, central to music, can be explained by the need to coordinate sound between more than one participant but not by individual display.[56] Recent evidence even suggests that music *reduces* sexual inclination: singing *lowers* men's and *raises* women's testosterone levels, a result compatible with a cooperative but not a competitive account of music's origins.[57]

Miller's search for evidence in support of his hypothesis, and the search for counter-evidence his statistical work has inspired in Brown and others, are both welcome ongoing research programs. There is no doubt that sexual selection does operate in *some* ways among humans. Wodaabe men in Nigeria and Niger are chosen by their women in the human equivalent of a lek dance and are unusually tall with strikingly big eyes, white teeth, and straight noses.[58] Such a stark example stands out by its difference from the human norm, but over thousands of generations sexual selection no doubt *has* played an important part in human life, especially, as Darwin and Richard Dawkins suggest, in the differentiation of superficial racial characteristics like face and hair,[59] and it may also serve as one factor in human art, especially visual art.

Ocher appears to have been sought for body decoration from as early as 120,000 years ago, and other body modifications, such as hairstyling, tattooing, scarification, and body piercing and the like have been practiced around the world for tens of thousands of years.[60] As the recent fashion for body piercing in Western countries highlights, such activity peaks at the ages of maximum reproductive opportunity. It makes biological sense that the visual arts should have started with the kind of display of the body most likely to have a sexual payoff. But notice here the difference from sexual selection in other species. In prehistoric times, before mirrors, and even now in the case of tattooing and other modifications, body and facial adornment often had to be not an individual practice but a social one. Songbirds do not chorus in support of their rivals, and bowerbirds do not help other males to construct their bowers. But from an early time, even at the closest to sexual selection we find in the arts, cooperation seems also to have been present in our highly social species. And as Kathryn Coe notes, elaborate body decoration in most societies serves primarily as a mark of affiliation and group identification.[61]

Marek Kohn and Steven Mithen have proposed that the knapping of Acheulian hand axes may be an even earlier, and sexually selected, precursor of visual art. The sheer number of hand axes found in some sites, the proportion that under microscopic examination show little or no sign of use, the high and perhaps excessive degree of symmetry and finish, and the existence of forms too large or small for apparent use, all suggest strongly that hand axes may have been refined to a degree far beyond need, in a way best explained in terms of sexual or social selection: as a display to others of prowess and judgment. Notice that this proposal, which Miller naturally endorses, has a detail absent in Miller's own arguments and reveals an awareness of the slow increments by which the first impulse of the visual arts may have developed.[62]

Art as sexual display does not explain *nothing* about art. But the very flexibility of human behavior suggests that sexual selection has been an extra gear for art, not the engine itself. In our species, unlike in peacocks or bowerbirds, there are scores of different criteria, many uncorrelated and some contradictory, by which females can choose male partners: muscularity or intelligence, competitiveness or cooperativeness, liveliness or calmness, zealousness or circumspection, practicality or imaginativeness, adventurousness or steadiness. In such circumstances sexual selection can have far less force than in creatures with much narrower criteria.

But there is one reason young men and women might especially want to look for a social entertainment system in each other: because of the playful interaction between infants and mothers or others at the start of all human lives that arises from, and ingrains more deeply in us, the unique importance of human shared attention (see the following section). With that disposition to sharing attention taken into account and admitted as the impetus for art, *then* sexual selection may explain an escalation of adaptations for sociality and for art.

Differential parental investment—higher male competitiveness, higher female choosiness—can then hint at part of the reason for the preponderance of males over females in art for public display, although women seem always to have participated in song, dance, weaving, and storytelling, especially near the home, as much as or more than men. Even if sexual selection for male artistic display has played a role in the arts, it should be stressed that this would not necessarily entail that males are more artistically capable. The genes necessary for good male performance would pass to both male and female descendants unless they happen to be located on the Y chromosome (1 chance in 23)—although they might then be activated only by sex-differentiated hormones, such as testosterone—while the genes necessary for female appreciation *cannot* be located on the Y chromosome and would therefore descend to offspring of both sexes. In *The Tale of Genji*, Genji wins a painting contest against his friend To no Chujo and, as a result, the adulation of many women.[63] But this novel, the world's first, and the pearl of Japanese literature, was written by a woman—and a mother.

Art as Adaptation 1: Communion and Community

Ellen Dissanayake has made the most persistent and extensive of all attempts to explain art in evolutionary terms. In *What Is Art For?* (1988) and *Homo Aestheticus*[64] she begins with an intuition, based on her wide knowledge of both Western and non-Western societies, that art matters to all people and therefore requires a biological explanation. Art should be recognized as a specieswide adaptation, she argues, for the following reasons:

1. It is universal in human societies. (She adduces a mass of cross-cultural evidence.)
2. It involves high commitments of time, resources, and energy. (Ditto.)
3. It produces strong pleasure and other intense emotions. (She notes in some detail that pleasure is the brain's sign of what has on average offered evolutionary benefit and that emotion is evolution's way of indicating importance.)
4. It is associated with biologically significant activities.
5. It develops reliably in all normal humans without special training.

Dissanayake also begins with another intuition, that modern Western art is a poor place to start thinking about art in biological terms. She argues that the rise of an art-for-art's-sake aesthetics in the late-eighteenth-century West makes it hard to understand art as an adaptation because it stresses the *non*functional, whereas in non-Western societies whole communities invest heavily in artistic activities that they feel to be not optional and peripheral but obligatory and central. The rise of the artistic avant-garde in the West in the last century and a half further obscures an understanding of art as a human universal because it involves an unprecedented degree of specialization, innovation, mechanical reproduction, and, therefore, exposure to examples of specialized artistic innovation. This saturation in turn drives some artists to still more radical innovation, even or perhaps especially if it runs counter to the cognitive preferences from which art arose.

In stressing both art as an adaptation and the remoteness of modern Western high art from the conditions in which art emerged, Dissanayake is surely correct. She is also correct to insist that art should be seen not so much in terms of *works* of art but as a behavior. But if art is an adaptive behavior, what is its function? Dissanayake knows, as she lists some of the functions proposed by anthropologists, ethologists, psychologists, and aestheticians, that there is no shortage of suggestions and no sign of convergence: art as direct, immediate experience or as mimesis, as the imitation of experience; as training for the unfamiliar or as defamiliarization; as a source of individual "mastery, security, and relief from anxiety," as a mode of individual display, or an assertion of individual prestige; as communication with others or a means of group identification; as providing a sense of meaning or order to the world or access to a supramundane world.[65]

In her own attempt to find art's highest common factor and its importance as part of the lives of all peoples, Dissanayake proposes describing art as "making special," as a behavior that she shrewdly observes has close affinities with two categories of biological activity (of "doing special," as it were) common in other species as well as our own: play and ritual. Play involves behavior outside the immediately functional, marked as such through particular forms of movement and expression, is pleasurable in itself and is therefore pursued for its own sake. Ritual, a key concept in animal behavior, as in the courtship rituals of many birds, involves behavior fixed and formalized, elaborated, exaggerated, and repeated for the sake of communicative clarity.

Because art in the Western art-for-art's-sake sense could never have directly become a biological adaptation, and because art nevertheless shows all the signs of being central enough to human lives to be adaptive, art therefore, Dissanayake proposes, *must* be "making special," it *must* have been associated with, and have enhanced, activities that mattered. But this does not follow. All animals engage in activities that matter to them, or they will fail to survive and reproduce. But they do not need art to make those activities matter: nature has ensured, through the motivation system of the emotions, that they perform what they must for their survival. And in the human case, art may embellish things of little importance and not those that matter most: ploughs have been crucial to agriculture and therefore to culture itself for millennia, yet they are almost never "artified," whereas in traditional cultures baubles or toys like stilts can be elaborately carved.

Dissanayake's repeated claim—that a society that treated as special any activities of prime importance to it would survive better than a society that did not—seems implausible. If the activities matter, the society already performs them; if it does not, it is already in danger. She writes: "making life-serving implements (tools, weapons) special both expressed and reinforced their importance to individuals and would have assured their more careful manufacture and use."[66] But hand axes already mattered among our hominid precursors, and they appear to have become essential to the way of life of *Homo erectus*. Overrefining their symmetry or toying with their scale, in the way Kohn and Mithen discuss, may have been early precursors of art and could be classed as "making special," but while this extra skill and effort may have earned the respect of others, it would not have clarified the importance of hand axes to groups that already relied on them.

"Making special" alone seems unable either to encompass all art or to explain its origins or adaptive force. But in her most recent book, *Art and Intimacy: How the Arts Began* (2000), Dissanayake has developed a much more cogent argument. Where Miller sees art as sexually selected, as something humans engage in so as to attract mates, Dissanayake here sees art as arising from the uniquely intimate contact of human parents, especially mothers, with their children. Dissanayake's "attunement" is close to my "attention" (which however allows more room for individual as well as shared attention).

For the first six months, infants have a love affair with human faces, voices, and touch. By about eight months, parent-infant "protoconversations" set the scene for the special nature of human sociality and for art. Aptly described by Dissanayake as multimedia performances, since they use eyes and faces, hands and feet, voice and movement, these protoconversations consist of rhythmic, finely attuned turn-taking and mutual imitation involving elaboration, exaggeration, repetition, and surprise, with each partner anticipating the other's response so as to coordinate their emotions in patterned sequence. From about nine to twelve months, infants tune into the attention and behavior of adults in new ways and try to have adults tune into theirs. By the end of their first year, they engage in joint attention (following another's hand or eyes or checking to see that the other follows its own) and in protodeclarative pointing (indicating an object or event simply for the sake of sharing attention toward it).[67] Human mothers and others provide a social entertainment system for infants, evolution apparently having selected for both adults and children who can turn the uniquely protracted dependency of human childhood into mutual delight.

With this crucial new addition, we can now return to the problem Dissanayake addresses in "making special." Her aim in proposing the term has been to distinguish art as practiced around the world, in mother-and-infant song-and-dance and a myriad other forms, from the Western elevation of art above life through the Kantian distinction between impractical art and the practical aspects of life.

Dissanayake is right to stress that this distinction is unhelpful, since to many peoples—even in the West (the icons in the Russian Orthodox tradition, for instance), let alone in tribal societies—art involves practices considered central and necessary to their lives. But rather than replacing the distinction between nonutilitarian art and the utilitarian with a distinction between "making special" and, implicitly, "leaving ordinary," I would suggest, we can understand art better by focusing on a distinction that has always been central to human understanding: the distinction between the physical and the nonphysical (the psychological, in modern terms; the spiritual, in older ones).

In one sense, this distinction is crumbling as science investigates the intricate connection between mind and brain. In another sense, cognitive anthropologists and developmental psychologists are exploring it in new ways as a fundamental dichotomy in human understanding of the world, even before language. New techniques make it possible to study how infant minds distinguish the ontological domains of inanimate and animate, bringing different expectations to and drawing different inferences from the two different domains (called "folk physics" and "folk psychology" in one set of terms; "theory of things" and "theory of mind" in another).[68]

From this and other recent findings, significant implications follow for understanding art and its relation to religion and ritual. Art has no immediate physical function but only an immediate psychical one: to appeal to attention and emotion. A decoration on a bowl does not change the bowl's physical capacity but does change its psychological appeal; a harvest song does not by itself gather crops but alters the attitude of the harvesters; a story does not bring about its own outcome but causes an audience to feel and respond as if they had witnessed the events. In each case, the effect is on those who encounter the artwork, whether design, music, or story.

In the initial and default case, across the world, art affects human beings, both active "artists" and reactive audiences. But many peoples believe that it will also have an effect on other kinds of beings in the spiritual world, beings presumed to respond in ways similar enough to *human* spirits that they too will be moved—and moved, perhaps, to intervene for, or not intervene against, those who have made the artwork or accord it respect.

Two points need to be stressed here. First, the impact on human beings is there from the first: the songs, shapes, or stories are, after all, designed to secure human attention. Second, the impact on—and indeed the very supposition of—imagined other beings also depends on art, on the power of story.

We crave one another's attention, but no one wishes to pay attention to a story that discloses only the banal and expected: one would be better off attending to the real world. To merit attention, stories select the striking: unusual characters or events or both. Recent research shows we remember best stories with characters who violate our categorial expectations, who cross one animal kind with another, who combine human and animal, or who separate the psychological from its usual physical embodiment.[69] Even now we attract attention in stories by crossing categories, by introducing aliens, mutants, and robots. And creatures with psychological powers but not limited to consistent physical embodiment or causation—spirits or gods—have been central to story from as far back as we can see.

We see our own agency as our prototype of cause: we want to move something, and we do. We make an early and lasting distinction between agents and nonagents, between the animate and the inanimate, and we are prone to overattribute agency: it is safer to err in that direction than in the other, to suppose a bush is a bear rather than the other way around.[70] And because we pay such extraordinarily close attention to one kind of agent, to others of our kind, we humans have uniquely evolved an understanding of false belief—a capacity to see that others, or ourselves, may conceive a situation differently from what it really is.[71] Because we understand false belief, because we can appreciate that we might not know the full situation, we crave the whole story; we seek an explanation that goes behind what we can see.

Spiritual agents as unseen causes are therefore not only memorable figures in story but offer us an apparent and eagerly sought completeness of explanation. Because *we* are moved by song, by images, by stories, because these things have been *designed* to move us, we suppose that these unseen forces may also be moved in similar ways. And because we can envisage the future in a vivid enough fashion to become anxious about uncertain possibilities, we are ready to move the unseen spirits to act more in our favor, or less in our disfavor, with the help of the art that so catches *our* attention and stirs *our* response.[72]

Because unseen spirits can be supposed to monitor what we do even when no one appears to be watching, a society-wide belief in such spiritual powers can help solve the problems of cooperation inherent in any individualized society— any society, that is, whose members are not genetically identical (like slime molds), very closely related (like ants or termites), or in loose aggregates (like mackerel or wildebeest). A human society unified by religion will usually be able to solve problems of cooperation more easily than another without.[73]

But if a society is bound by a common religion and indeed other common values that facilitate cooperation, a further problem emerges: that of ensuring that members of the society are genuinely committed to these shared beliefs. One way of doing this is through what biologists have studied in the animal world as "costly signaling."

Costly signals, although they can be used in the competition of sexual selection, have also been shown to have a powerful effect within many species in reinforcing group cooperation.[74] If a signal has low cost (as in the case of a mere display, promise, or claim), it can be easy to fake. High cost in terms of time, effort, or resources can serve as a guarantee of commitment (only those genuinely committed to the group will be prepared to make the commitment), and biological and historical human case studies show that groups that cement their cohesion by costly ritual can outcompete groups without such ritual.[75]

Costly signaling theory alone does not explain why such a costly activity as religious ritual should take an artistic form in humans. After all, ritualization of practices with high cost but little sensory appeal—prostration, prayer, recitation, offerings, tithes, fasting, sacrifice, mutilation, pilgrimage—can also serve as cohesive social signals. But ritual *with* art has several advantages over ritual without. Art may increase the time and energy costs in ritual preparation and, therefore, the signal value of the commitment, as in the striking example of the *mbari* houses of the Owerri Igbo which Dissanayake describes.[76] Art promises pleasure, engages the attention, stirs the emotions, and arouses pride and awe at the effects produced and the mastery exhibited. The very improbability of any artistic practice makes it a distinct marker, a contrast to the natural and to other rival groups, and hence in both respects a source of pride.

Art, therefore, though it begins in engaging the attention of other humans, can readily be commandeered both to engage the attention of putative spiritual beings and to ensure social cooperation at the human level, whether in the service of the gods or not. Dissanayake places a powerful stress on art as ritual, and Kathryn Coe emphasizes even more strongly that art has been traditionally used to solve the social problem of cooperation.[77]

In Dissanayake's or Coe's sense, traditional art is often far from nonutilitarian: it can have what seems the highest practical purpose possible—securing both the good will (or staving off the ill will) of the spiritual world and the focus of the group on these powerful and unseen agents. And as already noted, this "practicality" is not an illusion: case studies confirm that the advantages of social cohesion can easily repay the effort invested in ritual practice and outweigh the disadvantages of belief in nonexistent spiritual forces.

But even amplified by evidence unavailable to Dissanayake in the 1980s and early 1990s—physical versus psychological domains in cognitive anthropology and developmental psychology and multilevel selection and costly signaling in evolutionary biology—the social effects of religion and ritual cannot explain the *origin* of art. Without the art of storytelling, without the human impulse to catch and hold the attention of others through narratives that include agents with expectation-violating, larger-than-life powers, religion could not have arisen; without costume, architecture, and design, without dance and music, without verse and story, ritual could not pass beyond the penitential and sacrificial and engage the community in such awesome affirmations of its identity, values, and connection with forces beyond.

The religion and ritual to which Dissanayake tends to assimilate art in her first two books may not explain the origin of art—though her third book comes close to doing so—but this does not mean that once art began, social cohesion through group artistic traditions, including ritual traditions, could not become a powerful sustainer of art and, indeed, perhaps its main function, even in strict evolutionary terms, in many small-scale societies without specialist artists. The very power of art to move the spirit—Dissanayake cites a Dogon sculptor who reported he occasionally created something "that made everyone who saw it 'stop breathing' for a moment"[78]—makes art natural to associate with religion and ritual. I would therefore make an even stronger claim than Dissanayake's: that art has played a central function in human lives not only in itself but also in giving rise to religion and *then* reinforcing, through augmenting the impact of ritual, religion's power to cement group cohesion.

Yet if art can seem at its most powerful when tightly linked with religion and social cooperation, this does not mean that even in traditional societies art does not also persist in other ways closer to play or to trade than to ritual. We enjoy the sharing and shaping of attention, and although we may coordinate attention through ritualized art, we also, because we are not genetically identical, compete for attention. Especially as societies expand and diversify, and division of labor becomes widespread, art can become professionalized and secularized as well as communalized and spiritualized. At its highest, even secular art may retain religious art's sense of offering not just intense interest but deep explanation and exaltation and of drawing on a spiritual power somehow linking us through our artistic heritage. Or art may remain closer to a less exalted, less spiritualized, perhaps more playful form of catching the attention in popular and folk arts and crafts. Or it may, under the pressure for attention in a highly specialized world, lead even to avant-garde art, to questioning and debunking the heritage and shared values or to challenging tried and traditional ways of catching attention.

Instead of the mighty creatures of old story, the gods and demigods mingling with humans in the *Epic of Gilgamesh* and the *Mahabharata*, art can secularize itself to focus on outstanding humans like Genji or Hamlet, then on ordinary ones like Leopold Bloom or the Makioka sisters, then on subfunctional characters like Beckett's, or can fracture or altogether undermine character as a component of story, as in Robbe-Grillet or Godard. But art, whether before religion, in the overrefining of Paleolithic hand axes, or in societies held together by religious belief or in secularized modern or postmodern societies, always serves to engage attention. In identifying the source of our uncannily responsive attention to one another, and hence of our art as well as our social attunement, in the initial intimacy between infants and mothers or others, Dissanayake is surely right.

Art as Adaptation 2: Fiction as Mind Organization

Evolutionary psychology announced itself as a research program in the late 1980s and early 1990s in a series of manifestos by John Tooby and Leda Cosmides.[79] Tooby and Cosmides typify the strengths and weaknesses of strict evolutionary psychology: a probing analysis of the mind's information-processing needs, but in an abstract manner that often pays scant heed to the animals we emerge from or the humans we have become.

For many years Tooby and Cosmides considered art as a prime example of an evolutionary by-product, but they have recently rethought their position and proposed an adaptive explanation for art. Unlike Dissanayake, they work not from engagement with art but from inquiry about the mind; unlike Dissanayake, who encompasses all the arts, they focus especially on fiction, while still aiming (in their subtitle) "toward an evolutionary theory of aesthetics, fiction and the arts."[80]

They offer concrete grounds for supposing that fiction is adaptive:

1. Across cultures humans engage with pleasure in fictional worlds.
2. There is strong evidence of specialized cognitive design for coping with fiction:
   a. Fiction engages *"emotion systems while disengaging action systems."*[81]
   b. We decouple fictional information from factual, so that it cannot corrupt our knowledge stores, with the efficiency and effortlessness that tend to mark all evolved mental subroutines.
   c. The malfunction of a specialized cognitive system can indicate specialized cognitive design. The capacity to engage in pretend play, a forerunner of fiction, breaks down in autism but not in other kinds of mild cognitive dysfunction.
   d. An improbable feature offers better evidence of functional design than an expected consequence. That bone should be white can be predicted from its calcium content, which satisfies structural needs, so that there are no grounds for supposing the whiteness of bone serves some additional adaptive function. That minds should seek out accurate information seems equally predictable, yet this "'appetite for the true' model spectacularly fails" to match the frequent human preference for fiction over fact.[82]
   e. But it is not that our minds cannot or do not care to distinguish true information from false: in communication *intended* to be accepted as truthful, we pay keen attention to its accuracy.

Tooby and Cosmides propose that neurocognitive adaptations can operate in two ways, in ordinary functional modes and in organizational modes, such as play, learning, and perhaps dreaming, that help construct the mind. They nominate art as a fourth organizational mode. All such adaptations, they reason, should be scheduled for off-peak demands: when we are safe and fed, without obvious reproductive opportunities, and are "prevented by darkness or other restrictions from pursuing pressing instrumental goals, or impeded by (real) immaturity from producing useful work"[83]—all features pertinent to fiction.

Drawing on their other recent work, they note that humans operate not just with information true for the species in general but with the contingently true, with "the new worlds of the might-be-true, the true-over-there, the once-was-true, the what-others-believe-is-true, the true-only-if-I-did-that, the not-true-here, the what-they-want-me-to-believe-is-true, the will-someday-be-true, the certainly-is-not-true, the what-he-told-me, the seems-true-on-the-basis of-these-claims, and on and on."[84] Fiction, they propose, helps develop this key capacity of the mind to reason counterfactually.

Through their intense focus on art as an adaptation Tooby and Cosmides highlight markers of specific mental design that others have overlooked. Their consciousness that our minds were shaped by the demands of the past, not the present, also helps them clarify an important aspect of fiction's appeal. Since human minds evolved in a world where the main source of information was direct experience rather than the reformulations now possible through language and learning, we still process information more deeply "when we receive it in a form that resembles individual experience."[85]

Yet there are problems with the adaptive hypothesis they advance. Most obviously, the "organizational mode" would predict that interest in art should taper off beyond childhood, once the mind has been organized. But fiction in one form or another usually remains a passion or a pastime throughout life, and since Tooby and Cosmides attempt to account for all art as "organizational," we can also wonder why septuagenarians still throng classical concert halls and art galleries, and octogenarians and their elders share sing-alongs in old people's homes.

Tooby and Cosmides concentrate strongly on representation, which is only one component of art. Although they aim to elucidate art in general, their hypothesis does not account for music, likely to be the first of human arts. (Does music organize our ears to hear environmental sound? Surely not.) It also ignores the origins of the visual arts, likely to have begun not in representation but in bodily and facial adornment, in applying pigments, scarifying skin, modifying hair, filing teeth, all of which are still widespread behaviors—and reach high artistic refinement in Maori moko and Samoan tatu—and which presumably preceded masks and cave painting, let alone frescoes and canvases.

As for fiction itself, Tooby and Cosmides prove unpersuasive about its "organizational" effect. They assume that if fiction fulfills such a function, we will regularly prepare for common experience through fiction. Just as throwing rocks at pine cones readied our ancestors for throwing rocks at prey, they suggest, apparently seriously, that reading about the psychology of the characters in works like *The Possessed* may be a precursor to figuring out the psychology of members of our own families.[86] But we have to deal with others from infancy; we develop a theory of mind at about four, and we cannot understand key social aspects of fiction until our theory of mind matures. It is far more likely—as, indeed, developmental studies of narrative comprehension show[87]—that children learn to understand stories as their cognitive capacities develop in life, than that they learn to handle life through fiction. Tooby and Cosmides suggest that we can take from Cordelia the lesson that "overt emotional demonstrativeness is not a reliable cue to devotedness,"[88] but any child knows that a show of loving behavior is likely to increase parental solicitude, and even a fledgling bird knows to make its cries as loud as it can. Tooby and Cosmides seem to ignore actual experience for the sake of their theoretical model of adaptive function.

If their sense of the ultimate function of fiction seems doubtful, their sense of its proximate mechanism, our immediate motivation for fiction, is lost in fog. They propose that we attend to fiction because our minds detect that it will "have a powerfully organizing effect on our neurocognitive adaptations" even though it is not literally true.[89] But untruth per se does not make us attend to stories; indeed, it is a handicap they have to overcome. There are an infinite number of fictions that would interest no one (this tree is the daughter of a leather ball, and walked here overnight from the next hill . . .). The vague formulation of Tooby and Cosmides says nothing about why we want to tell or listen to stories, or how we choose which stories are worth our while.

Had they considered phylogeny and ontogeny as well as function, Tooby and Cosmides might have developed a more promising explanation of art in terms of shared attention. Our skill at decoupling,[90] which they rightly identify as a key to the power of human thought, first emerges as sociality evolves, in the decoupling of such serious behavior as aggression in rough-and-tumble social play, early in both mammalian phylogeny and human ontogeny.[91] Humans evolved into ultrasociality, and the capacity to decouple thought first reaches uniquely human levels in four-year-old children as their theory of mind unfurls and they begin to understand that their own earlier thoughts or those of others can be different from what they think now. This advance arises from the unique suite of human adaptations for shared, precise attention, which can explain why we want to focus so much on what others are doing, why we want to tell and listen to stories, and why we eventually become so adept, at higher levels, at the most rapid and nimble decoupling, at exploring, along with other imaginations, precise regions of possibility space far from the here and now. Tooby and Cosmides help to demonstrate the likelihood that art and fiction are adaptations, but they do not show why. But an explanation of art and fiction in terms of shared attention can account for both origin and function.

Conclusion

Only an evolutionary theory of art can explain why humans are so made that art matters so much to us, and perhaps why art has made such a difference to the success of our species.

Evolutionary analysis of art may or may not, finally, recognize art as an adaptation, but it will almost certainly show that art depends deeply on evolved features of human minds and behavior, and can link those investigating the arts to the rich research programs into human nature and human behavior currently under way in modern biology and psychology.

Evolutionary theories of art should be assessed on their capacity to generate testable predictions and withstand criticism and competition, to account for the evidence, and to explain art itself: its nature and purposes and impact, its kinds and range and content, its capacity to harness both tradition and innovation, the details of its particular canons and works, its interpretation and evaluation, and its relations to other human impulses, activities, and achievements and to other animal behaviors.

There are other evolutionary theories of art than those discussed here,[92] and other ways of relating evolution to art and literature than through an overarching theory of art as an adaptation. Much of the most promising work on literature and evolution, for instance, investigates one aspect of human nature as suggested by evolution (such as mate choice, male violence, or theory of mind) and examines literary works in this light or uses cross-cultural studies of stories to test evolutionary hypotheses about features of human behavior.[93]

But among evolutionary theories of art as a whole, those discussed here are the most influential to date and represent most major positions: adaptation or by-product, natural or sexual selection, or individual or social functions. All may have a role to play in a comprehensive evolutionary theory of art: Pinker's sharp sense of the mind's detailed design and of the value to the mind of the information we attend to and the ways we attend to it, and his stress on art's ingenious appeals to the adapted mind; Miller's arguments for the part sexual selection may have played in intensifying the artistic impulse and explaining the difference between male and female rates of producing public art; Tooby and Cosmides's alertness to art's role in developing the imaginative scope of decoupled human thought and extending the space in which we think, imagine, and feel; and most promising of all, Dissanayake's stress on human shared attention, which we can extend to suggest not only art's phylogenetic and ontogenetic origins but also its multiple functions, from catching and keeping up with attention through to social cohesion and individual and social creativity. And unlike other explanations, a theory of art focused on the sharing of attention can explain art as a whole, from its overall impact down to its fine-grained detail, even to the decisions individual artists make, in this line or that phrase, to maximize the attention, engagement, and response of an audience.

Joseph Carroll argues not only that literature represents the world but also that until recently it was the great repository of information about human nature.[94] That is not quite true: the great repository of information about human nature was the human mind, adapted intricately by evolution to understand other human minds. Nevertheless, literature was the great *public* repository of insight into human nature. "Trust Shakespeare," Antonio Damasio says, citing lines by the fallen Richard II, "to have been there before," to have made the distinction between emotion and feeling that Damasio himself, as a neuroscientist of the emotions, now wishes to propose.[95]

But if we were to value literature as the repository of shared knowledge of human nature, would this not raise the question: what role would remain for literature in a world where science can now offer considerably more objective explanations even of subjective human nature? Damasio points out that Shakespeare expresses gloriously the standard assumption that psychic feeling precedes somatic emotion, but he then adduces evidence to show that in fact emotion evolves before feeling in the course of evolution and of individual experience and that after neurological damage it is possible to lose feeling and not emotion, but not the other way around.

Science can explain human nature, but art's role is not to explain but to engage and to evoke. Scientists are approaching an evolutionary explanation of why laughter developed in humans and a neurophysiological explanation of how it operates, but they will not make us laugh by doing so or find a formula for being funny or make us laugh less in future because we now understand better why or how we laugh.[96] Similarly we have been shaped to savor art and stories more immediately, more viscerally, more emotionally than we can respond to new scientific explanations. Science can explain why and how art has come to matter, but that will not give science the emotional impact of art, nor allow it to find a formula for art, nor make art matter less. If anything, it will only clarify why and how art matters so much.

Notes

My thanks to Joseph Carroll, Stephen Davies, Ellen Dissanayake, Jonathan Gottschall, and David Sloan Wilson for thoughtful criticism of earlier drafts of this essay.

1. Dennett 2003, 183.
2. Mithen 1996, 172; Lewis-Williams 2002, 27.
3. Tooby and Cosmides 2001, 12.
4. Leitch et al. 2001.
5. Cited in Dutton 1995, 34.
6. D. E. Brown 1991; J. Carroll 1995, 405; see also 150–51 for critique; de Waal 2001.
7. Davies 2000, 200; Dutton 1993, 21; Dutton 1995, 35.
8. Dürer 1971, 24–25, cited in Dutton 1977, 392; Goethe, conversation

with Eckermann, January 31, 1827, cited Wright 2000, 155; Japanese, Pinker 2002, 408.

9. Williams 1966.

10. Cf. George Dickie, cited in Coe 2003, 108: "From ancient times to the present day, the great bulk of the theories of art have been functional."

11. Tinbergen 1963; Bekoff, Allen, et al. 2002, 60.

12. Pinker 1997, 525.

13. Jolly 1999, 186: "David Pilbeam of Harvard has been pointing out to students for years that evolution does not have to have an either-or explanation for every trait. Two good reasons are better than one."

14. Beginning with D. S. Wilson 1975. See Sober and Wilson 1998, D. S. Wilson 2002.

15. Echoes Boyd 2001. Among those who have recently foregrounded attention outside an evolutionary approach are Bordwell 1997; N. Carroll 1998; within such an approach: Aiken 1998; Bedaux and Cooke 1999; Cooke 1995, 1999; Coe 2003.

16. Dissanayake 2000.

17. Bekoff, Allen, et al. 2002, 205.

18. Hauser 2000, 211; Provine 2000, 93.

19. Stern 1977, 35–37; E. Morgan 1995, 104; Meltzoff and Moore 1995; Johnson, Booth, et al. 2001, 639.

20. Theory of Mind: Baron-Cohen 1995; Baron-Cohen, O'Riordan, et al. 1999; Baron-Cohen, Tager-Flusberg, et al. 2000. Multiple-order intentionality: Dennett [1991] 1993.

21. For the primate evolution of attention, see Chance 1988.

22. Eibl-Eibesfeldt 1982, 188; Bloom 2000, 89 comments that acceptance is as important to social animals as oxygen and food.

23. Bloom 2000, 166, 173; Chance and Larsen 1976 passim; Eibl-Eibesfeldt 1982; Moore and Dunham 1995 citing Chance and Jolly 1970; Bekoff, Allen, et al. 2002, 77.

24. Pinker 1997; Pinker 2002.

25. Pinker 1997, 539–42; 2002, 406. Here he develops a point made by Alexander 1989. But as Dissanayake 1992b notes: "I do not see that Alexander's scheme explains why scenarios should be packaged artfully rather than just presented" (100). Given Pinker's strong sense of the human design function, this should be apparent to him too: why do we not simply design schematic scenarios, and imagine consequences?

26. Pinker 1997, 525, 526, 539.

27. See Aiken 1998; in film, J. Anderson 1996; Bordwell and Carroll 1996; N. Carroll 1996. The work of Ernst Gombrich is the most sophisticated to show artistic trade-offs between one kind of psychological appeal and another.

28. Pinker 1997, 528–38.

29. Pinker in Glausiusz 2001, 4. Pinker indeed makes much of status, since he explains "the very uselessness of art" in terms of its value for indicating status: 1997, 522.

30. Pinker 1997, 528.

31. Here I agree with Dissanayake 1988, 1992a, 2000 and D. E. Brown 1991. For the most sophisticated version of the contrary view, see Shiner 2001.

32. Hernadi 2001, 64.

33. Flynn 1999.

34. Pinker 2002, 405.

35. Darwin 1871b.

36. Cronin 1991; Miller 2000b.

37. Trivers 1972; see Miller 2000b, 85–88.

38. Miller 2000b, 260–61.

39. Pinker 1997, 536; Darwin 1871b, 572.

40. Including Karl von Frisch (Griffin [1992] 2001, 99), William Hamilton (Hrdy 1999, 45) and Robin Fox (E. O. Wilson [1975] 2000, 569).

41. Miller 2000b, 7.

42. Miller 2000a, 334.

43. Miller 2000a, 355.

44. Miller 2000b, 77–78.

45. Wrangham and Peterson 1996.

46. Miller 2000b, 4, 29.

47. Miller 2000b, 250.

48. Dissanayake 1992b, 10–11.

49. Miller 2000b, 35.

50. Miller 1999; but see Fukui 2001.

51. Mothers singing: Trehub in Glausiusz 2001; infant preferences: Wallin, Merker, et al. 2000, 440; Hokusai: Lane 1989, 272.

52. Should you object to Homer and his blindness as legend, not history, other writers can take his place: Milton, Joyce, Borges. Miller overlooks the likelihood that many commit to the arts precisely to compensate for a lack of fitness in other areas, as in *The Gift of Stones* (1988), Jim Crace's thoughtful novel of Neolithic Britain, where a cripple takes up the role of storyteller.

53. Miller 2000b, 196.

54. S. Brown 2000a, 245–46.

55. See de Waal 2002; de Waal 2001, 26: "One could define language so narrowly that the babbling of a toddler does not fall under it, but does this mean that babbling has nothing to do with language? Narrow definitions neglect boundary phenomena and precursors, and they often mistake the tip of the iceberg for the whole."

56. S. Brown 2000a; S. Brown 2000b.

57. Fukui in Glausiusz 2001, 3.

58. Dutton 2000, 513.

59. Darwin 1871b, 2003.

60. Jolly 1999, 97–98 observes that human hair appears to have coevolved with preferences for hair styling.

61. Coe 2003.

62. Kohn and Mithen 1999. Kohn and Mithen were not the first to feel that flints were knapped to a point of "virtuoso elegance" (Loren Eisely 1979, in Dissaanyake 2000, 132).

63. Thiessen and Umezawa 1998, 302.

64. Dissanayake 1988, 1992b.

65. Dissanayake 1988, 64 ff; 1992a, 10, 84.

66. Dissanayake 1992a, 52; see also Dissanayake 1988, 103, 151; Dissanayake 2000, 145.

67. Stern 1977, 39; Barrett, Richert, et al. 2001, 51; Tomasello and Call 1997, 405, citing Stern 1985 and Trevarthen 1979; Dissanayake 2000, 7, 29; Povinelli and Preuss 1995, 422–23.

68. Cosmides and Tooby 1994; Spelke 1995; Caramazza and Shelton 1998; Wellman and Gelman 1998. For a review of the large literature on Theory of Mind, see Baron-Cohen 2000.

69. Atran 2002.

70. Atran 2002; Boyer 1994, 1996, 2001; Kinderman, Dunbar, et al. 1998.

71. For false belief, see Dennett 1978; Astington 1990; Perner 1991; Carruthers and Chamberlain 2000, 186.

72. For a discussion of the human capacity to "time-travel," including envisaging the future, see Suddendorf 1999.

73. Atran 2002; Boyer 2001; D. S. Wilson 2002.

74. See Miller 2000b; Zahavi and Zahavi 1997.

75. Sosis and Bressler 2000; D. S. Wilson 2002.

76. These take two years and much manpower to build and decorate but are left to decay immediately after the inauguration celebration: see Dissanayake 2000, 153.

77. Coe 2003. Coe offers an adaptive explanation of visual art in terms of the cooperative effects ancestor-worship can create among the ancestors' descendants, but she does not particularly explain the origins or features of visual art and underplays the amount of individual initiative and innovation even in traditional art.

78. Dissanayake 2000, 216.

79. Cosmides and Tooby 1989; 1992; Tooby and Cosmides 1989; 1990a, 1990b; 1992.

80. Tooby and Cosmides 2001.

81. Tooby and Cosmides 2001, 8.

82. Tooby and Cosmides 2001, 12.

83. Tooby and Cosmides 2001, 16–17.

84. Tooby and Cosmides 2001, 20; recent work: Cosmides and Tooby 2000a.

85. Tooby and Cosmides 2001, 24.

86. Tooby and Cosmides 2001, 21.

87. Berman and Slobin 1994.

88. Tooby and Cosmides 2001, 22.

89. Tooby and Cosmides 2001, 21.

90. Boyer 2001, 129 provides a clear explanation: "Worries about what would happen if the roof caved in and came crashing down on your head do not require the usual input (e.g., seeing the roof coming down) and do not produce the normal output (an attempt to dash off as fast as possible). This is why psychologists say that these thoughts are *decoupled* from their standard inputs and outputs."

91. Stern 1977, 4; Jolly 1999, 287.

92. See Cooke and Aiken 1999 for an annotated bibliography; Coe 2003.

93. See Bordwell and Carroll 1996 for a pertinent and astute discussion of the mid-range theories (cognitive rather than specifically evolutionary) rather than grand theory in film (rather than literature).

94. J. Carroll 1999a, 165.

95. Damasio 2003, 27.

96. Van Hooff and Preuschoft 2003; Damasio 2003; Boyd 2004.

Reverse-Engineering Narrative: Evidence of Special Design

Michelle Scalise Sugiyama

We must assume that storytelling is as old as mankind, at least as old as spoken language.

Joyce Carol Oates

The greater the number of generations in which a cultural behavior has been replicated, the greater is the probability of evidence of design.

Randy Thornhill and Craig Palmer

Introduction

Life as a hunter-gatherer is difficult, arduous, and dangerous. Given these conditions, why would our Upper Pleistocene ancestors bother to take the time to tell stories? For we can be pretty sure that they did. Anatomical evidence, as well as the very complexity and universality of the language faculty itself, suggest that language—a necessary condition for storytelling—is highly likely to have developed by the time *Homo sapiens* began spreading out of Africa 100,000 years ago.[1] Additionally, we know that humans were producing two- and three-dimensional representations of their environment (paintings on cave and cliff walls; carvings in stone, bone, and antler) by 32,000 B.P. and perhaps earlier.[2] Finally, archaeological evidence suggests that humans in southern Africa were using pigment symbolically (to paint their bodies and, possibly, to make marks on rocks and organic surfaces) between 120,000 and 100,000 years ago.[3] By the Middle Paleolithic, then, the potential for storytelling was well in place.

The antiquity of narrative is significant. It means that storytelling is a sufficiently ancient phenomenon to have evolved through the process of natural selection and that storytelling might serve an adaptive function—that is, it might have evolved in response to a problem that recurrently impinged upon human survival or reproduction throughout recent (i.e., Upper Pleistocene) human evolution. It is also possible that storytelling is a by-product—and unintended consequence—of adaptations that evolved to perform other functions. Both hypotheses have been examined[4] but not sufficiently to decisively rule out one or the other. Of course, we can never "prove" that narrative (or any organismic feature) is an adaptation; all we can do is ask whether or not it meets the criteria of complex adaptation—species-typicality, developmental reliability, a degree of complexity unlikely to have arisen by chance, and special design.[5] This essay addresses the latter criterion: Is narrative well-engineered to perform a fitness-promoting task?

In addressing this question, it is important to situate storytelling in its evolutionary context. Be it adaptation or by-product, storytelling is the product of a mind adapted to hunter-gatherer conditions, and it emerged when our ancestors practiced a foraging way of life.[6] Because many of these conditions no longer exist, it is possible that, in industrialized state societies, storytelling no longer serves its original purpose. Thus, adaptationist inquiries regarding narrative function are properly conceptualized not in terms of present-day applications but, rather, in terms of a problem of forager existence that storytelling might have solved.

The question of function can be usefully pursued through reverse-engineering—that is, inferring the function of the whole by examining the operation of its parts.[7] Anyone who has ever visited the junkyard and pondered the purpose of an unfamiliar object has practiced reverse-engineering. Why do we ponder thusly? Because such complexity is so obviously not accidental. Complexity is the product of deliberate design, and design implies intention: as tool-making primates, we cannot help but wonder, when confronted with an unfamiliar, painstakingly crafted object, "What is this for?" As evolutionary biologists and psychologists have discovered, the same logic applies to the component parts of organisms. Complex anatomical, physiological, and cognitive features—wings, immune systems, sonar—imply design. However, we must be careful not to take this analogy too far: whereas artifacts are designed by sentient beings with intentions and foresight, organic structures are "designed" by the blind and unpremeditated process of natural selection—that is, through the differential reproduction of variants over generations.

Reverse-engineering addresses another important issue. The dominant trend in adaptationist studies of art behaviors has been to examine them as a singular phenomenon. Dissanayake, for example, characterizes visual art, dance, and music as "rhythmic-modal elaboration"—that is, the transformation of everyday actions or materials through the use of "vivid description, repetition, and other rhythmic and modal devices of emphasis, added figuration, or intensification." The effect of this behavior, she argues, is to strengthen group solidarity and cooperation in times of crisis by "arousing interest, riveting joint attention, synchronizing bodily rhythms and activities, conveying messages with conviction and memorability, and ultimately indoctrinating and reinforcing right attitudes and behavior."[8] Coe proposes that visual art (for example, jewelry, textiles, basketry, masks, sand painting, and other traditional art objects) boosts the survival and reproduction odds of one's descendants and codescendants by fostering dynastic solidarity. In Coe's words, these objects function to "identify individuals who shared descent from a common ancestor and to encourage cooperative, unselfish behavior among all individuals so identified."[9] And Miller argues that painting, poetry, humor, music, and other forms of creative expression evolved as a means of exhibiting certain kinds of intelligence, which in turn functions as courtship display. The problem with these approaches, as Dissanayake herself admits, is that art "is notoriously difficult to define or to discuss with universal applicability."[10] Reverse-engineering offers a solution to this problem. If we think of art behaviors in terms of the cognitive and physical features involved in their generation or processing, we see that each employs very different parts of the mind and body: visual art engages our sense of sight (and to a lesser degree, touch) through the use of color, form, pattern, and texture; music engages our aural sense through the use of rhythm and tonality; and dance engages our kinesthetic sense through the use of physical movement, strength, balance, and endurance. On a biological level, then, art behaviors emerge as discrete phenomena. Thus, it cannot be assumed a priori that each of these behaviors performs the same function—or, indeed, any function at all.

Research on human aesthetic preferences also suggests that art behaviors are cognitively discrete.[11] Because the word "beautiful" can refer to almost anything attractive, we are misled into thinking that beauty is a homogeneous standard. But this is decidedly not the case—we use very different criteria to evaluate the beauty of, for example, a baby, a sunset, a dance, a bird's song, a flower's scent. As Tooby and Cosmides explain, those aspects of an object/phenomenon that we experience as beautiful are "cues which, in the environment in which humans evolved, signaled that it would have been advantageous to pay sustained sensory attention to it. . . . This includes everything from members of the opposite sex to game animals to the exhibition by others of intricate skills."[12] In other words, standards of beauty vary from object to object, behavior to behavior, phenomenon to phenomenon. For this reason, "there can be no general theory of the properties of things found beautiful—only a heterogeneous set of subsidiary theories."[13] Thus, the aspects of art objects/behaviors that we find beautiful (that is, which attract us to observe or participate in them), may very well differ from medium to medium; it follows that the functions of art behaviors might differ as well.

Anatomy of Narrative

In the case of narrative, we have what appears to be a complex—that is, "designed"—psychological structure that we suspect was used fairly regularly by

Upper Pleistocene foragers. This apparent complexity raises the question, what might this structure be designed to do? The answer to this question begins with the observation that storytelling involves communication: fundamentally verbal (and, for the majority of its existence, oral), storytelling requires at least two people, one to tell a story and one to listen to it.[14] In this formulation, I am making a distinction between the stories we tell in our heads (internal storytelling) and the stories we tell to others (external storytelling). Like my previous work, this essay addresses the latter phenomenon. For the purposes of the present exploration, it is not necessary to make fine cognitive distinctions between teller and listener: although storytelling talent varies from individual to individual, all normally developing humans capable of understanding stories are capable of telling stories, and vice versa. In other words, telling a story requires and engages the same cognitive software as listening to a story. Thus, I use the terms "narrative," "the narrative faculty," and "storytelling" interchangeably to refer to the human cognitive ability to generate and comprehend narrative.

If storytelling involves communication, what might it be designed to communicate? This is where reverse-engineering comes in: the first step is to identify the cognitive widgets and sprockets of storytelling, and the second is to figure out what they do. Fortunately, two independent lines of research have already done the first step for us—literary theory on the one hand and cognitive psychology on the other. The literary consensus is that stories consist of character, setting, actions, and events—linked temporally and/or causally—and conflict and resolution. *The Norton Anthology of Short Fiction*, for example, lists character, setting, action, complication, and coherence among the "truly basic characteristics of fiction."[15] Similarly, in a discussion of defining qualities of the short story, Oates mentions character, time, place, conflict, and resolution.[16] Psychological support for this view comes from story grammar research. Beginning in the 1960s, there was a burst of interest in how the mind constructs stories: various cognitive psychologists applied themselves to the task of identifying the constituent units of narrative and the rules (algorithms) for combining them, which they called *story grammars*. This research yielded a consensus regarding the essential components of narrative that parallels the literary one: the generation of narrative requires at least one character, setting, states and events, sequence, causal connections, goal-oriented action, and resolution.[17]

The reader might object that these components have been identified using Western literature and that we might expect hunter-gatherer stories to differ in construction. Evidence and common sense point to the opposite conclusion. The fact that we are able to translate stories from one culture to another is testimony to the universality of narrative structural components: although some cultural nuances or historical context may be lost in the process, the essence of the story—character and motive, events and constraints, actions and reactions, failure and triumph—comes through. If the components of narrative varied from culture to culture—if, for example, Yanomamö stories didn't have characters, or Mardudjara stories didn't have settings, or !Kung stories didn't have conflict—the stories of different cultures would be unintelligible to one another, and the fields of folklore and comparative literature could not exist. In my own reading of the oral narrative of a wide range of foraging peoples, I have yet to encounter a culture whose stories do not exhibit the same structural features as Western narrative.[18]

I know of only one anthropologist who offers evidence challenging this point. In his 1950 ethnography of the Siriono, Holmberg reports that, "After making one unsuccessful attempt after another to get informants to relate myths and tales, I was forced finally to conclude that this phase of culture was simply not developed, that there was no fund of folklore and mythology upon which to draw."[19] From the cynical perspective of a generation that has seen the debunking of Margaret Mead,[20] this conclusion seems a bit naive: the fact that the Siriono did not tell Holmberg any of their myths or tales does not necessarily mean they didn't have any to tell. Perhaps the Siriono misunderstood his request; perhaps he asked at inappropriate times; perhaps the Siriono considered their myths too sacred to relate to outsiders. Or perhaps Holmberg couldn't see the jungle for the trees, so to speak: his claim of Siriono narrative deficiency is immediately followed by a summary of the Siriono creation myth, "of which there are a number of variants." He goes on to report that Moon, the hero of the creation myth, is invoked to explain sundry natural phenomena. To take just one example, "Moon now lives in the sky. He is a great chief. He spends about half of his time hunting. During the dark of the moon the Siriono say that he is far away, hunting peccary." While these belief-statements are not in themselves a story, they sound as if they might be culled from one, and they definitely sound like myth. Holmberg may not have recognized these accounts as myth due to his own preconceived notions of what a mythology corpus ought to contain: "Although Moon is credited with having started everything in their culture, stories to account for these things were never told. I could get no supporting myths, for instance, for the origin of the world, the origin of men, or the origin of fire, even though informants were agreed that Moon was responsible for them."[21] Just because people don't tell stories about what the anthropologist thinks they ought to doesn't mean they don't tell stories at all.

Having identified the essential components of narrative, we can now turn to the task of identifying their respective functions. Neither literary scholars nor cognitive psychologists make much of the fact that stories are made out of words, yet, as noted previously, language is a necessary condition for storytelling. It is more than this, however: the verbalness of narrative is one of the things that distinguishes it from other art forms and, thus, goes to the issue of design and function. Some scholars would disagree with this conceptualization. Lloyd, for example, suggests that "any representational system can be a medium of narrative."[22] At first glance, this appears to be the case, but a simple thought experiment proves otherwise. Imagine Genghis Khan looking at a painting of the Ascension of Christ. Would he understand the story? The odds are against it. This is because nonverbal media, such as paintings and stained glass windows and statues, achieve their narrative effects through their reference to a story that the viewer already knows. If the great Khan knew that the painting depicted Christ and knew the story of Christ's life, then he would experience the painting as a story—or, more precisely, as an episode from the story of Christ. If he were not familiar with the story, he would experience the painting as a picture of a man who appears to be flying.

When deployed without verbal supplement, nonverbal expressive media (for example, visual art, dance, music) are actually quite inefficient narrative devices. This can be demonstrated with another thought experiment. Imagine early Homo sapiens trying to tell the story "Little Red Riding Hood" through the medium of paint. Our artist immediately encounters difficulty in representing the thoughts, beliefs, and motives of the characters as well as the relationships between them. This, in turn, makes it difficult to represent any but the most rudimentary of conflicts: even the simple fitness gamble at the heart of the story—risking one's skin to help one's kin—cannot be communicated because pictures cannot tell us why the little girl is taking a basket of food to the old woman.[23] A picture may be worth a thousand words, but sometimes a thousand pictures cannot match a few choice phrases.

If our artist uses music[24] or dance to tell her story, she encounters even more problems, beginning with the establishment of character. How does she convey to the audience that the main characters in "Little Red Riding Hood" are a little girl, her mother, her grandmother, a woodsman, and a wolf? Setting presents a similar obstacle: how does the artist communicate to the audience that the story is set in an isolated, dangerous forest? This information cannot be provided without the aid of props, scenery, and costume, and even then some story information would be resistant to communication: a key event in the plot of the story—the little girl telling the wolf that she is taking food to her ailing grandmother who lives all alone in the forest—cannot be hummed, drummed, whistled, danced, or mimed. As with visual art, narrative dance (for example, hula) and music (for example, *Peter and the Wolf*) depend either upon concurrent explication or upon audience foreknowledge of the story being performed. As Hagen and Bryant observe, music is a highly effective medium for communicating certain emotional states (for example, sadness, happiness, anger), but language is a much more effective medium for communicating common interests and political goals—that is, the beliefs, desires, and thoughts of human agents.[25] At best, then, the stories expressed through the visual and temporal arts are meaning-impoverished compared with those expressed through language.

So language is a necessary condition for narrative, but is it a sufficient one? Pinker characterizes language as "an unlimited set of messages of a certain kind (basically, hierarchical propositions involving human actions, beliefs, desires, and obligations; objects and their rough relative locations, motions, and forces; and the durations and relative times of events and states)."[26] It sounds as though language and narrative are more or less the same thing. However, not all utterances are stories: we use words for a diverse array of verbal tasks, such as conversation, lists, lectures, argument, interrogation, and lyric poetry. Moreover, the rules for making stories are different from those for making sentences.[27] Narrative elements cannot be combined according to any rules of noun-verb agreement, tense formation, inflection, and so on. Although cognitive psychologists have had only limited success in their efforts to delineate story grammar, it is clear that such a grammar must exist: stories are not simply random conglomerations of sentences. As Rumelhart puts it, "some higher level of organization takes place in stories that does not take place in strings of sentences."[28] In sum, language and story are not the same thing. Language is the medium of story, as metal is the medium of the internal combustion engine: engine parts are made of iron, steel, and aluminum; narrative parts are made of words and sentences. Mandler and Johnson refer to this level of narrative as the "surface structure," which they distinguish from "constituent structure"—that is, states, events, and actions and their temporal and causal relationships.[29]

Perhaps the most essential component of the constituent structure of narrative is action (also called "events"). According to Storey, sequence—that is, events that follow each other temporally—is the only characteristic of narrative that is universally agreed upon.[30] Holman's *Handbook to Literature*, for example, defines "story" as "actions in a time sequence" and "narrative" as "an account in prose or verse of an actual or fictional event or a sequence of such events."[31] And sequence—"the temporal ordering of narrated events"—is one of the two constraints on narrative form identified by Lloyd in his characterization of narrativity.[32] But what do critics and theorists mean by the terms "action" and "events"? Rumelhart defines "event" as "a change of state, or an action that people carry out" or "the reactions of animate (or anthropomorphized) objects to events in the world."[33] Mandler and Johnson similarly define "event" as any external or internal happening: "External events include actions of characters and changes of state in the world. Internal events include thoughts and plans, perceptions, and such peculiar phenomena as forgetting."[34] According to Holman, action is "the answer to the question, 'What happened?'"—that is, it is "what the characters say, do, think, or in some cases fail to do."[35] I have bombarded the reader with quotations here to make a point. These definitions have a common thread, and that thread is character: actions are *things that characters do,* and events are *things that happen to characters.*

As this observation suggests, temporally or causally linked events do not in themselves constitute a story. I suspect others would disagree with me. Turner, for example, argues that the wind blowing clouds through the sky, a child throwing a rock, a mother pouring milk into a glass, and a whale swimming through the water are "small spatial stories."[36] While I agree with Turner that cause-and-effect reasoning is a fundamental feature of both human cognition and storytelling, this capability does not in itself constitute narrative—at least, not in the sense that I am using the term. After all, chimpanzees, dolphins, mice, pigeons, and many other animals are capable of causal reasoning, yet we would hardly call this capability storytelling. As noted previously, narrative is quintessentially communicative—one person tells a story to another—whereas cause-and-effect reasoning is not. And, unlike cause-and-effect reasoning, narrative by definition involves characters.

In literary circles, the term "character" is "most often used to refer to a person in a fictional story."[37] In story grammar research, the terms "hero" and "protagonist" are more common, but they similarly imply human agency and consciousness. This is not to deny that animals and (more rarely) inanimate objects are used as characters in fiction. When used thusly, however, they are almost always anthropomorphized. Coyote, Anansi, Brer Rabbit, even Kafka's cockroach perceive and respond to the world with a human psyche. In myth, celestial bodies (for example, the sun or moon) and other natural phenomena (for example, the wind or a rainbow) are often characters, but they, too, tend to be anthropomorphized. In Siriono culture, for example, Moon (Yási) is conceptualized as a hunter, and the waxing and waning of the moon are explained in terms of his hunting activities. When he returns from a hunting trip, his face is dirty; he washes it a bit every day until it is completely clean (waxing moon). When he goes hunting again, his face gets a little dirtier each day, until it is completely covered with dirt (waning moon).[38]

When nonhuman characters are used but not anthropomorphized, the focus of the story tends to be the impact of this nonhuman "character" on human lives or affairs. In Barthelme's short story, "The Balloon," for example, narration focuses not on the balloon per se but on human responses to its presence: "There were reactions. Some people found the balloon 'interesting'"; "Daring children jumped, especially at those points where the balloon hovered close to a building"; "People began . . . to locate themselves in relation to aspects of the balloon."[39] Because he reveals from the outset that he is the person responsible for the appearance of the balloon, attention also focuses on the narrator and his intentions: "The balloon, beginning at a point on Fourteenth Street, the exact location of which I cannot reveal, expanded northward all one night, while people were sleeping, until it reached the Park. There, I stopped it," and "The balloon, I said, is a spontaneous autobiographical disclosure, having to do with the unease I felt at your absence."[40] Thus, the emphasis of the story is human action and reaction—the performance of a highly unusual act and the intellectual, emotional, and physical responses to it. If, as suggested previously, characters are agents—that is, causes of story action—then in Barthelme's story the agent is not the balloon but the narrator, who causes the balloon to come into being.

Thus, regardless of their outward form, the defining quality of story characters appears to be humanness—human thoughts, feelings, perceptions, and actions. As E. M. Forster writes (in reference to the novelist), "there are ninepins about whom he might tell the story, and tell a rattling good one, but no, he prefers to tell his story about human beings."[41] Scholes would appear to agree: "Virtually all stories are about human beings or humanoid creatures. Those that are not invariably humanize their material through metaphor and metonymy."[42] In a similar vein, Dunbar observes that stories "enable the reader to become a voyeur of the intimate lives of other individuals."[43] Bower and Morrow's observation that the psychological processes humans "use to explain and understand the actions of storybook characters are much the same as those they use to understand people's actions in everyday life"[44] implicitly acknowledges that characters are representations of the human psyche, as does Holman's comment that, "in fiction . . . the author reveals the characters of imaginary *persons*."[45] The function of character, then, is to illuminate the minds of our fellow human beings. As Booth puts it, narrative goes "beneath the surface of the action to obtain a reliable view of a character's mind and heart." Through this device, we are made privy to "motives directly and authoritatively without being forced to rely on those shaky inferences about other men which we cannot avoid in our own lives."[46]

The emphasis on human motives in characterization points to another key component of narrative: conflict. As Clayton writes: "Imagine this as a story: George wants someone to love. He walks into a room and meets Eloise. He loves her and is happy. Clearly that's not a story. There's desire but no obstacle, and without an obstacle, there's no conflict."[47] There is widespread, cross-disciplinary agreement on this point. Cognitive psychologists Black and Bower, for example, argue that the essence of "storiness" is the description of problems and of characters' plans for solving them.[48] Terrell, an archaeologist, writes that stories have "heroes and scoundrels, triumphs and defeats, trials and tribulations, conquests and achievements, winners and losers."[49] These general observations are borne out by particular ethnographic examples. Kpelle stories, for example, "never depict harmony or peace, rather there are continual conflicts between man and man, man and woman, and man and nature."[50] And in her work on Ju/'hoansi folklore, Biesele argues that conflict is key to making narrative memorable.[51]

Experimental evidence supports this hypothesis. Mandler and Johnson, for example, report that narrative passages containing goals without outcomes or complications without resolutions are recalled poorly or not at all.[52] Similarly, Bartlett's famous study of memory found that subjects modified or entirely omitted plot details that had no apparent relationship to the goal structure of the story.[53] And Gerrig claims that "making goal and plan inferences is a regular part of text comprehension."[54] Although their terms vary—problems and plans for solving them (Black and Bower), complications and resolutions (Mandler and Johnson), desires and obstacles (Clayton)—these scholars all make the same point: narrative conflict is rooted in human goals, obstacles to their achievement, and attempts to surmount those obstacles.

Narrative events and conflicts are rooted in time and space, or setting.[55] Setting has several dimensions: physical (for example, geographical location, topography, location of objects in relation to one another), temporal (for example, historical period, season, time of day), and social (for example, religious, moral, intellectual, legal climate).[56] However, setting is more than just where and when a story happens (for example, "A long time ago in a galaxy far, far away"): it both constrains and enables actions and events. The setting of "Little Red Riding Hood," for example, contributes to the little girl's vulnerability: she is traveling through woods where there are likely to be dangerous wild animals and where there are few if any people nearby to help her. In Hardy's *Jude the Obscure*, the laws and mores of the time (proscribing divorce) cause the lovers' unhappiness by preventing them from marrying legitimately. Setting, then, is not passive: it is a distinctive environment upon which characters act and to which they react.[57] On this view, setting is a representation of the potential sources of conflict in a given set of circumstances—that is, a localized representation of "the system of forces that regulate all possible action."[58]

The Function of the Whole

We now have the parts of narrative laid out before us like so many pieces of a car engine. What happens when we put all those parts back together again? In other words, if an engine is designed to make a car go, what is a story designed to do?

Let's review what we have learned about the function of individual story parts. We know that storytelling is verbal and interactive: it involves an exchange between storyteller and audience. We also know that, almost without exception, characters are representations of the human psyche; furthermore, characters give us special access to the human psyche that is not available to us in the real world. Finally, we know that conflict is an expression of human problems and plans for solving them, and that setting represents the specific conditions under which those plans are executed, thwarted, accomplished, or undone. The function of narrative, then, would appear to be the representation of the problems humans encounter in their lives and the constraints individuals struggle against in their efforts to solve them.[59] As Humphrey succinctly puts it, the storyteller models human behavior.[60]

Having reassembled the narrative apparatus, turned it on, and seen what it does, we are faced with a new question: Why spend time generating or processing representations of human beings and their problems? To put it in evolutionary terms, what possible benefit(s) does such a representational system offer to the Upper Pleistocene hunter-gatherer?

The fitness benefits of modeling human behavior are most succinctly expressed by the Boy Scout motto: be prepared. As any *Survivor* fan knows, finding food and water, building a shelter, preventing and treating injury and illness, and maintaining group cohesiveness is difficult and demanding work. Hunter-gatherer life is *Survivor* for real: a never-ending stream of tasks, obstacles, and hazards, the local solutions to which the individual is not born knowing. Acquiring this knowledge through firsthand experience is time-consuming, energy-intensive, and potentially dangerous; exclusive reliance upon such a method is unlikely to result in long life. Research on play in humans and other animals makes this same point. Lancy, for example, argues that, "If a young animal had to learn to fight during real fighting, it would be severely injured or killed. If it had to learn to hunt by hunting, it would starve. If it had to learn mothering by practicing on its own offspring, it would have a poor reproduction record."[61]

Tooby and Cosmides have arrived at the same conclusion by an alternative, highly intriguing route. They posit that fictional experiences function as "motivational guidance systems . . . designed to help construct adaptive brain circuitry, and to furnish it with the information, procedures, and representations it needs to behave adaptively when called upon to do so."[62] In other words, some of the information requisite to the development of a given adaptation may be stored in the environment of its bearer. The language faculty operates in this manner: a child must be exposed to language to acquire the ability to use and understand it.[63] Participating in imaginary worlds (for example, pretend play, stories, painting) may provide certain adaptations with critical "environmental" inputs that prepare them to perform as effectively as possible when needed. By "unleashing our reactions to potential lives and realities" Tooby and Cosmides argue, fiction enables us to "feel more richly and adaptively about what we have not actually experienced. This allows us not only to understand others' choices and inner lives better, but to feel our way more foresightfully to adaptively better choices ourselves."[64]

The folklore of contemporary foragers suggests that, indeed, narrative enables people to acquire information, rehearse strategies, or refine skills that are instrumental in surmounting real-life difficulties and dangers.[65] The information contained in narrative may be loosely divided into two categories: universal (that is, pertaining to human nature or the human condition) and local (that is, pertaining to location-specific physical or cultural conditions).[66] Stories commonly contain both kinds of information. Consider the Yanomamö tale "The Child-Armadillo, the Jaguar, and the Millipede." In this story, Millipede chides Jaguar for walking so noisily through the forest: "What noise you're making! If that's how you move people will hear you from far away and will lie in wait to shoot you with their arrows when you pass. . . . I walk slowly without making noise; I only crawl. I never make fallen branches snap." Jaguar wants to walk silently too, so "Millipede smoothed Jaguar's feet, rounded them off, and softened the soles."[67] This story tells the listener not to rely on sound to detect a jaguar's presence in the forest and points to an alternate means of doing so by calling attention to the jaguar's foot (and, hence, footprint). In so doing, it provides valuable information regarding a local predator. The story also points out the advantages of walking as quietly as possible when away from human settlement: if you travel noisily, you will not be able to hear potential threats, and jaguars and other predators—including enemy humans—may hear you from afar and lie in wait to kill you as you pass. This information has universal as well as local applications. On the local level, it identifies two specific predators (jaguars and humans), a specific attack strategy common to both species (forest ambush), and a preventive measure (walk softly).[68] On the universal level, the story underscores our vulnerability to predation and a concomitant safety rule: wherever potential predators may lurk (be they human or nonhuman), it pays to tread lightly and be vigilant.

By simulating a variety of social relationships, behaviors, and consequences, narrative also provides us with an opportunity to gain information about our social environment. Humans are highly gregarious: many of our most fundamental goals (friendship, alliance, status, trade, marriage, child rearing) by definition involve others. This means that we are highly dependent upon the cooperation of our fellows, who may either thwart or facilitate the achievement of those goals, depending on their own interests. Persuading others to cooperate with us and preventing others from antagonizing us depend upon accurately assessing or predicting their thoughts, feelings, motives, and reactions; indeed, several studies have explored the use of "mind reading" by both human and nonhuman primates to manipulate and deceive their fellows.[69] Clearly, then, a deep and broad understanding of human nature can greatly improve an individual's survival and reproduction prospects. Narrative offers a low-cost, readily available means of amplifying our social experience by enabling us to witness a variety of adaptively momentous actions (for example, rape, adultery, incest, conspiracy, homicide, ostracism) from multiple perspectives (for example, victim, perpetrator, accessory, kinsman, friend, enemy).

The ability to assess or predict the thoughts, feelings, motives, and reactions of our fellow humans is known as "theory of mind," and the part of the mind that performs this task is called the "theory of mind module" (TOMM).[70] Although evidence shows that the human mind contains mechanisms designed to respond to fundamental, recurrent social tasks (for example, face recognition, incest avoidance, paternity uncertainty, social exchange),[71] as noted previously, some adaptations depend upon environmental input for their development or successful implementation (for example, incest avoidance and language).[72] It may be that the development of TOMM is similarly dependent upon environmental input and that, by simulating human behavior and cognition (through its use of character), narrative increases the opportunities for such input. On this view, it is telling that the ability to create three-dimensional story characters (that is, characters with beliefs and desires) does not consistently manifest itself until approximately age four—that is, roughly when theory of mind emerges.[73] In their study of storytelling by children between the ages of two and five, Pitcher and Prelinger find that "as age progresses, both boys and girls (with no significant difference) attribute more detailed processes of thinking and of feeling, affect, or emotion to the characters in their stories."[74] Similarly suggestive is Leslie's argument that pretend play in two-year-old children is a precursor to the development of theory of mind: both operations entail the use of second-order representations—that is, representations of representations.[75] Significantly, children begin to engage in rudimentary storytelling—like pretend play, a form of pretense—around age two.[76] These observations, coupled with the fact that children with autism lack theory of mind and do not engage in pretend play,[77] suggest a feedback loop between storytelling and theory of mind: storytelling may help build or strengthen theory of mind, which in turn enriches storytelling, which further enriches theory of mind, and so on.

At the very least, it would appear that narrative provides us with the opportunity to expand our knowledge of human nature and the conditions that constrain it, both universal and local. Obviously, this system of information transmission depends upon some percentage of the population acquiring knowledge the hard way, through trial-and-error. Yet the possession of special knowledge conveys a fitness advantage that one would expect to be lost once such knowledge is shared. How do individuals benefit from sharing their hard-won experience?

Kin selection theory[78] provides one answer: by imparting wisdom to offspring, an individual benefits "all of its kin and descendants for generations, adding a huge pay-off to counterbalance the risks and costs of exploration."[79] The logic of reciprocal altruism points to another benefit of information sharing.[80] It is extremely unlikely that any one individual will be able to acquire through direct experience and in a timely fashion all the information she will need in her lifetime; thus, every individual may be expected at some point in her life to be in need of information. Because an individual will be more likely to receive information from others if she has shared information with them in the past, we would expect people to be motivated to share information with those whom they believe can be counted on to reciprocate. Lastly, our "Machiavellian intelligence"[81]—that is, the ability and inclination to deceive our fellows when it serves our fitness interests—points to a more sinister benefit of information sharing: narrative may be deployed strategically to influence the opinions, beliefs, and behavior of the audience in ways that serve the storyteller's ends.[82]

Discussion

The proposition that narrative is an information storage and transmission system is supported by anthropological research on cultural transmission, which indicates that, in foraging and other preindustrial cultures, individuals acquire the vast majority of their knowledge from other group members.[83] Indeed, Lancy claims that "we have what appears to be a universal tendency for the young to observe and imitate their elders" and that, among the Kpelle, "folklore clearly serves an enculturative function."[84] The flow of knowledge is not only from adult to child; adults often acquire information from other adults. For example, several anthropologists report that men increase their hunting knowledge not only by observing other hunters but by listening to them "tell the hunt" (that is, recount their hunting experiences):

> In storytelling around the campfire at night [Kalahari hunter-gatherer] men give graphic descriptions of hunts of the recent and distant past. To find animals requires all the information on their movements that can be gained from others' observations and the hunter's own interpretation of signs. Hunters will spend many hours discussing the habits and movements of animals.[85]

As Boyer observes, "One thing that modern humans did and still do vastly more than any other species is exchange information of all kinds. . . . The proper milieu in which humans live is that of information, especially information provided by other humans. It is their ecological niche."[86]

The notion that narrative simulates human experience is similarly noncontroversial: *mimesis* is an ancient and fundamental principle of literary theory.[87] From an adaptationist perspective, however, the question is not simply whether narrative transmits information—or whether narrative simulates human experience—but whether narrative is specially designed to transmit information by simulating human experience. Do other forms of creative expression perform the same task?

I argued previously that other art forms are less effective narrative media than storytelling. They are also less effective at holistic simulation of human experience. For example, while it clearly attempts to represent certain features of the human environment (for example, people, animals, landscape), visual art does not readily lend itself to the representation of internal states (for example, desires, motives, goals), causally linked events, or temporal sequence. Music and dance, on the other hand, are useful for representing the emotional state of the performer (for example, bellicosity, sexual arousal, anger, sadness) but not for representing more complex or targeted internal states (for example, suspicions of adultery, envy of a favored sibling, desire to usurp a chief), let alone the internal states of others. These media are also inadequate to the task of representing setting, temporal sequence, or causally linked events. Indeed, these media seem much better suited for emotional arousal or various kinds of display (for example, signaling social cohesion)[88] than for habitat simulation. Pantomime is similarly deficient: without language, it is extremely difficult to represent characters, objects, goals, or obstacles with particularity or precision. The identity of the persona being simulated is indeterminate, as are the time and place of the action. In sum, no other art form does all the things that narrative does. Neither visual art, sculpture, music, dance, nor pantomime effectively simulate the collective constraints on human fitness (people, animals, objects, events, phenomena, time, and topography), nor does any of these forms lend itself to the simulation of complex goals, obstacles, and their outcomes. In answer to our question, then, it would appear that narrative is uniquely well-suited to the task of simulating human experience, which in turn suggests that art behavior is not a homogeneous cognitive phenomenon.

Of course this does not "prove" that narrative is an adaptation: this question is far from being resolved. Nor does it speak to the question of whether or not other art forms are adaptations. What we can say at this point is that narrative appears to meet the criteria of special design. We can add the corollary that other art forms are not well-designed for holistic simulation of human experience. This is not to argue that other art forms do not serve as means of storing and transmitting information; on the contrary, some art behaviors appear to transmit information of various kinds.[89]

The conceptualization of art behaviors as information storage and transmission media is highly compatible with a constellation of ideas regarding the evolutionary trajectory of human intelligence. In their seminal 1987 essay, Tooby and DeVore argue that what distinguishes humans from other species is their occupation of the "cognitive niche"[90]—that is, our highly elaborated ability to manufacture, implement, and transmit cognitive models of our environment. Culture, they argue, is the transmission of these cognitive models between and across generations. This information-based view of culture is not new to anthropology. As Roberts wrote four decades ago,

> It is possible to regard all culture as information and to view any single culture as an "information economy" in which information is received or created, stored, retrieved, transmitted, utilized, and even lost. . . . Information is stored in the minds of . . . members and . . . artifacts. . . . Human storage systems have their limitations. . . . There is a limit to the amount of information any one individual or combination of individuals

can learn and remember. . . . [It] is safe to assert that no tribal culture is sufficiently small in inventory to be stored in one brain.[91]

What is new, however, is the addition of human life-history research to this discourse. Research and theory regarding the evolution of prolonged juvenility in humans points to two possible selection pressures that may have led to our occupation of the cognitive niche. One view posits that delayed maturity was selected for as humans began pursuing richer, more difficult-to-acquire resources, which demanded comparatively complex technologies and strategies. Prolonged juvenility allowed individuals to acquire and hone the foraging skill and knowledge needed to bring in these highly desirable but difficult-to-acquire resources. An alternate view proposes that prolonged juvenility allowed individuals to acquire and hone the social skills and knowledge requisite to survival and reproduction in the highly complex social world of humans.[92] Both views envision the extended human juvenile period as a means of acquiring a set of skills that, in adult life, boosted the individual's chances of surviving and reproducing. Thus, the cognitive niche hypothesis and the knowledge/skill-acquisition hypotheses are different sides of the same theoretical coin: the former identifies our zoological uniqueness and the latter explains how it might have evolved. Activities such as painting, narrative, song, dance, drama, proverbs, and games can be seen as different forms of cognitive modeling, serving collectively as a cognitive gymnasium whereby juveniles can acquire and exercise (and adults can expand and tone) the foraging and social skills required by existence as a highly gregarious, hunting-and-gathering animal.

One such cognitive workout is found in the Kpelle game *Kwa-tinaŋ*. In this game for two players, thirty-three stones are laid out in groups of three, four, and five in a cross formation, and the first player calls out instructions to the second player for removing the stones until all the stones have been removed. The catch is that the stones must be removed one at a time in a standard order while the caller has his back turned to the configuration.[93] This game requires the caller to construct a mental map of the configuration, which must be continually updated as stones are removed. Just as running strengthens the leg muscles, play of this sort might contribute to the development and strengthening of memory for spatial arrays, which—like strong legs—is essential for successful foraging. Unfortunately, quantitative ethnographic study of forager art and artists has been sorely neglected. Given the prominence of both human life history and cultural transmission in current evolutionary anthropological research, the documentation of hunter-horticulturalist art behavior is both a highly promising and a highly pressing task.

Notes

The epigraphs for this chapter are drawn from Oates 1992, 8 and Thornhill and Palmer 2000, 27.

1. See Dunbar 1996; P. Lieberman 1989; Miller 2000b, 260; Pinker 1994.

2. See Bahn, 1991, 1994; Chauvet, Deschamps, and Hillaire 1996; Dissanayake 2000; Gamble 1983; Mithen 1996, 156; Pfeiffer 1982.

3. See Knight, Power, and Watts 1995; Watts 1999.

4. Pinker 1997 discusses the arts, including fictional narrative, as by-products. Mithen 1996 argues that art, religion, and science are the by-product of the evolution of cognitive integration between four specialized kinds of human intelligence: technical, natural history, social, and linguistic. My work addresses the question of whether narrative could be an adaptation. See Scalise Sugiyama 1996, 2001a, 2001b. For an alternative to these views, see D. S. Wilson, this volume.

5. The classic work on this subject is Williams 1966.

6. See Scalise Sugiyama 2001c.

7. See Dennett 1995; Tooby and Cosmides 2001.

8. See Dissanayake 2000, 134, 139, as well as Dissanayake 1992b, 1995. For a variation on Dissanayake's hypothesis, see Boyd, this volume.

9. See Coe 2003, 3.

10. Miller 2000b, 131.

11. See Gangestad and Thornhill 1998; Orians and Heerwagen 1992; D. Singh 1993; Symons 1995.

12. Tooby and Cosmides 2001, 17.

13. Tooby and Cosmides 2001, 17; see also Thornhill 2003, 9.

14. See Scalise Sugiyama 1996, 2001a.

15. See Cassill 1981, xxi.

16. See Oates 1992, 7–8; see also Clayton 1984; Kermode 1981.

17. See Black and Bower 1980; Kintsch and van Dijk 1975; Labov and Waletzky 1967; Lehnert 1981; Mandler 1984; Mandler and Johnson 1977; Rumelhart 1975; Schank 1975; Thorndyke 1977.

18. See Scalise Sugiyama 1996, 2001a, 2001c. For a discussion of narrative universals, see Hogan 2003.

19. See Holmberg 1969.

20. See Freeman 1983.

21. See Holmberg 1969, 118–19.

22. See Lloyd 1989, 218.

23. For adaptationist treatments of this tale, see Scalise Sugiyama 1992, 2004, and forthcoming.

24. Archaeological evidence suggests that our ancestors were making music by the Upper Paleolithic Era: bone flutes have been found dating from 22,000 to

35,000 B.P., and possibly to 82,000 B.P. See Dissanayake 2000, 147; Lau et al., 1997. Studies also indicate that humans may have neural specializations for processing music. See, for example, Ayotte, Peretz, and Hyde 2002; Johnsrude, Penhune, and Zatorre 2000; Peretz 1996; Peretz and Morais 1993; Perry et al., 1999.

   25. See Hagen and Bryant 2003. Nota bene: By "music" I do not mean song. Owing to its verbal component, song is a hybrid medium, combining music, poetry, and/or narrative.

   26. See Pinker 1994, 279.

   27. See Rumelhart 1975; Thorndyke 1977.

   28. Rumelhart 1975, 212.

   29. See Mandler and Johnson 1977, 115.

   30. See Storey 1996. Se also Biesele 1993; Scholes 1980.

   31. See Holman 1980, 428, 284.

   32. See Lloyd 1989, 220.

   33. Rumelhart 1975, 215, 214.

   34. Mandler and Johnson 1977, 115.

   35. Holman 1980, 5.

   36. See M. Turner 1996, 13.

   37. Holman 1980, 74.

   38. Holmberg 1969, 119.

   39. See Barthelme 1987, 427–32, 427, 428, 431.

   40. Barthelme 1987, 427, 431.

   41. Forster 1972, 137.

   42. Scholes 1980, 206.

   43. Dunbar 1996, 6.

   44. See Bower and Morrow 1990, 48.

   45. Holman 1980, 75.

   46. See Booth 1983, 3.

   47. Clayton 1984, 13. See also Cassill 1981; Charters 1991; Oates 1992, 8.

   48. Black and Bower 1980. See also Kermode 1981; Kintsch and van Dijk 1975; Labov and Waletzky 1967; Lehnert 1981; Mandler 1984, 50–53; Mandler and Johnson 1977; Rumelhart 1975; Schank 1975; Thorndyke 1977.

   49. Terrell 1990, 4.

   50. Lancy 1996, 125.

   51. Biesele 1993.

   52. Mandler and Johnson 1977. See also Trabasso and Sperry 1985.

   53. Bartlett 1932.

   54. Gerrig 1988, 251–52.

   55. See Schank 1990; Thorndyke 1977.

   56. See Holman 1980.

57. For an extended treatment of the role of environment in literature see J. Carroll 2001b.

58. J. Carroll 1995, 136.

59. For discussion and detailed examples, see Scalise Sugiyama 1996, 2001a, 2001c. See also Pinker 1997, who despite arguing that storytelling is a by-product, nevertheless agrees that fiction is instructive and that it represents human problems and solutions: "Fictional narratives supply us with a mental catalogue of the fatal conundrums we might face someday and the outcomes of strategies we could deploy in them" (543). Carroll (p. 87) argues that the arts "simulate subjective human experience, map out social relations, evoke sexual and social interactions, depict the intimate relations of kin, and locate the whole complex and interactive array of human behavioral systems within models of the total world order."

60. Humphrey 1983, 67.

61. Lancy 1980, 482.

62. Tooby and Cosmides 2001, 16. Tooby and Cosmides define fiction very broadly, as "any representation intended to be understood as nonveridical, whether story, drama, film, painting, sculpture, and so on" (2001, 7).

63. See Pinker 1994.

64. Tooby and Cosmides 2001, 23.

65. The oral traditions of contemporary foraging peoples contain a wealth of local zoological, botanical, and topographical information that is difficult or costly to acquire at firsthand, which I have documented elsewhere; see Scalise Sugiyama 1996, 2001a, 2001c, 2004. Tonkinson makes a similar observation regarding the Dreamtime, which narrates the travels of ancestral beings from one place to another through hundreds of miles of desert. He argues that these tales familiarize the Mardudjara with the harsh and vast regions they must traverse to survive, providing them with landmarks and giving them a feeling for the distances between important locales. See Tonkinson 1978, 89.

66. Elsewhere I discuss the use of narrative to transmit general information regarding human nature and specific information regarding local constraints (see Scalise Sugiyama 2003). Briefly, I argue that, because all habitats present the same basic set of obstacles to survival and reproduction, we would expect any given literary setting to represent one or more adaptive problems ("the human condition"). However, because literary settings are representations of human habitats, and human habitats vary, we would expect local solutions to adaptive problems to vary in literature as they do in real life. On this view, then, we would expect narrative art to express both, human universals (for example, adaptive problems, cognitive adaptations) and cultural variation (for example, local solutions to adaptive problems).

67. Wilbert and Simoneau 1990, 291.

68. The Yanomamo live in prime jaguar habitat, and warfare, in the form of surprise raids, is a common feature of Yanomamo existence (see Chagnon 1979). These conditions obtain for other Amazonian groups, such as the Ache (see, for example, Hill and Hurtado 1996) and Shiwiar (Jivaro). The latter stress the importance of walking quietly in the jungle, instructing the uninitiated to "walk like a jaguar," and the ambush tactic described by Millipede is a recognized Jivaroan attack strategy (Lawrence Sugiyama, Associate Professor, Anthropology Department, University of Oregon, Eugene, personal communication).

69. See Byrne and Whiten 1988; Cheney and Seyfarth 1991; DeVore 1986; Scalise Sugiyama 1996; Whiten and Byrne 1997.

70. See Baron-Cohen, Leslie, and Firth 1985; Leslie 1987, 1991.

71. See, for example, Cosmides and Tooby 1992; Daly and Wilson 1988; Shepher 1971; Wolf 1970; Wolf and Huang 1980.

72. See Shepher 1971; Wolf 1970; Wolf and Huang 1980; and Pinker 1994.

73. See Baron-Cohen, Leslie, and Firth 1985; Leslie 1987; Shatz, Wellman, and Silber 1983.

74. Pitcher and Prelinger 1963, 158–59.

75. See Leslie 1987.

76. Pitcher and Prelinger 1963.

77. See Baron-Cohen 1995; Frith 1989; Tooby and Cosmides 2001.

78. See Hamilton 1964.

79. Tooby and DeVore 1987, 210.

80. See Trivers 1971.

81. See Byrne and Whiten 1988; Whiten and Byrne 1997.

82. See Scalise Sugiyama 1996.

83. See, for example, Fortes 1970; Hewlett and Cavalli-Sforza 1986; Ohmagari and Berkes 1997.

84. Lancy 1996, 83, 125.

85. See Liebenberg 1990, 80; see also Biesele 1978, 940; Blurton Jones and Konner 1976; Laughlin 1968, 308; Leacock 1954, 14; Nelson 1969, 374.

86. Boyer 2001, 325.

87. See, for example, Abrams 1953; J. Carroll 1995; Storey 1996.

88. See Hagen and Bryant 2003.

89. See, for example, Hagen and Bryant 2003; Miller 2000b; Mithen 1990.

90. Tooby and DeVore 1987, 207–8.

91. Roberts 1964, 438–39.

92. See, for example, Blurton Jones and Marlowe 2002; Bock and Kaplan 2001; Geary and Flinn 2001; Kaplan, Hill, Lancaster, and Hurtado 2000; Leigh 2001; Sugiyama 2004.

93. Lancy 1996, 104–5.

PART III

Darwinian Theory
and Scientific Methods

Can literary scholarship benefit not only from evolutionary theory but also from the quantitative methods scientists use to explore their fields of research? In many ways the premises of this section are more radical than those featured in previous sections. Two of the articles in this section (by Gottschall and by Kruger, Fisher, and Jobling) suggest that many (though by no means all) literary problems are best approached within the quantitative framework of scientific methodology. The implication, clearly unconventional in the context of humanities relativism, is that some literary problems have determinate answers that can be revealed through the use of the scientific method. The conclusions of these essays have relevance not only to the literary works under study but also to ancient and still-intense debates about human psychology and behavior—especially about gender and sexuality. At the heart of all three contributions in this section is the conviction that by drawing on Darwinian theory, literary scholars can contribute to scientific and literary knowledge at the same time. Literature—from classic novels to erotica to world folktales—is a vast, cheap, and virtually inexhaustible argosy of information about human nature—how it expresses itself species-typically and in particular cultural contexts. This resource has been largely overlooked by human scientists. Moreover, of the relatively few scientists who have used literature as data, most have relied on the qualitative methods of the humanities rather than on scientific quantification. The articles in this section argue that (1) the production of scientifically reliable information about literary works is possible, (2) specific literary hypotheses can be quantitatively tested, and (3) literary data can be mined as a precious trove of information for the scientific study of human behavior, psychology, cognition, and culture.

Quantitative Literary Study: A Modest Manifesto and Testing the Hypotheses of Feminist Fairy Tale Studies

Jonathan Gottschall

Part 1: Literary Studies and Quantitative Methods— a Modest Manifesto

In the early 1660s a London haberdasher of small wares named John Graunt—a self-made and self-educated man—had an inspiration. Since the sixteenth century London's Bills of Mortality had listed all "The Diseases and Casualties" of the week, partly to serve as an early warning system during plague time. For instance, during the week of April 11–18, 1665, one died from cancer, twenty-one from "dropsie," six from the hangman, fourteen from griping in the guts, eight from "rifing" of the lights, eight from stopping of the stomach, one from "wormes," and none from plague. Five months later, during the week of September 12–19, more died in almost every category and 7,165 died of plague.[1] The bills also provided sex ratio information on the total numbers of burials and christenings, the net increase or decrease in burials, and, incongruously, the amount of white and wheaten bread to be purchased for a penny or a half-penny.

In his *Natural and Political Observations Mentioned in a Following Index and Made upon the Bills of Mortality* (1662) Graunt noted that, while rich people used the bills at plague time to better "judge the necessity of their removal," most read them only to see "how the burials increased or decreased; and among the Casualties, what had happened rare, and extraordinary in the week currant; so as they might take the same as a Text to talk upon, in the next Company." Graunt suspected that the bills had potentially "greater uses" and proceeded to do something unprecedented: he went to the Hall of the Parish-Clerks and gathered copies of all bills on record. He meticulously compiled the information and organized it in tabular form so that it would be possible to compare births, diseases, and causes of death "by year, by season, by Parish, or other Division of the City." Based on his tables Graunt made 106 natural and/or political observations, "some concerning Trade

199

and Government, others concerning the Air, Countries, Seasons, Fruitfulness, Health, Diseases, Longevity, and the proportions between the Sex, and Ages of Mankinde."[2] Here are some of Graunt's discoveries, in his own words:

- That about one third of all that were quick die under five years old, and about thirty six per Centum under six.
- Annis 1603, and 1625, about a fifth part of the whole died, and eight times more than were born.
- That Purples, small-Pox, and other malignant Diseases fore-run the Plague.
- That not one in two thousand are Murthered in London.
- That Plagues always come in with King's Reigns is most false.
- That there are about six millions, and a half of people in England and Wales.
- That there are fourteen Males for thirteen Females in London, and in the Country but fifteen Males for fourteen Females.
- There being fourteen Males to thirteen Females, and Males being pro-lifique fourty years, and Females but twenty five, it follows that in effect there be 560 males to 325 Females.
- The said inequality is reduced by the latter marriage of the males, and their imployment in wars, Sea-voiage, and Colonies.
- Physicians have two Women Patients to one Man, and yet more Men die than Women.[3]

As might be inferred on the basis of this list, Graunt is now esteemed as a pioneer in fields as diverse as medicine, political science, sociology, demography, statistics, criminology, population biology, and others where the systematic study of populations (human or other) is vital. The methodology Graunt established allowed him "not onely to examine the Conceits, Opinions, and Conjectures, which upon view of a few scattered Bills I had taken up; but did also admit new ones, as I found reason, and occasion from my Tables."[4]

This insight represents a watershed moment in the development of the modern medical, life, and human sciences. Graunt was among the first to see that compiling and analyzing population-level data allows a researcher to systematically test the validity of his or her preconceptions and discover relationships in data that might otherwise be invisible.

Observations helped inaugurate a true and revolutionary Age of Discovery in the sciences of man and society. Graunt and his more mathematically sophisticated successors would discover, over the next 150 years or so, vast and unanticipated regularities in rates of birth, death, trade, mortality, murder, theft, disease, suicide, insanity, and more. These findings were often wholly unanticipated or perfectly opposed to expectation. For instance, Graunt himself discovered that, contrary to common prejudice, members of "the weaker sex" perished at lower rates in virtually every age cohort. Edmund Halley (1656–1742), of Halley's Comet fame, reported in astonishment that half of the souls in a sample of English towns perished before the age of seventeen. The self-styled "social physicist" Adolphe Quetlet (1796–1874) found many striking regularities in important areas of social and life history data, and he also discovered things that were more trivial but amazing nonetheless. For instance, he found that different breeds of intellectuals tended to have different average life expectancies. Natural philosophers in his sample tended to live the longest, outliving the shortest lived intellectuals, the poets, by fully eighteen years.

    Impressed with these regularities many nineteenth-century thinkers welcomed "the exciting prospect that the application of probability to empirical social data could produce a social physics to stand beside Newtonian natural philosophy."[5] Social scientists are more sober minded now; they have largely abandoned the extravagant Newtonian hopes of the statistical "age of exuberance."[6] But, in a real sense, the glacially paced development of what is known as "modern statistical methodology" over the course of 270 years—the conventional dates stretch from around 1650 to 1933—rivals those revolutions associated with the names of Darwin and Newton.[7] The slow creep of quantitative and statistical methods across disciplines of the natural and social sciences radically and irrevocably altered the way we seek, process, and evaluate information.

My argument is that literary studies is now in something quite like the position of those areas of knowledge that would become the social sciences before the advent of quantitative analysis of mass social phenomena. To read the history of the gradual coalescence of modern statistical methodology is to be constantly confronted with one salient fact: quantitative and statistical analyses have consistently revealed knowledge that could not otherwise have been known or, oftentimes, even suspected; these methods have continuously forced deep revision or outright abandonment of the most deeply seated and intuitively held convictions. To phrase my argument in the form of a prediction: if the community of literary scholars will make limited and judicious use of quantitative methodology, it will experience precisely the same benefits that have accrued to other human-related fields. Literary scholars will discover important things about literature that were previously unknown or unsuspected, and some of our most comfortable assumptions will be proven illusory or in need of significant revision. We can be confident in this prediction because this is exactly what has occurred in all other human-related disciplines that have wed quantification to their traditionally qualitative approaches, no matter how vigorously some initially protested that the subjects under study were fundamentally unquantifiable.

The main support for this argument will be presented in the form of a practical example. Inspired by the studies of Graunt and his many successors, this essay presents results of a "census" of world folktales—a description of "vital statistics" about certain broadly defined character types (males versus females, protagonists versus antagonists). The collected data is used to systematically test prominent feminist claims about folk and fairy tales that enjoy broad academic and popular credence and which are directly based on strong constructivist notions about human nature generally and gender specifically. The conclusion proposes practical steps for establishing a literary study in which more reliable and durable knowledge can be produced and accumulated. Before moving on to the empirical portion of the study, however, it is necessary to prepare the way by addressing some likely objections.

QUANTIFYING THE NOT EASILY QUANTIFIABLE

Those who seek to study literature quantitatively frequently hear two main objections. The first concern is based on the conviction that the really interesting questions in literary studies simply cannot be quantified. The second concern is that even if challenges associated with quantifying literary information could be overcome, quantitative analysis steamrolls over all of the complexity of individual characters and works that it is the main business of literary scholars to examine. It is objected that, while statistical generalization may be appropriate for fields of the social, human, and natural sciences, it is inappropriate for literary studies. Statistical generalization entails stark reductions of literary complexity and nuance and, in literary studies, complexity and nuance are bread and butter.

Statistical thinking has transformed the way economies and governments are managed, the way that illness is tracked, how the efficacy of drugs and medical procedures are established, and the way that crime is studied and punishment is assessed—in short, it has changed the way that investigators of strikingly diverse phenomena seek to find order in chaos. Thus it is interesting to see that precisely the same concerns literary scholars voice about quantification have been raised in nearly every human-related field to which it has been introduced (the main exception is psychology).[8] As the premier historian of statistics Stephen Stigler writes:

> In the 300 yrs since Newton's *Principia*, mathematical probability and statistics have found application in all the sciences—social, physical, biological. In each area where these ideas have been introduced there has been resistance as the protectors of the different realms have sought to prevent the "Queen of Sciences" [mathematics] from conquering new territory. The arguments against quantification have at times been sound and irrefutable, at other times ignorant and self-serving. At times, the

battles have been vicious, scorched earth affairs, at others, they have been carried out on the highest intellectual planes. This tension, between those who appreciate and wish to extend quantitative analysis and those who argue that only qualitative description can deal with the essence of all but the most limited questions that touch our lives persists today.[9]

Quantitative methodologies were resisted even in fields where, today, all would agree that they are absolutely vital. For example, none of us, today, would be eager to take a new drug or submit to a new medical procedure that had not been tested in a large-scale, double-blind study, and few would choose to consult a physician who relied purely on intuition, ignoring statistical studies on the characteristics of illnesses, the efficacy of treatments, and so forth. We would all prefer to consult the physician who combined excellent medical intuition, experience, and sensitivity to our individual medical histories with a firm and broad foundation in the scientific literature. Yet quantification initially met with staunch resistance in the field of medicine. Opponents objected that "the numerical method" denied "the variability of medical facts, which could only be fully appreciated through induction and medical intuition."[10] In short, opponents argued that medicine was an art form and that studies of populations were all but worthless because the physician's ultimate responsibility was to the individual patient. Statistics were good at describing the composite features of a population—an abstraction that Quetelet dubbed *l'homme moyen* (the average man)—but real patients weren't average men, they were all unique individuals.

A very similar description of the initial reaction to quantitative methods could be constructed for almost all other human-related fields where the value of those methods now goes mostly unquestioned. Critically, the point is not that investigators in these fields eventually discovered that everything could be reduced to numbers after all. Rather, they came to realize that quantitative and qualitative tools were both utterly indispensable for a reasonably complete exploration of their fields, each set of tools being appropriate for different types of questions.

Thus, while concerns about statistical generalization in literary study are perhaps natural, more quantitative research will be valuable for two principal reasons. First, and most obviously, quantitative analysis may help us do a better job of seeing patterns in complex literary works, or large populations of literary works, that might otherwise have been overlooked or underappreciated. As Anthony Kenny writes, the value of quantification can be likened to the value of aerial photography:

Photography from the sky can enable patterns to be detected which are obscured when one is too close to the ground: it enables us to see the wood despite the trees. So the statistical study of a text [or texts] can reveal broad patterns, macroscopic uniformities in a writer's work [or a population of works] which can escape notice as one reads word by word and sentence by sentence.[11]

The second reason is less intuitive and requires more explanation: the addition of a quantitative dimension to literary scholarship will substantially improve the power and precision of strictly qualitative work.

This point is best communicated by analogy with other fields where quantitative generalization about population-level traits is common. What if someone argued that psychology should not work toward reliable generalizations about human sexual attraction, aggression, social exchange, self-perception, and development, but rather it should focus exclusively on individual people? Psychologists should not base their conclusions on statistical trends in hundreds or thousands of subjects from diverse backgrounds. Rather, psychologists should study the individual person, get to know him in all his details, his family history, his formative experiences, his tendencies, biases, and so forth. Or, as another example, anthropologists should not make generalizations about social mores, kinship structures, and hierarchical patterns in different types of societies. Rather, anthropology should be confined exclusively to the study of individual cultures and subcultures.

This suggestion would, of course, be unwelcome in these fields. The typical psychologist or anthropologist would answer that studies at this level of particularity are indispensable: if you want to study human psychology or customs it would certainly be useful to do detailed research on individual people and cultures; case studies are valuable parts of psychology and anthropology. But, they would continue, such studies cannot be understood fully unless they can be placed within a broad, general context.

Of course, literary scholars appreciate that a researcher's grasp of the general shapes her or his ability to comprehend the particular. Judgments about individual characters, works, and authors are always influenced by a sense of the general. However, in literary studies general impressions are formed almost exclusively on the basis of qualitative impressions. Where formal studies of given literary populations exist (Victorian novels, femme fatales, Caribbean fiction, and so forth) quantitative studies account for a negligible portion of the total research. In many cases, this is because the problems addressed genuinely and stiffly resist quantification. In other cases, however, researchers are simply not in the habit of pursuing a quantitative response. Such responses are valuable because they are designed to control for subjectivity, selection, and confirmation biases, and, as such, they may help us do a better job of reaching accurate generalizations. This is not to suggest that quantitative tools do not have their own limitations or, much less, to argue that they are, as a rule, superior to qualitative approaches. That would be as meaningless as arguing that hammers are better than screwdrivers. It is a mistake to see quantitative and qualitative methods as competing alternatives; they are, on the contrary, entirely complementary. Each set of tools helps to make up for the inadequacies of the other.

Finally, the objection may arise that these arguments, like those of nineteenth-century "social physicists," are based on a false or strained analogy between literary study, where data are messy and complex, and fields where data are simpler and more straightforward. The abortive field of "social physics" failed to reduce human social life to a few fundamental laws because, in contrast to the phenomena studied by physicists, the forces governing human social life are vastly complex. But there is not a similar gulf in the complexity of phenomena studied by social scientists and literary scholars. Both fields explore exactly the same complicated things, although in different types of data sources: human social behavior, psychology, culture, and cognition as they manifest species typically and in specific cultural ecologies.[12] Literary studies *does* often deal in the unquantifiable and the not easily quantifiable, but in this it is not different from most other human-related fields, where a significant proportion of important questions are always best approached qualitatively. Sociologists, anthropologists, economists, and psychologists all face daunting challenges in attempting to assign numbers to different aspects of human behavior, society, culture, and psychology. These problems are never fully resolved. Rather, ideally, the problems are confronted, difficulties are minimized as much as is practical, and potential blind spots and inadequacies frankly acknowledged. These blind spots can then be addressed by other quantitative and qualitative approaches, and researchers can be most confident in their knowledge when different methods converge on the same results.

This may seem reasonable in theory, but how, in practice, do we assign numbers to the riot of information contained in literary works? In confronting this challenge, we can begin by consulting examples from the social sciences. A common problem across fields of the social sciences is that many sources of potentially valuable information come in text form: government documents, political speeches, personal advertisements, subject interviews, ethnographies, and so on. Traditionally, social scientists have attempted to extract information from these sources qualitatively, in much the same way that literary scholars extract information from literary works. However, over the last fifty or so years "content analysts" from diverse disciplines of the social and human sciences have been developing an increasingly large and sophisticated suite of methods for reducing some aspects of the information in text messages to a form suitable for quantitative analysis.[13] Thus the encouraging answer to the question posed at the head of this paragraph is that many different methods for quantitatively summarizing complicated text are already widely in use in other fields—to make a start, all we need do is apply them.

Obviously we cannot claim priority in our call for a more significant quantitative dimension in literary study. Over the last several decades attempts have repeatedly been made to establish quantification in literary study.[14] But despite their best efforts, advocates have never come close to mustering the critical mass required to move quantitative methods from the margins to the mainstreams of literary studies. The reasons for this are small and large. On the smaller side there are fears about the ease of "lying with statistics" (as though there were no sophists or charlatans prior to the mid–seventeenth century); there is significant concern in some quarters about the political and ideological ramifications of scientific methodologies (as though the "values" of science were mainly inherent in the tools rather than their wielders); and there is the practical fact that a stunningly high proportion of literary scholars honestly believe themselves to be mathematically disabled (as though elementary concepts taught in undergraduate statistics courses are beyond the faculties of people with the brains and discipline to earn doctorates).[15] While these and other issues are contributing factors, the most important impediment is the old and largely unexamined assumption that the objects literary scholars study, and the questions they ask, are of a fundamentally different character than those in all nonhumanities disciplines. This essay is an argument to the contrary.

We now move on to the empirical portion of this essay—a description of a large-scale content analysis of world folktales designed to test specific literary hypotheses. Like Graunt's *Observations*, this population-level portrait reveals some things that might not have been known before and strongly encourages reconsideration of important ideas that are widely taken for granted. However, this study is also like *Observations* in that it is an early and in many ways imperfect effort. This study amply suggests the potential of content analysis methodology in literary studies, but it does not represent a full realization of this potential. In segueing to the empirical study, it is difficult to improve on Graunt's humble introduction to his own *Observations*:

> How far I have succeeded in the Premisses, I now offer to the World's censure. Who, I hope will not expect from me, not professing Letters, things demonstrated with the same certainty, wherewith Learned men determine in their Scholes; but will take it well, that I should offer at a new thing . . . and that I have taken the pains, and been at the charge, of setting out those Tables, whereby all men may both correct my Positions, and raise others of their own: For herein I have, like a silly Scholeboy, coming to say my Lesson to the World (that Peevish, and Tetchie Master) brought a bundle of Rods wherewith to be whipt, for every mistake I have committed.[16]

Part 2: Testing the Hypotheses of Feminist Fairy Tale Studies

The defining empirical claim of classic feminist gender theory is that gender is primarily (if not exclusively) a product of nurture not nature. Behavioral, emotional, psychological, and even physical traits stereotypically associated with males and females have little basis in biology; they are products of the socialization environments particular to given types of societies. This understanding has shaped an immense body of feminist literary criticism and theory over the last several decades. Nowhere is this truer than in feminist analysis and critique of European fairy tales. While a minority of feminist scholars have advocated for fairy tales as a source of positive role models for young girls,[17] voices more numerous and loud have contended that gender patterns in European tales inflict profound damage upon the malleable minds of children, especially girls. Beginning with influential analyses by Simone de Beauvoir and Betty Friedan, feminists have argued that European tales are rife with stereotyped male and female ideals: men should be strong, active, and courageous; women should be beautiful, tractable, and passive.[18] These patterns not only reflect arbitrary cultural norms of the patriarchal west,[19] they also actively perpetuate them: fairy tales enforce "cultural norms that exalt [female] passivity . . . and perpetuate the patriarchal status quo"; they are manipulative "parables of feminine socialization"; they "exert awesome imaginative power over the female psyche"; they "prescribe female behavior"; they are "venomous" tools of "a patriarchal plot"; they preserve and "reinforce male hegemony in the civilizing process"; and they train women to be rape victims.[20]

   While the most prominent feminist work on the fairy tale was conducted in the 1970s and 1980s, its conclusions are still widely credited by educated laypersons and by scholars of the fairy tale. As evidence of the former, the conclusions of feminist fairy tale researchers have materially influenced several recently published collections of folk and fairy tales that are designed to correct for gender distortions in the classic European tales.[21] As evidence of the latter, *Marvels and Tales*, the leading journal of fairy tale studies, recently published a sympathetic special issue on feminist approaches to the fairy tale called *Fairy Tale Liberation—Thirty Years Later.*[22] To this issue the editor contributes a generally approving critical survey in which he shows that most of the core claims of feminist fairy tale studies continue to enjoy broad support.[23]

   The claim that European tales reflect and perpetuate the arbitrary gender norms of western patriarchal societies will be referred to, henceforth, as the social construction hypothesis (SCH). Every reasonable and plausible hypothesis should yield testable, or at least potentially testable, predictions.[24] The SCH is no exception. Since gender patterns in European fairy tales are said to reflect socially constructed differences between the sexes, the straightforward prediction of the SCH is that samples of traditional folktales from different culture areas around the world will evince markedly different patterns of female characterization than those identified in European tales. In short, the SCH predicts that an analysis of a culturally diverse sample will reveal diverse gender patterns.

DATA AND METHODS

Folktale collections were chosen so as to maximize the geographical variability of the sample as well as variability in levels of cultural complexity. Specialized collections focusing on specific themes, plots, or character types (for example, *Hopi Trickster Tales, Hero Tales of the South Slavs*) were rejected in favor of generic collections (*Hopi Folk Tales, Traditional Tales of the South Slavs*). All collections were of traditional tales originally transmitted through the oral tradition. In all, the study includes tales from forty-eight different culture areas from all inhabited continents, varying widely in ecology, geographic location, racial and ethnic composition, political systems, religious beliefs, and levels of cultural complexity. All non-English tales had been translated into English, and the sample ran the gamut from polished fairy tales to literal transcriptions of tales told in traditional contexts. Taken as a whole, the sample is a reasonable approximation of the universe of world folktales. A list of the collections and tales coded can be accessed by contacting the author or via the Internet at the following URL: http://www.science.mcmaster.ca/psychology/ehb/Gottschall(FolkTales).pdf.

Once suitable collections of tales were identified, each data collector (ten female and five male undergraduates at St. Lawrence University) scanned the thirty longest tales from each of three culture areas. (Several researchers were responsible for tales from four culture areas. They volunteered to code collections of tales that only arrived through interlibrary loan after the main portion of the study had been completed.) The thirty longest tales were chosen, rather than a random selection, to ensure a sample consisting of long, information-rich tales rather than short, information-poor tales. Since the emphasis of the inquiry was on the attributes of female characters, each of 1,440 tales was then scanned for the presence of a main female protagonist or a main female antagonist. A protagonist was defined as a character who plays a central role in the action and who the audience is led to root predominantly for rather than predominantly against. An antagonist was defined as a character who plays a central role in the action, who acts as an obstacle to the goals of the protagonist(s), and who the audience is led to root predominantly against rather than predominantly for. Any tale containing one or both of these character types was flagged for coding. This sampling procedure likely introduced some biases into the sample that will be discussed in the results section.

A coding form, reproduced in appendix 1, was developed to collect information on the main characters of all flagged tales. While male characters were not the main targets of the study, coding forms were also filled out for all main male protagonists and antagonists to provide a measuring stick for the characteristics of the females. In all, researchers completed 1,307 coding forms on 658 different tales. Of the completed forms, 568 were filled out for female protagonists, 392 for male protagonists, 197 for female antagonists, and 150 for male antagonists.

Data analysis is reported for the sample as a whole and for each of six geographical regions: (1) Europe, (2) East Eurasia, (3) North America, (4) South America, (5) Africa, and (6) the Insular Pacific combined with South East Asia and the Pacific Rim. (See appendix 2.) Our division of culture areas into geographical regions generally follows Murdock's precedent in the *World Ethnographic Sample* and the *Atlas of World Cultures*,[25] although it diverges in two significant ways. First, the analysis makes up for a shortfall of tales in Murdock's Insular Pacific region and a glut of tales in his East Eurasian region by grouping several culture areas in South East Asia and the Pacific Rim with tales from the Insular Pacific. Second, East African tales were grouped with Africa rather than with circum-Mediterranean tales. These divergences from Murdock result from the necessity of establishing regional samples of roughly equivalent size. Relatively small sample sizes meant that statistically meaningful culture-by-culture analyses could not be performed. Since most feminist critiques focus on Western European folktales, subanalyses were also performed for tales collected from Western European cultures to control for the possibility that different patterns of characterization in Eastern European tales could skew the results.

The sample was also divided into two broad levels of cultural complexity. The first level consists of tales that circulated primarily in unassimilated band and tribal societies, though the tales may have only been written down after assimilation. The second level consists of tales that, while they may have originated in nonstate societies, circulated for long periods in preindustrial state societies. Since the line between these categories can be fine, tales from culture areas that could not be confidently placed in one of these two categories were excluded from the calculation.

Finally, because a prominent claim of feminist scholars of folk and fairy tales is that patterns of characterization in European folk and fairy tales reflect the patriarchal biases of male editors and collectors (see discussion), subanalyses were performed for male-edited collections versus female-edited collections and for data gathered by female coders versus data gathered by male coders.

The main challenge in content analysis utilizing multiple coders is to maximize intercoder reliability—to ensure that different coders are using standardized criteria when scanning and coding. The following conventional steps were taken to promote intercoder reliability. First, coding questions focused on measures of the most salient aspects of characterization, avoiding questions demanding highly subjective responses. Second, detailed coding instructions were developed, as well as a coding dictionary defining all potentially ambiguous terms used in the coding form. Third, intercoder reliability was assessed in two formal tests. The first test assessed coder agreement in scanning an assortment of twenty-three culturally diverse tales for the presence of a main female protagonist or a main female antagonist. The second test assessed agreement in coding an assortment of eleven culturally diverse tales previously identified as containing either a main female protagonist or antagonist. Most practitioners strive for intercoder agreement rates of 80 percent or better and consider 70 percent to be the minimum level of adequacy.[26] Intercoder agreement in scanning tales was 89 percent while, for the variables discussed in this essay, agreement ranged from 75 to 94 percent with average agreement of 88 percent.

RESULTS

This section presents the results of six tests of predictions derived from the SCH related to the scarcity of main female characters, the passivity of female protagonists, the dearth of "heroic" female protagonists, the emphasis on the beauty of female protagonists, the emphasis on marriage, and the stigmatization of older female characters. In each case, data is analyzed to determine whether a specific pattern of gender representation claimed by feminist fairy tale scholars to be representative of European tales is also typical of the other subsamples. If the gender pattern is violated in any subsample the SCH is supported; if the pattern is consistent across subsamples then the SCH is undermined.

The Scarcity of Female Main Characters

A principal feminist claim is that there is a fundamental dearth of main female characters in European folktales relative to main male characters and that this reflects and perpetuates western ideals of female subordination and secondariness.[27] The representation of female protagonist main characters was estimated in two ways. The first estimation was reached by subtracting the number of tales with female protagonist main characters in the sample from the total number of tales scanned. (All pertinent questions from the coding form are listed in appendix 1.) However, this method may overestimate somewhat the representation of male protagonist main characters because it does not account for tales where main characters (like animals, plants, or forces of nature) may be represented as unsexed. In the second estimation, the tables of contents of all collections utilized in the study were consulted to determine the relative percentages of titles referring to male main characters versus female main characters. Any title that did not communicate definite information as to the sex of the tale's main character was excluded from the calculation. However, this method of estimation likely underestimates the representation of male main characters because it does not account for the fact that most folktales featuring anthropomorphized animals or forces of nature sex them as male. The results of both analyses confirm that female protagonist main characters are significantly underrepresented in the samples: by three to one in the first and two to one in the second. (See table 1.)

As stark as the discrepancies are, the likelihood exists that, due to the partic-

TABLE 1. PERCENTAGE OF MALE AND FEMALE MAIN CHARACTERS:
TWO METHODS OF ESTIMATION

	Estimation 1		Estimation 2	
	Male	Female	Male	Female
Overall	75	25**	67	33**
Europe	76	24**	66	33**
Western Europe	77	23**	68	32**
North America	82	18**	74	26**
South America	84	16**	68	32**
East Eurasia	74	26**	67	33**
Africa	62	38**	68	32**
Insular Pacific, etc.	73	27**	57	42*
Bands/tribes	70	30**	66	34**
Preindustrial states	75	25**	68	32**
Tales in male-edited collections	***	***	***	***
Tales in female-edited collections	***	***	***	***
Data collected by males	78**	22**	***	***
Data collected by females	83**	17**	***	***

* indicates $p < .05$
** indicates $p < .001$
*** impossible to calculate or n/a

ular sampling methodology we employed, these figures substantially *underestimate* the underrepresentation of female main characters. This is because all tales coded were first preselected for the presence of prominent female characters. A sample that was not thus presorted would likely have an even more extreme imbalance between main male and female characters.

Finally, these results have recently been replicated in computerized content analyses of a (different) culturally and geographically diverse sample of ninety collections of folktales from around the world. In these collections, male subject pronouns outnumbered their female equivalents by a ratio of three to one, and male terms (man, boy, uncle, etc.) outnumbered their female equivalents by roughly the same margin.[28] Together with the results of the present study, these findings strongly suggest that an underrepresentation of prominent female folktale characters is the rule across cultures.

The Passivity and Heroism of Main Female Protagonists

The claim that European fairy tales contain disproportionate numbers of passive female protagonists is perhaps the most pervasive and important in feminist fairy tale studies.[29] In the European tales, the argument goes, only female antagonists are active, communicating the message to girls and women that activity is bad and unfeminine while passivity is good, feminine, and worthy of rewards (like marriage and other happy endings). Coders were asked to judge whether each character was more accurately described as passive or active. (They also had the option of indicating that neither identification was appropriate.) Characters were identified as active if they took steps to personally resolve their problems and accomplish their goals. Characters were identified as passive if they simply

TABLE 2. PERSONALITY DESCRIPTORS OF MALE AND FEMALE PROTAGONISTS: PERCENT ACTIVE AND PHYSICALLY HEROIC

	Active		Physically Heroic	
	Male	Female	Male	Female
Overall	75	51**	29	9**
Europe	80	63*	32	9**
Western Europe	77	69	36	7
North America	76	49**	44	11**
South America	63	45*	17	6*
East Eurasia	68	36**	39	13**
Africa	77	51*	18	2**
Insular Pacific, etc.	85	61*	22	11
Bands/tribes	69	49**	31	7**
Preindustrial states	75	53**	34	11**
Tales in male-edited collections	76	50**	38	10**
Tales in female-edited collections	75	54*	34	9**
Data collected by males	83	50**	46	13**
Data collected by females	73	51**	31	9*

* indicates $p < .05$
** indicates $p < .001$

endured their problems, taking little or no action to resolve their complications or accomplish their goals.

With activity and passivity so defined, the results do vindicate the claim that active European female protagonists are less commonly encountered than active male protagonists. However, they lend no support to the claim that this state of affairs reflects arbitrary European norms. (See table 2.) Across all subsamples the percentage of active male protagonists significantly exceeds the percentage of active female protagonists. In fact, the European and Western European subsamples actually contained the highest proportions of active female protagonists in the study. In the European sample 62 percent of female protagonists were defined as active. And the Western European sample is the only sample in which differences in the levels of activity for male and female characters (77 percent and 69 percent, respectively) were statistically insignificant.

Closely related to claims about the overrepresentation of passive female characters, is the claim that female protagonists who accomplish their goals through physical heroism are less common than physically heroic male characters, again reflecting and reinforcing ideals of female passivity and disempowerment.[30] While European female protagonists were far less likely to be defined as physically heroic, this relationship was not unique to Europe but held steady across all the subsamples. (See table 2.) This finding is consistent with a tremendous amount of qualitative folktale scholarship on male hero tales around the world,[31] but neither this scholarship nor the present research implies that female protagonists were also less likely to express heroism in arenas not entailing physical courage, hardihood, or derring-do. It would be interesting to compare male and female ratings when using different definitions of heroism (for example, moral heroism) and activity/passivity than those used in the current study.

The Emphasis on Female Beauty

The putatively intense emphasis on the beauty of female protagonists is another phenomenon that deeply concerns feminist fairy tale scholars. European fairy tales are said to imply that "beauty is a girl's most valuable asset" and that "girls win the prize if they are fairest of them all; boys win if they are bold, active, and lucky."[32] Once again, the data agree with the perception that there is more emphasis on the beauty of female protagonists in European folktales relative to male protagonists. However, the data also show that this state of affairs is not confined to Europe. Coders were asked to indicate whether or not characters were portrayed as physically attractive or physically unattractive. (Characters were deemed physically attractive or unattractive not on the basis of the coders' judgments but solely on the judgments of characters and/or narrators in the works coded.) The appearance of a female protagonist explicitly defined as physically unattractive was a true statistical anomaly: just 8 of 1,440 tales included a main female protagonist explicitly defined as unattractive. While male protagonists were also overwhelmingly more likely to be defined as physically attractive than unattractive, information on this factor was much less likely to be conveyed if the character was male. Overall, 50 percent of tales featuring female protagonists contained explicit information on their physical attractiveness versus just 21 percent for male protagonists.

And even this significantly understates the preoccupation of folktales with the beauty of female protagonists because, in tales where information on attractiveness was communicated, there were roughly 50 percent more references per

TABLE 3. PHYSICAL ATTRACTIVENESS OF MALE AND FEMALE PROTAGONISTS

	Percent Attractive		Percent with Information on Attractiveness		Average Number of References to Attractiveness per Tale	
	Male	Female	Male	Female	Male	Female
Overall	96	97	22	49**	1.81	2.91**
Europe	94	100	37	65**	1.8	2.5*
Western Europe	100	100	37	86**	1.2	2.3
North America	100	91	7	39**	1.33	3.03*
South America	85	97	13	37**	2.2	2.5
East Eurasia	83	100*	22	63**	1.76	3.77**
Africa	100	97	24	47*	2.13	3.05
Insular Pacific, etc.	100	100	17	45*	1.33	2.25
Bands/tribes	96	95	13	37**	2.08	2.83**
Preindustrial states	98	96	29	64**	1.9	3.08**
Tales in male-edited collections	96	97	23	55**	1.85	3.16**
Tales in female-edited collections	100	97	35	49	2.0	2.77
Data collected by males	96	94	36	65**	1.81	3.03**
Data collected by females	98	98	19	51**	2.67	3.1

* indicates $p < .05$
** indicates $p < .001$

tale to the physical attractiveness of female characters than the physical attractiveness of male characters. While this finding disconfirms the notion that greater emphasis on female beauty is unique to European tales and European cultures, it should be noted that the emphasis on female beauty *was* particularly acute in the European subsamples. (See table 3.)

Finally, these findings have also recently been replicated by the content analysis of ninety collections of world folktales mentioned previously. Coders, aided by computerized content analysis software, found that there were almost always more references to female than male physical attractiveness, despite the fact that there were universally fewer prominent female characters in the collections.[33]

TABLE 4. EMPHASIS ON FINDING A SUITABLE MATE FOR MALE AND FEMALE PROTAGONISTS

	Married at Start		Married at Finish		Marriage Motive	
	Male	Female	Male	Female	Male	Female
Overall	25	24	66	66	50	50
Europe	10	8	90	87	61	50
Western Europe	7	7	90	89	54	50
North America	32	29	34	48	41	42
South America	35	38	57	66	55	54
East Eurasia	17	14	77	73	54	44
Africa	27	34	71	64	44	42
Insular Pacific, etc.	30	22	68	55	44	65
Bands/tribes	26	29	40	49	42	46
Preindustrial states	17	12	86	81	56	47
Tales in male-edited collections	17	20	70	69	54	46
Tales in female-edited collections	27	16	79	71	47	50
Data collected by males	30	15	64	65	48	42
Data collected by females	16	20	73	70	55	48

* indicates *p* < .05
** indicates *p* < .001

The Importance of Marriage

Feminist critics contend that "marriage is the fulcrum and major event of nearly every fairy tale; it is the reward for girls."[34] According to this line of argument, the damaging message of these tales is that happiness and success are not to be found within but must be conferred on a woman by a man. The data agree with the feminist perception that seeking and gaining a suitable mate is a primary challenge for the majority of female protagonists in European folktales. However, while European tales *do* place greater emphasis on marriage than tales contained in the other subsamples, marriage is a dominant theme in all of them. Moreover, the data do not support the contention that finding an appropriate mate is somehow more important for female characters than it is for male characters, not in Europe and not in the other subsamples. Across subsamples the majority of male and female protagonists who were not married at the beginning of the tales were married by the end. Additionally, the primary motive of a great proportion of protagonists of both sexes is finding and securing an appropriate mate. In short, across subsamples there were no statistically significant differences between male and female characters on these dimensions. (See table 4.)

The Stigmatization of Older Women

Finally, feminist critics claim that European fairy tales contain insidious messages about older women. Older women, more powerful and better able to challenge patriarchal institutions, are said to disproportionately inhabit antagonist roles.[35] This perception is confirmed by the data. However, once again, the pattern is not unique to Europe but holds true across subsamples. Overall, just 8 percent of female protagonists in the sample were identified as aged forty or over whereas 40 percent of female antagonists were identified as forty or over. Moreover, the data shows that in every subsample male antagonists were also older than male protagonists: overall, just 10 percent of male protagonists were identified as at least forty whereas 34 percent of male antagonists were identified as forty or older. Thus it is not so much *older women* who are stigmatized as *older people*. (See table 5.)

DISCUSSION

The SCH is anchored in the premise that gender-related patterns long, and largely accurately, observed in European fairy tales reflect the largely arbitrary gender arrangements of specific types of societies. This hypothesis generates the prediction that folktale traditions from different regions of the world, at different levels of cultural complexity, based on different political, religious, and economic systems, should evince substantially different gender-related patterns. That is, we should find regions of the world and types of societies where female characters are as active as male, where male beauty is emphasized as much as or more than

TABLE 5. PERCENTAGE OF FEMALE PROTAGONISTS AND ANTAGONISTS FALLING IN GIVEN AGE CATEGORIES

	Sexually Mature Teen or Twenties		Age Forty or Older	
	Female Protagonist	Female Antagonist	Female Protagonist	Female Antagonist
Overall	79	37**	8	40**
North America	71	38*	18	35
Europe	92	27**	4	64**
Western Europe	90	38**	3	52
South America	71	52	8	30*
East Eurasia	85	44**	4	29**
Africa	62	24**	12	48**
Insular Pacific, etc.	94	53**	2	33**
Bands/tribes	70	37**	13	39**
Preindustrial states	88	38**	3	44**
Tales in male-edited collections	81	40**	9	41**
Tales in female-edited collections	81	27**	6	31**
Data collected by males	82	35**	7	41**
Data collected by females	81	36**	8	45**

* indicates $p < .05$
** indicates $p < .001$

female, where females are as apt to be the swashbuckling heroes, and so forth. However, while the study revealed significant and important variation across sub-samples, the broad trends were never violated—not in the regional subsamples, not in the comparisons of band/tribal societies and preindustrial states, and not in samples divided by the sex of editors and coders.

Before the SCH is dismissed, however, one final complication must be addressed. Closely related to the SCH is the claim that gender patterns in the classic European fairy tales reflect the narrow biases of male editors who, consciously or unconsciously, chose tales, suppressed them, or redacted them until collections reflected the conservative patriarchal ideals of the late eighteenth and nineteenth centuries. In theory, this editorial manipulation hypothesis could be modified and extended to undermine confidence in the ability of this research to effectively test the SCH. Since western males have been responsible for gathering and editing most of the folktale collections that are available in English, the gender patterns revealed in this study could be considered more indicative of consistent patterns of collector/editor bias than legitimate patterns in the tales.

This conclusion seems unlikely for two reasons. First, it would require the assumption that the dozens of male and female folklorists, ethnographers, anthropologists, and other scholars who collected, edited, and translated the tales used in this study—despite their varying national, disciplinary, ideological, and historical backgrounds—made exactly the same type of editorial manipulations and that these manipulations radically altered the nature of the database. Second, the editorial manipulation hypothesis can be indirectly evaluated using the data in this study. Since the hypothesis posits sex-based bias, it predicts that we should find significantly different patterns of characterization in male-edited versus female-edited collections and perhaps even in data collected by males versus data collected by females. However, the variation across these subsamples is not always in the predictable direction, and it is consistent with naturally occurring variation across collections and cultures. In no case did results for male or female coders and editors violate the general patterns apparent in the other samples. In short, while these data do not conflict with the argument that European editors like Perrault, Lang, and the Grimms made significant alterations in the original source tales, they do not support the implication that, but for this meddling, the tales would portray significantly (if not radically) different gender patterns.

The most parsimonious explanation for the gender patterns revealed in this study is that distinct regularities in behavior, psychology, and gender predominate across human populations and are reflected in the world's folk literatures. While this conclusion is out of kilter with a humanities culture that is currently intent on emphasizing the diversity among human groups, it is consistent with the current state of knowledge in the human sciences and with the conclusions of previous generations of scholars, like Kluckhohn, who have studied regularities in world literature:

> The mere recurrence of certain motifs in varied areas separated geographically and historically tells us something about the human psyche. It suggests that the interaction of a certain kind of biological apparatus in a certain kind of physical world with some inevitables of the human condition brings about some regularities in the formation of imaginative products, of powerful images.[36]

This is not to deny the established fact of common cross-cultural borrowing and sharing of folktales.[37] It is to stress the equally well-established fact that diffusion cannot account for the many similarities in folktale traditions with little or no cultural contact.[38] And it is to contend that theories of diffusion tend to overlook an important point: folktales adapt so well to vastly different cultural ecologies because they speak to the common problems and preoccupations of the human condition—problems and preoccupations that are unbounded by culture.

While much more remains to be said of these results, explanations of individual trends in the data are beyond the scope of this essay.[39] For now, there is only space to note that the consistent patterns of sexual differentiation across various parameters of characterization are consistent with the new consensus across the human sciences that many aspects of gender previously considered products of arbitrary social conditioning are strongly influenced by biology and encountered across human cultures.[40] However, while the folktale patterns are inconsistent with the constructivist notion that individuals are mere products of their sociocultural contexts, they also provide no support for the orientation that is social constructivism's equally incomplete antithesis: biological determinism. While some variation in the data is due to random drift in relatively small samples, the often-considerable variability across subsamples testifies to human flexibility and the importance of physical and social environments in influencing the development of individuals and societies. The finding of (presumably) environmentally influenced variability within constraints is, instead, consistent with theories of human behavior and psychology that fall between what Mary Midgely calls the "rival fatalisms" of social and biological determinism.[41] These findings converge with emerging biosocial models of human behavior and psychology, which predict that patterns of human behavior, including gendered behavior, will bend significantly with pressures exerted by differing physical and social environments within the constraints of evolved human nature.[42]

CONCLUSION: METHOD, THEORY, AND THE ACCUMULATION OF KNOWLEDGE

Despite its long-standing popularity, the failure of the SCH may come as no great shock to many literary scholars. This is because, over the last several decades, literary scholars have expressed increasing skepticism in the very possibility of "real" knowledge. For instance, few literary scholars would be prepared to defend the notion that we now understand the ultimate functions of literary works, the persistence of archetypal themes, or the interpretation of individual works more definitively than we did 25, 250, or 2,500 years ago. While all knowledge, including scientific knowledge, is provisional and subject to future revision, humanists (with the arguable exception of those in historical branches of literary studies) have rarely managed to produce knowledge that can withstand the critiques of the next generation. In other words, there is little accumulation of knowledge in literary studies:

the line of work runs from generation to generation in continuous circles, bending to intellectual fashions and the rhetoric of powerful personalities.

But the way is clear for literary studies to begin laying up more reliable, durable, and intersubjective answers to the great variety of important questions that literary scholars ask and answer. A more vigorous and redoubtable literary studies can emerge if scholars take three practical steps. First, while not advocating a naive regression to the fantasy that intellectual inquiry can be utterly objective and value-neutral, literary scholars must reestablish contact with the ancient and fundamental tenet of all fields of intellectual inquiry that a researcher's prime moral and intellectual duty is, insofar as is possible, to keep his or her biases from influencing the theory, methods, or conclusions he or she credits. The SCH was promoted, and sustained for a period of more than thirty years, as much for ideological expedience as for its success in bringing coherence to information. Second, literary scholars must update their theoretical foundations to make them consistent with the current state of knowledge in the human sciences. Hard social constructivism is a failed theory, and the vast corpus of literary theory and analysis which continue to be based upon it, like the vast body of work founded on psychoanalytic concepts,[43] bears the mark of its failure. Third, more literary scholars should educate themselves about the strengths and weaknesses of quantitative methods and, where appropriate, seek to employ them in their own work. To reiterate: introducing a quantitative dimension—far from challenging the place of traditional methods of analysis—will serve to make them stronger and surer.

If these three steps are taken, literary studies can once again have impact outside of its own societies, conferences, and journals.[44] It can make more substantial contributions not only to the task of improving understanding of literary phenomena but, by exploiting its access to the vast and precious database about human behavior, psychology, cognition, and culture that is world literature, literary scholars can participate more fully in revealing the ultimate subject of the humanities: humans. The promise of this approach is suggested by the present research, which undermines central claims of constructivist scholarship, reveals undiscovered patterns of characterization in world folktales, and contributes to our understanding of the way that gender is organized in human societies.

Appendix 1: Pertinent Questions from Rating Form

1. Is the main character in this story (1) male or (2) female?
2. Is the character best described as a (1) protagonist, (2) antagonist, or (99) impossible to judge?
3. What is your best estimate of the character's age: (1) prepubescent (0–13), (2) sexually mature teenager, (3) twenties, (4) thirties, (5) forties, (6) fifties, (7) sixty or older, or (99) impossible to judge?

4. When the tale begins, is the character married? (1) Yes (2) No.
5. If the above answer is 2 (not married), does the character get married in the course of the tale? (1) Yes (2) No.
6. What is the character's main goal: (1) survival, (2) finding/keeping mate, (3) wealth or other material resource(s), (4) enhanced fame or social status, or (88) other?
7. Is the character more accurately defined as (1) passive (in the sense that he/she exemplifies patient endurance of troubles), or is he/she (2) active (in the sense that he/she actively pursues solutions to troubles), or (99) cannot answer?
8. Does the character accomplish his or her goal(s) through feats of physical heroism? (1) Yes (2) No.
9. Is the character (1) physically attractive, (2) unattractive, (3) average, or (99) is there no information on this topic?
10. Count up the number of references made to the character's physical attractiveness or unattractiveness. How many are there?

Appendix 2: Subsamples and Cultures

1. Overall (*n* = 658 tales): Aboriginal Australian, African American, Blackfoot, Chamacoco, China, Dena, East African Tribes, Gê, Germany, Guajiro, Gypsy (Roma), Haiti, Hawaii, Hopi, Hungary, India, Inuit, Iraq, Ireland, Iroquois, Israel, Japan, Korea, !Kung San, Maya, Mongolia, Navaho, New Guinea, Nigerian Tribes, Nivkalé, Norway, Palestine, Persia, Russia, Scotland, Siberian Indians, Sikuani, Sioux, Slovakia, Southern African Tribes, Tibet, Tlingit, Vietnam, West African Tribes, Yamana, Yanomami, Yugoslav.
2. North America (*n* = 101 tales): Blackfoot, Dena, Hopi, Inuit, Iroquois, Maya, Navaho, Sioux, Tlingit.
3. South America (*n* = 109 tales): Chamacoco, Gê, Guajiro, Nivkalé, Sikuani, Yamana, Yanomami.
4. Europe (*n* = 135 tales): Germany, Gypsy (Roma), Hungary, Ireland, Norway, Scotland, Slovakia, Yugoslavia.
5. Western Europe (*n* = 72 tales): Germany, Ireland, Norway, Scotland.
6. Africa (and diaspora) (*n* = 91 tales): African American, East African Tribes, Haiti, !Kung San, Nigerian Tribes, Southern African Tribes, West African Tribes.
7. East Eurasia (*n* = 144 tales): China, India, Iraq, Israel, Mongolia, Palestine, Persia, Russia, Siberia, Tibet.
8. Insular Pacific, Pacific Rim, and South East Asia (*n* = 78 tales): Aboriginal Australia, Hawaii, Japan, Korea, New Guinea, Vietnam.

9. Bands and tribes (n = 337 tales): Aboriginal Australia, Blackfoot, Dena, East African Tribes, Hawaii, Hopi, Inuit, Iroquois, !Kung San, Navaho, New Guinea, Nigerian Tribes, Siberian Indians, Sioux, Southern African Tribes, Tlingit, West African Tribes.
10. Preindustrial states (n = 291 tales): China, Germany, Gypsy (Roma), Hungary, India, Iraq, Ireland, Israel, Japan, Korea, Mongolia, Norway, Palestine, Persia, Russia, Scotland, Slovakia, Tibet, Vietnam, Yugoslav.
11. Male-analyzed tales (n = 141).
12. Female-analyzed tales (n = 517).
13. Tales from male-edited collections (n = 390).
14. Tales from female-edited collections (n = 158).

Notes

I would like to thank the persons responsible for collecting the data used in this essay: Rachel Berkey, Mitch Cawson, Carly Drown, Matthew Fleischner, Melissa Glotzbecker, Kimberly Kernan, Tyler Magnan, Kate Muse, Celeste Ogburn, Stephen Patterson, Christopher Skeels, Stephanie St. Joseph, Shawna Weeks, Alison Welsh, Erin Welch.

1. See Graunt 1665.
2. Graunt 1662, 1, 2, iv.
3. Graunt 1662, see index for full list.
4. Graunt 1662, 2.
5. Stigler 1986, 67; see also Stigler 1999; Porter 1986; McDonald 1993.
6. Porter 1986, 163.
7. See Stigler 1986, 381.
8. See Stigler 1986, 189–99.
9. Stigler 1986, 203.
10. Porter 1986, 159.
11. Kenny 1986, 116.
12. See McEwan, this volume.
13. For a historical survey see Neuendorf 2002, 27–46.
14. See, for instance, De Beaugrande 1989; Schmidt 1982, 1992; Martindale 1990, 1996. More recently, and prominently, Franco Moretti 2003, of Stanford University, has advanced a methodologically radical quantitative program "to delineate a transformation in the study of literature." Learned societies like the International Association for the Empirical Study of Literature and The International Association for Empirical Aesthetics as well as journals like *Poetics, Computers in the Humanities,* and *Empirical Studies in the Arts* (*ESA*) have now been in existence for decades. However, the societies are small and lack mainstream influence, and

Poetics and *ESA* are principally composed of articles written by and for psychologists and other human scientists who study aesthetics.

15. The common assumption that minds that gravitate toward language and literature are often unsuited for math receives a challenge from the history of statistics. A surprising number of the most influential figures in the development of "modern statistical methodology" were also competent scholars or producers of literature. For example, Quetlet wrote the libretto to an opera, a historical survey of romance, and much poetry. Karl Pearson (1857–1936), who is placed among the top two or three most important statisticians of all time, wrote plays and published articles on medieval German literature. Francis Ysidro Edgeworth (1845–1926), an important statistical innovator, had an outstanding literary as well as mathematical mind. He studied classics at Trinity College, Dublin, where he took first prizes in Greek prose and verse composition and was considered by his tutors to be the ablest man in the class. After he left Trinity with high honors, and before he embarked on a life of mathematical study, he supported himself as a teacher of Greek. Graunt's contemporary and close friend William Petty (1623–1687), a founder of "political arithmetic," was a professor of music at Gresham College who dabbled in the composition of Latin poetry. (Biographical details from Johnson and Kotz 1997; Stigler 1986.)

16. Graunt 1662, 2–3.

17. For example, Lurie 1970, 1971.

18. De Beauvoir 1953, 126, 128, 163, 167, 178; Friedan 1963, 118, 192.

19. See Zipes 1986, 3; for overviews see Haase 2000b and De Caro 1983.

20. Rowe 1986, 209; Kolbenschlag 1981, 3; Rowe 1986, 218; Helms 1987, 3; Daly 1978, 44; Zipes 1986, 9; Brownmiller 1975, 309–10.

21. Among others see Ragan 1998; Yolen and Guevera 2000; Tchana and Schart Hyman 2000.

22. Haase 2000a.

23. Haase 2000b.

24. Popper 1959.

25. Murdock 1957, 1981.

26. For overviews of content analysis methodology see Krippendorff 1980; Neuendorf 2002; Popping 2000; Weber 1990; West 2001.

27. For example, Ragan 1998, xxii–xxiv.

28. Gottschall, Callanan, Casamento, et al. 2004.

29. For example, M. Lieberman 1986; Lundell 1986; Stone 1986.

30. Yolen 2000.

31. J. Campbell 1968; Raglan 1936; Rank 1909; Thompson 1932–36, 1946.

32. M. Lieberman 1986, 188.

33. Gottschall, Callanan, Casamento, et al. 2004.

34. M. Lieberman 1986, 189; see also Orenstein 2002, 10; Rowe 1986, 271.

35. Bottigheimer 1980; M. Lieberman 1986, 196.

36. Kluckhohn 1959.

37. See Thomson 1932–36, 1946.

38. See Propp 1968; Thompson 1932–36, 1946; Tatar 1987.

39. Discussion of some of these trends is featured in Gottschall, Berkey, Drown, et al., 2004; Gottschall, Martin, Rea, and Quish 2004; Gottschall, Allison, DeRosa, and Klockeman 2004.

40. For accessible reviews see Fisher 1999; Halpern 2000; Hrdy 1999; Kimura 1999; Mealey 2000.

41. Midgely 1992.

42. See Barkow, Cosmides, and Tooby 1992; Pinker 2002; E. O. Wilson 1998.

43. See Crews 1997, 1999.

44. The fact that literary scholarship in the postmodern era has lost most of its relevance to the outside world has often been lamented. What is perhaps even more disturbing and telling is that literary scholarship has apparently *been steadily losing its relevance even for literary scholars*. As Stephen Greenblatt announced in his presidential address at the 2002 Modern Language Association convention, literary scholars have found it harder and harder to find publishers for their books mainly because literary scholars have stopped buying each other's books.

Proper Hero Dads and Dark Hero Cads: Alternate Mating Strategies Exemplified in British Romantic Literature

Daniel J. Kruger, Maryanne Fisher, and Ian Jobling

Contemporary literary research is generally not held to the standard of scientific responsibility. Although theories of human behavior in the sciences are adopted only after being supported by empirical testing, many literary researchers are not overly concerned with the empirical viability of the theories of behavior on which they base their work. Some appear to prefer one theory to another for subjective, political, or practical reasons. Many theories of behavior popular in contemporary literary research, such as Freudianism and Marxism, have been abandoned or have never been adopted in the human sciences because their premises are inconsistent with empirical evidence.[1] It is the constant testing of scientific theories against the facts of the real world that leads to real, if often frustratingly slow, progress in the human sciences. Scientific progress is cumulative; scientists seek to continually enhance the accuracy of ideas and sophistication of understanding through empirical research.

On the other hand, literary scholarship is not, for the most part, considered a cumulative discipline. But can it be? At the least, we propose that literary researchers could develop their theories of human cognition and behavior out of the best contemporary research on these subjects. At best, they could find ways of testing their interpretations of literary texts empirically. Because literary researchers are generally not trained in scientific methods and will continue not to be in the foreseeable future, it will be necessary for the time being for them to form partnerships with behavioral and social scientists (or to learn such methods themselves). Such collaborations are not useful only for literary researchers but also for behavioral and social scientists in that literature affords rich possibilities for testing and developing psychological theories. This article is the product of one such mutually productive collaboration. It provides an example of a scientifically grounded approach to literary study by empirically testing a specific literary interpretation that was, itself, derived from evolutionary theory on human sexuality.

Dad and Cad Mating Strategies

Recent research on human sexuality has suggested that humans, depending on context, have evolved to pursue either short-term or long-term mating strategies. There is a great deal of evidence to suggest that, unlike most mammals, humans are designed for long-term sexual relationships with substantial male parental investment in children. Human infants require a great deal of parental care, and children reared in father-absent households suffer much higher mortality rates than those who are reared in father-present homes, especially in preindustrial societies.[2] The sexual psychology of women also indicates that human sexuality has been shaped by long-term sexual relationships. A number of studies both in the United States and cross-culturally have shown that women regularly report being attracted to men who are socially respected, financially well-off, ambitious, industrious, dependable, emotionally stable, and romantic, all qualities that indicate the ability and willingness to sustain long-term, parentally investing relationships.[3]

However, there are also aspects of both men's and women's sexuality that show that we did not evolve exclusively to pursue long-term mating. The evidence for the importance of short-term mating in human evolution is most obvious in men who consistently demonstrate a marked desire for sexual variety.[4] Men are more likely than women not only to fantasize about having sex with multiple partners,[5] but also to seek out sex with multiple partners.[6] The fitness advantage of short-term sexual relationships is obvious for men: there is a linear relationship between the number of women with whom men have sex and the number of potential offspring. However, the disadvantage of this strategy, in human mating, is that the children of nonpaternally investing men would have a much higher mortality rate than the children of paternally investing men (especially in ancestral environments). Nevertheless, a successful philanderer would have been likely to sire a large number of children, some proportion of whom would likely survive, especially in a resource-rich environment. This strategy is known as the "cad" strategy among evolutionary theorists. It has been shown to be successful in some circumstances, such as when there is a small effect of male parental investment on female reproductive success due to the local ecology.[7]

It takes two to tango, and so, for a cad mating strategy to evolve in men, it would have had to be attractive to women as well. However, while the advantages of short-term mating are obvious for men, they may be less intuitively apparent for women. Why would an ancestral woman want to make the immense parental investment necessary to bear and raise a child when, without paternal investment, the child would have been more likely to die? The most common answer to this question is the "sexy son hypothesis."[8] When a woman mates with a cad, the genes that made the father successful as a cad would be passed on to her son (if she happens to have a son). Because this sexy son contains 50 percent of the mother's genetic material, he would, through his sexual success, increase his mother's fitness by giving her numerous grandchildren. Many theorists have hypothesized that women may, consequently, have evolved in some circumstances to prefer cues in men that show high sexual success, or "good genes," to cues of potential paternal investment.[9] It is also possible that women with a parentally investing mate would have extra-pair copulations with a cad in order to benefit from his genetic contribution. Research has shown that women currently involved in a committed relationship are more likely to engage in extra-pair copulations when they are ovulating and are less likely to use contraceptives during these liaisons.[10] Therefore, women may be trying to get the best of both worlds: genes from the cad and investment from the dad. Paternity studies indicate that 2 to 30 percent of children result from sex with someone other than a woman's husband across both modern and traditional societies,[11] providing evidence for a mixed-mating strategy among women.

This data should explode the myth that men are polygamous but women are monogamous. There are other reasons why females of many species might engage in extra-pair copulations, or have multiple regular partners, other than to have "sexy sons." Genetic diversity of offspring would provide an evolutionary hedge against an unpredictable environment, and an additional mate would be invaluable if the primary mate were sterile. An additional partner may provide a female with food or other resources that could enhance reproductive success and reduce her time and energy expenditures in foraging and the associated predation risk. Further, considering the possibility of infanticide or other abuse committed by male group members, a female may benefit from mating with multiple males to confuse paternity or otherwise give males an incentive not to harm her offspring.[12]

Men appear to specialize in either a short-term or long-term mating strategy. This argument has been made most convincingly by the anthropologists Patricia Draper and Henry Harpending and psychologist Jay Belsky, who have found that, cross-culturally, cads and dads show distinct clusters of personality traits that appear to be designed for success in their respective mating strategies. Draper and Harpending believe that cads and dads are different human morphs, just as workers and queens are different morphs of ants, and that whether a man becomes one or the other depends on an environmental trigger: the presence or absence of the father in the household where the son grows up. According to this theory, the presence or absence of a father in the boy's early environment indicates whether or not his society is one in which parental investment is the norm.

The sons of father-absent households will typically become cads, and those of father-present households will typically become dads.[13]

Although the literature describes a dichotomy between dads and cads, it is possible that men are distributed along a continuum of relative "dad- and cad-ness." It is also possible that one male's strategies could vary with age or environmental factors and that men could shift between mating effort and parental investment depending on the respective payoffs. Males may even provide paternal investment to a primary partner while, at the same time, exerting mating effort to obtain extra-pair copulations or secondary partners. However, there are constraints to these strategies; the cues that make cads attractive as sexual partners are, by design, difficult to fake. Thus a male who pursues a cad strategy without the requisite indicators of genetic fitness may not find much success.

One of the most reliable findings in the biological study of sexual behavior is that male sexual competitiveness is proportional to the degree of polygyny in a species.[14] Polygynous societies are more competitive than monogamous ones because the more women one man impregnates, the fewer opportunities for other men. For example, if one man impregnates fifteen women, he denies other men the opportunity to do so during the women's pregnancies and lactation periods. Consequently, the higher the degree of polygyny, the more intense the selection pressure on males to develop effective means of sexual competition. Draper, Harpending, and Belsky reason that because cads are more polygynous than dads, a dichotomy that may start in adolescent development, cads ought to be more highly sexually competitive than dads. Their review of the literature on the subject supports this view. Cross-culturally, men from father-absent households favor a sexually promiscuous mating strategy and are more misogynistic and reluctant to engage in parental investment; they are also violent, aggressive, rebellious, high in risk-taking, and at high risk of incarceration. Boys from father-present households are more likely to delay sexual experience, have positive attitudes toward and develop stable pair-bonds with women, have good relations with male peers, and accept authority, compared to boys from father-absent households.[15]

Draper, Harpending, and Belsky's account of the cad and dad mating strategies meshes well with research on women's mating strategies. If women had evolved exclusively to pursue long-term mateships, their sexual attraction would be uniform in all contexts; they would always prefer men who showed an ability and willingness to parentally invest in children. However, some recent studies show that women have *different* criteria for choosing long- and short-term mates, and the traits that they look for in short-term mates correspond quite well to the cad traits that Draper and Harpending have described. These results underscore the fact that women take an active role in sexual selection, contribute to differentiation in male mating strategies, and also address the ultimate question of why women would fall for "bad boys." Kelly and Dunbar found that women value bravery substantially more than kindness in short-term mates but that they value both qualities equally in long-term mates.[16] Also, for short-term mates, women desire men who prove themselves highly desirable to and sought after by other women, but these qualities are not nearly as important to them in long-term mates.[17] These results support the hypothesis that in choosing short-term mates women are unconsciously looking for risk-taking, sexually competitive males who will give them children with high genetic quality, including sons who resemble their sexy fathers.

High dominance traits are also associated with male promiscuity.[18] Dominant people have an upright bearing, move with ease and freedom, gaze at people fixedly and unashamedly, are more likely to infringe on other people's personal space than nondominants, and smile less often than nondominants because smiling is frequently a gesture of appeasement.[19] It is reasonable that dominance traits are part of the same cluster of characteristics as aggressiveness because dominance traits are essentially confrontational and challenging to others. Furthermore, Draper and Harpending's contention that cads are at high risk of incarceration makes sense given their relatively strong tendencies for risky behaviors, some of which may be considered criminal in contemporary state societies.

There is also some evidence that females, too, have evolved to pursue either a short-term or long-term mating strategy and that their developmental pathway is, again like males, influenced by early childhood environment. Belsky, Steinberg, and Draper have argued that the "attachment process," or the development of emotional bonds between child and parents, is a developmental psychological mechanism that evolved to evaluate life conditions and choose an appropriate reproductive strategy given probable future circumstances. Children who feel loved and welcomed by their parents experience "secure attachment;" those who feel unloved and unwelcomed experience one of the forms of "insecure attachment." Belsky, Steinberg, and Draper believe that fearful attachment to parents is an environmental cue that long-term monogamous relationships are not a viable strategy in the social world in which the child is growing up. Consequently, insecurely attached females are more likely to pursue short-term mating strategies than securely attached women and to prefer cads to dads. Their theory explains empirical findings that females who grow up in father-absent households, a major risk factor for insecure attachment, show earlier sexual activity than females from father-present households as well as a lack of interest or ability to form and maintain, long-term monogamous relationships.[20]

In conclusion, evidence indicates that both men and women have long- and short-term mating strategies. Men may be dads who attract women by showing their ability and willingness to parentally invest in children; these men tend to be compassionate, kind, romantic, and industrious. Alternatively, men may be cads who attract women by showing that they are highly competitive and will give women sons who show the same characteristics; these men are brave, aggressive, high in risk-taking, rebellious, and prone to be criminals. One of the most attractive characteristics of this theory is its correspondence to everyday experience. We have probably met men who try to attract women through a "nice guy" strategy by displaying kindness, sensitivity, and commitment, and we have also probably met men who try to attract women through macho dominance displays and risk-taking. By simply viewing women's responses to these men, most would agree that both of these strategies work some of the time. Women, too, appear to be designed for short- and long-term mating.

The Proper and the Dark Hero

The proper hero and the dark (or Byronic or Romantic) hero are the two major heroic types of the Romantic period.[21] Jobling has described the close correspondences between typical cad traits and the traits of the dark hero and between typical dad traits and those of the proper hero.[22]

Figuring most prominently in the novels and narrative poems of Walter Scott and Lord Byron, the dark hero is one of the distinctive character types of the British Romantic period. He appears in narratives set in the past or in distant lands and epitomizes Romanticism's glorification of rebellion and social alienation. George Staunton of Scott's *The Heart of Mid-Lothian* (1818) and Clement Cleveland of *The Pirate* (1821) are good examples of this character type. The dark hero is typically a violent, rebellious outlaw. Scott's dark heroes often participate in rebellions against the state, which are portrayed as expressing legitimate grievances against the government; George Staunton leads an uprising against a tyrannous police force in 1736 Edinburgh. Furthermore, dark heroes show evidence of dominance traits. They typically have a piercing and aggressive gaze and an unsmiling countenance. George Staunton, for example, has "a fiery eye . . . now turbid with melancholy, now gleaming with scorn, and now sparkling with fury."[23] Also typical of the dark hero are freedom and ease of bodily movement and a vaguely threatening self-confidence: "[Cleveland] advanced, with military frankness. . . . There was an air of success about Captain Cleveland which was mighty provoking. Young, handsome, and well assured, his air of nautical bluntness sat naturally and easily upon him."[24] As one would expect of men with these dominance traits, dark heroes are usually leaders. Staunton leads a band of outlaws who rebel against the police force of Edinburgh, and Cleveland leads a band of pirates.

Finally, dark heroes have a tendency to libertinism, rarely marry, and are almost always unhappy if they do marry. Clement Cleveland says, "I never saw a woman worth thinking twice about after the anchor was a-peak—on shore it is another thing; and I will laugh, sing, dance, and make love, if they like it, with twenty girls."[25] George Staunton has two children out of wedlock. He later ends up getting married, but the marriage is a failure because it is incompatible with his nature. Clement Cleveland states that pirates "enjoy the pleasures which chance throws in their way,"[26] revealing a fatalistic perspective that is concordant with the notion that a short-term strategy emerges when social support and resources in one's childhood environment are unpredictable.

The standard male lead in the narratives of this period is what Alexander Welsh calls the "proper hero" and Peter L. Thorslev, the "hero of sensibility."[27] This figure appears in most of the popular narratives of the time—there is always a proper hero in the novels of Ann Radcliffe and Walter Scott. This character resembles the typical hero in medieval romance and folktales in that the novels end with his happy marriage to a beautiful heroine and with a seemingly prosperous future. Again like the medieval romance and folktale hero, the proper hero's motives are kind and altruistic and in contrast to the egoism of villains and dark heroes. As John P. Farrell says of Scott's novels, the proper hero is "the good man" caught in a world of "egotistical fanaticisms."[28] In many respects, however, the proper hero is strikingly different from the traditional hero. Whereas it is the essence of the hero of folktale and romance to commit deeds of prowess in battle and to dominate the narrative, the proper hero is, in general, a weak and passive character who does not commit heroic actions. As Thorslev says, this type of hero "is distinguished not by daring exploits or superior intelligence, but quite simply by his capacities for feeling, mostly for the tender emotions—gentle and tearful love, nostalgia, and pervasive melancholy," and "he is set off from the general run of men by his very sensitivity."[29]

The proper hero is, as one would expect from this description, nonviolent and nonhomicidal. Welsh states, "there is ample evidence to support this rule. In the Waverley novels a [proper] hero never kills anyone."[30] Furthermore, proper heroes are low in dominance traits. They do not possess the commanding and striking presence of the dark hero and are rarely the center of attention in a group. As the contemporary critic William Hazlitt said, they "keep in the background and in a neutral posture, till they are absolutely forced to come forward, and it is then only with a very amiable reservation of modest scruples."[31]

Finally, the proper hero is entirely monogamous. Characteristically, he falls in love with the heroine at the beginning of the novel but is shy about confessing his love to her. He is then separated from the heroine for the body of the novel, which often covers several years, but continues to think of her the whole time. And at the end, the two lovers are rejoined and are married. The proper hero is of a highly parentally investing disposition. As the narrator says of Waverley, the proper hero of the eponymous novel by Scott, "the real disposition of Waverley, . . . notwithstanding his dreams of tented fields and military honour, seemed exclusively domestic."[32]

Hypotheses

This study provides empirical tests of predictions concordant with Jobling's hypothesis.[33] We predicted that female research participants would make relationship choices reflecting their understanding of the mating strategies and benefits likely to be conferred by dad and cad archetypes, respectively, proper and dark heroes in British Romantic literature. We expected women to find dark heroes (cads) more enticing for brief sexual relationships than long-term relationships and the reverse for proper heroes (dads). Therefore, the tendency to choose cads over dads should increase as the length of the hypothetical relationship decreases. We also predicted that women would prefer dads as suitable marriage partners for their daughters. Dads are more likely to invest heavily in offspring and are less likely to desert a family to pursue other women. In contrast, cads are more prone to leaving, and when the father is absent, the maternal grandparents could be expected to bear an increased burden on their resources. This increase in resource deployment toward their grandchildren would be expected to decrease the grandparents' inclusive fitness, as they would have fewer resources to invest in other offspring and grandchildren.

We also formed a hypothesis related to women's interpersonal attachment styles. Assuming that the attachment process is a mechanism for developing optimal reproductive strategies within particular environmental contingencies, we predicted that securely attached women would be more likely to focus on the benefits related to long-term relationships and insecurely attached women would be more likely to focus on the criteria valued in short-term relationships. Thus, insecurely attached women would have a stronger preference for cads than securely attached women.

Methods

We extracted two- to three-hundred-word descriptive passages of two proper heroes and two dark heroes from British novels of the Romantic period. Valancourt from Ann Radcliffe's *The Mysteries of Udolpho* (1794) and Edward Waverley from Walter Scott's *Waverley* (1814) represented proper heroes. George Staunton from Scott's *The Heart of Mid-Lothian* (1818) and Clement Cleveland from Scott's *The Pirate* (1821) represented dark heroes. To present short passages that directly discussed the heroes' features and personalities, the descriptions of two characters (Valancourt and Cleveland) were a composite, constructed with lines from different sections of each book.

Our participants were 257 ethnically and religiously diverse female introductory psychology students at a large Midwestern American university; 30 percent of participants were of Western European descent, 18.3 percent were of Eastern European descent, 7.4 percent were Latina, 6.6 percent were African American, 5.8 percent were East Asian or Pacific Islander, 3.1 percent were South Asian, 1.6 percent were Native American, 1.6 percent were Middle Eastern or Arab, and 27.7 percent cited mixed descent or other categories. The average age of participants was 18.73 years, with a standard deviation of 0.99 years. All participants completed the survey via the Internet and received course credit for their involvement.

For each passage, we provided participants with vocabulary keys that defined arcane words or phrases. The passages portrayed proper heroes as domestic, peaceable, bookish, moral, gentle, compassionate, frank, and shy; and cads were described as daring, arrogant, unconstrained, moody, passionate, rebellious, strong, defiant, humorous, confident, shrewd, vulgar, and slanderous but also successful with attractive women. (See the appendix for the composite passages as well as the vocabulary keys.)

Participants completed items for two dad/cad pairs: one pair was Waverley followed by George Staunton; the second pair was Valancourt followed by Clement Cleveland. Each type of passage was read first by half of the participants, the paired passages were separated by fifteen minutes of items not related to this study. After reading a passage, participants were asked to complete a short series of questions. The items, using a rating scale format, asked how well the participant thought she would like the character as a person; how well the character would like her; how well she and the character would get along; how well the character matched her personality; and how likely she would be to have a long-term committed relationship, a short-term relationship, and sex in a one-night stand with the character. In a forced-choice section, participants were asked to choose which character they would prefer for a three-week road trip, a formal date, sexual relations, marriage, and marriage to their hypothetical twenty-five-year-old daughter. Paired sample *t*-tests examined whether there was a statistically significant difference in participant ratings of dads and cads across paired passages, and binomial probabilities indicated statistically significant preferences in forced-choice items.

Every time a statistical inference is conducted, there is some possibility that the test will show a significant difference when in fact the result is only due to random variation. The more tests are used, the more likely there will be a false-positive result. We used the HC-Holm procedure to interpret our inferential results (Toothaker 1993); this is a procedure that allows for the examination of multiple comparisons while holding the probability of a false-positive result at the acceptable rate for just one comparison in the social sciences (= .05).[34] Because all effects presented are statistically significant, results are given as effect sizes, which indicate the practical significance, or strength, of the effect. Cohen outlines small (d = .20), medium (d = .50), and large (d = .80) effect sizes for the behavioral sciences (d indicates the magnitude of the effect in units of standard deviations). Most effect sizes in the behavioral and social sciences are small or medium.[35]

Each participant completed the Bartholomew four-category attachment inventory, which categorizes individuals as securely attached or one of three types of insecure attachment styles based on one's evaluation of oneself and others.[36] Fearfully attached individuals have a negative evaluation of both themselves and others; preoccupied individuals have a negative evaluation of themselves but a positive evaluation of others; dismissing individuals have a positive evaluation of themselves but a negative evaluation of others. Securely attached individuals have a positive evaluation of both themselves and others.

A one-way analysis of variance (ANOVA) tested whether participants with different attachment styles were more likely to have long-term committed, short-term, or one-night sexual relationships on the dad and cad evaluation items. Because the ANOVA only indicates whether there is at least one significant difference among the four attachment style groups, the Tukey-B post hoc comparison procedure was used to determine which groups, if any, significantly differed from each other. Point-biserial correlations tested whether participants with different attachment styles were significantly more prone to choose the dad or cad when selecting a mate for a prospective relationship.[37] A separate HC-Holm procedure was used for the analyses on attachment style.

Results

For both sets of passages, participants thought they would like the proper heroes more than the dark heroes, thought that the proper heroes would like them more than the dark heroes, and thought that the proper heroes better matched their personality than the dark heroes. (See table 1.) In the Waverley versus George Staunton comparison, participants had a moderate preference for a long-term committed relationship with the proper hero, no preference for a short-term relationship, and a moderate preference for a one-night sexual affair with the dark hero. In the Valancourt versus Clement Cleveland comparison, participants had a strong preference for a long-term committed relationship with the proper hero, a moderate preference for a short-term relationship with the proper hero, and no preference for a one-night sexual affair. In a forced choice between characters, participants preferred proper heroes for a formal date, marriage, and as a son-in-law in both sets of passages. (See table 2.) However, participants preferred the dark hero for sexual relations in one comparison and had no clear preference in the other. Participants preferred the proper hero for a three-week road trip in one comparison and had no significant preference in the other.

TABLE 1. COMPARISONS OF PARTICIPANT RATINGS OF DADS AND CADS

Waverley vs. George Staunton	Favors	*d*
Would like Waverley more than George Staunton	Dad	.52
Thought Waverley would like them more	Dad	.41
Would get along better with Waverley	Dad	.68
Waverley better matched their personality	Dad	.46
Preferred a long-term relationship with Waverley	Dad	.49
No preference for a short-term relationship	Draw	n.s.
Preferred to hook up sexually with George Staunton	Cad	.53
Valancourt vs. Clement Cleveland	Favors	*d*
Would like Valancourt more than Cleveland	Dad	.81
Thought Valancourt would like them more	Dad	.56
Would get along better with Valancourt	Dad	.76
Valancourt better matched their personality	Dad	.70
Preferred a long-term relationship with Valancourt	Dad	.94
Preferred a short-term relationship with Valancourt	Dad	.43
No preference for sexual relations	Draw	n.s.

Adapted from: D. J. Kruger, M. Fisher, and I. Jobling. 2003. "Proper and Dark Heroes as Dads and Cads: Alternative Mating Strategies in British Romantic Literature." *Human Nature* 14:305–17.

Women classified themselves as secure (125), fearful (46), preoccupied (45), and dismissing (40) on the Bartholomew attachment inventory. Fearful females were more likely to desire a one-night sexual affair with one of the dark heroes, George Staunton, than all the other women and were more likely to desire a short-term relationship with him than secure or dismissing women. (See table 3.) Fearful women were also more likely to desire a one-night sexual affair and short-term

TABLE 2. PERCENTAGE OF PARTICIPANTS FAVORING DADS AND CADS ACROSS CONTEXTS

Waverley vs. George Staunton	% Dad	% Cad	Favors
Three-week road trip to California	.60	.40	Dad
Formal date	.68	.32	Dad
Marriage	.81	.19	Dad
Sexual relations	.40	.60	Cad
Son-in-law	.87	.13	Dad
Valancourt vs. Clement Cleveland			
Three-week road trip to California	.54	.46	Draw
Formal date	.73	.27	Dad
Marriage	.83	.17	Dad
Sexual relations	.56	.44	Draw
Son-in-law	.91	.09	Dad

Adapted from: D. J. Kruger, M. Fisher, and I. Jobling. 2003. "Proper and Dark Heroes as Dads and Cads: Alternative Mating Strategies in British Romantic Literature." *Human Nature* 14:305–17.

TABLE 3. ATTACHMENT STYLE AND MATING STRATEGIES

	d
Fearful more likely to hook up sexually with George Staunton	.61
Fearful more likely to have a short-term relationship with George Staunton than secure or dismissing	.51
Fearful more likely to hook up sexually with Clement Cleveland	.68
Fearful more likely to have a short-term relationship with Clement Cleveland than dismissing or preoccupied	.71

relationship with the other dark hero, Clement Cleveland, than dismissing or pre-occupied women. In contrast, there were no significant differences by attachment style for the likelihood of forming long-term relationships with dark heroes or any significant effect of attachment style on relationships with proper heroes.

Discussion

The results of this experiment support our hypothesis that the dark hero and proper hero in British Romantic literature of the late eighteenth and early nineteenth centuries respectively represent cad and dad mating strategies. Modern day college women appear to easily identify the male archetypes represented by these characters nearly two centuries after their creation. Participants also usually indicated that they would make behavioral choices consistent with predictions from the evolutionary theory of alternative mating strategies in a life-history context.

We also found support for our other hypotheses. Women preferred proper hero "dads," who may be more likely to provide reliable support, for long-term relationships. However, the shorter the relationship in question, the more likely women were to choose dark hero "cads." Future research will attempt to determine whether women are consciously considering the potential genetic benefits to offspring when choosing cads. An inherent tendency toward an adaptive behavior will spread regardless of the subjective mental experience or lack thereof. Women might even choose cads for the sheer experiential pleasure of the relationship activities, without thinking of the consequences that would reliably occur without the use of modern contraceptives.

The participants' strongest preference was for the character type preferred as a son-in-law; they overwhelmingly chose the dad. It is striking that 60 percent of women would prefer to have sex with George Staunton, a cad, but only 13 percent would prefer to see him engaged to their twenty-five-year-old daughter (44 percent and 9 percent, respectively, for Clement Cleveland). It appears that participants would rather have a reliable provider (that is, "dad") as a son-in-law and preserve available resources for other children and grandchildren. The women in this study were similar in age to their imagined twenty-five-year-old daughter, and yet they were able to state a preference that would be appropriate for a potential grandmother. These findings concur with predictions of previous researchers that women may prefer a cad's "sexy" attributes for short-term relationships but still require paternal care and resources that a dad has to offer in a long-term relationship.

Apparently some characters were more desirable than others, regardless of their mating strategy. Our study employed actual descriptions of proper and dark heroes from British Romantic literature. This method contrasts with that found in typical social psychological experiments, where alternative versions of descriptive paragraphs are held consistent except for a few manipulated words. Although both sets of comparisons showed the predicted shift in preferences toward the cad as the length of relationship decreased (as indicated by effect sizes), Clement Cleveland's attractiveness only equaled Valancourt's for sexual relations. The difference in overall attractiveness may be due to factors such as differences in writing styles across authors or the attributions that were made to each character. An overall difference in the relative attractiveness of characters, combined with the predicted effect of male mating strategy by relationship duration, is the most parsimonious explanation for our findings. We encourage future researchers to examine the traits specifically associated with each personality type and how these traits interact to create the two profiles.

Interpersonal attachment style is thought to be the mediator of differential reproductive strategies emerging from environmental contingencies during development. We uncovered a relationship between attachment style and preferred characteristics of mating partners, such that fearfully attached women were the most likely to select the dark hero cad for a prospective relationship. Fearfully attached individuals are believed to have a negative evaluation of both themselves and others, which suggests that these women may judge the prospects of receiving long-term support from a male partner as unlikely. The negative self-evaluation may be related to one's perceived value as a mating partner, and those who perceive themselves to have lower values may have more concern about their mates leaving their relationship. Thus, fearfully attached women may believe it is better to mate with someone who is likely to provide genes that promote reproductive success in the current environment. These results are consistent with the belief that the attachment system evaluates conditions during childhood to guide mating strategies in adulthood. Fearfully attached women are more likely to experience disruptive social environments as children, which could indicate conditions appropriate for short-term mating strategies.

Some researchers may claim that our results reflect stereotypes deeply rooted in patriarchal Western family systems. We consider this explanation of our findings unlikely because, as discussed previously, anthropological research finds dad and cad morphs with distinct clusters of personality traits cross-culturally.[38] However, it would be worthwhile to replicate this experiment in a society where male parental investment has little effect on reproductive success. Women in these societies may be able to distinguish cad and dad types but may have a stronger preference for relationships with cads because cads would be more likely to enhance reproductive success, given the constraints of their local environments.

Some may also be wary of evolutionary explanations for behavior because of misconceptions about the implications of an evolutionary framework. An evolutionary approach does not imply genetic determinism. Evolutionary psychology explicitly acknowledges that human thought and behavior is the product of a complex interaction of genes and environment. Life-history theory in particular examines behavioral trajectories that are influenced by one's ontological experiences in social and ecological environments. The cad and dad theory of alternative mating strategies is, in fact, a description of the way in which an environmental factor (father-presence/absence) affects biological and psychological development.

Conclusion

Literary criticism relies on assumptions about human nature; however, these assumptions are often implicit and are rarely justified with empirical evidence. Literary critics typically interpret works in the context of local, contemporary events. Our project supports the notion that literature is an immense resource for examining evolutionary challenges and adaptations. Other areas of research in evolution and behavior, such as intergroup warfare, interpersonal politics, mate selection, and kin selection, are well represented in works of fiction and could be examined experimentally in studies with designs similar to this one. Furthermore, this project shows that there is no inherent incompatibility between literary research and the empirical methods employed in the human sciences. Many literary interpretations can be tested just as satisfactorily as psychological and anthropological hypotheses. Literary research with an empirical basis could help to increase the cumulative component of the field.

Darwinian literary criticism is an emerging theoretical approach that promises to promote consilience among the sciences and the humanities.[39] Evolutionary theory is the most powerful framework in the life sciences, is growing in prevalence in the social sciences, and could also provide a theoretical basis for the humanities. Although most Darwinian literary criticism so far produced uses evolutionary theory as a basis for standard qualitative literary interpretations, this project goes further in that it utilizes the empirical testing typical of the sciences.[40] In this study, we have shown that the mental adaptations of twenty-first-century college women enable them to properly interpret archaic character descriptions and make choices that would presumably promote their reproductive success.

Appendix

WAVERLEY (DAD 1)
His real disposition seemed exclusively domestic. While he was in the army, the other aristocrats often argued and fought amongst each other over who should

receive the greatest spoils of victory, but he was more annoyed than interested by these arguments. He was also not as concerned as his fellow warriors about military honor. As one of his acquaintances said of him, "High and perilous adventure is not his forte. He would never have been his celebrated ancestor Sir Nigel [a famous warrior], but only Sir Nigel's eulogist and poet. I will tell you where he will be at home and in his place—in the quiet circle of domestic happiness, lettered indolence, and elegant enjoyments of his family's estate. And he will refit his old library in the most exquisite Gothic taste, and garnish its shelves with the rarest and most valuable volumes; and he will draw plans and landscapes, and write verses, and rear temples, and dig grottoes; and he will stand in a clear summer night in the colonnade before the hall, and gaze on the deer as they stray in the moonlight, or lie shadowed by the boughs of the huge fantastic oaks; and he will repeat verses to his beautiful wife, who shall hang on his arm—and he will be a happy man."

Vocabulary Key
colonnade = a walkway with a row of pillars
disposition = character, temperament
eulogist = someone who writes a tribute to an important person
forte = specialty, strong point, gift
lettered indolence = learned idleness
Gothic = medieval style
perilous = risky, dangerous
"rear temples, and dig grottoes" = The person described in this passage is an eighteenth-century British nobleman, and the nobility of his time liked to design gardens that imitated ancient Greek and Roman ruins. Hence the temples and grottoes, which are artificial caves that the Greeks and Romans liked to design.

GEORGE STAUNTON (CAD 1)
He seemed about twenty-five years old. His carriage was bold and somewhat supercilious, his step easy and free, his manner daring and unconstrained. His features were uncommonly handsome, and all about him would have been interesting and prepossessing, but for that indescribable expression which habitual dissipation gives to the countenance, joined with a certain audacity in look and manner. The fiery eye, the abrupt demeanor, the occasionally harsh, yet studiously subdued tone of voice,—the features, handsome, but now clouded with pride, now disturbed by suspicion, now inflamed with passion—those dark hazel eyes which he sometimes shaded with his cap, as if he were averse to have them seen while they were occupied with keenly observing the motions and bearing of others—those eyes that were now turbid with melancholy, now gleaming with

scorn, and now sparkling with fury—was it the passions of a mere mortal that they expressed, or the emotions of a fiend who seeks, and seeks in vain, to conceal his fiendish designs under the borrowed mask of manly beauty? The whole partook of the mien, language, and port of the ruined archangel.

Vocabulary Key
audacity = boldness, daringness
carriage = bearing, gait
countenance = face
dissipation = debauchery, indulgence, immorality
mien = appearance, look
melancholy = depression
passions = emotions
port = the way one carries oneself, demeanor
prepossessing = attractive, handsome
supercilious = arrogant
turbid = cloudy, opaque
the ruined archangel = Lucifer, the Devil, who was cast out of heaven for rebelling against God

VALANCOURT (DAD 2)
He was a young soldier who was generally deemed to have good chances of rising in his profession. He passionately admired whatever is great and good in the moral world, and he expressed strong indignation at any criminal or mean action. He was also very gentle and compassionate toward anyone who had experienced misfortunes. People on meeting him were much pleased with his manly frankness, simplicity, and keen susceptibility to the grandeur of nature. He met a young girl named Emily St. Aubert while she was traveling with her father. He traveled with them for a few days and fell in love with Emily during the time. He was quite shy about declaring himself to her, and would merely hint at his love for her. For example, while he was alone with Emily looking at a beautiful landscape, he said, "These scenes soften the heart, like the notes of sweet music, and inspire that delicious melancholy which no person who had felt it once, would resign for the gayest pleasures. They waken our best and purest feelings, disposing us to benevolence, pity, and friendship. Those whom he love—I always seem to love more in such an hour as this."

Vocabulary Key
benevolence = good will, generosity
frankness = sincere, clearly evident

grandeur = greatness
indignation = righteous anger, annoyance
melancholy = sadness

CLEMENT CLEVELAND (CAD 2)

He was the captain of a ship. He was above the middle size and formed handsomely as well as strongly. He had a bold, sunburnt handsome countenance and a defiant manner that sometimes angered people. There was also an air of success about him which was very provoking. He had the bold and daring assumption of importance that is derived from success in adventures and the leadership of a ship's crew. He carried himself with military frankness and had an easy, lighthearted manner when in company. He had much natural shrewdness, a good sense of humor, an undoubting confidence in himself, and that enterprising hardihood of disposition which, without any other recommendable quality, very often leads to success with women. His acquaintances were often surprised by the coarse, daring way he talked to women, but some very attractive women responded to it. He was a man who had obviously lived in danger and spoke of it as sport. He was also sometimes dishonest; he was not averse to slandering a competitor's reputation in order to get what he wanted.

Vocabulary Key

Coarse = vulgar
countenance = face
defiant = bold, rebellious
frankness = sincere, clearly evident
shrewdness = cleverness
slandering = insulting, making a false and malicious statement

Notes

1. See J. Carroll 1995.
2. See Hill and Hurtado 1996; Geary 1998.
3. See Buss 1994; Gottschall, Martin, Rea, and Quish 2004.
4. See Schmitt et al. 2003.
5. See Buss 1994.
6. See Mealey 2000.
7. See Barash and Lipton 2001; Draper and Harpending 1982, 1988; Gangestad and Simpson 2000; Lancaster and Kaplan, 1992.
8. See Weatherhead and Robertson 1979.

9. See Barash and Lipton 2001; Cashdan 1994; Gangestad and Simpson 2000.

10. See Bellis and Baker 1990.

11. Voracek, Fisher, and Shackelford under submission.

12. See Hrdy 1999; R. L. Smith 1984.

13. See Draper and Harpending 1982, 1988; Draper and Belsky 1990.

14. See Divale and Harris 1976; Plavcan, 2000; Plavcan and van Schaik 1997; Plavcan, van Schaik, and Kappeler 1995.

15. For information in this paragraph see Draper and Harpending 1982, 1988; Draper and Belsky 1990.

16. See Dunbar and Kelly 2001.

17. See Buss 2000.

18. See Mazur, Halpern, and Udry 1994.

19. See Maclay and Knipe 1972; Sadalla, Kenrick, and Vershure 1987.

20. See Belsky, Steinberg, and Draper 1991; Chisholm 1999.

21. See Thorslev 1962; Welsh 1992.

22. See Jobling 2002.

23. Scott 1818, 115.

24. Scott 1822, 138, 142–43.

25. Scott 1822, 142.

26. Scott 1822, 254.

27. Welsh 1992; Thorslev 1962.

28. Farrell 1980, 85.

29. Thorslev 1962, 35, 39.

30. Welsh 1992, 150.

31. Hazlitt 1930, 252.

32. Scott 1814, 248.

33. Jobling 2002.

34. See Toothaker 1993.

35. See Cohen 1988.

36. From Bartholomew and Horowitz 1991.

37. For descriptions of these statistical matters see Holman 1993.

38. See Draper and Belsky 1990.

39. See E. O. Wilson 1998.

40. See also Gottschall, this volume.

Crossing the Abyss: Erotica and the Intersection of Evolutionary Psychology and Literary Studies

Catherine Salmon

When Don Symons and I wrote our book, *Warrior Lovers: Erotic Fiction, Evolution, and Female Sexuality*, we were asked to choose a phrase from it to go on the dust jacket. We chose, "To encounter erotica designed to appeal to the other sex is to gaze into the psychological abyss that separates the sexes."[1] At times, it seems that an even greater gulf separates the worlds of evolutionary psychology and literary studies, and yet, there is no good reason why that should be the case. Both fields have much to offer the other. For those interested in the study of human nature, literature, a product of our evolved human brains, is a bountiful source of data on human desires and dispositions, drawing attention to what is really important in our lives. But evolutionary psychology has something to offer literary studies as well. Many mainstream humanists have had a tendency to assume that human nature is constructed, that everything is nurture and nothing is nature. Recent research in cross-cultural anthropology and psychology suggests that this is incorrect, that almost everything that is important about human behavior and psychology always develops through a combination of nature and environment. One can't truly understand and interpret text without a deep understanding of basic human nature, those human universals that transcend cultural differences.

In this essay, I will try to illustrate the gifts these two fields can bring to each other, the insight evolutionary psychology can provide into the human nature that fuels literature itself, and the vast untapped source of data for psychologists that is literature. I will do so through an examination of recent developments in the evolutionary analysis of erotica, both that produced for a female audience (the romance novel) and the visual product (pornography) that is produced almost entirely for men. I will then address several of the literary and feminist perspectives on romance and pornography and how they would benefit from insights provided by an evolutionary perspective.

Unobtrusive Measures, or Using Erotica to Explore Human Sexuality

Before getting into the particulars of the pornography and romance genres, it's worth going over the rationale for using literature to examine human nature. Many kinds of data can illuminate our understanding of human behavior and, in particular, male and female sexual psychologies. All methods have their own strengths and weaknesses. Questionnaires and surveys, for instance, introduce a foreign element into what they are trying to measure and may not illicit a typical response.[2] One way to avoid such problems is to use a variety of different measures with different strengths and weaknesses. Unobtrusive measures (including the examination of literature) do not require the cooperation of a respondent and neither do they contaminate the response by introducing foreign elements.

Evolutionary psychologists have so far used unobtrusive measures to good effect. Daly and Wilson have used homicide statistics to illuminate the psychology of male sexual proprietariness;[3] Orians has used variation in real estate prices to shed light on the psychology of human landscape preferences;[4] Gorry has used an analysis of romance heroes to illustrate the essential ingredients of female mate choice;[5] and Salmon and Symons have examined esoteric genres of female-targeted erotica to explore the essential features of female sexual psychology.[6] The last three examples are clear illustrations of the potential gold mines of information about human nature to be found in free markets.

This view is quite different from the one that has dominated much of humanistic scholarship for the last few decades, one that has argued that markets create preferences as opposed to capitalizing on preexisting ones. And yet free markets clearly adapt products to our preferences through cycles of market research, consumer feedback, and economic competition. As a result, such products are a window into our natural preferences, our basic human desires. Evolutionarily inspired examinations of our diet and taste preferences illustrate that the success of fast food is not due simply to successful marketing techniques but to our evolved preference for foods high in fat and sugar. Across human history, such foods have been essential to our diet, though not in the quantities currently consumed, and physical work was required to obtain them.[7] As a result, those that were highly motivated to seek out such foods (those with a taste for sugar and fat) were more successful, leaving more children who shared their taste preferences. All humans alive today are the descendants of those fat and sugar fanciers, which is why foods high in fat and sugar are so difficult for us to resist.

Male-oriented pornography and female-oriented romance novels are multibillion dollar global industries whose products have been shaped in free markets by consumer preferences—by individuals who make an effort to acquire them. An evolutionary perspective suggests that what makes them successful or appealing to their audiences is how well they tap into basic male and female sexual psychologies.

Just as successful fast food chains provide products that take advantage of our human dietary psychology, successful producers of romance and pornography tap into our sexual psychology.

The World of Pornography

Commercial pornography exists in every industrialized society and in many developing societies as well. In the United States, the industry's annual revenues from video sales and rentals exceed four billion dollars per year, and porn videos account for more than 25 percent of the total video market.[8] Analyses of contemporary sexually explicit films reveal a fairly narrow range of themes and content. The utopian male fantasy realm depicted in pornography, dubbed "pornotopia" by historian Steven Marcus,[9] has remained essentially unchanged through time and space. Pornographic works survive from many ancient cultures, from Ancient Greek vase paintings to the wall paintings of Pompeii brothels to Renaissance sculptures.[10] They differ little in their essential nature or design from modern pornographic magazines or movies. In pornotopia, sex is all about lust and physical gratification, totally lacking in courtship, commitment, durable relationships, or mating effort. It is a world in which women are eager to have sex with strangers, easily sexually aroused, and always orgasmic. Porn videos contain minimal plot development, focusing instead on the sex acts themselves and emphasizing the display of female bodies, especially close-ups of faces (which display sexual arousal), breasts, and genitals. The majority focus almost entirely on sex, routinely representing "lesbianism, group sex, anal intercourse, oral-genital contact, and visible ejaculation."[11] Nonsexual interpersonal behavior is almost completely excluded. A content analysis of fifty random films reveals fellatio to be the most frequent act, followed by vaginal intercourse, with cunnilingus a distant third.[12] Sex scenes typically culminate with a male ejaculating on a female's body. The fact that videos and, in the last few years, the Internet so thoroughly dominate male-oriented erotica testifies to the deeply visual nature of male sexuality. Men tend to be sexually aroused by "objectified" visual stimuli. As a consequence, porn videos do not require the existence of a point-of-view character to be effective, and scenes of a woman alone, masturbating, are relatively common. The male viewer can imagine taking the sexually aroused woman out of the scene and having sex with her. Female porn stars manifest cues of high fertility in that they are young and physically attractive.

The Romance Novel

Although the romance novel has sometimes been called pornography for women, it is really the opposite of male-oriented porn. And like pornography, the fictional world of romance is remarkably unchanged over time, at least from the eighteenth century until now.[13] The goal of a romance novel's heroine is never sex for its own sake, much less impersonal sex with strangers. The core of a romance novel's plot is a love story in which the heroine overcomes all obstacles to find and win the heart of one man, her true love. Each romance must end with the establishment of a permanent bond.

Romances vary dramatically in the extent to which sexual activity is depicted, from not at all to highly explicit descriptions. Although the description of sexual activities is common in romances, it is not an essential ingredient. When sex is described, it serves the plot rather than replacing it. The hero discovers in the heroine a focus for his passion, which ties him to her, ensuring his fidelity. Sex scenes depict the heroine's control of the hero, and sexual activity is described subjectively, primarily through the heroine's emotions rather than through her physical responses or through visual imagery. The emotional focus of a romance is on love, commitment, and nurturing. Its final goal is the creation of a perfect union with the heroine's ideal mate, one who is strong yet nurturing.[14]

The Romance Hero

The characteristics of the heroes of successful romances shed considerable light on the psychology of female mate choice. As previously mentioned, these romances almost never feature gentle, sensitive, new-age guys. Instead, imagine Russell Crowe's heroic character Maximus in *Gladiator,* which brought women into the theaters in droves and saw Crowe's sex symbol status skyrocket.

Anthropologist April Gorry analyzed every description of the heroes of forty-five romance novels, developing an outline of the ideal romance hero.[15] In almost all cases she examined, the hero was older than the heroine. Heroes were always described as taller than the heroine and were most often muscular, handsome, strong, large, tanned, masculine, and energetic. Gorry also found that romance heroes exhibited cues of physical and social competence. They were described as sexually bold, calm, confident, impulsive, and, in a majority of novels, intelligent.

The essential characteristics of the hero of a successful romance novel have to do primarily with his physical appearance, physical and social competence, and intense love for the heroine. In contrast, being rich was not essential. When considering the psychological adaptations that underpin human female mate choice, it is worth considering that such things as money and formal education did not exist for the majority of human evolutionary history. The heroes of successful romance novels may or may not be rich, aristocratic, or well-educated, but they consistently possess characteristics that would have made them highly desirable mates over the course of human evolutionary history; they are tall, strong, handsome, healthy, intelligent, confident, competent men whose love for the heroine ensures that she and her children will reap the benefits of these qualities.

Why Are Pornography and Romance So Different?

If, over the course of human evolutionary history, most successful reproduction occurred within mateships and most mateships were monogamous (or serially monogamous), economic, and child-rearing partnerships, how is it possible for male and female sexual psychologies to differ as dramatically as commercial erotica would seem to imply they do?

The answer is that ancestral men and women differed qualitatively in some of the adaptive problems that they encountered in the domain of mating. However similar men's and women's typical parental investments may have been, the sexes differed dramatically in their minimum possible investments. For an ancestral female, the minimum possible investment consisted of an egg cell, nine months of gestation, the dangers of childbirth, several years of nursing, and continuing care postweaning until the child could survive on its own.[16] As ancestral males invested substantially in their wives' offspring (as most males do today), their typical parental investment was very high, but their minimum possible investment consisted of one internal ejaculation and a few minutes of their time. If a man sired a child in whom he did not invest he could have reproduced at almost no cost, if the child survived. Even if such opportunities rarely occurred in ancestral human populations, capitalizing on them when they did was so adaptive that males evolved a sexual psychology that makes low-cost sex with new women exciting to imagine and motivating to engage in.[17] Pornotopia is a fantasy realm, made possible by evolutionary-novel technologies, in which impersonal sex with a succession of high mate-value women is the norm rather than the rare exception.

Ancestral females, by contrast, had nothing to gain and much to lose from engaging in impersonal sex with random strangers and from seeking sexual variety for its own sake, and they had a great deal to gain from choosing their mates carefully. The romance novel is a tale of female mate choice in which the heroine will identify, win, and marry the hero, who embodies the characteristics that indicated high male mate value during the course of human evolutionary history.

Feminist Literary Approaches to Romance

It would be impossible in the space of this essay to cover all the literary perspectives on romance. Some of the conflicts between evolutionary and mainstream feminist views of women and sexuality have revolved around issues of women and power. Women can gain power by influencing men, but they can also gain it on their own. Considering that the gathering of food is primarily a female activity in most prestate societies, that there are some societies where males invest relatively little in women and their offspring, and that female kin groups are central in some primate and mammal societies, it is likely that female ancestors often took both of these paths. In a modern society that has restricted female options primarily to control through influencing men, females have two choices. They can exert as much control as possible through men (as often seen in romance novels), or they can work to gain control on their own (one feminist impulse).

I'm going to focus on what I see as the main feminist literary views, the first of which focuses on the romance as a form (or fantasy) of female empowerment. The romance inverts the power of patriarchal society by giving women power over men. The hero is incomplete and unsatisfied by life without the heroine. This view of the romance has been used in discussions of the works of Austin and Brontë as well as those published by Harlequin.[18] From this perspective, the hero is seen as the provider of physical and/or economic security, but the heroine is the one with the control, and the hero will do anything for her. From this perspective, if there is a battle between the sexes, the female wins.[19]

Other critics have focused on the impact the portrayal of women in romances has on readers. They have suggested that "romances don't help women to change their lives" and that "romances are subversive of women's lives, [they] encourage readers to succumb to stereotypical patterns that pacify and obscure women's legitimate frustrations in the performance of traditional roles, . . . and [they] encourage dependency on men and reinforce female passivity."[20] This is a far cry from the female empowerment view, where women are seen as seducing and transforming men. Other critics have argued for variations on Radway's claim that it is "tempting to suggest that romantic fiction must be an active agent in the maintenance of the ideological status quo because it ultimately reconciles women to patriarchal society and reintegrates them with its institutions."[21] It does this because each romance is a mythic account of how women must achieve fulfillment in a patriarchal society. Snitow suggests in the same vein that the message of the romance is that "pleasure for women is men."[22]

Much criticism has also focused on the damaging messages of romance. That bodice-rippers idealize rape, for example, giving the impression that the guy who hurts you is the one who loves you the most, and that the only socially acceptable form of adventure for women (as opposed to the many forms appropriate for men) is romance. As Juhase says, even today "romances continue to end with a kiss, not a promotion."[23]

Brownmiller and Greer both argue that romance is a reflection of dominant masculine ideology.[24] In Brownmiller's view, women are forced to conform, in Greer's, women choose their own bondage. Modleski falls somewhere in between, where romance is one of the strategies women use to adapt to circumscribed lives and to convince themselves that limitations are really opportunities.[25] They are a way to deal with women's fears of, and confusion over, masculine behavior in a world in which men learn to devalue women. In romance, that devaluation is only a mask, concealing the hero's love for the heroine.

What about Pornography Then?

Much feminist attention with regard to the meaning of erotica has focused on pornography.[26] The aim here has clearly not been to examine a wide range of reasons why men may enjoy pornography but, rather, to use it as evidence that men want to oppress women or take vicarious pleasure in images of female degradation of women. The arguments are made that pornography is morally wrong, that it is degrading to women, and that it not only leads to violence against women, it *is* violence against women. The point of this essay is not to spend time discussing all of these arguments. Other feminists have addressed many of these issues elsewhere quite eloquently, suggesting that rather than censoring pornography we should encourage women to produce their own erotic material, asserting their own sexual needs.[27] There has been disagreement among feminists who see in pornography the erosion of existing norms and applaud it for that[28] and those who instead see it as the expression and confirmation of an anti-female perspective.[29] Some feminists have also suggested that the pornography industry is "bad" for the actresses, that it may not degrade all women but that it does degrade the actresses involved. This is one area where evolutionary minded thinking and feminist thinking run parallel. The porn actress is involved in a profession, often because of financial need, that runs counter to the main currents of female sexual psychology and decreases her desirability for the type of stable, pair-bonded relationships she might prefer. On the other hand, few express concern over the plight of male porn actors.

However, there are two particular criticisms I would like to comment on more fully because evolutionary-minded thinking can prevent us from making some unwarranted assumptions and encourage scientific testing of our theories.

Diamond, for example, suggested that pornographic material demeans women by depicting them as "malleable, obsessed with sex, and willing to engage in any sexual act with any available partner."[30] In fact, like prostitution, porn is often said to evidence male contempt for, or lack of respect for, women. But there exists an ideal test case for such claims: gay male porn. If these claims were accurate, we would expect gay male porn either not to exist at all or, if it did exist, to differ in significant ways from straight male porn. (For example, it might emphasize the development of enduring relationships or be less relentlessly focused on genitals.) But, in fact, gay and straight porn are essentially identical, differing only in the sex of the actors. In fact, gay porn often gives the impression of being more "real" than straight porn: for one thing, the actors in gay porn almost invariably seem to be having a genuinely good time, which is not always true of the actresses in straight porn; for another, the impersonal sex depicted in gay porn is not very different from the real life sexual relations of many gay men.[31]

In the same vein, the so called "money-shot," or external ejaculation, is also said to be evidence of male contempt for women, despite its equal frequency in gay porn. A better explanation for its ubiquitous nature might focus on the nature of male sexual arousal and the importance of visual proof of satisfaction. Facial expressions display sexual pleasure (one reason for the frequent close-ups of female faces in heterosexual porn), but the only proof of male sexual satisfaction is ejaculation; if the male ejaculates inside his female costar, the audience doesn't see that. As a result, climaxes in pornographic videos are typically external. There are many "non-reproductive" acts in porn, but it is important to remember that finding pleasure in sexual behavior (especially intercourse) is what evolution would have selected for. Engaging in a variety of acts, as long as some vaginal penetration was involved at some point, would not have been maladaptive.

The argument that viewing pornography leads to violence against women was raised a long time ago and still persists despite the quantity of research done to date that generally disconfirms the idea. There has been a great deal of work on the issue of negative attitudes toward women on the part of men after viewing pornography. In 1997, for instance, Davis reported that men who viewed sexually explicit films did not have negative attitudes toward women's rights nor were they more accepting of marital or date rape.[32] At least one examination of convicted sex offenders' experiences with porn concluded that they did not differ from those of other incarcerated males.[33] And, when Kutchinski examined the incidence of rape in several societies that have lenient attitudes toward pornography, he concluded that increased availability was not associated with increased reports of rape in Denmark, Sweden, West Germany, or the United States.[34] It is also worth mentioning that sexual violence is fairly uncommon in pornography, despite the common claims of its opponents.[35] And Sweden and Denmark, countries with high gender equality and low levels of violence against women, have some of the most liberal attitudes toward pornography.[36] In the United States, those states with the greatest gender inequality, also happen to have the lowest circulation of pornography.[37]

How Can Evolutionary Thinking Inform the Interpretation of Romance and Pornography?

If, as I have suggested previously, feminist thinking on pornography and romance has often gone astray, I would suggest that it is, at times, a focus on politics that is at the heart of this confusion, whether the view be that patriarchy is the root of all evil, that "Pornography is the Theory, Rape is the Practice,"[38] or that women should be encouraged to explore their own sexuality.[39] Much of this comes down to women's rights, concern about economic equality, or demonization of male sexuality. The question is, do the political debates get to the heart of why romance plots are so predictable and have such an enduring appeal to women? Why the romance hero is what he is? Or why pornography is so appealing to men and why most porno movies seem very similar to each other? This is where an evolutionary perspective can shine some light.

Over human evolutionary history, there have been numerous problems we have had to solve to survive and reproduce. Our adaptations, including our sexual psychologies, are the solutions—those behaviors (or psychological mechanisms) that make us more likely to survive and reproduce than the next person. And when it comes down to reproduction, the adaptive problems that faced males and females were significantly different.

As mentioned previously, ancestral men and women differed dramatically in the minimum possible investment they could make in an offspring if that off-spring was to have a chance of surviving. As a result, ancestral males could have reproduced at almost no cost if they impregnated a woman to whom they were not married and produced a child in which they did not invest. Ancestral females never encountered an opportunity for low-cost reproduction, the minimum possi-ble female parental investment was very large. Selection would have favored psy-chological adaptations that function to promote the pursuit of low-cost reproductive opportunities in men but not in women. In women, we would expect more of a focus on mechanisms designed to evaluate the willingness of men to commit investment.

These differences explain many aspects of pornography, in particular the endless parade of young, sexually attractive, and willing women. Promiscuous tendencies are shared by males of other species as well. Most are more than will-ing to mate with any female who is interested and accessible.[40] Likewise, it explains the focus of the romance on finding the perfect mate, which reflects the importance of paternal investment to the survival of offspring.[41] Choosing the best mate possible has always been vitally important to women. Critics some-times point to economic inequality (as experienced by the readers) as the source of this need to pair bond in romance, but it is not only economically disadvan-taged women who read romances. When one considers the mate choices of wealthy women, they seem to desire the same things in a man that poorer women do.[42] In fact, money itself would not have been relevant for ancestral women; possession of other resources, or the ability to obtain them, would have been. This is why the romance hero is always strong and capable of handling any situa-tion. He is typically a protector, not necessarily a stockbroker or lawyer.

The possessiveness the romance hero displays toward the heroine is also more satisfactorily explained from the evolutionary than the standard feminist perspective. His proprietary impulses stem not from a general desire to control women but, rather, from a specific desire to have control over female sexuality. Because of internal fertilization, a human male can never be positive a child is his own. On the other hand, no woman should ever have reason to doubt (modern technology aside) that the child emerging from her womb is indeed her biological child. As a result, males of all species tend to engage in behavior designed to increase certainty of paternity, everything from mate guarding to copulatory plugs (thankfully, more common in insects than in primates).[43]

An evolutionary perspective not only allows us to make predictions and explanations about the appeal and characteristics of mainstream erotic genres, it also allows us to make predictions about genres for a homosexual audience and, perhaps, to better explain more esoteric genres which at first glance might not seem to fit the typical mold.

A Test Case: Slash Fiction

If a comparison of gay porn to heterosexual porn highlights what is really essential to male sexual psychology, a comparison of mainstream romance with a subgenre known as "slash" can perhaps do the same for female sexual psychology. At first glance, slash might appear to pose a problem to the evolutionary psychology perspective. Slash fiction refers to romantic/erotic narratives written almost exclusively by and for women in which both protagonists are expropriated male media characters. Popular pairings include Kirk and Spock from the original *Star Trek* series, Starsky and Hutch, from the show of the same name, Clark Kent and Lex Luthor from UPN's *Smallville,* and Sam and Frodo from *Lord of the Rings.* Although slash protagonists fall in love and have sex with each other, they are typically depicted as heterosexual, sometimes as bisexual, and occasionally as homosexual. The term "slash" arose from the convention of using a stroke or slash between the men's names to signify their relationship (Kirk/Spock or K/S). It is mostly disseminated over the Internet, although there is also a small print market through which collections of stories and novels are sold at conventions and through the mail. A similar Japanese genre, Yaoi, focuses on romantic relationships between boys or young men, where the protagonists are Japanese anime or comic book characters. Yaoi is based on a long historical tradition of "boy's love" stories in Japan,[44] and the main consumers are also female, usually young women.

The typical literary or popular culture approach to slash has mainly focused on the pornographic aspects of slash, though there are exceptions. In one of the earliest academic articles on slash, "Pornography by Women, for Women, with Love," Joanna Russ documented the existence of male/male romance stories in the form of K/S. She focused on the lifelong monogamous relationship depicted in most K/S and argued that slash represents a new kind of pornography, written by and for women. She noted that slash stories are about lovers who take a "personal interest in each other's minds, not only each other's bodies" and who develop an "exclusive commitment to one another."[45] While many slash stories contain detailed descriptions of sexual acts, the emphasis is on the emotional nature of these acts, in stark contrast to the impersonal couplings of male-oriented pornography. Russ also perceptively observed that these stories are not really about male homosexuality; rather, they depict a female fantasy of sexuality acted out on and by male bodies. Slash cannot be described, simply, as gay porn written by women.

Patricia Frazer Lamb and Diana Veith have argued that slash is really a type of androgynous romance, a reworking of romance conventions to create a loving relationship between equals, which, they believe, cannot exist between men and women in a patriarchal society. They emphasize the telepathic bond that Kirk and Spock often share in K/S stories, and they note that these characters mix and match traditional masculine and feminine traits.[46]

Two of the most widely read academic writers on slash are Constance Penley and Henry Jenkins. Penley has proposed several explanations of why women write such narratives, including the hypotheses that slash readers and writers are "alienated" from their own bodies, that the slash pairing avoids the inherent inequalities of the romance-novel formula, and that slash fans are "retooling" masculinity by creating sensitive but not wimpy protagonists.[47] Jenkins adds to this that "slash is not so much a genre about sex as it is a genre about the limitations of traditional masculinity and about reconfiguring male identity."[48]

What can evolutionary psychology add to this picture? Can it present a different view of the appeal of slash? I think it can, in fact, present a simpler view of the appeal of these characters and their relationships. To a large extent, slash follows the conventions of the typical romance, with some interesting exceptions.

Academic students of slash, while always interesting and often insightful, have sometimes reached flawed conclusions because their focus was too narrow. For example, some theorists have written about slash as if it consisted only of Kirk/Spock, assuming that certain features of K/S, such as its "utopian" aspects, characterize all slash rather than being a reflection of the ideals of the Star Trek universe's creator in particular. Most television series that are "slashed" do not share this vision and, therefore, neither does the slash that they inspire.

The most serious deficit resulting from the insufficiently comparative nature of most academic slash theory is the failure to see slash as another form of women's romance fiction. In a rush to show that slash, and its fans, are "different," academic theorists have largely ignored the similarities between slash and mainstream romances.

The average slash story is, no doubt, more sexually graphic than the average romance novel. But graphic sex is not an essential ingredient of either genre. Although slash stories may include detailed descriptions of sexual acts, the emphasis always is on the emotional quality of the sex rather than on physical sensations, just as it is in mainstream romances. In slash, as in mainstream romances, sex occurs within committed relationships as part of an emotionally meaningful exchange, and the story of developing love takes precedence over anatomical details. In mainstream romances and slash alike, sex serves the plot, whereas in male-oriented porn it is the other way around. Furthermore, the artwork that illustrates many slash stories is unabashedly romantic and highly reminiscent of romance-novel cover art; it may portray nudity, but it almost never portrays penetration.

The love relationships depicted in slash are undoubtedly egalitarian, but whether these relationships are more egalitarian than those depicted in mainstream romances is highly questionable. Most readers and writers of mainstream romances would argue vehemently that the hero/heroine relationship *is* egalitarian. Despite the hero's much greater physical strength, he does not wield more power within the couple's relationship than the heroine does, and their dissimilar character traits can be considered complementary. And in slash, although battle-of-the-sexes themes are relatively muted, they are still present. As in mainstream romances, issues of commitment are explored ("Does he really love me?"), and a naturally promiscuous masculine sexuality is transformed and harnessed by the power of love to create a permanent, intimate, nurturing, monogamous bond.

The theme of exclusivity that permeates mainstream romances (as evidenced in possessiveness, jealousy, and monogamy) is equally common in slash. And in academic analyses of the romance novel much is made of the heroine's giving her virginity to the hero. It is a common slash convention for one or both protagonists—who usually have had a great deal of sexual experience with women—to have no sexual experience with men. In both genres the loss of "virginity" provides emotional resonance, affirming the couple's commitment to a bond they share with no one else. The prevalence and popularity in slash of so-called "first time" stories echoes the core theme of the romance novel: the search for the one right partner and the resolution of that search in sexual union.

The romance hero, according to Barlow and Krentz, is "a man in every sense of the word, and for most women the word man reverberates with thousands of years of connotative meanings which touch upon everything from sexual prowess, capacity for honor/loyalty, to an ability to protect and defend the family unit. He is no weakling . . . he will be forced in the course of the plot to prove his commitment to the relationship."[49] This description also characterizes slash protagonists. They are men "in every sense of the word," cops, space explorers, secret agents, and each must prove that his love is strong enough to survive not only the plot twists typical of cop/spy/science-fiction stories but also the conflicts that arise from the fact that he and his partner are (usually) heterosexual. These include internal conflict with the protagonist's own self-image as well as external conflict with friends, family, coworkers, and an often homophobic world. If their love survives that, it can survive anything, including the ravages of time.

Final Comments

It is clear that an analysis of the essential ingredients of pornography and romance provides insight into male and female sexual psychologies, insights that complement the results of surveys and experimental studies. Free markets are a window into our evolved human nature. But from a literary or popular culture perspective, what can an evolutionary perspective offer toward an understanding of erotica?

For one thing, it highlights the importance of looking at the impact of human nature, of not focusing entirely on nurture, of recognizing that both are relevant to most human actions and emotions. It is important to remember that an evolutionary perspective is best at predicting large statistical truths; it does not explain every anomaly. But if one takes into account the ancestral problems men and women faced, and the adaptations that evolved to deal with them, many if not all of the characteristics of pornography (from the anonymous sex with a variety of partners to the money shot) and romance (with its focus of the importance of choosing the "right" man) make perfect sense without invoking highly specific cultural pressures or the ravages of patriarchy (which both must develop in some sense from human nature in any case). And this perspective allows us to make predictions about erotica for specialized audiences and can explain the ways in which they are similar or different from mainstream forms in a more parsimonious way. Bringing an evolutionary perspective to literary studies can only enrich the field and provoke more discussion between two disciplines which should have been talking all along.

Notes

1. Salmon and Symons 2001.
2. Webb, Campbell, Schwartz, and Sechrest 1966.
3. For an overview see Daly and Wilson 1988.
4. Orians 1980.
5. Gorry 1999.
6. Salmon and Symons 2001.
7. Nesse and Williams 1994; Rozin 1976; Eaton, Eaton, and Konner 1997.
8. Morais 1999.
9. Marcus 1966.
10. Bullough and Bullough 1995; Paglia 1990.
11. Hebditch and Anning 1988.
12. Brosius, Weaver, and Staab 1993.
13. Mussell 1984.

14. Radway 1984.
15. Gorry 1999.
16. Barrett, Dunbar, and Lycett 2002.
17. For an overview see Symons 1979.
18. Clair 1992.
19. Radway 1984.
20. Mussell 1984, 17.
21. Radway 1984, 217.
22. Snitow 1979, 150.
23. Juhasz 1994, 10.
24. Brownmiller 1975; Greer 1971.
25. Modleski 1982.
26. For overviews see Dworkin 1989; Brownmiller 1975; MacKinnon 1989.
27. McElroy 1995; Russ 1985.
28. McElroy 1995; Kipnis 1996.
29. Brownmiller 1975; Dworkin 1989; MacKinnon 1989.
30. S. Diamond 1985.
31. Symons 1979; Bailey, Gaulin, Agyei, and Gladue 1994; Mahay, Laumann, and Michaels 2000.
32. Davis 1997.
33. Marshall 1989.
34. Kutchinski 1991.
35. Monk-Turner and Purcell 1999.
36. Kutchinski 1991.
37. Baron 1990.
38. L. Segal 1990.
39. McElroy 1995.
40. For overview see Barrett, Dunbar, and Lycett 2002.
41. Hill and Hurtado 1996.
42. Buss 1989; Wiederman and Allgeier 1992.
43. For an overview see Alcock 2001a.
44. McHarry 2003; Thorn 1997.
45. Russ 1985, 85.
46. Frazer Lamb and Veith 1986.
47. Penley 1991.
48. Jenkins 1992, 191.
49. Barlow and Krentz 1992.

Afterword

Denis Dutton

Works of literary criticism and theories of literature are portrayals and under-standings of the human mind's storytelling capacities. Think of them as an anal-ogy with visual portrayals—drawings and paintings—of the human body. A period spent teaching in the fine arts department of my university has provided me with a useful lesson or two in this connection. Much art practice today for-sakes, for better or worse, accurate, "hand-guided" representation of the world. Fine arts students, attracted to such techniques as graphic collage and sculptural construction, influenced by modernism and the easy use of computers, no longer immerse themselves in life drawing as students once did. Whether or not this is a justifiable development, it is certainly understandable: the human body and the human face are very hard to draw, much harder than natural objects, landscape features, and most artifacts.

There are two notable reasons for this difficulty. First, whatever the myriad ends the body evolved for, being easy to render with pencil or paintbrush was not one of them. There may be aspects of the human form that make drawing eas-ier—the most obvious is its left/right symmetry—but they come about as acci-dents of an evolution that was governed by other factors in how it constructed and adapted the skeleton and musculature.

What's worse, human beings already possess an evolved ability to *read* the body, especially the face, with the utmost acuity. The visual sensitivity required to establish and recognize eye contact by normal-sighted individuals ought to astound us: the angular difference in arc degrees between an eye that is looking at you across a room and one that isn't would be close to immeasurable. Yet we are able to distinguish eye contact, catching a glance at a distance, as a normal part of everyday life. We also have a constant, lifelong awareness of the positions and appearance of arms, hands, and fingers—a sense of their posture and gestural meanings—that is complex and subtle. An artist's inability to draw well will therefore reveal itself most immediately in badly rendered faces and hands: draw-ing your neighbor's house or dog or lawnmower is so much less testing than drawing your neighbor. (This challenge is often resolved by lazy art students who render a figure as facing away from the viewer, Casper David Friedrich–style, with hands conveniently in pockets.)

I raise this in analogy: just as ordinary experience of the human form sets a high bar for any artist who would draw it, so our lifetime experience with narrative sets a high bar for anyone who would theorize about it. We grow up as audiences, tellers, and critics of jokes, gossip, fairy tales, plays, movies, anecdotes, novels, poems, and histories. These narrative objects, which reflect immensely complex interests and capacities, are universal in genesis if not in every instanced type. Literary theories of any kind have to stand up against our highly developed, preexisting sense of the uses and pleasures of stories. We know too much already to be persuaded by any over-simple, one-dimensional account—from a philosopher, scientist, or literature professor—that isolates some aspects of stories and discounts others that we know in experience to be important.

This stubborn fact, however, has tended to be ignored in literary theory since its very beginnings. Anyone who teaches the history of aesthetics is in the business of surveying a long series of exaggerated, partial, one-sided, all-or-nothing claims purporting to explain the nature of art and its creation. It is a tendency most conspicuously present in Plato—who stressed the social utility of art—but is also found to some extent in Aristotle—who concentrated on *mimesis*—and in the early sections of Kant's Third Critique, where the disinterested contemplation of form is so stressed. (In later sections, Kant's thesis becomes more richly complex.) Closer to our time, Tolstoy's obsessive concentration on the communicative functions of art, including artistic sincerity, is a good example of the single-dimension tendency. Tolstoy, like all the others, is useful to study (and a pleasure to teach) because he captured a crucial aspect of art and articulated its importance with passion and insight. His theory, however, is far from adequate to the totality of art, ignoring form. In just as provocative a manner, the formal values ignored by Tolstoy became the centerpiece of Clive Bell's *Art*, famous for the wild claim that the subject matter of a painting is "irrelevant" to its aesthetic value. Defending his thesis, Bell writes, "You will notice that people who cannot feel pure aesthetic emotions remember pictures by their subjects; whereas people who can, as often as not, have no idea what the subject of a picture is. They have never noticed the representative element, and so when they discuss pictures they talk about the shapes of forms and the relations and quantities of colours."[1] Did you ever come across anyone who, in their experience of a painting could remember blue rectangles, green mottled areas, and pinkish brown smudges but couldn't recall if they were cars or trees or people?

By the second half of the twentieth century such weirdness and extremism had become a ticket to academic success, particularly in literary theory. From Freud to the New Criticism through Deconstruction to postcolonial theory and varieties of social-constructionist feminism, the careerist pattern in literary theory has been to reduce all artistic value to a single essential set of factors and, conversely, to declare whole categories of putative aesthetic interests and features irrelevant or inimical to critical understanding. No single critical approach has triumphed out of this, but the three most influential—Freudianism, Marxism, and deconstruction—did, as Joseph Carroll observes, seem to offer a combined comprehensive understanding of art and the human condition: "Freudianism provides an explanatory apparatus for individual identity and sexual and family relations, Marxism for social history, and deconstruction for the cosmic nature of things. Together, these three forms of explanation cover the whole field of human experience, and each also promises to provide a key to deep forces that have been repressed and disguised—for the sake of psychic economy, class interest, or rational order."[2]

These familiar reductionisms (they are also forms of determinism) have come to constitute the comfortable, daily methodological bread of academic critics and theorists. It should therefore not surprise anyone that the first accusation to be made against any new, potentially powerful and attractive competing theory is that it must be "reductionism" and "determinism." That's the only kind of thinking most literary theorists know. And that is why it is so important to declare that, as David Sloan Wilson makes clear in his essay, evolutionary psychology does not propose or intend to reduce art to a small set of psychic determinants, that evolutionary aesthetics opens the field to a valid, scientifically acceptable creative constructivism. To recover the innate interests and capacities that have enabled and driven music, art, drama, and literature to develop into the staggeringly vast arrays of work and performance they have become is not to impose on them a new determinism. The deep syntactic structures posited by Chomskyan linguistics have not been shown to be a constraint on poetic freedom, and there is no reason to expect constraints to emerge from an aesthetics informed by Darwinism. A fundamental underlying, universal structure of domain-specific intelligence, continuous with a general intelligence, innate tendencies toward emotional reactions to environmental situations and cues, a grasp of cognitive capacities such as memory and pattern recognition, a basic topography of the emotions, and an inventory of more-or-less permanent innate human interests—all of these factors are now within the reach of aesthetic theory. This does not threaten art or its criticism or predictively set limits on what is in principle progressively possible in the arts. In this sense, it is not antimodernist, denying, for instance, *Finnegans Wake* a place in a pantheon of artistic greatness. It may predict that plotted stories, comic and tragic, on themes of love and death will probably demonstrate their long-term attractiveness to most literary audiences, including audiences for theater and film. But this is a long way from claiming that Dickens is a greater writer than Joyce, even if it might explain why Dickens can be expected to be more popular than Joyce into the foreseeable future as fodder for films.

Evolutionary aesthetics does not, in fact, invalidate reductionisms so much as enrich and elucidate them, providing a framework that can show the extent of their truth and explain their limitations. Here is an example of what I mean, in the form of an episode from recent aesthetics. In the philosophy of art, formalism remains a complex set of ideas that validate some of our deepest intuitions about art but systematically deny or exclude others. "Pure" aesthetics, it holds, is essentially about form and structure. There's an intuitive appeal to this formalistic way of thinking through aesthetics, and our profession has been in its spell at least since Kant. More important, many strains of modernism in art, literature, and music have more or less adopted the Kantian intuition that the essence of aesthetic appreciation lies in the contemplation of pure form. But there are counterintuitions, and in aesthetics as elsewhere in philosophy, academic careers are built out of reconciling such conflicts of intuition or showing that they are unreal or showing why one side is decisively right and the other wrong.

Under the debates about formalism there lurks a question that has been seldom seriously asked during the last fifty years: Where do the intuitions come from? For instance, back in the 1970s aestheticians began to examine the question of what might be wrong (if anything) with art forgery. Arthur Koestler and Alfred Lessing, assuming the formalist position, had claimed there was nothing wrong with forgeries so long as they were "aesthetically" indistinguishable from originals or, anyway, looked as good as originals. To reject the aesthetically excellent forgery, so the Lessing/Koestler position went, was mere snobbery.[3]

In an article responding to their argument, I appealed to an imagined experience: the acute sense of deflation and disappointment you'd feel if you learned that a dazzling virtuoso piano recording you'd much admired had in fact been faked, speeded up electronically. From this I built up a general view of art as necessarily involving performance and achievement.[4] An intrinsic part of the experience of listening to a pianist perform a difficult work is our background knowledge of the difficulty of the playing: our response is not to a high number of notes per second but to notes per second performed by ten fingers on a keyboard. (This explains why showers of notes in electronic music can never sound "fast" and thrill us in the same way that a virtuoso pianist can.)

I still think I was right, but my argument contained an awkward gap. It depended on an impressive psychological effect—a shock, a sense even of betrayal when you discover that the virtuoso's recording is not what you thought it was. But I had no way to explain the existence of this shock. At least one writer, Leonard B. Meyer, had treated the admiration of technique as a contingent cultural construct (as though we could envision a culture where practiced skill was *not* admired).[5] Yet Meyer's response seemed implausible, though it fit the normal pattern of social-constructivist theories. Contrary to Meyer's implication, the admiration of technique, of feats of virtuosity, is a cross-cultural, universal value. It infects not only the arts but potentially all human activity, for example, oratory, hunting skills, and sporting activities everywhere. The admiration of high skill, particularly in areas involving public performance, is too widespread and persistent to be "explained" by appeals to culture. The real question is, why do cultures everywhere come to encourage an intuitive admiration of skill?

Today, as *The Literary Animal* demonstrates, there is a substantial psychological literature that we can apply to philosophical ruminations on origins of our intuitions, including the feelings and emotions expressed, aroused, or represented in aesthetic experience. In the case of the admiration of technique, the universality of this phenomenon has as much of an evolutionary basis as the general liking for fatty and sweet foods. There can be no doubt that skill-developing, skill-admiring peoples survived better than competitors in the Pleistocene Age. But beyond natural selection, it is probable that sexual selection has played a major role in the evolution of the admiration of technique, with our ancestors tending to find attractive as mates individuals who could demonstrate a range of manual or intellectual skills. Many philosophers have been reluctant to psychologize such values if that means naturalizing them as stable components of an evolved human nature. But why? What's so much better about using "culture" as the one-size-fits-all explanation for basic values in the arts?

Consider the famous Komar and Melamid experiment to create the favorite paintings for various peoples around the world, derived from poll results. The preference-driven paintings they put together are a hoot (George Washington shares a Hudson River scene with a hippo), but they inadvertently back up independent research on cross-cultural preferences in landscapes and landscape pictures.[6] There is a cross-culturally established list of elements which are desired by human beings in landscapes—water, variegated open areas with climbable trees, large wild or domestic mammals, pathways or riverbanks that disappear into an inviting distance (so-called way-finding elements), and so forth. Beyond psychological lab tests, these preferred landscape elements show up both in landscape calendars and in the design of private gardens and public parks worldwide. Komar and Melamid back this up, but then so does the history of landscape painting in both Europe and Asia.

Such developments represent an exciting challenge to aesthetics and literary theory. The issues are fascinating. Why not work with psychologists to understand better cross-cultural preferences in picture content? Are there psychological mechanisms that account for the intense satisfactions of group singing or of sharing an artistic experience as the member of an audience? Can we identify and statistically analyze recurrent themes or plot devices in drama and literature? How does the admiration of skill manifest itself in disparate activities spread across cultures, and how might a more global perspective elucidate our understanding of the adulation given to pop idols or virtuoso pianists?

Evolutionary psychologists insist that wherever an intense pleasure is found in human life, there is likely some reproductive or survival advantage connected with it. Whatever their practical values, art and literature can deliver intense pleasure. Moreover, they utilize vast amounts of money, time, and effort on the part of creators and audiences. Why? Literary theorists, aestheticians, it's time to start explaining. Just repeating the mantra that "it's all culture" has become tedious and empty.

Answers to the ultimate questions for this inquiry remain intriguingly uncertain, despite the data and insights of *The Literary Animal*: "What in the end is the evolutionary function of art and literature?" and the connection question, "What are the prehistoric sources of the impulse to create art and literature?" Answers are so far provisional and may forever remain so. (This is not so remarkable: we may never be certain how we got an appendix.) Some thinking moves in the direction of regarding the pleasure as a byproduct of cognitive capacities that have important survival value. Others see art itself as central for increasing survival potential in the period of early human evolution. Some view its function as lying in its communal dimension, while others emphasize its connections to individual assertion in courtship and sex. Experimental evidence will have bearing on how these and other positions are ultimately sorted out. We can look at other cultures and other epochs and venture to generalize across traditions wherever evidence warrants. Whatever answers we finally achieve, I am certain they will reflect the fact that each of the major theories of art offered by the history of aesthetics has emphasized an important, if incomplete, truth about the nature of art. The objective now within our reach would be a naturalist aesthetics grounded in a valid human psychology that not only explained art but explained the appeal of varying, and sometimes contradictory, traditional theories of art. A Darwinian aesthetics will therefore be multilayered, true to the myriad relations between separate aspects of the creation and experience of art and literature. None of the great thinkers who have applied their minds to art have been entirely wrong, but no theory of art which ignores or denies the natural, evolved basis for the aesthetic response can ever be entirely right.

Wittgenstein remarked that philosophy leaves everything as it is. Everything, he might have added, except our understanding. Adequate theories of art also leave the arts as they are, to make their own way in the world, which they will in any event. In the meantime, much new and original research, empirical and speculative, remains to be done. For aesthetics and literary theory, the future begins here.

Notes

1. Bell 1914.
2. J. Carroll 1998.
3. Koestler 1965; Lessing 1967.
4. Dutton 1979.
5. Meyer 1967.
6. See Wypijewski 1997.

Works Cited

Abrams, M. H. 1953. *The Mirror and the Lamp: Romantic Theory and the Critical Tradition.* London: Oxford University Press.

———. 1986. "Poetry, Theories Of." In *Princeton Encyclopedia of Poetic Terms,* edited by Alex Preminger et al., 203–14. Princeton: Princeton University Press.

Ahearn, Edward J. 1987. *Marx and Modern Fiction.* New Haven: Yale University Press.

Aiello, L. C., and P. Wheeler. 1995. "The Expensive Tissue Hypothesis." *Current Anthropology* 36:199–211.

Aiken, N. 1998. *The Biological Origins of Art.* Westport, Conn.: Praeger.

Alcock, J. 2001a. *Animal Behavior: An Evolutionary Approach.* 7th ed. Sunderland, Mass.: Sinauer.

———. 2001b. *The Triumph of Sociobiology.* Oxford: Oxford University Press.

Alexander, R. D. 1979. *Darwinism and Human Affairs.* Seattle: University of Washington Press.

———. 1987. *The Biology of Moral Systems.* Hawthorne, New York: Aldine de Gruyter.

———. 1989. "The Evolution of the Human Psyche." In *The Human Revolution: Behavioral and Biological Perspectives on the Origins of Modern Humans,* edited by P. Mellars and C. Stringer, 455–513. Princeton: Princeton University Press.

———. 1990. "Epigenetic Rules and Darwinian Algorithms: The Adaptive Study of Learning and Development." *Ethology and Sociobiology* 11:241–303.

Anderson, Joseph D. 1996. *The Reality of Illusion: An Ecological Approach to Cognitive Film.* Carbondale: Southern Illinois University Press.

Anderson, Malte. 1994. *Sexual Selection.* Princeton: Princeton University Press.

Armstrong, Isobel. 1990. Introd. to *Pride and Prejudice,* by Jane Austen. New York: Oxford University Press.

Armstrong, Nancy. 1981. "Inside Greimas's Square: Literary Characters and Cultural Constraints." In *The Sign in Music and Literature,* edited by Wendy Steiner, 52–66. Austin: University of Texas Press.

———. 1987. *Desire and Domestic Fiction: A Political History of the Novel.* New York: Oxford University Press.

Astington, J. W. 1990. "Narrative and the Child's Theory of Mind." In *Narrative Thought and Narrative Language,* edited by B. Britton and A. Pellegrini. Hillsdale N.J.: Erlbaum.

Atran, Scott. 1990. *Cognitive Foundations of Natural History: Towards an Anthropology of Science*. Cambridge: Cambridge University Press.

———. 2002. *In Gods We Trust: The Evolutionary Landscape of Religion*. New York: Oxford University Press.

Auerbach, Nina. 1978. *Communities of Women: An Idea in Fiction*. Cambridge, Mass.: Harvard University Press.

Aunger, R., ed. 2000. *Darwinizing Culture: The Status of Memetics as a Science*. Oxford: Oxford University Press.

Austen, Jane. 1994. *Sense and Sensibility* and *Pride and Prejudice*. New York: St. Martin's.

———. 2000. *Pride and Prejudice: An Authoritative Text, Background, and Sources*. 3rd ed. Edited by Donald Gray. New York: Norton.

Ayotte, J., I. Peretz, and K. Hyde. 2002. "Congenital Amusia: A Group Study of Adults Afflicted with a Music-specific Disorder." *Brain* 125:238–51.

Bahn, P. G. 1991. "Pleistocene Images Outside of Europe." *Proceedings of the Prehistoric Society* 57:99–102.

———. 1994. "New Advances in the Field of Ice Age Art." In *Origins of Anatomically Modern Humans*, edited by M. H. Nitecki and D. V. Nitecki, 121–32. New York: Plenum Press.

Bailey, J. Michael. 1997. "Are Genetically Based Individual Differences Compatible with Species-wide Adaptations?" In *Uniting Psychology and Biology: Integrative Perspectives on Human Development*, edited by Nancy L. Segal, Glenn E. Weisfeld, and Carol C. Weisfeld, 81–100. Washington: American Psychological Association.

———. 1998. "Can Behavior Genetics Contribute to Evolutionary Behavioral Science?" In *Handbook of Evolutionary Psychology: Ideas, Issues, Applications*, edited by Charles Crawford and Dennis L. Krebs, 211–33. Mahway, N.J.: Lawrence Erlbaum Associates.

Bailey, J. M., S. Gaulin, Y. Agyei, and B. Gladue. 1994. "Effects of Gender and Sexual Orientation on Evolutionarily Relevant Aspects of Human Mating Psychology." *Journal of Personality and Social Psychology* 66:1081–93.

Barash, D. P. 1997. "In Search of Behavioral Individuality." *Human Nature* 8:153–69.

Barash, D. P., and J. E. Lipton. 2001. *The Myth of Monogamy: Fidelity and Infidelity in Animals and People*. New York: Freeman.

Barkow, J. H. 1990. "Beyond the DP/DSS Controversy." *Ethology and Sociobiology* 11:341–51.

Barkow, J., L. Cosmides, and J. Tooby, eds. 1992. *The Adapted Mind*. Oxford: Oxford University Press.

Barlow, L., and J. A. Krentz. 1992. "Beneath: The Hidden Codes of Romance." In *Dangerous Men and Adventurous Women*, edited by J. A. Krentz, 15–30. Pennsylvania: University of Pennsylvania Press.

Baron, L. 1990. "Pornography and Gender Equality: An Empirical Analysis." *Journal of Sex Research* 27:3.

Baron-Cohen, S. 1995. *Mindblindness: An Essay on Autism and Theory of Mind*. Cambridge, Mass.: Bradford/MIT Press.

———. 2000. "Theory of Mind and Autism: A Fifteen-Year-Review." *Understanding Other Minds: Perspectives from Developmental Cognitive Neuroscience*, edited by S. Baron-Cohen, H. Tager-Flusberg, and D. Cohen, 3–20. Oxford: Oxford University Press.

Baron-Cohen, Simon, Alan Leslie, and U. Firth. 1985. "Does the Autistic Child Have a Theory of Mind?" *Cognition* 21:37–46.

Baron-Cohen, S., M. O'Riordan, et al. 1999. "Recognition of Faux Pas by Normally Developing Children and Children with Asperger Syndrome or High-functioning Autism." *Journal of Autism and Developmental Disorders* 29:407–18.

Baron-Cohen, S., H. Tager-Flusberg, et al., eds. 2000. *Understanding Other Minds: Perspectives from Developmental Cognitive Neuroscience*. Oxford: Oxford University Press.

Barrett, J. L., R. Richert, et al. 2001. "God's Beliefs Versus Mother's: The Development of Nonhuman Agent Concepts." *Child Development* 72:50–65.

Barrett, L., R. Dunbar, and J. Lycett. 2002. *Human Evolutionary Psychology*. Princeton, N.J.: Princeton University Press.

Barrow, John D. 1995. *The Artful Universe*. Oxford: Clarendon Press.

Bartels, Andreas, and Semir Zeki. 2000. "The Neural Basis of Romantic Love." *Neuroreport* 11:3829–34.

Barthelme, Donald. 1987. "The Balloon." In *The Short Story: 30 Masterpieces*, edited by Beverly Lawn, 427–32. New York: St. Martin's Press.

Bartholomew, K., and L. M. Horowitz. 1991. "Attachment Styles among Young Adults: A Test of a Four-Category Model." *Journal of Personality and Social Psychology* 61:226–44.

Bartlett, F. C. 1932. *Remembering*. Cambridge: Cambridge University Press.

Bate, J. 1997. *The Genius of Shakespeare*. London: Macmillan.

Beall, Anne E., and Robert J. Sternberg. 1995. "The Social Construction of Love." *Journal of Social and Personal Relationships* 12:417–38.

Bedaux, J. B., and B. Cooke, eds. 1999. *Sociobiology and the Arts*. Amsterdam: Rodopi.

Bekoff, M., and C. Allen. 2002. "The Evolution of Social Play: Interdisciplinary Analyses of Cognitive Processes." In *The Cognitive Animal: Empirical and Theoretical Perspectives on Animal Cognition*, edited by M. Bekoff, C. Allen, and G. M. Burghardt, 429–35. Cambridge, Mass.: Bradford/MIT Press.

Bekoff, M., C. Allen, et al., eds. 2002. *The Cognitive Animal: Empirical and Theoretical Perspectives on Animal Cognition*. Cambridge, Mass.: Bradford/MIT Press.

Bell, Clive. 1914. *Art*. London: Chatto and Windus.

Bellis, M., and R. Baker. 1990. "Do Females Promote Sperm Competition: Data for Humans." *Animal Behavior* 40:197–99.

Belsey, Catherine. 2002. "Making Space: Perspective Vision and the Lacanian Real." *Textual Practice* 16:31–55.

Belsky, J., L. Steinberg, and P. Draper. 1991. "Childhood Experience, Interpersonal Development, and Reproductive Strategy: An Evolutionary Theory of Socialization." *Child Development* 62:647–70.

Berman, R. A., and D. I. Slobin. 1994. *Relating Events in Narrative: A Crosslinguistic Developmental Study.* Hillsdale, N.J.: Lawrence Erlbaum.

Betzig, Laura L. 1986. *Despotism and Differential Reproduction: A Darwinian View of History.* Hawthorne, N.Y.: Aldine de Gruyter.

———. 1998. "Not Whether to Count Babies, but Which." In *Handbook of Evolutionary Psychology: Ideas, Issues, Applications,* edited by Charles Crawford and Dennis L. Krebs, 265–73. Mahway, N.J.: Lawrence Erlbaum Associates.

Bickerton, D. 1990. *Language and Species.* Chicago: University of Chicago Press.

Biesele, Megan. 1978. "Sapience and Scarce Resources: Communication Systems of the !Kung and Other Foragers." *Social Science Information* 17:921–47.

———. 1993. *Women Like Meat: The Folklore and Foraging Ideology of the Kalahari Ju/'Hoan.* Bloomington: Indiana University Press.

Black, John B., and Gordon H. Bower. 1980. "Story Understanding as Problem-Solving." *Poetics* 9:223–50.

Bloch, R. Howard. 1991. *Medieval Misogyny and the Invention of Western Romantic Love.* Chicago: University of Chicago Press.

Bloom, H. 2000. *Global Brain: The Evolution of Mass Mind from the Big Bang to the 21st Century.* New York: John Wiley.

Blurton Jones, Nicholas, and Melvin J. Konner. 1976. "!Kung Knowledge of Animal Behavior." In *Kalahari Hunter-Gatherers,* edited by Richard B. Lee and Irven DeVore, 325–48. Cambridge: Harvard University Press.

Blurton Jones, Nicholas, and Frank Marlowe. 2002. "Selection for Delayed Maturity. Does It Take Twenty Years to Learn to Hunt and Gather?" *Human Nature* 13:199–238.

Bock, J., and H. Kaplan. 2001. "Fertility Theory: The Embodied Capital Theory of Life History Evolution." In *International Encyclopedia of the Social and Behavioral Sciences, Volume on Demography,* Vol. 3.3, Article 155, edited by J. M. Hoem, 5561–68. New York: Elsevier Science.

Booth, Wayne C. 1983. *The Rhetoric of Fiction.* Chicago: University of Chicago Press.

———. 1996. "Distance and Point of View: An Essay in Classification." In *Essentials of the Theory of Fiction,* edited by Michael J. Hoffman and Patrick D. Murphy, 116–33. Durham, N.C.: Duke University Press.

Bordwell, D. 1997. *On the History of Film Style*. Cambridge, Mass.: Harvard University Press.

Bordwell, D., and N. Carroll, eds. 1996. *Post-Theory: Reconstructing Film Studies*. Madison: University of Wisconsin Press.

Bottigheimer, Ruth. 1980. "The Transformed Queen: A Search for the Origins of Negative Female Archetypes in Grimms' Fairy Tales." *Amsterdamer Beitrage zur neuren Germanistik* 10:1–12.

———. 1982. "Tale Spinners: Submerged Voices in Grimms' Fairy Tales." *New German Critique* 27:141–50.

Bouchard, Thomas J. 1994. "Genes, Environment, and Personality." *Science* 264:1700–1.

———. 1997. "The Genetics of Personality." In *Handbook of Psychiatric Genetics*, edited by Kenneth Blum and Ernest P. Noble, 267–90. Boca Raton, Fla.: CRC Press.

Bower, Gordon H., and Daniel G. Morrow. 1990. "Mental Models in Narrative Comprehension." *Science* 247:44–48.

Bowlby, John. 1982. *Attachment and Loss*. Vol.1, *Attachment*. New York: Basic Books.

———. 1997. *Attachment and Loss*. Vol.1, *Attachment*. London: Pimlico.

Boyd, Brian. 1998. "Jane, Meet Charles: Literature, Evolution, and Human Nature." *Philosophy and Literature* 22:1–30.

———. 2001. "The Origin of Stories: *Horton Hears a Who*." *Philosophy and Literature* 25:197–214.

———. 2004. "Laughter and Literature: A Play Theory of Humor." *Philosophy and Literature* 28:1–22.

Boyd, R., and P. Richerson. 1985. *Culture and the Evolutionary Process*. Chicago: University of Chicago Press.

Boyer, P. 1994. *The Naturalness of Religious Ideas*. Berkeley and Los Angeles: University of California Press.

———. 1996. "What Makes Anthropomorphism Natural: Intuitive Ontology and Cultural Representations." *Journal of the Royal Anthropological Institute* 2:83–97.

———. 2001. *Religion Explained: The Evolutionary Origins of Religious Thought*. New York: Basic Books.

Bradley, A. C. 1929. *A Miscellany*. London: Macmillan.

Branden, N. 1989. *Judgement Day*. Boston: Houghton Mifflin.

Brauner, S. 2001. *Fearless Wives and Frightened Shrews: The Construction of the Witch in Early Modern Germany*. Amherst: University of Massachusetts Press.

Bridgeman, Bruce. 2003. *Psychology and Evolution: The Origins of Mind*. Thousand Oaks, Calif.: Sage.

Bristol, R. Curtis. 2001. "What Freud Taught Us about Passionate Romantic

Love." In *The Psychoanalytic Century: Freud's Legacy for the Future*, edited by David E. Scharff. New York: Other Press.

Brook, P. 1968. *The Empty Space*. London: Penguin.

Brosius, H. B., J. B. Weaver, and J. F. Staab. 1993. "Exploring the Social and Sexual 'Reality' of Contemporary Pornography." *Journal of Sex Research* 30:161–70.

Brown, D. E. 1991. *Human Universals*. Philadelphia: Temple University Press.

———. 2000. "Human Universals and Their Implications." In *Being Humans: Anthropological Universality and Particularity in Transdisciplinary Perspectives*, edited by N. Roughley, 156–74. New York: Walter de Gruyter.

Brown, S. 2000a. "Evolutionary Models of Music: From Sexual Selection to Group Selection." *Perspectives in Ethology* 13:231–81.

———. 2000b. "The 'Musilanguage' Model of Music Evolution." In *The Origins of Music*, edited by S. Brown, B. Merker, and N. L. Wallin, 271–300. Cambridge, Mass.: Bradford/MIT Press.

Brownmiller, S. 1975. *Against Our Will*. New York: Bantam.

Brownstein, Rachel M. 1988. "Jane Austen: Irony and Authority." *Women's Studies* 15:57–70.

Bruner, J. 2002. *Making Stories: Law, Literature, Life*. New York: Farrar, Straus, and Giroux.

Brunetière, F. 1894/1914. *The Law of the Drama*. New York: Columbia College.

Bullough, V. L., and B. Bullough. 1995. *Sexual Attitudes: Myths and Realities*. New York: Prometheus Books.

Buss, D. M. 1989. "Sex Differences in Human Mate Preferences: Evolutionary Hypothesis Testing in 37 Cultures." *Behavioral and Brain Sciences* 12:1–49.

———. 1990. "Toward a Biologically Informed Psychology of Personality." *Journal of Personality* 58:1–16.

———. 1994. *The Evolution of Desire: Strategies of Human Mating*. New York: Basic Books.

———. 1995. "Evolutionary Psychology: A New Paradigm for Psychological Science." *Psychological Inquiry* 6:1–30.

———. 1999. *Evolutionary Psychology: The New Science of the Mind*. Boston: Allyn and Bacon.

———. 2000. *The Dangerous Passion: Why Jealousy Is as Necessary as Love and Sex*. New York: Free Press.

Butler, Marilyn. 1975. *Jane Austen and the Ear of Ideas*. Oxford: Clarendon.

Byrne, Richard W., and Andrew Whiten. 1988. *Machiavellian Intelligence: Social Expertise and the Evolution of Intellect in Monkeys, Apes and Humans*. Oxford: Clarendon.

Campbell, Anne. 2002. *A Mind of Her Own: The Evolutionary Psychology of Women*. Oxford: Oxford University Press.

Campbell, D. T. 1960. "Blind Variation and Selective Retention in Creative Thought and Other Knowledge Processes." *Psychological Review* 67:380–400.

————. 1974. "Evolutionary Epistemology." In *The Philosophy of Karl Popper,* edited by P. A. Scilpp, 413–63. LaSalle, Ill.: Open Court Publishing.

Campbell, J. 1968. *The Hero with a Thousand Faces.* Princeton: Princeton University Press.

Caramazza, A., and J. R. Shelton. 1998. "Domain-Specific Knowledge Systems in the Brain: The Animate-Inanimate Distinction." *Journal of Cognitive Neuroscience* 10:1–34.

Carey, S., and E. Spelke. 1994. "Domain-Specific Knowledge and Conceptual Change." In *Mapping the Mind: Domain Specificity in Cognition and Culture,* edited by L. A. Hirschfeld and S. A. Gelman, 169–200. Cambridge: Cambridge University Press.

Carroll, J. 1995. *Evolution and Literary Theory.* Columbia: University of Missouri Press.

————. 1998. Review of John Ellis's Literature Lost: Social Agendas and the Corruption of the Humanities, in *Times Literary Supplement,* no. 4967 (June 12): 27.

————. 1999a. "The Deep Structure of Literary Representations." *Evolution and Human Behavior* 20:159–73.

————. 1999b."The Deep Structure of Literary Representations." *Evolution and Human Behavior* 20:159–73.

————. 1999c. "Wilson's *Consilience* and Literary Study." *Philosophy and Literature* 23:393–413.

————. 2001a. "Human Universals and Literary Meaning: A Sociobiological Critique of *Pride and Prejudice, Villette, O Pioneers!, Anna of the Five Towns,* and *Tess of the d'Urbervilles." Interdisciplinary Literary Studies* 2:9–27.

————. 2001b. "The Ecology of Victorian Fiction." *Philosophy and Literature* 25:295–313.

————. 2001c. "Universalien in der Literaturwissenschaft (Universals in Literary Study)." In *Universalien und Konstruktivismus,* edited by Peter M. Hejl, 235–56. Frankfurt am Main: Suhrkamp.

————. 2002. "Organism, Environment, and Literary Representation." *Interdisciplinary Studies in Literature and Environment* 9:27–45.

————. 2003. "Adaptationist Literary Study: An Emerging Research Program." *Style* 36:596–617.

Carroll, N. 1996."Prospects for Film Theory: A Personal Assessment." In *Post-Theory: Reconstructing Film Studies,* edited by D. Bordwell and N. Carroll, 37–68. Madison: University of Wisconsin Press.

————. 1998. *A Philosophy of Mass Art.* Oxford: Clarendon.

Carruthers, P., and A. Chamberlain, eds. 2000. *Evolution and the Human Mind.* Cambridge: Cambridge University Press.

Cashdan, E. 1994. "Women's Mating Strategies." *Evolutionary Anthropology* 5:134–43.

Cassill, R. V. 1981. "Talking about Fiction." In *The Norton Anthology of Short Fiction*, edited by R. V. Cassill, xxi–xxxiii. New York: Norton.

Chagnon, Napoleon. 1979. *Yanomamö: The Fierce People.* New York: Holt, Rinehart, and Winston.

Chagnon, Napoleon, and William Irons, eds. 1979. *Evolutionary Biology and Human Social Behavior: An Anthropological Perspective.* North Scituate, Mass.: Duxbury Press.

Chance, M. R. A. 1988. *Social Fabrics of the Mind.* Hove, Sussex: Lawrence Erlbaum.

Chance, M. R. A. and C. Jolly. 1970. *Social Groups of Monkeys, Apes and Men.* New York: Dutton.

Chance, M. R. A., and R. R. Larsen, eds. 1976. *The Social Structure of Attention.* London: John Wiley.

Charney, Maurice. 2000. *Shakespeare on Love and Lust.* New York: Columbia University Press.

Charters, Ann. 1991. "The Elements of Fiction." In *The Story and Its Writer: An Introduction to Short Fiction*, 3–5. Boston: Bedford Books.

Chauvet, Jean-Marie, Eliette Brunel Deschamps, and Christian Hillaire. 1996. *Dawn of Art: The Chauvet Cave: The Oldest Known Paintings in the World.* New York: H. N. Abrams.

Cheney, D. L., and R. M. Seyfarth. 1991. "Truth and Deception in Animal Communication." In *Cognitive Ethology: The Minds of Other Animals*, edited by C. A. Ristau, 127–51. Hillsdale, N.J.: Erlbaum.

Chiappe, Dan. 2000. "Metaphor, Modularity, and the Evolution of Conceptual Integration." *Metaphor and Symbol* 15:137–58.

Chiappe, Dan, and Kevin MacDonald. Under submission. The Evolution of Domain-general Mechanisms in Intelligence and Learning.

Chisholm, J. S. 1999. *Death, Hope and Sex: Steps to an Evolutionary Ecology of Mind and Morality.* Cambridge, England: Cambridge University Press.

Chomsky, N. 1956. "Three Models for the Description of Language." *IRE Transactions on Information Theory* 2:13–54.

Clair, D. 1992. "Sweet Subversions." In *Dangerous Men and Adventurous Women*, edited by J. A. Krentz, 15–30. Pennsylvania: University of Pennsylvania Press.

Clayton, John J. 1984. Preface to *The Heath Introduction to Fiction*, edited by John Clayton, 1–34. Lexington, Mass.: D.C. Heath.

Coe, Kathryn. 2003. *The Ancestress Hypothesis: Visual Art as Adaptation.* New Brunswick, N.J.: Rutgers University Press.

Cohen, J. 1988. *Statistical Power Analysis for the Behavioral Sciences.* New York: Academic Press.

Cook, V. 1976. "Lord Raglan's Hero—A Coss-Cultural Critique." *Florida Anthropologist* 87:147–54.

Cooke, B. 1995. "Microplots: The Case of *Swan Lake.*" *Human Nature* 6:183–96.

——. 1999. "The Promise of a Biothematics." In *Sociobiology and the Arts,* edited by Jan Baptist Bedaux and Brett Cooke, 43–62. Amsterdam: Editions Rodopi.

——. 2002. *Human Nature in Utopia: Zamyatin's "We."* Evanston: Northwestern University Press.

Cooke, B., and N. Aiken. 1999. "Selectionist Studies of the Arts: An Annotated Bibliography." In *Biopoetics: Evolutionary Explorations in the Arts,* edited by B. Cooke and F. Turner, 433–64. Lexington, Ky.: International Conference on the Unity of the Sciences.

Cornelius, Randolph R. 1996. *The Science of Emotion: Research and Tradition in the Psychology of Emotions.* Upper Saddle River, N.J.: Prentice-Hall, 1996.

Cosmides, L., and J. Tooby. 1989. "Evolutionary Psychology and the Generation of Culture, Case Study: A Computational Theory of Social Exchange." Pt. 2. *Ethology and Sociobiology* 10:51–97.

——. 1992. "Cognitive Adaptations for Social Exchange." In *The Adapted Mind: Evolutionary Psychology and the Generation of Culture,* edited by J. H. Barkow, L. Cosmides, and J. Tooby, 163–228. New York: Oxford University Press.

——. 1994. "Origins of Domain Specificity: The Evolution of Functional Organization." In *Mapping the Mind: Domain Specificity in Cognition and Culture,* edited by L. Hirschfeld and S. A. Gelman, 85–116. Cambridge: Cambridge University Press.

——. 1997. "Evolutionary Psychology: A Primer." University of California, Santa Barbara, Center for Evolutionary Psychology. http://www.psych.ucsb.edu/research/cep/primer.html (accessed June 1, 2004).

——. 2000a. "The Cognitive Neuroscience of Social Reasoning." In *The New Cognitive Neurosciences,* edited by M. S. Gazzaniga, 1259–70. Cambridge, Mass.: Bradford/MIT Press.

——. 2000b. "Evolutionary Psychology and the Emotions." In *Handbook of Emotions,* edited by M. Lewis and J. M. Haviland-Jones, 91–115. New York: Guilford Press.

Costa, P. T., and T. A. Widiger, eds. 2002. *Personality Disorders and the Five-Factor Model of Personality.* 2nd ed. Washington: American Psychological Association.

Crawford, Charles. 1998. "Environments and Adaptations: Then and Now." In *Handbook of Evolutionary Psychology: Ideas, Issues, Applications,* edited by Charles Crawford and Dennis L. Krebs, 275–302. Mahway, N.J.: Lawrence Erlbaum Associates.

Crews, Frederick, et al. 1997. *The Memory Wars: Freud's Legacy in Dispute.* New York: New York Review of Books.

——, ed. 1999. *Unauthorized Freud: Doubters Confront a Legend.* New York: Penguin.

————. 2001a. *Postmodern Pooh.* New York: North Point Press.

————. 2001b. "Saving Us from Darwin." Pt. 1. *New York Review of Books,* October 4: 24–27.

————. 2001c. "Saving Us from Darwin." Pt. 2. *New York Review of Books,* October 18: 51–55.

————. 2002. "Saving Us from Darwin: Interview with Frederick Crews." By Glenn Branch. *Reports of the National Center for Science Education* 22 (6): 27–30. November–December.

————. 2003. "Psychoanalysis and Literary Criticism." *Proceedings of the Modern Language Association* 118:615–16.

Cronin, H. 1991. *The Ant and the Peacock: Altruism and Sexual Selection from Darwin to Today.* Cambridge: Cambridge University Press.

Cross, T. P., and C. H. Slover, eds. 1936. *Ancient Irish Tales.* New York: Henry Holt.

Daly, Mary. 1978. *Gyn/Ecology: The Metaethics of Radical Feminism.* Boston: Beacon.

Daly, M., and M. Wilson. 1988. *Homicide.* Hawthorne, N.Y.: Aldine.

————. 1990. "Is Parent-Offspring Conflict Sex-linked? Freudian and Darwinian Models." *Journal of Personality* 58:163–89.

————. 1994. "The Evolutionary Psychology of Male Violence." In *Male Violence,* edited by J. Archer. London: Routledge.

Damasio, Antonio. 1994. *Descartes' Error: Emotion, Reason, and the Human Brain.* New York: G. P. Putnam.

————. 2003. *Looking for Spinoza: Joy, Sorrow and the Feeling Brain.* Orlando, Fla.: Harcourt.

Darwin, Charles. 1859. *On the Origin of Species by Means of Natural Selection.* Edited by Joseph Carroll. Peterborough, Ontario: Broadview, 2003.

————. 1871a. *The Descent of Man, and Selection in Relation to Sex.* Introd. by John Tyler Bonner and Robert M. May. Princeton: Princeton University Press, 1981.

————. 1871b. *The Descent of Man, and Selection in Relation to Sex.* London: Gibson Square, 2003.

Davies, S. 2000. "Non-Western Art and Art's Definition." In *Theories of Art Today,* edited by N. Carroll, 199–216. Madison: University of Wisconsin Press.

Davis, K. A. 1997. "Voluntary Exposure to Pornography and Men's Attitudes Toward Feminism and Rape." *Journal of Sex Research* 34:131–37.

Dawkins, R. 2003. Introd. to *The Descent of Man and Selection in Relation to Sex,* by Charles Darwin. London: Gibson Square.

Deacon, T. W. 1998. *The Symbolic Species.* New York: Norton.

De Beaugrande, Robert. 1989. "Toward the Empirical Study of Literature: A Synoptic Sketch of a New Society." *Poetics* 18:7–27.

De Beauvoir, Simone. 1953. *The Second Sex.* New York: Knopf.

De Caro, Francis. 1983. *Women and Folklore: A Bibliographic Study.* Westport, Conn.: Greenwood Press.

Degler, Carl. 1991. *In Search of Human Nature: The Decline and Revival of Darwinism in American Social Thought*. New York: Oxford University Press.

DeGraff, Amy. 1987. "The Fairy Tale and Women's Studies: An Annotated Bibliography." *Marvels and Tales* 1:76–82.

Dennett, D. C. 1978. *Brainstorms*. Cambridge, Mass.: Bradford/MIT Press.

———. 1990. "Memes and the Exploitation of the Imagination." *Journal of Aesthetics and Art Criticism* 48:127–35.

———. [1991] 1993. *Consciousness Explained*. London, Penguin.

———. 1995. *Darwin's Dangerous Idea: Evolution and the Meanings of Life*. London: Penguin.

———. 2003. *Freedom Evolves*. New York: Viking.

DeVore, Irven. 1986. "Deception in the Natural Communication of Chimpanzees." In *Deception: Perspectives on Human and Nonhuman Deceit*, edited by R. W. Mitchell and N. S. Thompson, 221–44. Albany: State University of New York Press.

de Waal, F. B. M. 1996. *Good Natured: The Origins of Right and Wrong in Humans and Other Animals*. Cambridge, Mass.: Harvard University Press.

———. 2001. *The Ape and the Sushi Master: Cultural Reflections of a Primatologist*. New York: Basic Books.

———. 2002. "Evolutionary Psychology: The Wheat and the Chaff." *Current Directions in Psychological Science* 116:187–91.

Diamond, Lisa. 2003. "What Does Sexual Orientation Orient? A Biobehavioral Model Distinguishing Romantic Love and Sexual Desire." *Psychological Review* 110:173–92.

Diamond, S. 1985. "Pornography: Image and Reality." In *Women Against Censorship*, edited by V. Burstyn, 40–57. Vancouver, Canada: Douglas and McIntyre.

Digman, J. M. 1990. "Personality Structure: Emergence of the Five-Factor Model." *Annual Review of Psychology* 41:417–40.

Dissanayake, E. 1988. *What Is Art For?* Seattle: University of Washington Press.

———. 1992a. *Art and Intimacy: How the Arts Began*. Seattle: University of Washington Press.

———. 1992b. *Homo Aestheticus: Where Art Comes from and Why*. Seattle: University of Washington Press.

———. 1995. "Chimera, Spandrel, or Adaptation: Conceptualizing Art in Human Evolution." *Human Nature* 6:99–117.

———. 2000. *Art and Intimacy: How the Arts Began*. Seattle: University of Washington Press.

———. 2003. "Art in Global Context: An Evolutionary/Functionalist Perspective for the Twenty-first Century." *International Journal of Anthropology* 18:245–58.

Divale, W. T., and M. Harris. 1976. "Population, Warfare, and the Male-Supremacist Complex." *American Anthropologist* 78:521–38.

Drakakis, J. 2002. *Alternative Shakespeares*. London: Routledge.

Draper, P. 1989. "African Marriage Systems: Perspectives from Evolutionary Ecology." *Ethology and Sociobiology* 10:145–69.

Draper, P., and J. Belsky. 1990. "Personality Development in Evolutionary Perspective." *Journal of Personality* 58:141–61.

Draper, P., and H. Harpending. 1982. "Father Absence and Reproductive Strategy: An Evolutionary Perspective." *Journal of Anthropological Research* 38:252–73.

———. 1988. "A Sociobiological Perspective on the Development of Human Reproductive Strategies." In *Sociobiological Perspectives on Human Development*, edited by K. B. MacDonald, 340–72. New York: Springer.

Duckworth, Alistair. 1971. *The Improvement of the Estate: A Study in Jane Austen's Novels*. Baltimore: Johns Hopkins University Press.

Dunbar, R. I. M. 1988. *Primate Social Systems*. London: Chapman and Hall.

———. 1993. "Coevolution of Neocortical Size, Group Size and Language in Humans." *Behavioural and Brain Sciences* 16:681–735.

———. 1996. *Grooming, Gossip, and the Evolution of Language*. London: Faber and Faber.

Dunbar, R. I. M., A. Marriott, and N. D. C. Duncan. 1997. "Human Conversational Behavior." *Human Nature* 8:231–46.

Dutton, D. 1977. "Art, Behavior, and the Anthropologists." *Current Anthropology* 183:387–407.

———. 1979. "Artistic Crimes." *British Journal of Aesthetics* 19:302–41.

———. 1993. "Tribal Art and Artifact." *Journal of Aesthetics and Art Criticism* 511:13–21.

———. 1995. "Mythologies of Tribal Art." *African Arts* 28:32–43.

———. 2000. "But They Don't Have Our Concept of Art." In *Theories of Art Today*, edited by N. Carroll, 217–38. Madison: University of Wisconsin Press.

Dworkin, A. 1989. *Pornography: Men Possessing Women*. New York: Penguin.

Easterlin, Nancy. 2000. "Psychoanalysis and the 'Discipline of Love.'" *Philosophy and Literature* 24:261–79.

Eaton, S. B., S. B. Eaton III, and M. J. Konner. 1997. "Paleolithic Nutrition Revisited: A Twelve-Year Retrospective on Its Nature and Implications." *European Journal of Clinical Nutrition* 51:207–16.

Eaves, L. J., H. J. Eysenck, and N. G. Martin. 1989. *Genes, Culture, and Personality: An Empirical Approach*. London: Harcourt.

Ehrlich, Paul R. 2000. *Human Natures: Genes, Cultures, and the Human Prospect*. Washington, D.C.: Island/Shearwater.

Eibl-Eibesfeldt, I. 1982. "Warfare, Man's Indoctrinability and Group Selection." *Zeitschrift für Tierpsychologie* 60:177–98.

———. 1989. *Human Ethology*. Hawthorne, N.Y.: Aldine de Gruyter.

Ekman, Paul. 2003. *Emotions Revealed: Recognizing Faces and Feelings to Improve Communication and Emotional Life.* New York: Henry Holt.

Ekman, Paul, and Richard J. Davidson, eds. 1994. *The Nature of Emotion: Fundamental Questions.* New York: Oxford University Press.

Elster, Jon. 1999. *Alchemies of the Mind: Rationality and the Emotions.* Cambridge: Cambridge University Press.

Evans, D. 1996. *An Introductory Dictionary of Lacanian Psychoanalysis.* London and New York: Routledge.

———. 1998. "From Kantian Ethics to Mystical Experience: An Exploration of Jouissance." In *Key Concepts of Lacanian Psychoanalysis,* edited by Dany Nobus, 1–28. London: Rebus Press.

———. 1999. *Introducing Evolutionary Psychology.* London: Icon.

Eysenck, H. J. 1979. *The Structure and Measurement of Intelligence.* Berlin: Springer-Verlag.

———. 1980. "The Biosocial Nature of Man." *Journal of Social and Biological Structures* 3:125–34.

———. 1995. *Genius: The Natural History of Creativity.* Cambridge: Cambridge University Press.

Eysenck, Hans J., and Michael W. Eysenck. 1985. *Personality and Individual Differences: A Natural Science Approach.* New York: Plenum.

Farrell, J. P. 1980. *Revolution as Tragedy: The Dilemma of the Moderate from Scott Toarnold.* Ithaca, N.Y.: Cornell University Press.

Ferry, David. 1993. *Gilgamesh: A New Rendering in English Verse.* New York: Farrar, Straus, Giroux.

Fisher, Helen. 1994. *Anatomy of Love: A Natural History of Mating, Marriage, and Why We Stray.* New York: Fawcett Columbine.

———. 1995. "The Nature and Evolution of Romantic Love." In *Romantic Passion: A Universal Experience?* edited by William Jankowiak, 23–41. New York: Columbia University Press.

———. 1999. *The First Sex: The Natural Talents of Women and How They Are Changing the World.* New York: Random House.

———. 2004. *Why We Love: The Nature and Chemistry of Romantic Love.* New York: Henry Holt.

Fitzgerald, Robert, trans. 2004. *The Iliad.* New York: Farrar, Straus, and Giroux.

Flynn, J. R. 1999. "Searching for Justice: The Discovery of IQ Gains over Time." *American Psychologist* 54:5–20.

Foley, Robert. 1996. "The Adaptive Legacy of Human Evolution: A Search for the Environment of Evolutionary Adaptedness." *Evolutionary Anthropology* 4:194–203.

Forster, E. M. 1972. "Flat and Round Characters and 'Point of View.'" In *Twentieth Century Literary Criticism,* edited by David Lodge, 136–45. London: Longman.

Fortes, Meyer. 1970. "Social and Psychological Aspects of Education in Taleland."
    In *From Child to Adult*, edited by J. Middleton, 14–74. Garden City, N.Y.: Nat-
    ural History Press.

Fox, Robin. 1983. *The Red Lamp of Incest*. Notre Dame: Notre Dame University
    Press.

———. 1993. *Reproduction and Succession: Studies in Anthropology, Law and Society*. New
    Brunswick: Transaction Publications.

———. 1997. "Sexual Conflict and Epic Narrative." In *Conjectures and Confronta-
    tions: Science, Evolution, Social Concern*. New Brunswick: Transaction Publica-
    tions.

———. 2000. Introd. to *Ancient Society*, by L. H. Morgan. New Brunswick: Trans-
    action Publications.

Foyster, Elizabeth. 1999. *Manhood in Early Modern England: Honour, Sex, and Marriage*.
    London: Longman.

Fraiman, Susan. 1989. "The Humiliation of Elizabeth Bennet." In *Refiguring the
    Father: New Feminist Readings of Patriarchy*, edited by Patricia Yaeger and Beth
    Kowaleski-Wallace, 168–87. Carbondale: Southern Illinois University Press.

Frank, R. H. 1988. *Passions within Reason: The Strategic Role of the Emotions*. New York:
    Norton.

Frazer Lamb, P. and D. Veith. 1986. "Romantic Myth, Transcendence, and Star
    Trek Zines." In *Erotic Universe: Sexuality and Fantastic Literature*, edited by
    D. Palumbo, 235–56. Westport, Conn.: Greenwood Press.

Freeman, Derek. 1983. *Margaret Mead and Samoa: The Making and Unmaking of an
    Anthropological Myth*. Cambridge: Harvard University Press.

Friedan, Betty. 1963. *The Feminine Mystique*. New York: Dell Publishing.

Frith, U. 1989. *Autism: Explaining the Enigma*. Oxford: Basil Blackwell.

Fromm, Harold. 2003. "The New Darwinism in the Humanities: Back to Nature
    Again." Pt. 2. *Hudson Review* 56:315–27.

Fukui, N. 2001. *Is Music the Peacock's Tail?* Paper presented at annual meeting of the
    Human Behavior and Evolution Society, London.

Gallup, G. G. 1970. "Chimpanzees: Self-Recognition." *Science* 167:86–87.

Gamble, Clive. 1983. "Culture and Society in the Upper Palaeolithic of Europe."
    In *Hunter-Gatherer Economy in Prehistory: A European Perspective*, edited by Geoff
    Bailey, 210–11. Cambridge: Cambridge University Press.

Gangestad, S., and J. A. Simpson. 2000. The Evolution of Human Mating: Trade-
    offs and Strategic Pluralism. *Brain and Behavioral Sciences* 23:573–644.

Gangestad, S., and R. Thornhill. 1998. "Menstrual Cycle Variation in Women's
    Preferences for the Scent of Symmetrical Men." *Proceedings of the Royal Society
    of London Series B* 265:927–33.

Gardner, H. A. 1972. *The Quest for Mind: Piaget, Levi-Strauss, and the Structuralist Move-
    ment*. New York: Random House.

Gaulin, Steven J. C., and Donald H. McBurney. 2001. *Psychology: An Evolutionary Approach.* Saddle River, N.J.: Prentice Hall.

Geary, D. 1998. *Male, Female: The Evolution of Human Sex Differences.* Washington, D.C.: American Psychological Association.

Geary, David, and Mark Flinn. 2001. "Evolution of Human Parental Behavior and the Human Family." *Parenting: Science and Practice* 1:5–61.

Geary, David C., and Kelly J. Huffman. 2002. "Brain and Cognitive Evolution: Forms of Modularity and Functions of Mind." *Psychological Bulletin* 128:667–98.

Gerrig, Richard J. 1988. "Text Comprehension." In *The Psychology of Human Thought,* edited by Robert J. Sternberg and Edward E. Smith, 242–66. Cambridge: Cambridge University Press.

Gillis, John. 1985. *For Better, for Worse: British Marriages, 1600 to the Present.* Oxford: Oxford University Press.

Glausiusz, J. 2001. "The Genetic Mystery of Music." *Discover Magazine* 22 (8), August.

Gorry, A. 1999. "Leaving Home for Romance: Tourist Women's Adventures Abroad." Ph.D. diss., University of California at Santa Barbara.

Gottschall, Jonathan. 2001. "Homer's Human Animal: Ritual Combat in the *Iliad.*" *Philosophy and Literature* 25:278–94.

———. 2004. "Literary Universals and the Sciences of the Mind." *Philosophy and Literature* 28:202–17.

Gottschall, Jonathan, E. Allison, J. DeRosa, and K. Klockeman. 2004. "Can Literary Studies Be Scientific? Results of an Empirical Search for the Virgin-Whore Dichotomy." *Interdisciplinary Literary Studies* 6.

Gottschall, Jonathan, R. Berkey, C. Drown, M. Fleischner, M. Glotzbecker, K. Kernan, T. Magnan, K. Muse, C. Ogburn, C. Skeels, S. St. Joseph, S. Weeks, A. Welch, E. Welch. 2004. "Patterns of Characterization in Folk Tales Across Geographic Regions and Levels of Cultural Complexity: Literature as a Neglected Source of Quantitative Data." *Human Nature* 15:365–82.

Gottschall, Jonathan, C. Callanan, N. Casamento, N. Gladd, K. Manganini, T. Milan-Robertson, P. O'Connell, K. Parker, N. Riley, V. Stucker, A. Tapply, C. Wall, A. Webb. 2004. "World Literature's Missing Daughters." Paper presented at the annual meeting of the North Eastern Modern Language Association, Pittsburgh.

Gottschall, J., J. Martin, J. Rea, and H. Quish. 2004. "Sex Differences in Mate Choice Criteria Are Reflected in Folk Tales from Around the World and in Historical European Literature." *Evolution and Human Behavior* 25:102–12.

Gould, S. J., and R. C. Lewontin. 1979. "The Spandrels of San Marco and the Panglossian Paradigm: A Critique of the Adaptationist Program." *Proceedings of the Royal Society of London* B 205:581–98.

————. 1994. "Evolution as Fact and Theory." In *Hen's Teeth and Horse's Toes*, edited by S. J. Gould. New York: Norton.

Gowing, Laura. 1996. *Domestic Dangers: Women, Words, and Sex in Early Modern London.* Oxford: Clarendon.

Graunt, John. 1662. *Natural and Political Observations Mentioned in a Following Index and Made upon the Bills of Mortality.* London: Martin, Allestry and Dicas.

————. 1665. *London's Dreadful Visitation.* London: E. Cotes.

Greer, G. 1971. *The Female Eunuch.* New York: McGraw-Hill.

Griffin, D. [1992] 2001. *Animal Minds: Beyond Cognition to Consciousness.* Chicago: University of Chicago Press.

Griffin, D., and K. Bartholomew. 1994. "Models of the Self and Other: Fundamental Dimensions Underlying Measures of Adult Attachment." *Journal of Personality and Social Psychology* 67:430–45.

Griffiths, Paul E. 1997. *What Emotions Really Are: The Problem of Psychological Categories.* Chicago: University of Chicago Press.

Haase, D., ed. 2000a. "Fairy Tale Liberation—Thirty Years Later." 2000. Special issue, *Marvels and Tales: Journal of Fairy-Tale Studies* 14.

————. 2000b. "Feminist Fairy Tale Scholarship: A Critical Survey and Bibliography." *Marvels and Tales: Journal of Fairy-Tale Studies* 14:15–63.

Hagen, Edward, and Gregory Bryant. 2003. "Music and Dance as a Coalition Signaling System." *Human Nature* 14:21–51.

Halliday, E. M. 1960. "Narrative Perspective in 'Pride and Prejudice.'" *Nineteenth-Century Fiction* 15:65–71.

Halpern, Diane. 2000. *Sex Differences in Cognitive Abilities.* Mahwah, New Jersey: Erlbaum.

Hamilton, W. D. 1964. "The Genetical Evolution of Social Behavior." Pts. 1 and 2. *Journal of Theoretical Biology* 7:1–52.

Handler, Richard, and Daniel Segal. 1990. *Jane Austen and the Fiction of Culture: An Essay on the Narration of Social Realities.* Tucson: University of Arizona Press.

Harbage, A. 1964. *Annals of English Drama, 975–1700.* London: Methuen.

Harding, D. W. 1940. "'Regulated Hatred': An Aspect in the Work of Jane Austen." *Scrutiny* 8:346–47, 351–54, 362.

Hauser, M. 2000. *Wild Minds: What Animals Really Think.* London: Allen Lane/Penguin.

Hawkes, T. 1992. *Meaning by Shakespeare.* London: Routledge.

Hazlitt, W. 1930. "Why the Heroes of Romances Are Insipid." In *The Complete Works of William Hazlitt*, vol. 17, edited by P. P. Howe, 246–54. London: Dent.

Heaney, Seamus, trans. 2000. *Beowulf: A New Verse Translation.* New York: Norton.

Hebditch, D., and N. Anning. 1988. *Porn Gold: Inside the Pornography Business.* London: Faber and Faber.

Helms, Cynthia. 1987. "Storytelling, Gender and Language in Folk/Fairy Tales: A Selected Annotated Bibliography." *Women and Language* 10:3–11.

Hernadi, P. 2001. "Literature and Evolution." *Substance* 94/95, 55–71.

Herrnstein, R. J., and C. Murray. 1994. *The Bell Curve: Intelligence and Class Structure in American Life.* New York: Free Press.

Hewlett, Barry S., and L. L. Cavalli-Sforza. 1986. "Cultural Transmission among Aka Pygmies." *American Anthropologist* 88:922–34.

Hill, Kim, and Magdalena Hurtado. 1996. *Ache Life History: The Ecology and Demography of a Foraging People.* Hawthorne, N.Y.: Aldine De Gruyter.

Hinton, Alexander Laban. 1999. "Outline of a Bioculturally Based, 'Processual' Approach to the Emotions." In *Biocultural Approaches to the Emotions,* edited by Alexander Laban Hinton, 299–328. Cambridge: Cambridge University Press.

Hoeniger, F. David. 1992. *Medicine and Shakespeare in the English Renaissance.* Newark: University of Delaware Press.

Hogan, Patrick. 2003. *The Mind and Its Stories: Narrative Universals and Human Emotion.* Cambridge: Cambridge University Press.

Hogan, Robert, John Johnson, and Stephen Briggs, eds. 1997. *Handbook of Personality Psychology.* San Diego: Academic Press.

Holman, Hugh C. 1980. *A Handbook to Literature.* 4th ed. Indianapolis: Bobbs-Merrill.

Holmberg, Allan R. 1969. *Nomads of the Long Bow: The Siriono of Eastern Bolivia.* Garden City, N.Y.: Natural History Press.

Homer. *The Iliad.* 1974. Translated by Robert Fitzgerald. Oxford: University Press.

———. *The Iliad.* 1990. Translated by Robert Fagles. New York: Viking.

———. *The Iliad.* 1999. Translated by. A. T. Murray, revised by William F. Wyatt. Cambridge: Harvard University Press.

———. *The Odyssey.* 1996. Translated by Robert Fagles. New York: Viking.

Hopkins, Lisa. 1998. *The Shakespearean Marriage.* Basingstoke: Macmillan.

Howell, D. C. 1997. *Statistical Methods for Psychology.* 4th ed. San Diego, Calif.: Academic Press.

Hrdy, S. B. 1999. *Mother Nature: A History of Mothers, Infants, and Natural Selection.* New York: Pantheon.

Hughes, A. L. 1993. *Evolution and Human Kinship.* Oxford: Oxford University Press.

Humphrey, Nicholas. 1983. *Consciousness Regained.* Oxford: Oxford University Press.

Hutton, J., ed. 1982. *Aristotle's Poetics.* New York: Norton.

Irons, William. 1979. "Cultural and Biological Success." In *Evolutionary Biology and Human Social Behavior: An Anthropological Perspective,* edited by Napoleon A. Chagnon and William Irons, 257–72. North Scituate, Mass.: Duxbury Press.

———. 1990. "Let's Make Our Perspective Broader Rather than Narrower: A Comment on Turke's 'Which Humans Behave Adaptively, and What Does It Matter?'" *Ethology and Sociobiology* 11:361–74.

———. 1998. "Adaptively Relevant Environments Versus the Environment of Evolutionary Adaptedness." *Evolutionary Anthropology* 6:194–204.

Jankowiak, William, ed. 1995. *Romantic Passion: A Universal Experience?* New York: Columbia University Press.

Jankowiak, William, and Ted Fischer. 1998. "A Cross-Cultural Perspective on Romantic Love." *Ethnology* 31 (1992): 149–55. Reprinted in *Human Emotions: A Reader*, edited by Jennifer M. Jenkins, Keith Oatley, and Nancy L. Stein, 55–62. Oxford: Blackwell.

Jenkins, H. 1992. *Textual Poachers: Television Fans and Participatory Culture*. New York: Routledge.

Jensen, Arthur R. 1998. *The G Factor: The Science of Mental Ability*. Westport, Conn.: Praeger.

Jobling, Ian. 2001a. "The Psychological Foundations of the Hero-Ogre Story: A Cross-Cultural Study." *Human Nature* 12:247–72.

———. 2001b. "Personal Justice and Homicide in Scott's *Ivanhoe*: An Evolutionary Psychological Perspective." *Interdisciplinary Literary Studies* 2:29–43.

———. 2002. "Byron as Cad." *Philosophy and Literature*. 26:296–311.

Johnson, Claudia L. 1988. *Jane Austen: Women, Politics, and the Novel*. Chicago: University of Chicago Press.

Johnson, Norman, and Samuel Kotz. 1997. *Leading Personalities in Statistical Sciences: From the Seventeenth Century to the Present*. New York: John Wiley and Sons.

Johnson, S., A. Booth, et al. 2001. "Inferring the Goals of a Non-Human Agent." *Cognitive Development* 16:637–56.

Johnsrude, I., V. Penhune, and R. Zatorre. 2000. "Functional Specificity in Right Human Auditory Cortex for Perceiving Pitch Direction." *Brain* 123:155–63.

Jolly, A. 1999. *Lucy's Legacy: Sex and Intelligence in Human Evolution*. Cambridge, Mass.: Harvard University Press.

Jones, Douglas. 2003a. The Generative Psychology of Kinship, Part I: Cognitive Universals and Evolutionary Psychology. *Evolution and Human Behavior* 24:303–19.

———. 2003b. The Generative Psychology of Kinship, Part II: Generating Variation from Universal Building Blocks with Optimality Theory. *Evolution and Human Behavior* 243:20–350.

Juhasz, S. 1994. *Reading from the Heart: Women, Literature and the Search for True Love*. New York: Penguin.

Kaplan, H., K. Hill, J. Lancaster, and A. M. Hurtado. 2000. "A Theory of Human Life History Evolution: Diet, Intelligence, and Longevity." *Evolutionary Anthropology* 9:156–85.

Kelly, S., and R. I. M. Dunbar. 2001. "Who Dares Wins: Heroism Versus Altruism in Women's Mate Choice." *Human Nature* 12:89–105.

Kenny, Anthony. 1986. *A Stylometric Study of the New Testament.* Oxford: Oxford University Press.

Kendrick, Douglas T., Edward K. Sadalla, and Melanie R. Trost. 1997. "Evolution, Traits, and the Stages of Human Courtship: Qualifying the Parental Investment Model." In *Human Nature: A Critical Reader,* edited by Laura Betzig, 213–24. Oxford: Oxford University Press.

Kermode, Frank. 1981. "Secrets and Narrative Sequence." In *On Narrative,* edited by W. J. T. Mitchell, 79–97. Chicago: University of Chicago Press.

Keverne, E. B., N. Martensz, and B. Tuite. 1989. "Beta-Endorphin Concentrations in Cerebrospinal Fluid in Monkeys Are Influenced by Grooming Relationships." *Psychoneuroendocrinology* 14:155–61.

Kimura, D. 1999. *Sex and Cognition.* Cambridge, Mass.: MIT Press.

Kinderman, P., R. Dunbar, et al. 1998. "Theory of Mind Deficits and Causal Attributions." *British Journal of Psychology* 89:191–204.

Kinsella, Thomas. 1969. Introd. to *The Táin: Translated from the Irish Epic Táin Bó Cualigne.* 1969. New York: Oxford University Press.

Kintsch, Walter, and Teun A. van Dijk. 1975. "Toward a Model of Text Comprehension and Production." *Psychological Review* 85:363–94.

Kipnis, L. 1996. *Bound and Gagged: Pornography and the Politics of Fantasy in America.* New York: Grove.

Kluckhohn, Clyde. 1959. "Recurrent Themes in Myths and Mythmaking." *Daedelus* 88:268–79.

Knight, Chris, Camilla Power, and Ian Watts. 1995. "The Human Symbolic Revolution: A Darwinian Account." *Cambridge Archaeological Journal* 5:75–114.

Koestler, Arthur. 1965. "The Aesthetics of Snobbery." *Horizon* 8:50–53.

Kohn, M., and S. Mithen. 1999. "Handaxes: Products of Sexual Selection?" *Antiquity* 73:518–26.

Kolbenschlag, Madonna. 1981. *Kiss Sleeping Beauty Goodbye: Breaking the Spell of Feminine Myths and Models.* Toronto: Bantam.

Konner, Melvin. 1982. *The Tangled Wing: Biological Constraints on the Human Spirit.* London: Heinemann.

Kott, J. 1974. *Shakespeare Our Contemporary.* New York: Norton.

Krippendorff, K. 1980. *Content Analysis: An Introduction to Its Methodology.* Beverly Hills: Sage Publications.

Kudo, H., and R. I. M. Dunbar. 2001. "Neocortex Size and Social Network Size in Primates." *Animal Behavior* 62:711–22.

Kutchinski, B. 1991. "Pornography and Rape: Theory and Practice? Evidence from Crime Data in Four Countries Where Pornography Is Easily Available." *International Journal of Law and Psychiatry* 14:147–64.

Labouet, H. 1929. "La parente a plaisanteries en Afrique occidentale." *Africa* 2:244–54.

Labov, William, and Joshua Waletzky. 1967. "Narrative Analysis: Oral Versions of Personal Experience." In *Essays on the Verbal and Visual Arts*, edited by June Helm, 12–44. Seattle: University of Washington Press.

Lacan, J. 1949. "The Mirror Stage as Formative of the Function of the I." In Jacques Lacan, *Écrits: A Selection*. Translated by Alan Sheridan, 8–29. London: Tavistock, 1977.

———. 1953a. "The Function and Field of Speech and Language in Psychoanalysis." In Jacques Lacan, *Écrits: A Selection*. Translated by Alan Sheridan, 30–113. London: Tavistock, 1977.

———. 1953b. "Some Reflections on the Ego." *International Journal of Psychoanalysis*. 34:11–17.

———. 1953–54. *The Seminar: Book I, Freud's Papers on Technique, 1953–4*. Translated by John Forrester. Cambridge: Cambridge University Press, 1987.

———. 1954–55. *The Seminar: Book II, The Ego in Freud's Theory and in the Technique of Psychoanalysis, 1954–5*. Translated by Sylvana Tomaselli. Cambridge: Cambridge University Press, 1988.

———. 1972–73. *Le Séminaire: Livre XX, Encore, 1972–73*, edited by Jacques-Alain Miller. Paris: Seuil.

Lancaster, J. B., and H. Kaplan. 1992. "Human Mating and Family Formation Strategies: The Effects of Variability among Males in Quality and the Allocation of Mating Effort and Parental Investment." In *Topics in Primatology*. Vol.1, *Human Origin*, edited by Toshisada Nishida, 21–33. New York: Springer.

Lancy, David F. 1980. "Play in Species Adaptation." *Annual Review of Anthropology* 9:471–95.

———. 1996. *Playing on the Mother Ground*. New York: Guilford Press.

Lane, R. 1989. *Hokusai: Life and Work*. New York: E. P. Dutton.

Langland, Elizabeth. 1984. *Society in the Novel*. Chapel Hill: University of North Carolina Press.

Lau, Beverly, Bonnie Blackwell, Henry Schwarcz, Ivan Turk, and Joel Blickstein. 1997. "Dating a Flautist? Using ESR (Electron Spin Resonance) in the Mousterian Cave Deposits at Divje Babe I, Slovenia." *Geoarchaeology* 12:507–36.

Laughlin, W. 1968. "Hunting: An Integrating Biobehavior System and Its Evolutionary Importance." In *Man the Hunter*, edited by R. B. Lee and I. DeVore, 304–20. Chicago: Aldine.

Leacock, E. 1954. "The Montagnais 'Hunting Territory' and the Fur Trade." *American Anthropological Association Memoir 78*.

Leaska, Mitchell A. 1996. "The Concept of Point of View." In *Essentials of the Theory of Fiction*, edited by Michael J. Hoffman and Patrick D. Murphy, 158–71. Durham, N.C.: Duke University Press.

LeDoux, Joseph. 1996. *The Emotional Brain: The Mysterious Underpinnings of Emotional Life*. New York: Simon and Schuster.

Lehnert, Wendy G. 1981. "Plot Units and Narrative Summarization." *Cognitive Science* 4:293–331.

Leigh, S. R. 2001. "Evolution of Human Growth." *Evolutionary Anthropology* 10:223–36.

Leitch, V. B., et al., eds. 2001. *The Norton Anthology of Theory and Criticism*. New York: Norton.

Leslie, Alan. 1987. "Pretense and Representation in Infancy: The Origins of 'Theory of Mind.'" *Psychological Review* 94:84–106.

———. 1991. "The Theory of Mind Impairment in Autism: Evidence for a Modular Mechanism of Development?" In *Natural Theories of Mind: Evolution, Development and Simulation of Everyday Mindreading*, edited by Andrew Whiten, 63–78. Oxford: Blackwell.

Lessing, Alfred. 1967. "What Is Wrong with a Forgery?" In *Aesthetic Inquiry: Essays on Art Criticism and the Philosophy of Art*, edited by Monroe Beardsley and Herbert Schueller. Belmont, California: Dickenson.

Levin, Richard. 1993. "On Defending Shakespeare, 'Liberal Humanism,' Transcendent Love, and Other 'Sacred Cows' and Lost Causes." *Textual Practice* 7:50–55.

Levins, R., and R. C. Lewontin. 1987. *The Dialectical Biologist*. Cambridge, Mass.: Harvard University Press.

Lewes, George Henry. 1859. "The Novels of Jane Austen." *Blackwood's Magazine* 86:99–113.

Lewis, Michael, and Jeannette M. Haviland, eds. 2000. *Handbook of Emotions*. 2nd ed. New York: Guilford Press.

Lewis-Williams, D. 2002. *The Mind in the Cave: Consciousness and the Origins of Art*. London: Thames and Hudson.

Liebenberg, Louis. 1990. *The Art of Tracking*. Claremont, South Africa: D. Philip.

Lieberman, Marcia. 1986. "Some Day My Prince Will Come: Female Acculturation Through the Fairy Tale." In *Don't Bet on the Prince: Contemporary Feminist Fairy Tales in North America and England*, edited by Jack Zipes. New York: Methuen.

Lieberman, P. 1989. "The Origins of Some Aspects of Human Language and Cognition." In *The Human Revolution: Behavioural and Biological Perspectives on the Origins of Modern Humans*, edited by P. Mellars and C. Stringer, 391–414. Edinburgh: Edinburgh University Press.

Litvak, Joseph. 1992. "Delicacy and Disgust, Mourning and Melancholia, Privilege and Perversity: '*Pride and Prejudice*.'" *Qui Parle* 6:35–51.

Litz, A. Walton. 1965. *Jane Austen: A Study of Her Artistic Development*. New York: Oxford University Press.

Lloyd, Dan. 1989. *Simple Minds.* Cambridge: MIT Press.

Loomba, A., and M. Orkin, eds. 1998. *Post-Colonial Shakespeares.* London: Routledge.

Love, Glen. 2003. *Practical Ecocriticism: Literature, Biology, and the Environment.* Charlottesville: University of Virginia Press.

Low, Bobbi S. 1998. "The Evolution of Human Life Histories." In *Handbook of Evolutionary Psychology: Ideas, Issues, Applications,* edited by Charles Crawford and Dennis L. Krebs, 131–61. Mahway, N.J.: Lawrence Erlbaum Associates.

———. 2000. *Why Sex Matters: A Darwinian Look at Human Behavior.* Princeton: Princeton University Press.

Lundell, Torborg. 1986. "Gender-Related Biases in the Type and Motif Indexes of Aarne and Thompson." In *Fairy Tales and Society: Illusion, Allusion, and Paradigm,* edited by Ruth Bottigheimer. Philadelphia: University of Pennsylvania Press.

Lurie, Alison. 1970. "Fairy Tale Liberation." *New York Review of Books.* December 17, 42–44.

———. 1971. "Witches and Fairies: Fitzgerald to Updike." *New York Review of Books* December 2, 6–11.

Lyons, Charles. 1971. *Shakespeare and the Ambiguity of Love's Triumph.* The Hague: Mouton.

MacDonald, Kevin. 1990. "A Perspective on Darwinian Psychology: The Importance of Domain-General Mechanisms, Plasticity, and Individual Differences." *Ethology and Sociobiology* 12:449–80.

———. 1995a. "The Establishment and Maintenance of Socially Imposed Monogamy in Western Europe." *Politics and the Life Sciences* 14:3–46.

———. 1995b. "Evolution, the Five-Factor Model, and Levels of Personality." *Journal of Personality* 63:525–67.

———. 1997. "Life History Theory and Human Reproductive Behavior: Environmental/Contextual Influences and Heritable Variation." *Human Behavior* 8:327–59.

———. 1998a. "Evolution and Development." In *The Social Child,* edited by Anne Campbell and Steven Muncer, 21–49. Hove, East Sussex: Psychology Press.

———. 1998b. "Evolution, Culture, and the Five-Factor Model." *Journal of Cross-Cultural Psychology* 29:119–49.

MacKinnon, C. 1989. *Toward a Feminist Theory of the State.* Cambridge, Mass.: Harvard.

Maclay, G., and H. Knipe. 1972. *The Dominant Man: The Pecking Order in Human Society.* New York: Delacorte.

Mahay, J., E. O. Laumann, and S. Michaels. 2000. "Race, Gender, and Class in Sexual Scripts." In *Sex, Love, and Health in America: Private Choices and Public Poli-*

cies, edited by E. O. Laumann and R. T. Michael. Chicago: University of Chicago Press.

Mamet, D. 1998. *Three Uses of the Knife: On the Nature and Purpose of Drama.* New York: Random House.

Mandler, Jean. 1984. *Scripts, Stories, and Scenes: Aspects of Schema Theory.* Hillsdale, N.J.: Lawrence Erlbaum Associates.

Mandler, Jean M., and Nancy S. Johnson. 1977. "Remembrance of Things Parsed: Story Structure and Recall." *Cognitive Psychology* 9:111–51.

Marcus, Steven. 1966. *The Other Victorians: A Study of Sexuality and Pornography in Mid-nineteenth Century England.* New York: Basic Books.

Marshall, W. D. 1989. "Pornography and Sex Offenders." In *Pornography: Research Advances and Policy Considerations,* edited by D. Zillman and J. Bryant, 185–214. Hillsdale, N.J.: Erlbaum Associates.

Martindale, Colin. 1990. *The Clockwork Muse: The Predictability of Artistic Change.* New York: Basic Books.

———. 1996. "Empirical Questions Deserve Empirical Answers." *Philosophy and Literature* 20:347–61.

Mazur, A., C. Halpern, and J. R. Udry. 1994. "Dominant Looking Male Teenagers Copulate Earlier." *Ethology and Sociobiology* 15:87–94.

McCrae, Robert R., ed. 1992. "The Five-Factor Model: Issues and Applications." *Journal of Personality* Special Issue, 60.

McCrae, Robert R., and Paul T. Costa. 1997. "Conceptions and Correlates of Openness to Experience." In *Handbook of Personality Psychology,* edited by Robert Hogan, John Johnson, and Stephen Briggs, 826–47. San Diego: Academic Press.

McDonald, Lynn. 1993. *The Early Origins of the Social Sciences.* Montreal and Kingston, Canada: McGill-Queen's University Press.

McElroy, A. 1995. *XXX: A Woman's Right to Pornography.* New York: St. Martin's Press.

McGuire, Michael, and Alfonso Troisi. 1998. *Darwinian Psychiatry.* New York: Oxford University Press.

McHarry, M. 2003. "Yaoi: Redrawing Male Love." *The Guide,* November.

Mealey, Linda. 2000. *Sex Differences: Developmental and Evolutionary Strategies.* San Diego: Academic Press.

Meltzoff, A. N., and M. K. Moore. 1995. "Infants' Understanding of People and Things: From Body Imitation to Folk Psychology." In *The Body and the Self,* edited by J. L. Bermúdez, A. Marcel, and N. Eilan, 43–70. Cambridge, Mass.: Bradford/MIT Press.

Meyer, Leonard. 1967. "Forgery and the Anthropology of Art." In *Music, the Arts, and Ideas,* edited by Leonard Meyer. Chicago: University of Chicago Press.

Midgely, Mary. 1992. "Rival Fatalisms." In *Sociobiology Examined,* edited by A. Montague. Oxford: Oxford University Press.

Miller, Geoffrey. 1998. "How Mate Choice Shaped Human Nature: A Review of Sexual Selection and Human Evolution." In *Handbook of Evolutionary Psychology: Ideas, Issues, and Applications,* edited by Charles Crawford and Dennis Krebs, 87–129. London: Lawrence Erlbaum Associates.

———. 1999. "Sexual Selection for Cultural Displays." In *The Evolution of Culture: An Interdisciplinary View,* edited by R. Dunbar, C. Knight, and C. Power. New Brunswick, N.J.: Rutgers University Press.

———. 2000a. "Evolution of Human Music Through Sexual Selection." In *The Origins of Music,* edited by. S. Brown, B. Merker, and N. L. Wallin, 329–60. Cambridge, Mass.: Bradford/MIT Press.

———. 2000b. *The Mating Mind: How Sexual Choice Shaped the Evolution of Human Nature.* New York: Doubleday.

Miller, George. 1956. "The Magical Number Seven, Plus or Minus Two." *Psychological Review.* 63:81–97.

Mithen, Steven J. 1990. *Thoughtful Foragers: A Study of Prehistoric Decision Making.* Cambridge: Cambridge University Press.

———. 1996. *The Prehistory of the Mind: A Search for the Origins of Art, Religion and Science.* London: Thames and Hudson.

———. 2001. "The Evolution of Imagination: An Archaeological Perspective." *Substance* 30:28–54.

Modleski, T. 1982. *Loving with a Vengeance: Mass-produced Fantasies for Women.* Hamden, Conn.: Archon.

Moncrieff, Hope. 1978. *Romance and Legend of Chivalry.* New York: Bell Publishing.

Monk-Turner, E., and H. C. Purcell. 1999. "Sexual Violence in Pornography: How Prevalent Is It?" *Gender Issues* 17:58–68.

Moore, C., and P. J. Dunham, eds. 1995. *Joint Attention: Its Origins and Role in Development.* Hillsdale, N.J.: Lawrence Erlbaum.

Morais, R. C. 1999. "Porn Goes Public." *Forbes* 163:214–21.

Moretti, Franco. 2003. "Graphs, Maps, and Trees: Abstract Models for Literary History." *New Left Review* 24.

Morgan, E. 1995. *The Descent of the Child: Human Evolution from a New Perspective.* Oxford: Oxford University Press.

Morgan, Susan. 1980. *In the Meantime: Character and Perception in Jane Austen's Fiction.* Chicago: University of Chicago Press.

Mudrick, Marvin. 1952. *Jane Austen: Irony as Defense and Discovery.* Princeton: Princeton University Press.

Murdock, G. P. 1957. "World Ethnographic Sample." *American Anthropologist* 59:664–88.

———. 1981. *Atlas of World Cultures.* Pittsburgh: University of Pittsburgh Press.

Mussell, K. 1984. *Fantasy and Reconciliation: Contemporary Formulas of Women's Romance Fiction.* Westport, Conn.: Greenwood Press.

Naoya, S. 1987. *The Paper Door and Other Stories.* Translated by Jane Dunlop. Tokyo: Charles E. Tuttle.

Neely, Carol Thomas. 1985. *Broken Nuptials in Shakespeare's Plays.* New Haven: Yale University Press.

Nelson, Richard K. 1969. *Hunters of the Northern Ice.* Chicago: University of Chicago Press.

Nesse, Margaret. 1995. Guinevere's Choice. *Human Nature* 6:145–63.

Nesse, R. M., and K. Berridge. 1997. "Psychoactive Drug Use in Evolutionary Perspective." *Science* 277:63–65.

Nesse, R. M., and G. C. Williams. 1994. *Why We Get Sick.* New York: Random House.

Nettle, D. 1998. *The Fyem Language of Northern Nigeria.* Munich: Lincom Europa.

———. 2005. "The Wheel of Fire and the Mating Game: Explaining the Origins of Tragedy and Comedy." *Journal of Cultural and Evolutionary Psychology.*

Neuendorf, K. 2002. *The Content Analysis Guidebook.* Thousand Oaks, Calif.: Sage Publications.

Newell, A., and H. Simon. 1956. "The Logic Theory Machine." *Ire Transactions on Information Theory* 2:61–79.

Newman, Karen. 1983. "Can This Marriage Be Saved: Jane Austen Makes Sense of an Ending." *Journal of English Literary History* 50:693–708.

Newton, Judith Lowder. 1981. *Women, Power, and Subversion: Social Strategies in British Fiction, 1774–1860.* Athens: University of Georgia Press.

Nisbett, R. 2003. *Geography of Thought.* New York: Free Press.

Nisbett, R., I. Choi, K. Peng, and A. Norenzayan. 2001. "Culture and Systems of Thought: Holistic versus Analytic Cognition." *Psychological Review* 108:291–310.

Nisbett, R., and D. Cohen. 1996. *Culture of Honor.* New York: Westview Press.

Nordlund, Marcus. 2002. "Consilient Literary Interpretation." *Philosophy and Literature* 26:312–33.

Oates, Joyce Carol. 1992. Introd. to *The Oxford Book of American Short Stories,* edited by Joyce Carol Oates, 3–16. Oxford: Oxford University Press.

Ohmagari, Kayo, and Fikret Berkes. 1997. "Transmission of Indigenous Knowledge and Bush Skills among the Western James Bay Cree Women of Subartic Canada." *Human Ecology* 25:197–222.

Ong, W. 1988. *Orality and Literacy: The Technologizing of the Word.* London: Routledge.

Orenstein, Catherine. 2002. *Little Red Riding Hood Uncloaked: Sex, Morality, and the Evolution of a Fairy Tale.* New York: Basic Books.

Orians, G. 1980. "Habitat Selection: General Theory and Applications to Human

Behavior." In *The Evolution of Human Social Behavior,* edited by J. S. Lockhard, 49–66. Chicago: Elsevier.

Orians, Gordon H., and Judith H. Heerwagen. 1992. "Evolved Responses to Landscapes." In *The Adapted Mind,* edited by Jerome Barkow, Leda Cosmides, and John Tooby, 556–79. New York: Oxford University Press.

O'Rourke, James. 1992. "'Rule in Unity' and Otherwise: Love and Sex in *Troilus and Cressida.*" *Shakespeare Quarterly* 43:139–58.

Ovid, Publius Naso. 1947. *The Art of Love and Other Poems.* Translated by J. H. Mozley. London: Heinemann.

Pagels, E. 1995. *The Origin of Satan.* Princeton: Princeton University Press.

Paglia, C. 1990. *Sexual Personae: Art and Decadence from Nefertiti to Emily Dickinson.* New Haven, Conn.: Yale University Press.

Palmer, Jack A., and Linda K. Palmer. 2002. *Evolutionary Psychology: The Ultimate Origins of Human Behavior.* Boston: Allyn and Bacon.

Panksepp, Jaak. 1998. *Affective Neuroscience: The Foundations of Human and Animal Emotions.* New York: Oxford University Press.

Pearson, Lu Emily. 1966. *Elizabethan Love Conventions.* London: Allen and Unwin.

Penley, C. 1991. "Brownian Motion: Women, Tactics, and Technology." In *Technoculture,* edited by. C. Penley and A. Ross, 135–61. Minneapolis: University of Minnesota Press.

Pennebaker, J. W. 1997. *Opening Up: The Healing Power of Emotional Expression.* New York: Guilford.

Pennebaker, J. W., and J. D. Seagal. 1999. "Forming a Story: The Health Benefits of Narrative." *Journal of Clinical Psychology* 55:1243–54.

Peretz, I. 1996. "Can We Lose Memory for Music? The Case of Music Agnosia in a Non-Musician." *Journal of Cognitive Neurosciences* 8:481–96.

Peretz, I., and J. Morais. 1993. "Specificity for Music." In *Handbook of Neuropsychology,* vol. 8, edited by F. Boller and J. Grafman, 373–90. New York: Elsevier.

Perner, J. 1991. *Understanding the Representational Mind.* Cambridge, Mass.: Bradford/MIT Press.

Perry, D., R. Zatorre, M. Petrides, B. Alivisatos, E. Meyer, and A. Evans. 1999. "Localization of Cerebral Activity During Simple Singing." *Neuroreport* 10:3979–84.

Pervin, Lawrence. 1990. "A Brief History of Modern Personality Theory." In *Handbook of Personality: Theory and Research,* edited by Lawrence A. Pervin, 3–18. New York: Guilford Press.

———. 2003. *The Science of Personality.* 2nd ed. New York: Oxford University Press.

Pervin, Lawrence A., and Oliver P. John, eds. 1999. *Handbook of Personality: Theory and Research.* 2nd ed. New York: Guilford Press.

Pfeiffer, John. 1982. *The Creative Explosion.* New York: Harper and Row.

Phelan, James. 1989. *Reading People, Reading Plots: Characters, Progression, and the Interpretation of Narrative.* Chicago: University of Chicago Press.

Pinker, Steven. 1994. *The Language Instinct: How the Mind Creates Language.* New York: William Morrow.

———. 1995. "Language Is a Human Instinct." In *The Third Culture: Scientists on the Edge,* edited by John Brockman, 223–38. New York: Simon and Schuster.

———. 1997. *How the Mind Works.* New York: Norton.

———. 2002. *The Blank Slate: The Modern Denial of Human Nature.* New York: Viking.

Pitcher, Evelyn Goodenough, and Ernst Prelinger. 1963. *Children Tell Stories: An Analysis of Fantasy.* New York: International Universities Press.

Plavcan, J. M. 2000. "Inferring Social Behavior from Sexual Dimorphism in the Fossil Record." *Journal of Human Evolution* 39:327–44.

Plavcan, J. M., and C. P. van Schaik. 1997. "Interpreting Hominid Behavior on the Basis of Sexual Dimorphism." *Journal of Human Evolution* 32:345–74.

Plavcan, J. M., C. P. van Schaik, and P. M. Kappeler. 1995. "Competition, Coalitions and Canine Size in Primates." *Journal of Human Evolution* 28:245–76.

Plotkin, H. 1994. *Darwin Machines and the Nature of Knowledge.* Cambridge, Mass.: Harvard University Press.

Poovey, Mary. 1984. *The Proper Lady and the Woman Writer: Ideology as Style in the Works of Mary Wollstonecraft, Mary Shelley, and Jane Austen.* Chicago: University of Chicago Press.

Popper, Karl. 1959. *The Logic of Scientific Discovery.* London: Hutchinson.

Popping, Roel. 2000. *Computer-Assisted Text Analysis.* London: Sage Publications.

Porter, Theodore. 1986. *The Rise of Statistical Thinking, 1820–1900.* Princeton, N.J.: Princeton University Press.

Potts, Richard. 1998. "Variability Selection in Hominid Evolution." *Evolutionary Anthropology* 7:81–96.

Pound, N. 2002. "Male Interest in Visual Cues of Sperm Competition Risk." *Evolution and Human Behavior* 23:443–66.

Povinelli, D. J., and T. M. Preuss. 1995. "Theory of Mind: Evolutionary History of a Cognitive Specialization." *Trends in Neuroscience* 18:418–24.

Propp, Vladimir. 1968. *Morphology of the Folktale,* translated by Laurence Scott. Austin, Texas: University of Texas Press.

Provine, R. R. 2000. *Laughter: A Scientific Investigation.* London: Faber and Faber.

Pujol, Jesús, Anna López, Joan Deus, et al. 2002. "Anatomical Variability of the Anterior Cingulate Gyrus and Basic Dimensions of Human Personality." *Neuroimage* 15:847–55.

Radcliffe, A. 1794. *The Mysteries of Udolpho.* Oxford: Oxford University Press, 1998.

Radway, J. 1984. *Reading the Romance: Women, Patriarchy, and Popular Literature.* Chapel Hill: University of North Carolina Press.

Ragan, K. 1998. Introd. to *Fearless Girls, Wise Women, and Beloved Sisters: Heroines in Folktales from Around the World*, edited by K. Ragan. New York: Norton.

Raglan, F. R. S. 1936. *The Hero: A Study in Tradition, Myth, and Drama*. London: Methuen.

Rank, O. 1909. *The Myth of the Birth of the Hero*. Translated by F. Robbins and S. Jelliffe. New York: Journal of Nervous and Mental Disease Publishing.

Raymond, James. 1982. "Rhetoric: The Method of the Humanities." *College English* 44:778–83.

Richerson, Peter J., and Robert Boyd. 2000. "Climate, Culture, and the Evolution of Cognition." In *The Evolution of Cognition*, edited by Cecilia Heyes and Ludwig Huber, 329–46. Cambridge, Mass.: MIT Press.

Ridley, Matt. 1999. *Genome: Autobiography of a Species in 23 Chapters*. New York: HarperCollins.

———. 2003. *Nature via Nurture*. New York: Harper Collins.

Roberts, John M. 1964. "The Self-Management of Cultures." In *Explorations in Cultural Anthropology*, edited by Ward H. Goodenough, 433–54. New York: McGraw-Hill.

Rossano, Matthew J. 2003. *Evolutionary Psychology: The Science of Human Behavior and Evolution*. Hoboken, N.J.: John Wiley and Sons.

Rougemont, Denis de. 1939. *L'amour et l'occident*. Paris: Librairie Plon.

Rowe, Karen. 1986. "Feminism and Fairy Tales." In *Don't Bet on the Prince: Contemporary Feminist Fairy Tales in North America and England*, edited by Jack Zipes. New York: Methuen.

Rozin, P. 1976. "The Selection of Food by Rats, Humans, and Other Animals." In *Advances in the Study of Behavior*, edited by J. Rosenblatt, R. A. Hinde, and E. Shaw, vol. 6, 21–76. New York: Academic Press.

Rumelhart, David. 1975. "Notes on a Schema for Stories." In *Representation and Understanding: Studies in Cognitive Science*, edited by Daniel G. Bobrow and Allan Collins, 211–36. New York: Academic.

Rushton, J. Philippe. 1995. *Race, Evolution, and Behavior: A Life History Perspective*. New Brunswick, N.J.: Transaction.

Russ, J. 1985. *Magic Mommas, Trembling Sisters, Puritans and Perverts: Feminist Essays*. Trumansburg, N.Y.: Crossing Press.

Sadalla, E. K., D. T. Kenrick, and B. Vershure. 1987. "Dominance and Heterosexual Attraction." *Journal of Personality and Social Psychology* 52:730–38.

Salmon, C., and D. Symons. 2001. *Warrior Lovers: Erotic Fiction, Evolution and Female Sexuality*. London: Weidenfeld and Nicolson.

Sarich, Vincent, and Frank Miele. 2004. *Race: The Reality of Human Differences*. Boulder, Colo.: Westview Press.

Scalise Sugiyama, Michelle. 1992. "Discipline and Punishment: 'Little Red Riding

Hood' as Evolutionary Fable." Paper presented at the annual meeting of the Philological Association of the Pacific Coast, San Diego.

———. 1996. On the Origins of Narrative: Storyteller Bias as a Fitness-Enhancing Strategy." *Human Nature* 7:403–25.

———. 2001a. "Food, Foragers, and Folklore: The Role of Narrative in Human Subsistence." *Evolution and Human Behavior* 22:221–40.

———. 2001b. "New Science, Old Myth: An Evolutionary Critique of the Oedipal Paradigm." *Mosaic* 34:121–36.

———. 2001c. "Narrative Theory and Function: Why Evolution Matters." *Philosophy and Literature* 25:233–54.

———. 2003. "Cultural Variation Is Part of Human Nature: Literary Universals, Context-Sensitivity and 'Shakespeare in the Bush.'" *Human Nature* 14:383–96.

———. 2004. "Predation, Narration, and Adaptation: 'Little Red Riding Hood' Revisited." *Interdisciplinary Literary Studies* 5:108–27.

———. Forthcoming. "Cultural Relativism in the Bush: Towards a Theory of Narrative Universals." *Human Nature*.

———. Forthcoming. "Lions and Tigers and Bears: Predators as a Folklore Universal." In *Wellsprings*, edited by F. Turner and Leighton B. Cooke.

Schank, Roger C. 1975. "The Structure of Episodes in Memory." In *Representation and Understanding: Studies in Cognitive Science*, edited by Daniel G. Bobrow and Allan Collins, 237–72. New York: Academic.

———. 1990. *Tell Me a Story: A New Look at Real and Artificial Memory*. New York: Scribner's.

Schmidt, S. J. 1982. *Foundations of an Empirical Study of Literature: Components of Basic Theory*. Hamburg, Germany: Helmut, Buske, Verlag.

———. 1992. "Looking Back—Looking Ahead: Literary Studies: Trends in the Nineties," *Poetics* 21:1–4.

Schmitt, D. P., and 118 Members of the International Sexuality Description Project. 2003. "Universal Sex Differences in the Desire for Sexual Variety: Tests from 52 Nations, 6 Continents, and 13 Islands." *Journal of Personality and Social Psychology* 85:85–104.

Scholes, Robert. 1980. "Language, Narrative and Antinarrative." In *On Narrative*, edited by W. Mitchell, 200–8. Chicago: Chicago University Press.

Scott, W. 1814. *Waverley*. Oxford: Oxford University Press, 1986.

———. 1818. *The Heart of Mid-Lothian*. New York: Holt, 1969.

———. 1822. *The Pirate*. New York: Funk and Wagnalls, 1900.

Segal, L. 1990. *Slow Motion: Changing Masculinities, Changing Men*. New Brunswick, N.J.: Rutgers Press.

———. 1997. "Twin Research Perspective on Human Development." In *Uniting Psychology and Biology: Integrative Perspectives on Human Development*, edited by

Nancy L. Segal, Glenn E. Weisfeld, and Carol C. Weisfeld, 145–73. Washington: American Psychological Association.

———. 1999. *Entwined Lives: Twins and What They Tell Us about Human Behavior.* New York: Dutton.

Segal, Nancy L., and Kevin B. MacDonald. 1998. "Behavioral Genetics and Evolutionary Psychology: Unified Perspective on Personality Research." *Human Biology* 70:159–84.

Seligman, Daniel. 1992. *A Question of Intelligence: The IQ Debate in America.* New York: Carol.

Shakespeare, William. 1998. *Complete Works. The Arden Shakespeare,* edited by Richard Proudfoot, Ann Thompson, and David Scott Kastan. Walton-on-Thames: Thomas Nelson and Sons.

Shatz, Marilyn, Henry M. Wellman, and Sharon Silber. 1983. "The Acquisition of Mental Verbs: A Systematic Investigation of the First Reference to Mental State." *Cognition* 14:301–21.

Shaver, Phillip, Cindy Hazan, and Donna Bradshaw. 1988. "Love as Attachment: The Integration of Three Behavioral Systems." In *The Psychology of Love,* edited by Robert J. Sternberg and Michael L. Barnes, 68–99. New Haven: Yale University Press.

Shepher, Joseph. 1971. "Mate Selection among Second Generation Kibbutz Adolescents and Adults: Incest Avoidance and Negative Imprinting." *Archives of Sexual Behavior* 1:293–307.

Shiner, Larry. 2001. *The Invention of Art: A Cultural History.* Chicago: University of Chicago Press.

Singer, Irving. 1984. *The Nature of Love.* Vol. 2. Chicago: University of Chicago Press.

Singer, Peter. 1999. *A Darwinian Left: Politics, Evolution, and Cooperation.* New Haven: Yale University Press.

Singh, D. 1993. "Adaptive Significance of Female Physical Attractiveness: Role of Waist-to-Hip Ratio." *Journal of Personality and Social Psychology* 65:293–307.

Singh, Nagendra Kumar. 1997. *Divine Prostitution.* Delhi: A. P. H. Publishing.

Smith, Johanna M. 1993. "'I Am a Gentleman's Daughter': A Marxist-Feminist Reading of *Pride and Prejudice.*" In *Approaches to Teaching Austen's "Pride and Prejudice,"* edited by Marcia McClintock Folsom, 67–73. New York: Modern Language Association of America.

———. 2000. "The Oppositional Reader and *Pride and Prejudice.*" In *A Companion to Jane Austen Studies,* edited by Laura Cooner Lambdin and Robert Thomas Lambdin, 27–40. Westport, Conn.: Greenwood Press.

Smith, R. L. 1984. "Human Sperm Competition." In *Sperm Competition and the Evolution of Animal Mating Systems,* edited by R. Smith, 601–59. New York: Academic Press.

Smuts, B. B., D. L. Cheney, R. M. Seyfarth, R. W. Wrangham, and T. T. Struh-saker. 1987. *Primate Societies.* Chicago: Chicago University Press.

Snitow, A. B. 1979. "Mass Market Romance: Pornography for Women Is Different." *Radical History Review* 20:141–61.

Sober, E., and D. S. Wilson. 1998. *Unto Others: The Evolution and Psychology of Unselfish Behavior.* Cambridge, Mass.: Harvard University Press.

Sokal, A., and A. Bricmont. 1998. *Intellectual Impostures.* London: Profile Books.

Sompayrac, L. M. 1999. *How the Immune System Works.* Malden, Mass.: Blackwell Science.

Sosis, R., and E. Bressler. 2000. "Cooperation and Commune Longevity." *Cross-Cultural Research* 34:71–88.

Spelke, E. 1995. "Initial Knowledge: Six Suggestions." In *Cognition on Cognition,* edited by J. Mehler and S. Franck, 433–47. Cambridge, Mass.: Bradford/MIT Press.

Sperber, D. 1994. "The Modularity of Thought and the Epidemiology of Representations." In *Mapping the Mind: Domain Specificity in Cognition and Culture,* edited by L. A. Hirschfeld and S. A. Gelman, 39–67. Cambridge: Cambridge University Press.

Sperber, D., and D. Wilson. 1988. *Relevance: Communication and Cognition.* Oxford, Basil Blackwell.

Špinka, M., R. C. Newberry, et al. 2001. "Mammalian Play: Training for the Unexpected." *Quarterly Journal of Biology* 762:141–68.

Spiro, Melford. 1987. *Culture and Human Nature,* edited by Benjamin Kilborne and L. L. Langness. Chicago: University of Chicago Press.

Stanislavsky, C. 1948. *An Actor Prepares.* New York: Theatre Arts Books.

Stern, D. 1977. *The First Relationship: Mother and Infant.* Cambridge, Mass.: Harvard University Press.

Sternberg, R. J. 1998. *Love Is a Story.* New York: Oxford University Press.

Sternberg, Robert J., and Michael L. Barnes, eds. 1988. *The Psychology of Love.* New Haven: Yale University Press.

Stigler, Stephen. 1986. *The History of Statistics: The Measurement of Uncertainty Before 1900.* Cambridge: Harvard University Press.

———. 1999. *Statistics on the Table: The History of Statistical Concepts and Methods.* Cambridge: Harvard University Press.

Stiller, J., D. Nettle, and R. I. M. Dunbar. 2003. The Small World of Shakespeare's Plays. *Human Nature* 14:397–408.

Stone, Kay. 1986. "Feminist Approaches to the Interpretation of Fairy Tales." *Fairy Tales and Society: Illusion, Allusion, and Paradigm,* edited by Ruth Bottigheimer. Philadelphia: University of Pennsylvania Press.

Storey, Robert. 1996. *Mimesis and the Human Animal: On the Biogenetic Foundations of Literary Representation.* Evanston, Ill.: Northwestern University Press.

Suddendorf, T. 1999. "The Rise of the Metamind." In *The Descent of Mind: Psychological Perspectives on Hominid Evolution*, edited by M. C. Corballis and S. E. G. Lea, 218–60. Oxford: Oxford University Press.

Sugiyama, Lawrence. 2004. "Illness, Injury, and Disability among Shiwiar Forager-Horticulturalists: Implications of Health Risk Buffering for the Evolution of Human Life History." *American Journal of Physical Anthropology* 123:371–89.

Sulloway, F. J. 1996. *Born to Rebel: Birth Order, Family Dynamics, and Creative Lives*. New York: Vintage.

Symons, Donald. 1979. *The Evolution of Human Sexuality*. Oxford: Oxford University Press.

———. 1989. "A Critique of Darwinian Anthropology." *Ethology and Sociobiology* 10:131–44.

———. 1992. "On the Use and Misuse of Darwinism in the Study of Human Behavior." In *The Adapted Mind: Evolutionary Psychology and the Generation of Culture*, edited by Jerome Barkow, Leda Cosmides, and John Tooby, 137–62. New York: Oxford University Press.

———. 1995. "Beauty Is in the Adaptations of the Beholder: The Evolutionary Psychology of Human Female Sexual Attractiveness." In *Sexual Nature, Sexual Culture*, edited by P. R. Abramson and S. D. Pinkerton. Chicago: University of Chicago Press.

The Táin. 1969. Translated by Thomas Kinsella. New York: Oxford University Press.

Tanner, Tony. 1986. *Jane Austen*. Cambridge, Mass.: Harvard University Press.

Tatar, Maria. 1987. *The Hard Facts of the Grimms' Fairy Tales*. Princeton, N.J.: Princeton University Press.

Taylor, G. 1989. *Reinventing Shakespeare*. Oxford: Grove Press.

Tchana, Katrin, and Trina Schart Hyman. 2000. *The Serpent Slayer and Other Stories of Strong Women*. Boston: Little, Brown.

Terrell, J. 1990. "Storytelling and Prehistory." *Archaeological Method and Theory* 2:1–29.

Thiessen, D., and Y. Umezawa. 1998. "The Sociobiology of Everyday Life: A New Look at a Very Old Novel." *Human Nature* 93:293–320.

Thomas, Vivian. 1987. *The Moral Universe of Shakespeare's Problem Plays*. London: Croom Helm.

Thompson, Stith. 1932–36. *Motif-Index of Folk-Literature*. Bloomington: Indiana University Press.

———. 1946. *The Folktale*. New York: Dryden Press.

Thorn, M. 1997. "What Japanese Girls Do with Manga and Why." Paper presented at the annual meeting of the *Japanese Anthropological Society of Australia*.

Thorndyke, Perry. 1977. "Cognitive Structures in Comprehension and Memory of Narrative Discourse." *Cognitive Psychology* 9:77–110.

Thornhill, R. 1998. "Darwinian Aesthetics." In *Handbook of Evolutionary Psychology: Ideas, Issues, and Applications*, edited by C. Crawford and D. L. Krebs, 543–72. Mahwah, N.J.: Lawrence Erlbaum Associates.

———. 2003. "Darwinian Aesthetics Informs Traditional Aesthetics." In *Evolutionary Aesthetics*, edited by Eckart Voland and Karl Grammar, 9–35. Berlin: Springer.

Thornhill, R., and Craig Palmer. 2000. *A Natural History of Rape: Biological Bases of Sexual Coercion*. Cambridge: MIT Press.

Thorslev, P. L. 1962. *The Byronic Hero: Types and Prototypes*. Minneapolis: University of Minnesota Press.

Tierney, P. 2000. *Darkness in El Dorado: How Scientists and Journalists Devastated the Amazon*. New York: Norton.

Tiger, Lionel. 1968. *Men in Groups*. London: Thomas Nelson.

Tinbergen, N. 1951. *The Study of Instinct*. Oxford: Clarendon Press.

———. 1963. "On Aims and Methods in Ethology." *Zeitschrift für Tierpsychologie* 20:410–33.

Tomasello, M., and J. Call. 1997. *Primate Cognition*. New York: Oxford University Press.

Tonkinson, Robert. 1978. *The Mardudjara Aborigines: Living the Dream in Australia's Desert*. New York: Holt, Rinehart and Winston.

Tooby, J., and L. Cosmides. 1989. "Evolutionary Psychology and the Generation of Culture, Part I: Theoretical Considerations." *Ethology and Sociobiology* 10:29–49.

———. 1990a. "The Past Explains the Present: Emotional Adaptations and the Structure of Ancestral Environments." *Ethology and Sociobiology* 11:375–424.

———. 1990b. "On the Universality of Human Nature and the Uniqueness of the Individual: The Role of Genetics and Adaptation." *Journal of Personality* 58:17–67.

———. 1992. "The Psychological Foundations of Culture." In *The Adapted Mind: Evolutionary Psychology and the Generation of Culture*, edited by Jerome Barkow, Leda Cosmides, and John Tooby, 19–136. New York: Oxford University Press.

———. 2001. "Does Beauty Build Adapted Minds? Toward an Evolutionary Theory of Aesthetics, Fiction and the Arts." *Substance* 94/95:6–27.

Tooby, John, and Irven DeVore. 1987. "The Reconstruction of Hominid Behavioral Evolution Through Strategic Modeling." In *The Evolution of Human Behavior: Primate Models*, edited by Warren Kinzey, 183–237. Albany: SUNY Press.

Toothaker, L. E. 1993. *Multiple Comparison Procedures*. Newbury Park, Calif.: Sage.

Trabasso, Tom, and Linda L. Sperry. 1985. "Causal Relatedness and Importance of Story Events." *Journal of Memory and Language* 24:595–611.

Trevarthen, C. 1979. "Communication and Cooperation in Early Infancy: A Description of Primary Intersubjectivity." In *Before Speech: The Beginning of Human Communication*, edited by M. Bullowa. Cambridge: Cambridge University Press.

Trivers, Robert S. 1971. "The Evolution of Reciprocal Altruism." *The Quarterly Review of Biology* 46:35–57.

———. 1972. "Parental Investment and Sexual Selection." In *Sexual Selection and the Descent of Man 1871–1971*, edited by Bernard G. Campbell, 136–79. Chicago: Aldine.

———. 1985. *Social Evolution*. Menlo Park: Benjamin/Cummings.

Turke, Paul W. 1990. "Which Humans Behave Adaptively, and Why Does It Matter?" *Ethology and Sociobiology* 11:305–39.

Turner, F. 1992. *Natural Classicism: Essays on Literature and Science*. Charlottesville: University of Virginia Press.

Turner, F., and E. Pöppel. 1988. "Metered Poetry, the Brain, and Rime." In *Beauty and the Brain: Biological Aspects of Aesthetics*, edited by I. Rentschler, B. Hertzberger, and D. Epstein, 71–90. Basel: Birkhäuser.

Turner, Mark. 1996. *The Literary Mind*. New York: Oxford University Press.

Van Ghent, Dorothy. 1953. *The English Novel: Form and Function*. New York: Holt, Rinehart, Winston.

Van Hooff, J., and S. Preuschoft. 2003. "Laughter and Smiling: The Intertwining of Nature and Culture." In *Animal Social Complexity: Intelligence, Culture, and Individualized Societies*, edited by F. B. M. de Waal and Peter L. Tyack, 260–87. Cambridge, Mass.: Harvard University Press.

Veyne, Paul. 1982. L'homosexualité à Rome. "Sexualités occidentales." Special issue of *Communications*, 35, Phillipe Ariès, André Béjin, eds. Paris: Editions du Seuil.

Voracek, M., M. L. Fisher, and T. K. Shackelford. Under submission. "Sex Differences in Subjective Estimates of Nonpaternity Rates in Austria."

Waal, F. B. M. D. 1996. *Good Natured: The Origins of Right and Wrong in Humans and Other Animals*. Cambridge, Mass.: Harvard University Press.

———. 2001. *The Ape and the Sushi Master: Cultural Reflections of a Primatologist*. New York: Basic Books.

———. 2002. "Evolutionary Psychology: The Wheat and the Chaff." *Current Directions in Psychological Science* 116:187–91.

Wallin, N. L., B. Merker, et al., eds. 2000. *The Origins of Music*. Cambridge, Mass.: Bradford/MIT Press.

Watts, Ian. 1999. "The Origin of Symbolic Culture." In *The Evolution of Culture*, edited by Robin Dunbar, Chris Knight, and Camilla Power, 113–46. New Brunswick, New Jersey: Rutgers University Press.

Weatherhead, P. J., and R. J. Robertson. 1979. "Offspring Quality and the Polygyny Threshold: 'The Sexy Son Hypothesis.'" *American Naturalist* 113:201–8.

Webb, E., D. T. Campbell, R. Schwartz, and L. Sechrest. 1966. *Unobtrusive Measures: Non-Reactive Research in the Social Sciences*. Chicago: Rand McNally.

Weber, R. P. 1990. *Basic Content Analysis*. 2nd ed. Newbury Park, California: Sage Publications.

Weiderman, M. W., and E. R. Allgerier. 1992. "Gender Differences in Mate Selection Criteria: Sociobiological or Socioeconomic Explanation?" *Ethology and Sociobiology* 13:115–24.

Weiner, J. 1994. *The Beak of the Finch: A Story of Evolution in Our Time*. New York: Knopf.

Wellman, H. W., and S. A. Gelman. 1998. "Knowledge Acquisition in Foundational Domains." In *Handbook of Child Psychology*. Vol. 2, *Cognition, Perception and Language*, edited by D. Kuhn and R. Siegler, 523–73. New York: Wiley.

Welsh, A. 1992. *The Hero of the Waverley Novels, with New Essays on Scott*. Princeton, N.J.: Princeton University Press.

West, M. 2001. *Theory, Method, and Practice in Computer Content Analysis*. New York: Ablex Publishing.

West-Eberhard, M. J. 2003. *Developmental Plasticity and Evolution*. Oxford: Oxford University Press.

Whiten, Andrew, and Richard W. Byrne. 1997. *Machiavellian Intelligence II: Extensions and Evaluations*. Cambridge: Cambridge University Press.

Wiggins, Jerry S., ed. 1996. *The Five-Factor Model of Personality: Theoretical Perspectives*. New York: Guilford Press.

Wilbert, Johannes, and Karin Simoneau. 1990. *Folk Literature of the Yanomami Indians*. Los Angeles: UCLA Latin American Center Publications.

Williams, George C. 1966. *Adaptation and Natural Selection*. Princeton: Princeton University Press.

Wilson, D. S. 1975. "A Theory of Group Selection." *Proceedings of the National Academy of Sciences* 72:143–46.

———. 1994. "Adaptive Genetic Variation and Human Evolutionary Psychology." *Ethology and Sociobiology* 15:219–35.

———. 1999. "Tasty Slice—but Where Is the Rest of the Pie?" *Evolution and Human Behavior* 20:279–87.

———. 2002. *Darwin's Cathedral: Evolution, Religion and the Nature of Society*. Chicago: University of Chicago Press.

Wilson, E. O. 1998. *Consilience: The Unity of Knowledge*. New York: Knopf.

———. [1975] 2000. *Sociobiology: The New Synthesis*. Cambridge, Mass.: Belknap.

Wilson, Margo, and Martin Daly. 1992. "The Man Who Mistook His Wife for a Chattel." In *The Adapted Mind: Evolutionary Psychology and the Generation of Cul-

ture, edited by Jerome H. Barkow, Leda Cosmides, and John Tooby, 289–322. Oxford: Oxford University Press.

———. 1997. "Life Expectancy, Economic Inequality, Homicide, and Reproductive Timing in Chicago Neighborhoods." *British Medical Journal* 314:1271–74.

Wilson, T. D. 2002. *Strangers to Ourselves: Discovering the Adaptive Unconscious.* Cambridge, Mass.: Harvard University Press.

Wolf, Arthur. 1970. "Childhood Association and Sexual Attraction: A Further Test of the Westermarck Hypothesis." *American Anthropologist* 72:503–15.

Wolf, Arthur, and Chieh-shan Huang. 1980. *Marriage and Adoption in China, 1845–1945.* Stanford: Stanford University Press.

Woolf, Virginia. 1925. *The Common Reader: First Series.* New York: Harcourt, Brace, and World, 1953.

Wrangham, R., and D. Peterson. 1996. *Demonic Males: Apes and the Origins of Human Violence.* Boston: Houghton Mifflin.

Wright, R. 2000. *Nonzero: The Logic of Human Destiny.* London: Little Brown.

Wylie, Judith. 2000. "Dancing in Chains: Feminist Satire in *Pride and Prejudice.*" *Persuasions: Journal of the Jane Austen Society of North America* 22:62–69.

Wypijewski, J., ed. 1997. *Painting by Numbers: Komar and Melamid's Scientific Guide to Art.* New York: Farrar, Straus and Giroux.

Yolen, Jane. 1998. Foreword to *Fearless Girls, Wise Women, and Beloved Sisters: Heroines in Folktales from Around the World,* edited by Kathleen Ragan. New York: Norton.

———. 2000. "An Open Letter to My Daughter and Granddaughters." In *Not One Damsel in Distress: World Folktales for Strong Girls,* edited by Jane Yolen. San Diego, Calif.: Harcourt.

Yolen, Jane, and Susan Guevera. 2000. *Not One Damsel in Distress: World Folktales for Strong Girls.* San Diego, Calif.: Harcourt.

Zahavi, A., and A. Zahavi. 1997. *The Handicap Principle: A Missing Part of Darwin's Puzzle.* Oxford: Oxford University Press.

Zipes, Jack. 1979–80. "Who's Afraid of the Brother's Grimm? Socialization and Politi[ci]zation Through Fairy Tales." *The Lion and the Unicorn* 3:4–56.

———. 1983a. *Fairy Tales and the Art of Subversion: The Classical Genre for Children and the Process of Civilization.* New York: Wildman.

———. 1983b. *The Trials and Tribulations of Little Red Riding Hood.* New York: Bergin and Garvey Publishers.

———. 1986. Introd. to *Don't Bet on the Prince: Contemporary Feminist Fairy Tales in North America and England,* edited by Jack Zipes. New York: Methuen.

Contributors

Brian Boyd, University Distinguished Professor in the Department of English, University of Auckland, is known for his award-winning work on Vladimir Nabokov, translated into seven languages. He has also published on Renaissance drama; on American, English, Irish, New Zealand, and Russian fiction; on children's fiction; and on evolutionary approaches to play, humor, and literature. His next book will be a study of evolution, cognition, and fiction with detailed examples from Homer to the 1990s.

Joseph Carroll teaches English at the University of Missouri–St. Louis. He has published books on Matthew Arnold and Wallace Stevens, and for the past several years he has been working to establish a Darwinian paradigm for literary study. In *Evolution and Literary Theory*, he set evolutionary theory in sharp contrast with poststructuralism, and in *Literary Darwinism: Evolution, Human Nature, and Literature*, he collected the essays in which he has subsequently tracked and helped guide the development of Darwinian literary studies. He has also edited an edition of Darwin's *Origin of Species*. He is currently working on using Darwinism for the study of Victorian fiction.

Frederick Crews is Professor of English Emeritus at the University of California, Berkeley. His writings include *Skeptical Engagements, The Critics Bear It Away: American Fiction and the Academy, The Memory Wars: Freud's Legacy in Dispute*, and the satires *The Pooh Perplex* and *Postmodern Pooh*. He is also the editor of *Unauthorized Freud: Doubters Confront a Legend*.

Denis Dutton teaches the philosophy of art at the University of Canterbury, New Zealand. For twenty-five years he has edited the influential journal of theory and criticism *Philosophy and Literature*. He is also the editor of the *Arts and Letters Daily*, a leading site for intellectual content on the Internet that has been hailed by *The Guardian* as the best website in the world. Dutton has written extensively on, among other things, the intersections between aesthetics and evolutionary theory.

Dylan Evans trained and practiced as a Lacanian psychoanalyst in Buenos Aires, London, and Paris before receiving a Ph.D. in philosophy from the London School of Economics. He did postdoctoral research in philosophy at Kings College

London and in robotics at the University of Bath before moving to the University of the West of England where he is currently Senior Lecturer in Intelligent Autonomous Systems. His research interests include the study of emotions in humans and the attempt to endow robots with artificial emotions. He is the author of six books, including *An Introductory Dictionary of Lacanian Psychoanalysis*, *Introducing Evolutionary Psychology*, *Emotion: The Science of Sentiment*, and *Placebo: Mind over Matter in Modern Medicine*.

Maryanne L. Fisher received a Ph.D. from York University in Toronto and is currently an assistant professor at St. Mary's University in Halifax, Canada. Her research primarily focuses on women's mating strategies, spanning the topics of female intrasexual competition, attractiveness, hormonal influences, romantic relationship factors, and cross-cultural mate preferences.

Robin Fox is University Professor of Social Theory at Rutgers University, where he founded the Department of Anthropology in 1967. Educated at the London School of Economics and Harvard, he did fieldwork in the New Mexico Pueblos and in the West of Ireland and taught at the universities of Exeter and London. He wrote *Kinship and Marriage*, which has remained the major text on the subject, and thirteen other books, including *The Imperial Animal* with Lionel Tiger. His latest is *Participant Observer: Memoir of a Transatlantic Life*.

Jonathan Gottschall received a Ph.D. in English from Binghamton University. He has published articles on Homer, on the study of literature from an evolutionary perspective, and on quantitative approaches to literary study. He has also published human science research on wartime rape, rape-pregnancy, and the controversy over evolutionary study of rape; literature as a source of quantitative data; mate preferences; and cross-cultural universals. He is currently putting finishing touches on his book *The Rape of Troy: Evolution, Violence, and the World of Homer*.

Ian Jobling has a Ph.D. in comparative literature from SUNY Buffalo and has written articles examining folktales and the Victorian novel from a Darwinian perspective. He now works as a writer and webmaster in the Washington D.C. area.

Daniel J. Kruger earned an M.A. and a Ph.D. in social psychology at Loyola University Chicago with projects integrating social psychology with evolutionary theory. He is currently a researcher at the University of Michigan, where he works on projects ranging from applied health research to investigations of the psychological indicators of life-history attributes and their correspondence with behavioral strategies. His evolutionary research interests include altruism, competition, cooperation, life history, mating strategies, mortality patterns, risk taking, and applications for social and ecological sustainability.

Ian McEwan's works have earned him worldwide critical acclaim. He won the Somerset Maugham Award in 1976 for his first collection of short stories, *First Love, Last Rites*; the Whitbread Novel Award in 1987 and Prix Fémina Etranger in 1993 for *The Child in Time*; and Germany's Shakespeare Prize in 1999. He has been shortlisted for the Booker Prize for Fiction three times, winning the award for *Amsterdam* in 1998. His novel *Atonement* received the WH Smith Literary Award in 2002, the National Book Critics' Circle Fiction Award in 2003, the Los Angeles Times Prize for Fiction in 2003, and the Santiago Prize for the European Novel in 2004. He is also a prolific essayist who has written frequently on advances in the realm of evolution and human behavior. His novel *Enduring Love* follows a science journalist reporting on evolutionary psychology and revolves thematically around the biology of altruism. McEwan currently lives in London, where he has recently completed a new novel, *Saturday*, based on a day in the life of a neurosurgeon.

Daniel Nettle is presently employed as a lecturer in psychology at the University of Newcastle upon Tyne, where he focuses on the evolutionary origins of cognition and creativity. The latter is the subject of his recent book *Strong Imagination: Madness, Creativity and Human Nature* as well as several of his articles. He has also authored three books on linguistics. Nettle once made his living as a playwright and actor who specialized in Shakespearean roles.

Marcus Nordlund is a postdoctoral research fellow in English literature at Uppsala University and an associate professor of the same subject at Gothenburg University, Sweden. He is currently completing a biocultural study of love in seven plays by William Shakespeare.

Catherine Salmon is an assistant professor in the psychology department at the University of Redlands in California. Her research interests include parental investment and birth order, reproductive suppression and dieting behavior, and human sexuality and pornography. She is the coauthor with Don Symons of *Warrior Lovers*, a book on sexuality, evolution, and erotic fiction.

Michelle Scalise Sugiyama is an affiliate of the English department and the Institute for Cognitive and Decision Sciences at the University of Oregon, Eugene. She studied at the Center for Evolutionary Psychology at the University of California, Santa Barbara, where she received a Ph.D. in literature in 1997. Integrating theory and research from anthropology, evolutionary biology, and cognitive psychology, her work seeks to understand narrative in terms of the cognitive architecture that underlies it, the conditions under which it emerged, and the role it played in ancestral human life.

David Sloan Wilson, a professor of biology and anthropology at Binghamton University, is an evolutionary biologist who studies humans along with other species. He is best known for championing the theory of multilevel selection, in which adaptation and natural selection can occur at all levels of the biological hierarchy. Additional interests include the nature of individual differences and evolutionary processes that involve nongenetic inheritance mechanisms. He publishes in psychology, anthropology, and philosophy journals in addition to his mainstream biological research. His books include *The Natural Selection of Populations and Communities*, *Unto Others: The Evolution and Psychology of Unselfish Behavior* (with Elliott Sober), and *Darwin's Cathedral: Evolution, Religion, and the Nature of Society*.

Edward O. Wilson was born in Birmingham, Alabama, in 1929, attended schools mostly in the South, and graduated from the University of Alabama in 1949. He went on to Harvard University to earn a Ph.D. and has been on the faculty there ever since. In 2001 he became a University Research Professor Emeritus and the Honorary Curator of Insects. His scholarly activities have spanned many areas of biology and the human sciences from systematics and ecology of ants to biogeography, sociobiology, and the philosophy of consilience. His more than one hundred awards in science and letters have included two Pulitzer Prizes, the U.S. National Medal of Science, and the Crafoord Prize, given by the Royal Swedish Academy of Sciences to recognize disciplines not covered by the original Nobel Prize.

RETHINKING THEORY

GENERAL EDITOR

Gary Saul Morson

CONSULTING EDITORS

Robert Alter
Frederick Crews
John M. Ellis
Caryl Emerson